Kerr's Cost Data for Landscape Construction

1994
Unit prices for site development
14th Edition

Edited by
Norman L. Dietrich, ASLA, PE, AICP
KERR ASSOCIATES

Contributing Editors
Tracy Anderson-Burger
Deborah Dietrich-Smith
Daniel Smith
David A. Wilford

 VAN NOSTRAND REINHOLD
New York

ISBN 0-442-01808-8

I(T)P™ Van Nostrand Reinhold is a division of International Thomson Publishing, Inc.
    The ITP logo is a trademark under license

Printed in the United States of America

For more information, contact:

Van Nostrand Reinhold
115 Fifth Avenue
New York, NY 10003

Chapman & Hall
2-6 Boundary Row
London
SE1 8HN
United Kingdom

Thomas Nelson Australia
102 Dodds Street
South Melbourne, 3205
Victoria, Australia

Nelson Canada
1120 Birchmount Road
Scarborough, Ontario
Canada M1K 5G4

Chapman & Hall GmbH
Pappelallee 3
69469 Weinheim
Germany

International Thomson Publishing Asia
221 Henderson Road #05-10
Henderson Building
Singapore 0315

International Thomson Publishing Japan
Hirakawacho Kyowa Building, 3F
2-2-1 Hirakawacho
Chiyoda-ku, 102 Tokyo
Japan

International Thomson Editores
Seneca 53
Col. Polanco
11560 Mexico D.F. Mexico

96 97 98 99 EDWLT 10 9 8 7 6 5 4 3 2

CONTENTS

1994

CONTENTS

APPENDIX

PREFACE

The Book

This is the fourteenth edition of COST DATA FOR LANDSCAPE CONSTRUCTION from the editorial team at Kerr Associates. Our objective is to provide all the cost information needed to estimate the construction costs of projects designed or specified by landscape architects. Each edition is completely revised based on new surveys of labor and material costs.

For those who still use a pencil to do cost estimates, estimating worksheets laid out for use with this book may be reproduced from the sample in the back of the book.

Let us know what you need for your estimating and how we can improve the usefulness of COST DATA FOR LANDSCAPE CONSTRUCTION.

Good estimating!

KERR ASSOCIATES

Norman L. Dietrich, ASLA, PE, AICP
Editor

The Editors   1993

The editor-in-chief is Norman L. Dietrich, an Associate Professor of Landscape Architecture at Iowa State University. Professor Dietrich is a registered landscape architect and civil engineer in several states. He has also taught landscape architecture design and construction at Michigan State University and Texas A & M University.

He is a member of the American Society of Landscape Architects, American Society of Civil Engineers and American Institute of Certified Planners. He was founder and president of Norman L. Dietrich Associates (now Dietrich-Bailey Associates), a landscape architecture, planning and civil engineering firm in Plymouth, Michigan.

Tracy Anderson-Burger is the assistant editor for this COST DATA FOR LANDSCAPE ARCHITECTURE. She received her Bachelor of Landscape Architecture degree from Iowa State versity and a MS in Civil Engineering from the University of Florida.

Deborah Dietrich-Smith is the contributing editor for the plant materials. She received a Bachelor of Science (Botany) from Central Michigan University. Daniel Smith provided the labor cost data.

David A. Wilford assisted with the programming and formatting for the desktop publishing of CDLC.

INTRODUCTION

COST DATA FOR LANDSCAPE CONSTRUCTION contains current landscape construction cost information for landscape architects, architects, engineers, cost estimators, and property managers. This information is in the form of average unit prices for a broad variety of landscape construction items for use in the preparation of construction cost estimates. We have made every effort to reflect current costs.

The information in this book is designed to be primarily used by designers and cost estimators for preparing cost estimates for projects that will be bid competitively. It may also be useful to planners who need to know the costs of complete recreational facilities and to contractors who may find the productivity data of interest. We do not suggest that the contractor use the actual cost data contained here. Under some conditions this could prove unprofitable. But the data may be useful for comparison, and the format helpful for the initial development of a time accounting system.

There are many factors which affect actual construction costs. Particularly wide variations in bids are commonly found in the landscape construction industry. However, if instructions are carefully followed, a total cost derived from the data in this book will usually fall inside the bid range.

No guaranty, warranty or representation is made by Kerr Associates, or the editors as to the correctness or sufficiency of any information in this book. Kerr Associates and the editors assume no liability in connection with the use of this book. Nothing contained in this book shall be construed as a recommendation for any product or process.

Master Format

COST DATA FOR LANDSCAPE CONSTRUCTION is organized in accordance with the MasterFormat of the Construction Specifications Institute (CSI). The book's format will correspond closely with specifications following the CSI format for easy reference. Due to the specialized nature of the book, only the MasterFormat divisions which are relevant to site, recreation, and landscape development are covered.

The Sections of the MasterFormat Divisions are divided further into categories of operations and materials. Costs are arranged by individual item in each category. Subdivisions of size or of equipment used are indented below the item description. To find a specific item, refer to its CSI Division and Section, or refer to the index at the back of the book.

Cost Data

Very detailed cost data is necessary for developing construction plans and specifications. However, such detailed information is inconvenient for developing preliminary estimates for studies of early stages of project design. For this reason, two types of costs are provided: Unit Prices and Composite Costs.

Unit Prices

The major portion of the data is made up of unit prices for detailed items representing a broad spectrum of materials and methods. These detailed basic costs can be combined as needed to conform to the specific project requirements. They are most useful for estimating in the late stages of project design and for estimating from final plans and specifications.

Composite Costs

COMPOSITE COSTS

In addition to these detailed construction items, most sections begin with a category entitled "Composite Costs." This category will always be highlighted with a gray tone as you see over this paragraph. It contains items which are composites of the more detailed items. They are most useful for developing preliminary cost estimates when exact conditions, materials, and methods are not yet known.

Many of the composite cost items are illustrated in Appendix S, "Illustrated Composites". These illustrations can help the estimator to visualize the composite cost item, and find the assembly that comes closest to the item being estimated. The composites which are illustrated in Appendix S are identified with asterisks (***) next to the line item description.

Between the many detailed basic costs, and the composite costs, this book covers a range of detail all the way from a single operation, such as the placing of mulch, to the construction of a complete facility, such as a golf course.

THE DATA

For most items there are eight columns of information: KEY; DESCRIPTION; UNIT; CREW and EQUIPMENT; PER DAY; INSTALLATION COST; MATERIALS COST; and TOTAL COST.

Description

The DESCRIPTION column specifies the construction items for which the costs are provided. The description may be followed by indented subdivisions listing options in material size, installation equipment, or methods. Items in the "COMPOSITE COSTS" categories may be followed by subdivisions listing ranges of quantities which reflect the unit cost savings made possible through economies of scale of larger projects.

Unit

The UNIT column lists the unit of measurement upon which the unit prices and the per day output are based. APPENDIX A is the key to the unit abbreviations. APPENDIX D lists the factors for converting units.

Crew and Equipment

The capital letters in the CREW and EQUIPMENT column refer to the construction trade codes in APPENDIX B, and represent the types of workers or trades involved in the item or operation. The number before each letter is the number of that type of worker on the typical crew. The two digit numbers to the right of the comma are equipment codes. APPENDIX C is the key to the equipment codes and lists their daily rate. Often more than one piece of equipment is used per item. Sometimes the equipment code is continued on the next line.

For example, 1A1G1L,22,33 means that the crew is composed of one medium equipment operator (A), one light equipment operator (G), and one laborer (L). This crew would use a 300 HP bulldozer (22) and a 15 CY motor scraper (33) to perform this construction task.

The typical crews for each item were determined by input from construction contractors, and equipment and materials manufacturers. Actual crew size and makeup can vary greatly for a number of reasons, such as union rules or local custom. Crews shown here are generally the smallest possible cost effective crew for that particular item of work. Often the actual crew will be larger, but installation costs should not be affected by this. Supervisory personnel are not included in the crew. The additional costs for supervision are considered here to be an overhead item.

Per Day

The PER DAY output is the average number of units that the defined crew can install in one 8-hour day. The average per day output was determined with the assistance of construction contractors, and materials and equipment manufacturers. Actual per day output can vary greatly because of management competence, weather, union rules or local custom, job duration, etc. The per day output data represented here are averages from sources around the nation and as such, represent good guides.

Installation Cost

The INSTALLATION COST column provides the cost of installation per unit. This cost is derived from the daily rates for the workers and equipment defined in the CREW and EQUIPMENT column, divided by the per day output. The labor rates used for installation costs are an average of labor rates for each trade in 28 major U.S. metropolitan areas with an added factor for insurance and taxes. These rates were obtained from the U.S. Department of Labor prevailing wage rate determinations, and they include all fringe benefits. The national average daily labor rates by trade are shown in APPENDIX B, along with local adjustment factors and actual labor rates by trade for each of the 28 metropolitan areas.

The daily equipment costs used here are derived from the weekly rental rate divided by 5, plus the hourly operating cost times 8 hours. We assume the rental rate to be a reasonable representation of the cost of owning the equipment. Actual rental rates vary throughout the United States. The rental rates used to develop the equipment costs were derived from cost recovery rates considering purchase price, depreciation, maintenance costs, overhead costs, and average annual use hours for equipment in average to excellent condition.

The hourly operating cost for each piece of equipment includes fuel, lubrication, maintenance, repairs, and tread wear. Equipment operator costs are not included in the total equipment cost. Total daily equipment costs are shown in APPENDIX C.

THE DATA

The MATERIALS COST column provides the cost of materials per unit. Materials prices were obtained from manufacturers' and suppliers' quotations for this edition, and were then averaged for the United States. Materials costs provided include an average factor for shipping and delivery, which assumes the job site is in or near a metropolitan area. Some materials costs include a factor for waste at the job site.

Total Cost

The TOTAL COST is the sum of the installation cost and materials cost per unit, with a percentage added for subcontractor's overhead and profit. Markup for overhead and profit can vary depending on economic conditions and other factors. An overhead and profit markup of 25 percent has been used, except in the Planting, Fountain, and Irrigation Sections where 35 percent is used. The landscape contractor typically has a higher overhead than other types of contractors due to the relatively small size of most landscape contracts, and the highly seasonal nature of the work, hence the higher markup.

Plant Materials Data

The Planting Section contains the results of a national survey of plant materials prices conducted especially for this Edition. High, low and average prices for many species and varieties of trees, shrubs and ground covers are provided. The materials included are for the most part those commonly available in their hardiness zones. The plant materials prices include the landscape contractor's overhead and profit markup and the cost of shipment to the site. They do not include installation costs. See the detailed Instructions Section below for directions on calculating the total cost of plant materials and on substituting local quotes for the survey data.

Step One: Job Review

The first step toward an accurate cost estimate is a thorough review of the job. During this step, assess the appropriate level of detail for the estimate. The estimator must take care to select costs that are of a degree of detail consistent with the stage of design. Final plans call for a very detailed estimate, with accurate quantity takeoffs and with the construction items broken down to the most detailed components for which unit prices are available. Planning studies and preliminary design require less detail and are easily prepared using the Composite Cost data at the beginning of most sections.

Step Two: Quantity Take-Off

An accurate quantity take-off is crucial. Make a list of construction items from the plans and specifications, checking against COST DATA FOR LANDSCAPE CONSTRUCTION to see that they match, and keeping in mind the level of detail. Record this list on a copy of the cost estimating worksheet.

The quantity of each item listed must then be accurately determined. APPENDIX F, "Area Calculation," may be useful for this step. Depending on the particular items included in the plans, the following appendices may also be useful: Material Weights; Soil Expansion and Compaction; Planting Pit Volumes; Backfill Volumes; Board Measure; and Reinforcing Steel. Be sure that the measurement unit used is the same as the unit used in the tables for the particular item. Round any fractions of units up to full units.

Step Three: Unit Prices

Assign a unit price to each item. If unit prices are to be adjusted for the job locality, installation costs and materials costs must be listed separately on the cost estimate worksheet, otherwise just record the total unit price for each item. Be careful to choose the construction method or equipment type and size most consistent with the scale of the job and with the requirements of the specifications. Always try to use the unit price for the most cost effective piece of equipment, unless site conditions or equipment availability will not allow it. Consider cost effectiveness on a total job basis: While a larger piece of equipment may not be the best for a certain task considered alone, if it is the best equipment for another task in the same subcontract, then it may become cost effective for other tasks as well, because it must be mobilized anyway.

SELECTING EQUIPMENT SIZE

To determine the most cost effective of two different sizes or types of equipment for a particular task, divide the difference in mobilization cost by the difference in the total unit price. The resulting figure is the number of units at which the higher mobilization cost is justified, and the larger equipment becomes more cost effective.

For example, clearing large tracts of light brush can be done by brush saw or a 150 HP bulldozer. If the mobilization cost of the brush saw is $0.00 and the mobilization cost of the bulldozer is $279.00, then the difference is $279.00. If the total unit price of clearing brush is $12.30 per MSF for the brush saw and $5.80 per MSF for the bulldozer, then the difference in total unit price is $6.50 per MSF. Divide the difference in mobilization costs by the difference in unit costs to find the number of units at which the higher mobilization cost of the larger equipment is offset by its lower unit cost. $279.00 divided by $6.50/MSF = 43 MSF. In this example, the 150 HP bulldozer is more cost effective than the brush saw for projects over 50 MSF. When calculating this break-even point make sure that the unit prices are based on the same unit.

INSTALLED PLANT MATERIAL COSTS

The composite plant costs in the Planting Section include an average cost for the particular type and size of plant material, as indicated in the item DESCRIPTION. If desired, this average cost may be subtracted from the composite cost, and a more exact figure for a specific species added back in. To use the detailed installation costs, it is necessary to add the plant material cost to them. The plant material costs in the Planting Section already include a markup for contractor's overhead and profit and include the cost of shipment from the nursery.

For example, the composite cost of a 2" caliper shade tree planted with on-site topsoil backfill is $292.00. If the specific variety of shade tree is known, then its material cost can be substituted for the average shade tree cost in the composite. The Acer platanoides "Crimson King" average material cost is $171, which includes the normal markup. Subtracting the $146 material cost (listed in the composite description for a 2" caliper tree) leaves $146 for installation. So the $171 "Crimson King" cost plus the $146 installation cost totals $317 including overhead and profit. This is a more accurate composite cost for the provision and installation of this variety of shade tree.

Alternately, the $171.00 material cost of the "Crimson King" could be added to a group of detailed installation costs, which reflect the final planting details and specifications, for the most accurate cost estimate.

INSTRUCTIONS

The unit prices may be adjusted for the location of the project when a high level of accuracy is needed or if local construction costs differ greatly from the national averages.

The information in APPENDIX B, "Labor," may be used to adjust installation costs to reflect local labor rates. A quick way to do this is to apply the appropriate local labor rate adjustment factor, from APPENDIX B, to the installation cost of each item.

For example, to adjust the total unit cost of a 50' aluminum flagpole to reflect labor rates in metropolitan Atlanta, Georgia, multiply the installation cost per unit by the adjustment factor. $233.61 x 0.641 = $149.74 = adjusted installation cost per pole. Next add the adjusted installation cost to the materials cost and increase the sum by 25 percent to calculate the adjusted total unit cost. $149.74 + $2440 = $2589.74, $2589.74 x 1.25 = $3237.19 per pole. Use a 35 percent markup when adjusting the cost of planting, irrigation, or fountain items.

The most precise way to adjust unit prices to compensate for local labor rates is to calculate the daily crew cost using the actual daily labor rates for each trade. The number and type of workers in each crew for each construction item is cited in the CREW and EQUIPMENT column. See the previous section, THE DATA, for directions on interpreting the CREW and EQUIPMENT codes. APPENDIX B is the key to the crew codes.

Find the actual local daily labor rate for each trade on the crew from APPENDIX B. Multiply the daily rate by the number of that type of worker on the crew to get the total daily cost of that trade. Repeat for all the trades on the crew. Next add the daily cost of all the trades on the crew to find the total adjusted daily crew cost.

Next compute the total daily equipment cost for the item. The equipment code key and daily rates are in APPENDIX C. Directions on interpreting the equipment codes are in the previous section, THE DATA. Add the daily rates for each type of

equipment cited in the CREW and EQUIPMENT column for the item to find the total daily equipment cost. There are no local adjustment factors provided for equipment costs.

Add the total adjusted daily crew cost to the total daily equipment cost, and divide the sum by the PER DAY output to find the adjusted installation cost per unit. Next add the adjusted installation cost to the materials cost and multiply the sum by 1.25 or 1.35 to find the adjusted total unit cost. Most sections use a 25 percent markup for overhead and profit, except the Planting, Irrigation, and Fountain sections which use a 35 percent markup. See the TOTAL column heading over each item to find the appropriate markup.

The U.S. Department of Labor prevailing wage determinations used here generally reflect union rates. If it is known that non-union labor is commonly used in the job locality, these rates should be adjusted. As a guide, non-union rates average from 25 to 33 percent lower than union rates. The labor rates in APPENDIX B can be adjusted as the year progresses using one of the several reliable national indexes which periodically provide information on the percentage change in labor rates.

The installation costs make no allowance for overtime or high travel expenses. If the job is remote from a metropolitan area, travel and per diem expenses may be required for special trade and must be given consideration in preparation of the estimate.

Also, if the job site is remote from a metropolitan area, extra shipping charges may increase the costs of some materials, and this must be given consideration by the estimator.

To use local quotes on plant materials instead of the survey data, add a markup of up to 35 percent to the quoted wholesale price to cover the landscape contractor's shipping costs and overhead and profit. Retail price quotes do not need to be marked up further.

Step Five: Mobilization Costs

Equipment mobilization and demobilization costs must be included in the estimate. Make a list of the equipment called for in the CREW and EQUIPMENT column of each item included in the plans and specifications. Include the mobilization cost from

APPENDIX C, "Equipment," once for each piece of equipment. The mobilization costs listed in APPENDIX C include demobilization costs.

Step Six: Summation

Figure the total cost for the total quantity of each item required, then add the item totals and mobilization costs to find the bottom line total. Add general contractor's overhead and profit when appropriate. General contractor's overhead and profit can

vary from close to 0 percent to 20 percent, depending on market and economic conditions. Ten percent is a good average to use for cost estimating. Add on contingency if desired. Check your calculations.

02070 Selective Demolition

KEY	DESCRIPTION	UNIT	CREW AND EQUIPMENT	PER DAY	INSTALLATION COST	MATERIALS COST	TOTAL + 25%
10	**WALL REMOVAL**						
	Remove concrete wall, load or pile						
	non-reinforced						
100	by hand	CF	2L	35	11.66		14.60
110	air tools	CF	2G3L,12,86	300	5.09		6.40
120	reinforced	CF	2G3L,12,86	230	6.64		8.30
	Remove concrete block wall, load or pile						
	cavity						
130	by hand	CF	2L	55	7.42		9.30
140	air tools	CF	2G3L,12,86	760	2.01		2.51
	solid						
150	by hand	CF	2L	45	9.07		11.30
160	air tools	CF	2G3L,12,86	620	2.46		3.08
	Remove brick wall, load or pile						
170	by hand	CF	2L	45	9.07		11.30
180	air tools	CF	2G3L,12,86	280	5.45		6.80
	Remove stone wall, load or pile						
	mortared						
190	by hand	CF	2L	40	10.20		12.80
200	air tools	CF	2G3L,12,86	280	5.45		6.80
	dry set						
210	by hand	CF	2L	60	6.80		8.50
220	air tools	CF	2G3L,12,86	460	3.32		4.15
20	**PAVEMENT AND CURB REMOVAL**						
	Remove concrete pavement, load or pile						
	non-reinforced						
	3"-4" thick						
100	by hand	SY	2L	10	40.81		51.00
110	air tools	SY	2G3L,12,86	140	10.90		13.60
120	backhoe/loader	SY	1G2L,13	150	5.12		6.40
	5"-6" thick						
130	by hand	SY	2L	6.3	64.77		81.00
140	air tools	SY	2G3L,12,86	90	16.96		21.20
150	backhoe/loader	SY	1G2L,13	95	8.08		10.10
160	demolition hammer	SY	2G2L,14,87	320	4.18		5.20
	7"-8" thick						
170	air tools	SY	2G3L,12,86	70	21.81		27.30
180	demolition hammer	SY	2G2L,14,87	240	5.57		7.00
	mesh reinforced						
	3"-4" thick						
190	air tools	SY	2G3L,12,86	100	15.27		19.10
200	backhoe/loader	SY	1G2L,13	140	5.48		6.90
	5"-6" thick						
210	air tools	SY	2G3L,12,86	65	23.48		29.40
220	backhoe/loader	SY	1G2L,13	90	8.53		10.70
230	demolition hammer	SY	2G2L,14,87	230	5.82		7.30
	7"-8" thick						
240	air tools	SY	2G3L,12,86	50	30.53		38.20
250	demolition hammer	SY	2G2L,14,87	170	7.87		9.80
	rod reinforced						
	5"-6" thick						
260	air tools	SY	2G3L,12,86	55	27.75		34.70
270	demolition hammer	SY	2G2L,14,87	180	7.43		9.30
	7"-8" thick						
280	air tools	SY	2G3L,12,86	40	38.16		47.70
290	demolition hammer	SY	2G2L,14,87	140	9.55		11.90
	Remove bituminous pavement, load or pile						
	2"-3" thick						
300	by hand	SY	2L	20	20.40		25.50
310	air tools	SY	2G3L,12,86	330	4.63		5.80
320	backhoe/loader	SY	1G2L,13	350	2.19		2.74

02070 Selective Demolition

DEMOLITION

KEY	DESCRIPTION	UNIT	CREW AND EQUIPMENT	PER DAY	INSTALLATION COST	MATERIALS COST	TOTAL + 25%
	4"-6" thick						
330	by hand	SY	2L	13	31.39		39.20
340	air tools	SY	2G3L,12,86	160	9.54		11.90
350	backhoe/loader	SY	1G2L,13	210	3.66		4.57
360	demolition hammer	SY	2G2L,14,87	410	3.26		4.08
	8"-10" thick						
370	air tools	SY	2G3L,12,86	90	16.96		21.20
380	demolition hammer	SY	2G2L,14,87	310	4.31		5.40
	Remove brick pavement, load or pile						
	dry set						
390	by hand	SY	2L	38	10.74		13.40
400	backhoe/loader	SY	1G2L,13	420	1.83		2.29
	mortared						
410	by hand	SY	2L	12	34.01		42.50
420	air tools	SY	2G3L,12,86	170	8.98		11.20
430	backhoe/loader	SY	1G2L,13	180	4.27		5.30
	Remove concrete curb, load or pile						
	non-reinforced						
440	by hand	LF	2L	24	17.00		21.30
450	air tools	LF	2G3L,12,86	190	8.03		10.00
460	backhoe/loader	LF	1G2L,13	300	2.56		3.20
	reinforced						
470	air tools	LF	2G3L,12,86	110	13.88		17.30
480	backhoe/loader	LF	1G2L,13	170	4.52		5.60
	Remove granite curb, load or pile						
490	for reuse	LF	1G2L,13	170	4.52		5.60
500	for disposal	LF	1G2L,13	300	2.56		3.20
	Remove wood curb, load or pile						
510	by hand	LF	2L	50	8.16		10.20
520	backhoe/loader	LF	1G2L,13	500	1.54		1.92
30	**FENCE REMOVAL**						
	Remove chain link fence, load or pile						
	for reuse						
100	7' high or under	LF	2L	230	1.77		2.22
110	over 7' high	LF	2L	150	2.72		3.40
	for disposal						
120	7' high or under	LF	2L	470	0.87		1.09
130	over 7' high	LF	2L	310	1.32		1.65
	Remove barbed wire fence, load or pile						
140	3-strand	LF	2L	540	0.76		0.94
150	5-strand	LF	2L	350	1.17		1.46
160	Remove wood fence, 6' high or under, load or pile	LF	2L	460	0.89		1.11

02110 Site Clearing						1994
KEY	DESCRIPTION	UNIT	CREW AND EQUIPMENT	PER DAY	INSTALLATION COST	MATERIALS COST / TOTAL + 25%
00	**COMPOSITE COSTS**					
	Clear brush and saplings, medium density					
	load, haul and dump					
100	1 acre or less	MSF				35.60
110	over 1 acre	MSF				25.80
120	over 10 acres	Ac				800.00
	Clear timber up to 1' diameter, medium density, pile					
	load, haul and dump					
130	1 acre or less	MSF				110.00
140	over 1 acre	MSF				61.00
150	over 10 acres	Ac				2200.00
	burn on site					
160	1 acre or less	MSF				94.00
170	over 1 acre	MSF				24.80
180	over 10 acres	Ac				880.00
	Clear and grub timber up to 1' dia., medium density, pil					
	load, haul and dump					
190	1 acre or less	MSF				167.00
200	over 1 acre	MSF				62.00
210	over 10 acres	Ac				2830.00
	burn on site					
220	1 acre or less	MSF				127.00
230	over 1 acre	MSF				29.20
240	over 10 acres	Ac				1070.00
10	**CLEARING**					
	Clear and pile brush and saplings					
	light density					
100	by hand	SY	1L	620	0.33	0.41
110	brush saw	MSF	1L,83	22	9.84	12.30
120	50 HP bulldozer	MSF	1G,20	60	7.41	9.30
130	150 HP bulldozer	MSF	1G,21	140	4.68	5.80
	medium density					
140	by hand	SY	1L	370	0.55	0.69
150	brush saw	MSF	1L,83	13	16.65	20.80
160	50 HP bulldozer	MSF	1G,20	55	8.09	10.10
170	150 HP bulldozer	MSF	1G,21	130	5.04	6.30
	heavy density					
180	by hand	SY	1L	250	0.82	1.02
190	brush saw	MSF	1L,83	9	24.05	30.10
200	50 HP bulldozer	MSF	1G,20	48	9.26	11.60
210	150 HP bulldozer	MSF	1G,21	110	5.95	7.40
	Clear & pile timber up to 1' dia., 75-100% hardwoods					
	light density					
220	by hand	MSF	1G4L,18,82,82	42	34.99	43.70
230	150 HP tractor	MSF	1G,21	120	5.46	6.80
240	300 HP tractor	MSF	1G,22	190	5.39	6.70
	medium density					
250	by hand	MSF	1G4L,18,82,82	25	58.79	73.00
260	150 HP tractor	MSF	1G,21	100	6.55	8.20
270	300 HP tractor	MSF	1G,22	170	6.03	7.50
	heavy density					
280	by hand	MSF	1G4L,18,82,82	17	86.45	108.00
290	150 HP tractor	MSF	1G,21	75	8.73	10.90
300	300 HP tractor	MSF	1G,22	130	7.88	9.90
	plus heavy vines, add					
310	by hand	MSF			19.88	24.90
320	150 HP tractor	MSF			1.92	2.40
330	300 HP tractor	MSF			1.58	1.97

SITE PREPARATION

KEY	DESCRIPTION	UNIT	CREW AND EQUIPMENT	PER DAY	INSTALLATION COST	MATERIALS COST	TOTAL + 25%
	Clear & pile timber up to 1' dia., 25-50% hardwoods						
	light density						
340	by hand	MSF	1G4L,18,82,82	55	26.72		33.40
350	150 HP tractor	MSF	1G,21	130	5.04		6.30
360	300 HP tractor	MSF	1G,22	210	4.88		6.10
	medium density						
370	by hand	MSF	1G4L,18,82,82	33	44.53		56.00
380	150 HP tractor	MSF	1G,21	120	5.46		6.80
390	300 HP tractor	MSF	1G,22	190	5.39		6.70
	heavy density						
400	by hand	MSF	1G4L,18,82,82	22	66.80		84.00
410	150 HP tractor	MSF	1G,21	85	7.70		9.60
420	300 HP tractor	MSF	1G,22	140	7.32		9.10
	plus heavy vines, add						
430	by hand	MSF			16.03		20.00
440	150 HP tractor	MSF			1.92		2.40
450	300 HP tractor	MSF			1.58		1.97
	Clear & pile timber up to 1' dia., 0-25% hardwoods						
	light density						
460	by hand	MSF	1G4L,18,82,82	80	18.37		23.00
470	150 HP tractor	MSF	1G,21	140	4.68		5.80
480	300 HP tractor	MSF	1G,22	220	4.66		5.80
	medium density						
490	by hand	MSF	1G4L,18,82,82	47	31.27		39.10
500	150 HP tractor	MSF	1G,21	130	5.04		6.30
510	300 HP tractor	MSF	1G,22	210	4.88		6.10
	heavy density						
520	by hand	MSF	1G4L,18,82,82	31	47.41		59.00
530	150 HP tractor	MSF	1G,21	100	6.55		8.20
540	300 HP tractor	MSF	1G,22	170	6.03		7.50
	plus heavy vines, add						
550	by hand	MSF			12.33		15.40
560	150 HP tractor	MSF			1.92		2.40
570	300 HP tractor	MSF			1.58		1.97
	Cut and pile hardwood trees over 1' diameter (add to above per MSF cost)						
	1'-2' diameter						
580	by hand	Ea	1G4L,18,82,82	80	18.37		23.00
590	150 HP tractor	Ea	1G,21	290	2.26		2.82
600	300 HP tractor	Ea	1G,22	780	1.31		1.64
	2'-3' diameter						
610	by hand	Ea	1G4L,18,82,82	16	91.85		115.00
620	150 HP tractor	Ea	1G,21	60	10.91		13.60
630	300 HP tractor	Ea	1G,22	160	6.40		8.00
	3'-4' diameter						
640	by hand	Ea	1G4L,18,82,82	8	183.70		230.00
650	150 HP tractor	Ea	1G,21	29	22.58		28.20
660	300 HP tractor	Ea	1G,22	95	10.79		13.50
	4'-6' diameter						
670	by hand	Ea	1G4L,18,82,82	2.5	587.85		730.00
680	300 HP tractor	Ea	1G,22	60	17.08		21.30
	Cut and pile softwood trees over 1' diameter (add to above per MSF cost)						
	1'-2' diameter						
690	by hand	Ea	1G4L,18,82,82	150	9.80		12.20
700	150 HP tractor	Ea	1G,21	550	1.19		1.49
710	300 HP tractor	Ea	1G,22	1460	0.70		0.88
	2'-3' diameter						
720	by hand	Ea	1G4L,18,82,82	30	48.99		61.00
730	150 HP tractor	Ea	1G,21	110	5.95		7.40
740	300 HP tractor	Ea	1G,22	290	3.53		4.42

KEY	DESCRIPTION	UNIT	CREW AND EQUIPMENT	PER DAY	INSTALLATION COST	MATERIALS COST	TOTAL + 25%
	3'-4' diameter						
750	by hand	Ea	1G4L,18,82,82	15	97.98		122.00
760	150 HP tractor	Ea	1G,21	50	13.09		16.40
770	300 HP tractor	Ea	1G,22	170	6.03		7.50
	4'-6' diameter						
780	by hand	Ea	1G4L,18,82,82	5	293.93		367.00
790	300 HP tractor	Ea	1G,22	60	17.08		21.30
20	**STUMP REMOVAL**						
	Grub & pile stumps up to 1' dia., 75-100% hardwoods						
	light density						
100	1 CY backhoe	MSF	1G1L,15	310	2.38		2.98
110	150 HP tractor	MSF	1G,21	480	1.36		1.70
120	300 HP tractor	MSF	1G,22	770	1.33		1.66
	medium density						
130	1 CY backhoe	MSF	1G1L,15	220	3.36		4.20
140	150 HP tractor	MSF	1G,21	420	1.56		1.95
150	300 HP tractor	MSF	1G,22	690	1.49		1.86
	heavy density						
160	1 CY backhoe	MSF	1G1L,15	110	6.72		8.40
170	150 HP tractor	MSF	1G,21	300	2.18		2.73
180	300 HP tractor	MSF	1G,22	510	2.01		2.51
	plus heavy vines, add						
190	1 CY backhoe	MSF			1.41		1.76
200	150 HP tractor	MSF			0.48		0.60
210	300 HP tractor	MSF			0.40		0.50
	Grub & pile stumps up to 1' dia., 25-50% hardwoods						
	light density						
220	1 CY backhoe	MSF	1G1L,15	410	1.80		2.25
230	150 HP tractor	MSF	1G,21	520	1.26		1.57
240	300 HP tractor	MSF	1G,22	820	1.25		1.56
	medium density						
250	1 CY backhoe	MSF	1G1L,15	280	2.64		3.30
260	150 HP tractor	MSF	1G,21	460	1.42		1.78
270	300 HP tractor	MSF	1G,22	750	1.37		1.71
	heavy density						
280	1 CY backhoe	MSF	1G1L,15	140	5.28		6.60
290	150 HP tractor	MSF	1G,21	340	1.93		2.41
300	300 HP tractor	MSF	1G,22	580	1.77		2.21
	plus heavy vines, add						
310	1 CY backhoe	MSF			1.37		1.71
320	150 HP tractor	MSF			0.48		0.60
330	300 HP tractor	MSF			0.40		0.50
	Grub & pile stumps up to 1' dia., 0-25% hardwoods						
	light density						
340	1 CY backhoe	MSF	1G1L,15	580	1.27		1.59
350	150 HP tractor	MSF	1G,21	560	1.17		1.46
360	300 HP tractor	MSF	1G,22	880	1.16		1.46
	medium density						
370	1 CY backhoe	MSF	1G1L,15	410	1.80		2.25
380	150 HP tractor	MSF	1G,21	520	1.26		1.57
390	300 HP tractor	MSF	1G,22	820	1.25		1.56
	heavy density						
400	1 CY backhoe	MSF	1G1L,15	200	3.69		4.62
410	150 HP tractor	MSF	1G,21	410	1.60		2.00
420	300 HP tractor	MSF	1G,22	670	1.53		1.91
	plus heavy vines, add						
430	1 CY backhoe	MSF			0.96		1.20
440	150 HP tractor	MSF			0.48		0.60
450	300 HP tractor	MSF			0.40		0.50

SITE PREPARATION

KEY	DESCRIPTION	UNIT	CREW AND EQUIPMENT	PER DAY	INSTALLATION COST	MATERIALS COST	TOTAL + 25%
	Grub and pile hardwood stumps over 1' diameter (add to above per MSF cost)						
	1'-2' diameter						
460	1 CY backhoe	Ea	1G1L,15	10	73.87		92.00
470	150 HP tractor	Ea	1G,21	1180	0.55		0.69
480	300 HP tractor	Ea	1G,22	3140	0.33		0.41
	2'-3' diameter						
490	1 CY backhoe	Ea	1G1L,15	6	123.12		154.00
500	150 HP tractor	Ea	1G,21	240	2.73		3.41
510	300 HP tractor	Ea	1G,22	630	1.63		2.03
	3'-4' diameter						
520	1 CY backhoe	Ea	1G1L,15	4.4	167.90		210.00
530	150 HP tractor	Ea	1G,21	120	5.46		6.80
540	300 HP tractor	Ea	1G,22	380	2.70		3.37
	4'-6' diameter						
550	1 CY backhoe	Ea	1G1L,15	3.1	238.30		298.00
560	150 HP tractor	Ea	1G,21	38	17.23		21.50
570	300 HP tractor	Ea	1G,22	230	4.46		5.60
	Grub and pile softwood stumps over 1' diameter (add to above per MSF cost)						
	1'-2' diameter						
580	1 CY backhoe	Ea	1G1L,15	19	38.88		48.60
590	150 HP tractor	Ea	1G,21	2190	0.30		0.37
600	300 HP tractor	Ea	1G,22	5830	0.18		0.22
	2'-3' diameter						
610	1 CY backhoe	Ea	1G1L,15	11	67.16		84.00
620	150 HP tractor	Ea	1G,21	440	1.49		1.86
630	300 HP tractor	Ea	1G,22	1170	0.88		1.09
	3'-4' diameter						
640	1 CY backhoe	Ea	1G1L,15	8	92.34		115.00
650	150 HP tractor	Ea	1G,21	220	2.98		3.72
660	300 HP tractor	Ea	1G,22	700	1.46		1.83
	4'-6' diameter						
670	1 CY backhoe	Ea	1G1L,15	6	123.12		154.00
680	150 HP tractor	Ea	1G,21	70	9.35		11.70
690	300 HP tractor	Ea	1G,22	250	4.10		5.10
30	**DISPOSAL**						
	Load cleared brush and saplings on truck						
	light density						
100	by hand	MSF	2L	440	0.93		1.16
110	1/2 CY wheel loader	MSF	1G1L,10	1090	0.63		0.79
120	1 1/2 CY wheel loader	MSF	1G1L,12	2180	0.37		0.46
	medium density						
130	by hand	MSF	2L	260	1.57		1.96
140	1/2 CY wheel loader	MSF	1G1L,10	650	1.06		1.32
150	1 1/2 CY wheel loader	MSF	1G1L,12	1310	0.61		0.76
	heavy density						
160	by hand	MSF	2L	170	2.40		3.00
170	1/2 CY wheel loader	MSF	1G1L,10	440	1.57		1.96
180	1 1/2 CY wheel loader	MSF	1G1L,12	870	0.92		1.15
	Load cleared timber up to 1' diameter on truck						
	light density						
190	1 3/4 CY track loader	MSF	1G2L,18,82	150	6.98		8.70
200	3 CY track loader	MSF	1G4L,19,82,82	280	5.68		7.10
	medium density						
210	1 3/4 CY track loader	MSF	1G2L,18,82	100	10.47		13.10
220	3 CY track loader	MSF	1G4L,19,82,82	200	7.95		9.90
	heavy density						
230	1 3/4 CY track loader	MSF	1G2L,18,82	50	20.94		26.20
240	3 CY track loader	MSF	1G4L,19,82,82	100	15.90		19.90

02110 Site Clearing

KEY	DESCRIPTION	UNIT	CREW AND EQUIPMENT	PER DAY	INSTALLATION COST	MATERIALS COST	TOTAL + 25%
	Load cut trees over 1' diameter on truck (add to above per MSF cost)						
	1'-2' diameter						
250	1 3/4 CY track loader	Ea	1G2L,18,82	40	26.18		32.70
260	3 CY track loader	Ea	1G4L,19,82,82	120	13.25		16.60
	2'-3' diameter						
270	1 3/4 CY track loader	Ea	1G2L,18,82	20	52.36		65.00
280	3 CY track loader	Ea	1G4L,19,82,82	40	39.74		49.70
	3'-4' diameter						
290	1 3/4 CY track loader	Ea	1G2L,18,82	5	209.43		262.00
300	3 CY track loader	Ea	1G4L,19,82,82	12	132.47		166.00
	4'-6' diameter						
310	1 3/4 CY track loader	Ea	1G2L,18,82	2.4	436.32		550.00
320	3 CY track loader	Ea	1G4L,19,82,82	6	264.94		331.00
	Load grubbed stumps up to 1' diameter on truck						
	light density						
330	1 3/4 CY track loader	MSF	1G2L,18	600	1.72		2.15
340	3 CY track loader	MSF	1G3L,19	1140	1.19		1.49
	medium density						
350	1 3/4 CY track loader	MSF	1G2L,18	420	2.46		3.07
360	3 CY track loader	MSF	1G3L,19	800	1.70		2.12
	heavy density						
370	1 3/4 CY track loader	MSF	1G2L,18	210	4.92		6.10
380	3 CY track loader	MSF	1G3L,19	400	3.39		4.24
	Load grubbed stumps over 1' diameter on truck (add to above per MSF cost)						
	1'-2' diameter						
390	1 3/4 CY track loader	Ea	1G2L,18	160	6.45		8.10
400	3 CY track loader	Ea	1G3L,19	480	2.83		3.53
	2'-3' diameter						
410	1 3/4 CY track loader	Ea	1G2L,18	80	12.91		16.10
420	3 CY track loader	Ea	1G3L,19	160	8.48		10.60
	3'-4' diameter						
430	1 3/4 CY track loader	Ea	1G2L,18	20	51.64		65.00
440	3 CY track loader	Ea	1G3L,19	48	28.27		35.30
	4'-6' diameter						
450	1 3/4 CY track loader	Ea	1G2L,18	10	103.28		129.00
460	3 CY track loader	Ea	1G3L,19	24	56.53		71.00

Haul and dump, see Appendix I

Burn cleared timber and/or grubbed stumps on site, use loading cost plus 25 percent

02115 Selective Clearing

KEY	DESCRIPTION	UNIT	CREW AND EQUIPMENT	PER DAY	INSTALLATION COST	MATERIALS COST	TOTAL + 25%
00	COMPOSITE COSTS						
	Fell and buck tree, grub stump, load, haul and dump						
	open area						
100	6" diameter	Ea					124.00
110	12" diameter	Ea					222.00
120	18" diameter	Ea					309.00
130	24" diameter	Ea					409.00
140	36" diameter	Ea					570.00
	congested area						
150	6" diameter	Ea					303.00
160	12" diameter	Ea					411.00
170	18" diameter	Ea					650.00
180	24" diameter	Ea					810.00
190	36" diameter	Ea					1040.00

SITE PREPARATION

02115 Selective Clearing — 1994

KEY	DESCRIPTION	UNIT	CREW AND EQUIPMENT	PER DAY	INSTALLATION COST	MATERIALS COST	TOTAL + 25%
	Prune tree, load, haul and dump trimmings						
200	6" diameter	Ea					58.00
210	12" diameter	Ea					122.00
220	18' diameter	Ea					177.00
230	24" diameter	Ea					235.00
240	36" diameter	Ea					348.00
	Strip sod, load, haul and dump						
250	1 MSF or less	SY					4.36
260	over 1 MSF	SY					0.69
270	over 1 acre	MSF					77.00
10	**TREE REMOVAL**						
	Fell and buck tree, chip small branches						
	open area						
100	6" diameter	Ea	3L,82,84	30	25.22		31.50
110	9" diameter	Ea	3L,82,84	22	34.39		43.00
120	12" diameter	Ea	3L,82,84	17	44.50		56.00
130	18" diameter	Ea	3L,82,84	12	63.04		79.00
140	24" diameter	Ea	3L,82,84	9	84.05		105.00
150	30" diameter	Ea	3L,82,84	7	108.07		135.00
160	36" diameter	Ea	3L,82,84	6	126.08		158.00
170	48" diameter	Ea	3L,82,84	5	151.30		189.00
	congested area						
	6" diameter						
180	by hand	Ea	3L,82,84	16	47.28		59.00
190	aerial lift truck	Ea	1D2L,08,82,84	21	46.16		58.00
	9" diameter						
200	by hand	Ea	3L,82,84	11	68.77		86.00
210	aerial lift truck	Ea	1D2L,08,82,84	14	69.24		87.00
	12" diameter						
220	by hand	Ea	3L,82,84	8	94.56		118.00
230	aerial lift truck	Ea	1D2L,08,82,84	11	88.13		110.00
	18" diameter						
240	by hand	Ea	3L,82,84	5	151.30		189.00
250	aerial lift truck	Ea	1D2L,08,82,84	7	138.49		173.00
	24" diameter						
260	by hand	Ea	3L,82,84	4	189.12		236.00
270	aerial lift truck	Ea	1D2L,08,82,84	5	193.88		242.00
	30" diameter						
280	by hand	Ea	3L,82,84	3.2	236.40		296.00
290	aerial lift truck	Ea	1D2L,08,82,84	4	242.35		303.00
	36" diameter						
300	by hand	Ea	3L,82,84	2.7	280.18		350.00
310	aerial lift truck	Ea	1D2L,08,82,84	3.5	276.97		346.00
	48" diameter						
320	by hand	Ea	3L,82,84	2	378.25		473.00
330	aerial lift truck	Ea	1D2L,08,82,84	2.6	372.85		466.00
20	**STUMP REMOVAL**						
	Chip stump to below groundline						
100	6" diameter	Ea	1L,85	55	6.26		7.80
110	9" diameter	Ea	1L,85	46	7.48		9.30
120	12" diameter	Ea	1L,85	40	8.60		10.80
130	18" diameter	Ea	1L,85	32	10.75		13.40
140	24" diameter	Ea	1L,85	27	12.74		15.90
150	30" diameter	Ea	1L,85	23	14.96		18.70
160	36" diameter	Ea	1L,85	20	17.20		21.50
170	48" diameter	Ea	1L,85	16	21.50		26.90
	Grub stump						
	6" diameter						
180	by hand	Ea	3L	4	153.02		191.00
190	1 CY backhoe	Ea	1G1L,15	40	18.47		23.10

02115 Selective Clearing — 1994

KEY	DESCRIPTION	UNIT	CREW AND EQUIPMENT	PER DAY	INSTALLATION COST	MATERIALS COST	TOTAL + 25%
	9" diameter						
200	by hand	Ea	3L	3.4	180.03		225.00
210	1 CY backhoe	Ea	1G1L,15	27	27.36		34.20
	12" diameter						
220	by hand	Ea	3L	3	204.03		255.00
230	1 CY backhoe	Ea	1G1L,15	20	36.94		46.20
	18" diameter						
240	by hand	Ea	3L	2.4	255.04		319.00
250	1 CY backhoe	Ea	1G1L,15	13	56.83		71.00
	24" diameter						
260	by hand	Ea	3L	2	306.05		383.00
270	1 CY backhoe	Ea	1G1L,15	10	73.87		92.00
	30" diameter						
280	by hand	Ea	3L	1.7	360.05		450.00
290	1 CY backhoe	Ea	1G1L,15	8	92.34		115.00
	36" diameter						
300	by hand	Ea	3L	1.5	408.06		510.00
310	1 CY backhoe	Ea	1G1L,15	7	105.53		132.00
	48" diameter						
320	by hand	Ea	3L	1.2	510.08		640.00
330	1 CY backhoe	Ea	1G1L,15	5	147.75		185.00
30	**SHRUB REMOVAL**						
	Cut shrubs or trees under 4" diameter						
100	5' height	Ea	1L,82	95	2.30		2.87
110	10' height	Ea	1L,82	48	4.55		5.70
120	15' height	Ea	1L,82	32	6.83		8.50
130	20' height	Ea	1L,82	24	9.10		11.40
	Cut and chip shrubs or trees under 4" diameter						
140	5' height	Ea	2L,82,84	130	4.25		5.30
150	10' height	Ea	2L,82,84	65	8.50		10.60
160	15' height	Ea	2L,82,84	43	12.85		16.10
170	20' height	Ea	2L,82,84	32	17.26		21.60
40	**TREE PRUNING**						
	Prune trees						
	6" diameter						
100	by hand	Ea	2L,84	15	35.87		44.80
110	aerial lift truck	Ea	1D1L,08,84	20	37.55		46.90
	9" diameter						
120	by hand	Ea	2L,84	10	53.81		67.00
130	aerial lift truck	Ea	1D1L,08,84	13	57.77		72.00
	12" diameter						
140	by hand	Ea	2L,84	7	76.87		96.00
150	aerial lift truck	Ea	1D1L,08,84	10	75.10		94.00
	18" diameter						
160	by hand	Ea	2L,84	4.9	109.81		137.00
170	aerial lift truck	Ea	1D1L,08,84	7	107.28		134.00
	24" diameter						
180	by hand	Ea	2L,84	3.7	145.42		182.00
190	aerial lift truck	Ea	1D1L,08,84	4.9	153.26		192.00
	30" diameter						
200	by hand	Ea	2L,84	3	179.35		224.00
210	aerial lift truck	Ea	1D1L,08,84	3.9	192.56		241.00
	36" diameter						
220	by hand	Ea	2L,84	2.5	215.22		269.00
230	aerial lift truck	Ea	1D1L,08,84	3.3	227.57		284.00
	48" diameter						
240	by hand	Ea	2L,84	1.9	283.19		354.00
250	aerial lift truck	Ea	1D1L,08,84	2.4	312.91		391.00

SITE PREPARATION

KEY	DESCRIPTION	UNIT	CREW AND EQUIPMENT	PER DAY	INSTALLATION COST	MATERIALS COST	TOTAL + 25%
50	**SOD STRIPPING**						
	Strip sod						
100	by hand	SY	1L	160	1.28		1.59
110	18" sod cutter	MSF	1L,70	42	8.91		11.10
120	1/2 CY wheel loader	MSF	1G,10	70	6.92		8.70
130	1 CY wheel loader	MSF	1G,11	150	3.66		4.58
140	50 HP bulldozer	MSF	1G,20	220	2.02		2.53
150	150 HP bulldozer	MSF	1G,21	430	1.52		1.90
60	**DISPOSAL**						
	Stack or load bucked trees						
	6" diameter						
100	by hand	Ea	3L	24	25.50		31.90
110	1 1/2 CY wheel loader	Ea	1G2L,12	48	20.89		26.10
	9" diameter						
120	by hand	Ea	3L	16	38.26		47.80
130	1 1/2 CY wheel loader	Ea	1G2L,12	32	31.34		39.20
	12" diameter						
140	by hand	Ea	3L	12	51.01		64.00
150	1 1/2 CY wheel loader	Ea	1G2L,12	24	41.78		52.00
	18" diameter						
160	by hand	Ea	3L	8	76.51		96.00
170	1 1/2 CY wheel loader	Ea	1G2L,12	16	62.67		78.00
180	boom truck	Ea	1D2L,07	13	80.39		100.00
	24" diameter						
190	by hand	Ea	3L	6	102.02		128.00
200	1 1/2 CY wheel loader	Ea	1G2L,12	12	83.56		104.00
210	boom truck	Ea	1D2L,07	10	104.50		131.00
	30" diameter						
220	by hand	Ea	3L	4.8	127.52		159.00
230	1 1/2 CY wheel loader	Ea	1G2L,12	10	100.28		125.00
240	boom truck	Ea	1D2L,07	8	130.63		163.00
	36" diameter						
250	by hand	Ea	3L	4	153.02		191.00
260	1 1/2 CY wheel loader	Ea	1G2L,12	8	125.35		157.00
270	boom truck	Ea	1D2L,07	6	174.17		218.00
	48" diameter						
280	by hand	Ea	3L	3	204.03		255.00
290	1 1/2 CY wheel loader	Ea	1G2L,12	6	167.13		209.00
300	boom truck	Ea	1D2L,07	4.8	217.71		272.00
	Load grubbed stumps						
	6" diameter						
310	by hand	Ea	3L	60	10.20		12.80
320	1 1/2 CY wheel loader	Ea	1G2L,12	120	8.36		10.40
	9" diameter						
330	by hand	Ea	3L	44	13.91		17.40
340	1 1/2 CY wheel loader	Ea	1G2L,12	85	11.80		14.70
	12" diameter						
350	by hand	Ea	3L	35	17.49		21.90
360	1 1/2 CY wheel loader	Ea	1G2L,12	70	14.33		17.90
	18" diameter						
370	by hand	Ea	3L	24	25.50		31.90
380	1 1/2 CY wheel loader	Ea	1G2L,12	48	20.89		26.10
390	boom truck	Ea	1D2L,07	38	27.50		34.40
	24" diameter						
400	by hand	Ea	3L	18	34.01		42.50
410	1 1/2 CY wheel loader	Ea	1G2L,12	37	27.10		33.90
420	boom truck	Ea	1D2L,07	30	34.83		43.50
	30" diameter						
430	1 1/2 CY wheel loader	Ea	1G2L,12	30	33.43		41.80
440	boom truck	Ea	1D2L,07	24	43.54		54.00

KEY	DESCRIPTION	UNIT	CREW AND EQUIPMENT	PER DAY	INSTALLATION COST	MATERIALS COST	TOTAL + 25%
	36" diameter						
450	1 1/2 CY wheel loader	Ea	1G2L,12	25	40.11		50.00
460	boom truck	Ea	1D2L,07	20	52.25		65.00
	48" diameter						
470	1 1/2 CY wheel loader	Ea	1G2L,12	19	52.78		66.00
480	boom truck	Ea	1D2L,07	15	69.67		87.00
	Stack or load tree prunings						
490	6" diameter	Ea	2L	48	8.50		10.60
500	9" diameter	Ea	2L	32	12.75		15.90
510	12" diameter	Ea	2L	24	17.00		21.30
520	18" diameter	Ea	2L	16	25.50		31.90
530	24" diameter	Ea	2L	12	34.01		42.50
540	30" diameter	Ea	2L	10	40.81		51.00
550	36" diameter	Ea	2L	8	51.01		64.00
560	48" diameter	Ea	2L	6	68.01		85.00
	Pile sod on site or load on truck						
570	by hand	SY	1L	190	1.07		1.34
580	1/2 CY wheel loader	MSF	1G,10	65	7.46		9.30
590	1 CY wheel loader	MSF	1G,11	130	4.23		5.30
600	1 1/2 CY wheel loader	MSF	1G,12	190	3.13		3.91

Haul and dump, see Appendix I

EARTHWORK

KEY	DESCRIPTION	UNIT	CREW AND EQUIPMENT	PER DAY	INSTALLATION COST	MATERIALS COST	TOTAL + 25%
00	**COMPOSITE COSTS**						
	Rough grade and scarify subgrade, furnish and spread topsoil, and fine grade						
	4" deep						
100	1000 SF or less	SY					14.50
110	over 1000 SF	SY					6.90
120	over 1 acre	MSF					406.00
	6" deep						
130	1000 SF or less	SY					15.30
140	over 1000 SF	SY					8.20
150	over 1 acre	MSF					463.00
	Rough grade and scarify subgrade, spread topsoil from stockpile, and fine grade						
	4" deep						
160	1000 SF or less	SY					12.00
170	over 1000 SF	SY					4.44
180	over 1 acre	MSF					129.00
	6" deep						
190	1000 SF or less	SY					15.20
200	over 1000 SF	SY					4.49
210	over 1 acre	MSF					139.00
10	**TOPSOIL STRIPPING**						
	Strip and stockpile topsoil, 4" depth						
	50' maximum haul						
105	by hand	SY	2L	75	5.44		6.80
110	1/2 CY wheel loader	MSF	1G,10	8	60.59		76.00
115	50 HP bulldozer	MSF	1G,20	29	15.33		19.20
	150' maximum haul						
120	by hand	SY	2L	60	6.80		8.50
125	1/2 CY wheel loader	MSF	1G,10	4.9	98.92		124.00
130	50 HP bulldozer	MSF	1G,20	13	34.21		42.80
135	150 HP bulldozer	MSF	1G,21	37	17.69		22.10
140	300 HP bulldozer	MSF	1G,22	80	12.81		16.00
	300' maximum haul						
145	150 HP bulldozer	MSF	1G,21	24	27.28		34.10
150	300 HP bulldozer	MSF	1G,22	55	18.63		23.30
	500' maximum haul						
155	300 HP bulldozer	MSF	1G,22	36	28.46		35.60
160	10 CY towed scraper	MSF	1A,30	27	28.66		35.80
165	15 CY towed scraper	MSF	1A,31	55	14.25		17.80
170	20 CY towed scraper	MSF	1A,32	60	19.73		24.70
	1000' maximum haul						
175	10 CY towed scraper	MSF	1A,30	22	35.17		44.00
180	15 CY towed scraper	MSF	1A,31	42	18.66		23.30
185	20 CY towed scraper	MSF	1A,32	47	25.19		31.50
190	15 CY motor scraper, 1/4 push dozer	MSF	1A1G,22,33	55	28.02		35.00
195	10 CY elevating scraper	MSF	1A,34	46	16.61		20.80
200	20 CY elevating scraper	MSF	1A,35	65	19.91		24.90
	Strip and stockpile topsoil, 6" depth						
	50' maximum haul						
205	by hand	SY	2L	50	8.16		10.20
210	1/2 CY wheel loader	MSF	1G,10	5	96.94		121.00
215	50 HP bulldozer	MSF	1G,20	22	20.21		25.30
	150' maximum haul						
220	by hand	SY	2L	41	9.95		12.40
225	1/2 CY wheel loader	MSF	1G,10	3.4	142.56		178.00
230	50 HP bulldozer	MSF	1G,20	9	49.41		62.00
235	150 HP bulldozer	MSF	1G,21	29	22.58		28.20
240	300 HP bulldozer	MSF	1G,22	65	15.76		19.70

02210 Grading

KEY	DESCRIPTION	UNIT	CREW AND EQUIPMENT	PER DAY	INSTALLATION COST	MATERIALS COST	TOTAL + 25%
	300' maximum haul						
245	150 HP bulldozer	MSF	1G,21	18	36.37		45.50
250	300 HP bulldozer	MSF	1G,22	40	25.62		32.00
	500' maximum haul						
255	300 HP bulldozer	MSF	1G,22	24	42.70		53.00
260	10 CY towed scraper	MSF	1A,30	23	33.65		42.10
265	15 CY towed scraper	MSF	1A,31	44	17.81		22.30
270	20 CY towed scraper	MSF	1A,32	50	23.68		29.60
	1000' maximum haul						
275	10 CY towed scraper	MSF	1A,30	17	45.52		57.00
280	15 CY towed scraper	MSF	1A,31	33	23.75		29.70
285	20 CY towed scraper	MSF	1A,32	37	32.00		40.00
290	15 CY motor scraper, 1/5 push dozer	MSF	1A1G,22,33	45	33.39		41.70
295	10 CY elevating scraper	MSF	1A,34	36	21.22		26.50
300	20 CY elevating scraper	MSF	1A,35	55	23.52		29.40
	Strip and stockpile topsoil, 8" depth						
	50' maximum haul						
305	by hand	SY	2L	39	10.46		13.10
310	1/2 CY wheel loader	MSF	1G,10	4.2	115.41		144.00
315	50 HP bulldozer	MSF	1G,20	18	24.71		30.90
	150' maximum haul						
320	by hand	SY	2L	31	13.16		16.50
325	1/2 CY wheel loader	MSF	1G,10	2.6	186.43		233.00
330	50 HP bulldozer	MSF	1G,20	7	63.53		79.00
335	150 HP bulldozer	MSF	1G,21	24	27.28		34.10
340	300 HP bulldozer	MSF	1G,22	55	18.63		23.30
	300' maximum haul						
345	150 HP bulldozer	MSF	1G,21	14	46.77		58.00
350	300 HP bulldozer	MSF	1G,22	32	32.02		40.00
	500' maximum haul						
355	300 HP bulldozer	MSF	1G,22	21	48.80		61.00
360	10 CY towed scraper	MSF	1A,30	19	40.73		51.00
365	15 CY towed scraper	MSF	1A,31	38	20.63		25.80
370	20 CY towed scraper	MSF	1A,32	43	27.53		34.40
	1000' maximum haul						
375	10 CY towed scraper	MSF	1A,30	14	55.27		69.00
380	15 CY towed scraper	MSF	1A,31	27	29.03		36.30
385	20 CY towed scraper	MSF	1A,32	30	39.46		49.30
390	15 CY motor scraper, 1/6 push dozer	MSF	1A1G,22,33	37	39.92		49.90
395	10 CY elevating scraper	MSF	1A,34	29	26.34		32.90
400	20 CY elevating scraper	MSF	1A,35	47	27.53		34.40
	Strip and stockpile topsoil, 10" depth						
	50' maximum haul						
405	by hand	SY	2L	32	12.75		15.90
410	1/2 CY wheel loader	MSF	1G,10	3.4	142.56		178.00
415	50 HP bulldozer	MSF	1G,20	15	29.65		37.10
	150' maximum haul						
420	by hand	SY	2L	25	16.32		20.40
425	1/2 CY wheel loader	MSF	1G,10	2.1	230.81		289.00
430	50 HP bulldozer	MSF	1G,20	6	74.12		93.00
435	150 HP bulldozer	MSF	1G,21	20	32.74		40.90
440	300 HP bulldozer	MSF	1G,22	45	22.77		28.50
	300' maximum haul						
445	150 HP bulldozer	MSF	1G,21	12	54.56		68.00
450	300 HP bulldozer	MSF	1G,22	27	37.95		47.40
	500' maximum haul						
455	300 HP bulldozer	MSF	1G,22	17	60.28		75.00
460	10 CY towed scraper	MSF	1A,30	17	45.52		57.00
465	15 CY towed scraper	MSF	1A,31	33	23.75		29.70
470	20 CY towed scraper	MSF	1A,32	37	32.00		40.00

| | 02210 Grading | | | | | | 1994 |

KEY	DESCRIPTION	UNIT	CREW AND EQUIPMENT	PER DAY	INSTALLATION COST	MATERIALS COST	TOTAL + 25%
	1000' maximum haul						
475	10 CY towed scraper	MSF	1A,30	12	64.49		81.00
480	15 CY towed scraper	MSF	1A,31	23	34.08		42.60
485	20 CY towed scraper	MSF	1A,32	26	45.53		57.00
490	15 CY motor scraper, 1/7 push dozer	MSF	1A1G,22,33	32	45.58		57.00
495	10 CY elevating scraper	MSF	1A,34	25	30.55		38.20
500	20 CY elevating scraper	MSF	1A,35	41	31.56		39.40
	Strip and stockpile topsoil, 12" depth						
	50' maximum haul						
505	by hand	SY	2L	27	15.11		18.90
510	1/2 CY wheel loader	MSF	1G,10	2.9	167.14		209.00
515	50 HP bulldozer	MSF	1G,20	13	34.21		42.80
	150' maximum haul						
520	by hand	SY	2L	21	19.43		24.30
525	1/2 CY wheel loader	MSF	1G,10	1.8	269.28		337.00
530	50 HP bulldozer	MSF	1G,20	4.7	94.62		118.00
535	150 HP bulldozer	MSF	1G,21	18	36.37		45.50
540	300 HP bulldozer	MSF	1G,22	40	25.62		32.00
	300' maximum haul						
545	150 HP bulldozer	MSF	1G,21	10	65.47		82.00
550	300 HP bulldozer	MSF	1G,22	23	44.55		56.00
	500' maximum haul						
555	300 HP bulldozer	MSF	1G,22	15	68.31		85.00
560	10 CY towed scraper	MSF	1A,30	15	51.59		64.00
565	15 CY towed scraper	MSF	1A,31	29	27.03		33.80
570	20 CY towed scraper	MSF	1A,32	33	35.87		44.80
	1000' maximum haul						
575	10 CY towed scraper	MSF	1A,30	11	70.35		88.00
580	15 CY towed scraper	MSF	1A,31	20	39.19		49.00
585	20 CY towed scraper	MSF	1A,32	22	53.81		67.00
590	15 CY motor scraper, 1/8 push dozer	MSF	1A1G,22,33	28	51.60		64.00
595	10 CY elevating scraper	MSF	1A,34	21	36.37		45.50
600	20 CY elevating scraper	MSF	1A,35	36	35.94		44.90
15	**BULK SITE EXCAVATING AND FILLING**						
	Rip hardpan soil						
100	150 HP tractor, ripper	BCY	1G,21	10160	0.06		0.08
110	300 HP tractor, ripper	BCY	1G,22	18310	0.06		0.07
	Excavate and fill balanced quantities on site, light or medium soil, compaction not included						
	50' maximum haul						
120	by hand, light soil	BCY	2L	8	51.01		64.00
130	by hand, medium soil	BCY	2L	6	68.01		85.00
140	1/2 CY wheel loader	BCY	1G,10	130	3.73		4.66
150	50 HP bulldozer	BCY	1G,20	560	0.79		0.99
	150' maximum haul						
160	by hand, light soil	BCY	2L	7	58.29		73.00
170	by hand, medium soil	BCY	2L	5	81.61		102.00
180	1/2 CY wheel loader	BCY	1G,10	80	6.06		7.60
190	50 HP bulldozer	BCY	1G,20	250	1.78		2.22
200	150 HP bulldozer	BCY	1G1L,21	950	0.90		1.13
210	300 HP bulldozer	BCY	1G1L,22	1950	0.63		0.79
	300' maximum haul						
220	150 HP bulldozer	BCY	1G1L,21	460	1.87		2.33
230	300 HP bulldozer	BCY	1G1L,22	1070	1.15		1.44
	500' maximum haul						
240	300 HP bulldozer	BCY	1G1L,22	680	1.81		2.26
250	10 CY towed scraper, 1/2 push dozer	BCY	1A1G1L,21,30	620	2.31		2.89
260	15 CY towed scraper, 1/3 push dozer	BCY	1A1G1L,22,31	1160	1.29		1.62
270	20 CY towed scraper, 1/3 push dozer	BCY	1A1G1L,22,32	1330	1.43		1.79

KEY	DESCRIPTION	UNIT	CREW AND EQUIPMENT	PER DAY	INSTALLATION COST	MATERIALS COST	TOTAL + 25%
	1000' maximum haul						
280	10 CY towed scraper, 1/3 push dozer	BCY	1A1G1L,21,30	420	3.25		4.07
290	15 CY towed scraper, 1/4 push dozer	BCY	1A1G1L,22,31	760	1.89		2.36
300	20 CY towed scraper, 1/5 push dozer	BCY	1A1G1L,22,32	870	2.07		2.58
310	15 CY motor scraper, 1/2 push dozer	BCY	1A1G1L,22,33	1440	1.35		1.68
320	10 CY elevating scraper	BCY	1A1L,34	910	1.06		1.33
330	20 CY elevating scraper	BCY	1A1L,35	1830	0.82		1.02
	2000' maximum haul						
340	15 CY motor scraper, 1/2 push dozer	BCY	1A1G1L,22,33	1110	1.75		2.18
350	10 CY elevating scraper	BCY	1A1L,34	660	1.47		1.83
360	20 CY elevating scraper	BCY	1A1L,35	1380	1.09		1.36
	4000' maximum haul						
370	15 CY motor scraper, 1/3 push dozer	BCY	1A1G1L,22,33	780	2.32		2.90
380	10 CY elevating scraper	BCY	1A1L,34	460	2.10		2.63
390	20 CY elevating scraper	BCY	1A1L,35	990	1.51		1.89
	Excavate and fill balanced quantities on site, heavy soil, compaction not included						
	50' maximum haul						
400	by hand	BCY	2L	4.6	88.71		111.00
410	1/2 CY wheel loader	BCY	1G,10	110	4.41		5.50
420	50 HP bulldozer	BCY	1G,20	440	1.01		1.26
	150' maximum haul						
430	by hand	BCY	2L	4.2	97.16		121.00
440	1/2 CY wheel loader	BCY	1G,10	65	7.46		9.30
450	50 HP bulldozer	BCY	1G,20	190	2.34		2.93
460	150 HP bulldozer	BCY	1G1L,21	740	1.16		1.45
470	300 HP bulldozer	BCY	1G1L,22	1530	0.80		1.00
	300' maximum haul						
480	150 HP bulldozer	BCY	1G1L,21	360	2.39		2.98
490	300 HP bulldozer	BCY	1G1L,22	840	1.46		1.83
	500' maximum haul						
500	300 HP bulldozer	BCY	1G1L,22	540	2.28		2.84
510	10 CY towed scraper, 1/2 push dozer	BCY	1A1G1L,21,30	500	2.87		3.58
520	15 CY towed scraper, 1/3 push dozer	BCY	1A1G1L,22,31	930	1.61		2.02
530	20 CY towed scraper, 1/3 push dozer	BCY	1A1G1L,22,32	1060	1.79		2.24
	1000' maximum haul						
540	10 CY towed scraper, 1/3 push dozer	BCY	1A1G1L,21,30	340	4.02		5.00
550	15 CY towed scraper, 1/4 push dozer	BCY	1A1G1L,22,31	610	2.35		2.94
560	20 CY towed scraper, 1/5 push dozer	BCY	1A1G1L,22,32	690	2.60		3.25
570	15 CY motor scraper, 1/2 push dozer	BCY	1A1G1L,22,33	1130	1.71		2.14
580	10 CY elevating scraper	BCY	1A1L,34	710	1.36		1.70
590	20 CY elevating scraper	BCY	1A1L,35	1440	1.04		1.30
	2000' maximum haul						
600	15 CY motor scraper, 1/2 push dozer	BCY	1A1G1L,22,33	870	2.23		2.78
610	10 CY elevating scraper	BCY	1A1L,34	520	1.86		2.33
620	20 CY elevating scraper	BCY	1A1L,35	1080	1.39		1.73
	4000' maximum haul						
630	15 CY motor scraper, 1/3 push dozer	BCY	1A1G1L,22,33	620	2.92		3.65
640	10 CY elevating scraper	BCY	1A1L,34	360	2.69		3.36
650	20 CY elevating scraper	BCY	1A1L,35	780	1.92		2.40
20	**BULK EXCAVATING**						
	Excavate and pile soil						
	light or medium soil						
100	by hand, light soil	BCY	2L	15	27.20		34.00
110	by hand, medium soil	BCY	2L	9	45.34		57.00
120	1/2 CY wheel loader	BCY	1G,10	230	2.11		2.63
130	1 CY wheel loader	BCY	1G1L,11	450	1.67		2.09
140	1 1/2 CY wheel loader	BCY	1G1L,12	680	1.17		1.47
150	3/4 CY track loader	BCY	1G1L,16	410	1.56		1.95

	02210 Grading						1994
KEY	DESCRIPTION	UNIT	CREW AND EQUIPMENT	PER DAY	INSTALLATION COST	MATERIALS COST	TOTAL + 25%
160	1 CY track loader	BCY	1G1L,17	550	1.31		1.63
170	1 3/4 CY track loader	BCY	1G1L,18	970	0.85		1.07
180	3 CY track loader	BCY	1G1L,19	1660	0.57		0.71
190	50 HP bulldozer	BCY	1G,20	560	0.79		0.99
200	150 HP bulldozer	BCY	1G1L,21	1900	0.45		0.56
210	300 HP bulldozer	BCY	1G1L,22	4300	0.29		0.36
	heavy soil						
220	by hand	BCY	2L	7	58.29		73.00
230	1/2 CY wheel loader	BCY	1G,10	180	2.69		3.37
240	1 CY wheel loader	BCY	1G1L,11	350	2.15		2.69
250	1 1/2 CY wheel loader	BCY	1G1L,12	530	1.51		1.88
260	3/4 CY track loader	BCY	1G1L,16	320	2.00		2.50
270	1 CY track loader	BCY	1G1L,17	430	1.67		2.09
280	1 3/4 CY track loader	BCY	1G1L,18	760	1.09		1.36
290	3 CY track loader	BCY	1G1L,19	1300	0.73		0.91
300	50 HP bulldozer	BCY	1G,20	440	1.01		1.26
310	150 HP bulldozer	BCY	1G1L,21	1490	0.58		0.72
320	300 HP bulldozer	BCY	1G1L,22	3380	0.36		0.45
	Excavate and load soil						
	light or medium soil						
330	by hand, light soil	BCY	2L	8	51.01		64.00
340	by hand, medium soil	BCY	2L	4.9	83.28		104.00
350	1/2 CY wheel loader	BCY	1G,10	210	2.31		2.89
360	1 CY wheel loader	BCY	1G1L,11	410	1.84		2.30
370	1 1/2 CY wheel loader	BCY	1G1L,12	620	1.29		1.61
380	3/4 CY track loader	BCY	1G1L,16	370	1.73		2.16
390	1 CY track loader	BCY	1G1L,17	490	1.47		1.83
400	1 3/4 CY track loader	BCY	1G1L,18	860	0.96		1.20
410	3 CY track loader	BCY	1G1L,19	1480	0.64		0.80
	heavy soil						
420	by hand	BCY	2L	3.7	110.29		138.00
430	1/2 CY wheel loader	BCY	1G,10	160	3.03		3.79
440	1 CY wheel loader	BCY	1G1L,11	330	2.28		2.86
450	1 1/2 CY wheel loader	BCY	1G1L,12	490	1.63		2.04
460	3/4 CY track loader	BCY	1G1L,16	300	2.13		2.66
470	1 CY track loader	BCY	1G1L,17	390	1.84		2.30
480	1 3/4 CY track loader	BCY	1G1L,18	690	1.20		1.50
490	3 CY track loader	BCY	1G1L,19	1190	0.80		1.00
	Load piled soil						
	light or medium soil						
500	by hand, light soil	BCY	1L	9	22.67		28.30
510	by hand, medium soil	BCY	1L	5	40.81		51.00
520	1/2 CY wheel loader	BCY	1G,10	230	2.11		2.63
530	1 CY wheel loader	BCY	1G,11	450	1.22		1.53
540	1 1/2 CY wheel loader	BCY	1G,12	680	0.87		1.09
550	3/4 CY track loader	BCY	1G,16	520	0.84		1.04
560	1 CY track loader	BCY	1G,17	690	0.75		0.93
570	1 3/4 CY track loader	BCY	1G,18	1220	0.51		0.64
580	3 CY track loader	BCY	1G,19	2080	0.36		0.45
	heavy soil						
590	by hand	BCY	1L	4.5	45.34		57.00
600	1/2 CY wheel loader	BCY	1G,10	180	2.69		3.37
610	1 CY wheel loader	BCY	1G,11	350	1.57		1.96
620	1 1/2 CY wheel loader	BCY	1G,12	530	1.12		1.40
630	3/4 CY track loader	BCY	1G,16	420	1.04		1.29
640	1 CY track loader	BCY	1G,17	560	0.92		1.15
650	1 3/4 CY track loader	BCY	1G,18	970	0.64		0.81
660	3 CY track loader	BCY	1G,19	1670	0.45		0.56

Haul and dump, see Appendix I

KEY	DESCRIPTION	UNIT	CREW AND EQUIPMENT	PER DAY	INSTALLATION COST	MATERIALS COST	TOTAL + 25%
	Grade at dump						
	light or medium soil						
670	by hand, light soil	BCY	1L	40	5.10		6.40
680	by hand, medium soil	BCY	1L	35	5.83		7.30
690	1/2 CY wheel loader	BCY	1G,10	240	2.02		2.52
700	50 HP bulldozer	BCY	1G,20	670	0.66		0.83
710	150 HP bulldozer	BCY	1G,21	2280	0.29		0.36
720	300 HP bulldozer	BCY	1G,22	5160	0.20		0.25
	heavy soil						
730	by hand	BCY	1L	27	7.56		9.40
740	1/2 CY wheel loader	BCY	1G,10	190	2.55		3.19
750	50 HP bulldozer	BCY	1G,20	530	0.84		1.05
760	150 HP bulldozer	BCY	1G,21	1790	0.37		0.46
770	300 HP bulldozer	BCY	1G,22	4060	0.25		0.32
25	**BULK FILLING**						
100	Common borrow	CCY				6.00	7.50
	Load borrow at pit, haul and dump, see Appendix I						
	Spread dumped soil, compaction not included						
	light or medium soil						
110	by hand, light soil	CCY	1L	35	5.83		7.30
120	by hand, medium soil	CCY	1L	30	6.80		8.50
130	1/2 CY wheel loader	CCY	1G,10	240	2.02		2.52
140	50 HP bulldozer	CCY	1G,20	670	0.66		0.83
150	150 HP bulldozer	CCY	1G1L,21	2280	0.38		0.47
160	300 HP bulldozer	CCY	1G1L,22	5160	0.24		0.30
	heavy soil						
170	by hand	CCY	1L	23	8.87		11.10
180	1/2 CY wheel loader	CCY	1G,10	210	2.31		2.89
190	50 HP bulldozer	CCY	1G,20	530	0.84		1.05
200	150 HP bulldozer	CCY	1G1L,21	1750	0.49		0.61
210	300 HP bulldozer	CCY	1G1L,22	4060	0.30		0.38
30	**COMPACTION**						
	Compact bulk fill, minimal compaction						
100	50 HP bulldozer	CCY	1G,20	2850	0.16		0.20
110	150 HP bulldozer	CCY	1G,21	5680	0.12		0.14
120	300 HP bulldozer	CCY	1G,22	13500	0.08		0.09
35	**LOOSENING ROCK**						
	Drill rock for blasting, etc.						
	soft rock (use 0.5 LF of drilling per BCY of Rock)						
100	by hand	LF	2L	16	25.50		31.90
110	air tools, 2"	LF	1G3L,86	310	3.25		4.06
120	air tools, 2 1/2"	LF	1G3L,86	230	4.38		5.50
130	crawler drill	LF	2G1L,23	500	3.13		3.91
	medium rock (use 1 LF of drilling per BCY of rock						
140	by hand	LF	2L	13	31.39		39.20
150	air tools, 2"	LF	1G3L,86	210	4.79		6.00
160	air tools, 2 1/2"	LF	1G3L,86	160	6.29		7.90
170	crawler drill	LF	2G1L,23	350	4.47		5.60
	hard rock (use 1.5 LF of drilling per BCY of rock)						
180	by hand	LF	2L	9	45.34		57.00
190	air tools, 2"	LF	1G3L,86	150	6.71		8.40
200	air tools, 2 1/2"	LF	1G3L,86	110	9.15		11.40
210	crawler drill	LF	2G1L,23	240	6.51		8.10

EARTHWORK

KEY	DESCRIPTION	UNIT	CREW AND EQUIPMENT	PER DAY	INSTALLATION COST	MATERIALS COST	TOTAL + 25%
	Blast rock						
220	soft rock	BCY	3L	400	1.53	0.60	2.66
230	medium rock	BCY	4L	400	2.04	1.15	3.99
240	hard rock	BCY	3L	200	3.06	2.01	6.30
250	Rip rock	BCY	1G,22	5250	0.20		0.24
40	**ROCK EXCAVATION AND FILLING**						
	Excavate and fill loosened rock on site						
	50' maximum haul						
100	by hand	BCY	2L	4.6	88.71		111.00
110	1/2 CY wheel loader	BCY	1G,10	105	4.62		5.80
120	50 HP bulldozer	BCY	1G,20	245	1.82		2.27
	150' maximum haul						
130	by hand	BCY	2L	4.2	97.16		121.00
140	1/2 CY wheel loader	BCY	1G,10	62	7.82		9.80
150	50 HP bulldozer	BCY	1G,20	110	4.04		5.10
160	150 HP bulldozer	BCY	1G,21	415	1.58		1.97
170	300 HP bulldozer	BCY	1G,22	855	1.20		1.50
	300' maximum haul						
180	150 HP bulldozer	BCY	1G,21	200	3.27		4.09
190	300 HP bulldozer	BCY	1G,22	470	2.18		2.73
	500' maximum haul						0.00
200	300 HP bulldozer	BCY	1G,22	300	3.42		4.27
	Excavate and pile loosened rock						
210	by hand	BCY	2L	7	58.29		73.00
220	1/2 CY wheel loader	BCY	1G,10	175	2.77		3.46
230	3/4 CY wheel loader	BCY	1G,16	275	1.58		1.98
240	1 CY track loader	BCY	1G,17	365	1.41		1.76
250	1 3/4 CY track loader	BCY	1G,18	645	0.97		1.21
260	3 CY track loader	BCY	1G,19	1100	0.68		0.85
270	50 HP bulldozer	BCY	1G,20	245	1.82		2.27
280	150 HP bulldozer	BCY	1G,21	630	1.04		1.30
290	300 HP bulldozer	BCY	1G,22	1890	0.54		0.68
	Excavate and load loosened rock						
300	by hand	BCY	2L	3.7	110.29		138.00
310	1/2 CY wheel loader	BCY	1G,10	125	3.88		4.85
320	3/4 CY wheel loader	BCY	1G,16	220	1.98		2.47
330	1 CY track loader	BCY	1G,17	295	1.74		2.18
340	1 3/4 CY track loader	BCY	1G,18	445	1.40		1.75
350	3 CY track loader	BCY	1G,19	890	0.84		1.05
	Haul and dump, see Appendix I						
45	**ROUGH GRADING**						
	Rough grade site						
	light or medium soil						
100	by hand, light	SY	1L	190	1.07		1.34
110	by hand, medium	SY	1L	165	1.24		1.55
120	small motor grader	SY	1G1L,36	470	1.47		1.83
130	large motor grader	SY	1G1L,37	945	0.81		1.02
140	50 HP bulldozer	SY	1G,20	825	0.54		0.67
150	150 HP bulldozer	SY	1G1L,21	2775	0.31		0.39
160	300 HP bulldozer	SY	1G1L,22	6295	0.20		0.24
	heavy soil						
170	by hand	SY	1L	130	1.57		1.96
180	small motor grader	SY	1G1L,36	375	1.84		2.30
190	large motor grader	SY	1G1L,37	755	1.02		1.27
200	50 HP bulldozer	SY	1G,20	660	0.67		0.84
210	150 HP bulldozer	SY	1G1L,21	2220	0.39		0.48
220	300 HP bulldozer	SY	1G1L,22	5035	0.24		0.31
	Remove rocks and debris from soil surface						
230	by hand	SY	1L	400	0.51		0.64
240	rock picker, tractor drawn	MSF	1G,51	350	0.98		1.23

KEY	DESCRIPTION	UNIT	CREW AND EQUIPMENT	PER DAY	INSTALLATION COST	MATERIALS COST	TOTAL + 25%
50	**TOPSOILING**						
	Scarify subgrade						
105	by hand	SY	1L	500	0.41		0.51
110	6' disk	MSF	1G,50	195	1.51		1.89
115	12' disk	MSF	1G,51	390	0.88		1.10
120	Purchase natural topsoil, delivered to site	CCY				17.90	22.40
	Load, haul and dump topsoil, delivered to site, see Appendix I						
	From stockpile spread topsoil 2" deep						
	50' maximum haul						
125	by hand	SY	2L	135	3.02		3.78
130	1/2 CY wheel loader	MSF	1G,10	13	37.29		46.60
135	50 HP bulldozer	MSF	1G,20	43	10.34		12.90
	150' maximum haul						
140	by hand	SY	2L	110	3.71		4.64
145	1/2 CY wheel loader	MSF	1G,10	9	53.86		67.00
150	50 HP bulldozer	MSF	1G,20	22	20.21		25.30
155	150 HP bulldozer	MSF	1G1L,21	50	17.17		21.50
160	300 HP bulldozer	MSF	1G1L,22	100	12.29		15.40
	300' maximum haul						
165	150 HP bulldozer	MSF	1G1L,21	37	23.21		29.00
170	300 HP bulldozer	MSF	1G1L,22	78	15.75		19.70
	500' maximum haul						
175	300 HP bulldozer	MSF	1G1L,22	58	21.19		26.50
180	10 CY towed scraper	MSF	1A1L,30	33	29.63		37.00
185	15 CY towed scraper	MSF	1A1L,31	70	14.11		17.60
190	20 CY towed scraper	MSF	1A1L,32	77	18.02		22.50
	1000' maximum haul						
195	10 CY towed scraper	MSF	1A1L,30	29	33.72		42.10
200	15 CY towed scraper	MSF	1A1L,31	59	16.74		20.90
205	20 CY towed scraper	MSF	1A1L,32	64	21.69		27.10
210	15 CY motor scraper, 1/3 push dozer	MSF	1A1G1L,22,33	72	25.13		31.40
215	10 CY elevating scraper	MSF	1A1L,34	64	15.12		18.90
220	20 CY elevating scraper	MSF	1A1L,35	83	18.05		22.60
	From stockpile spread topsoil 4" deep						
	50' maximum haul						
225	by hand	SY	2L	75	5.44		6.80
230	1/2 CY wheel loader	MSF	1G,10	8	60.59		76.00
235	50 HP bulldozer	MSF	1G,20	29	15.33		19.20
	150' maximum haul						
240	by hand	SY	2L	61	6.69		8.40
245	1/2 CY wheel loader	MSF	1G,10	4.9	98.92		124.00
250	50 HP bulldozer	MSF	1G,20	13	34.21		42.80
255	150 HP bulldozer	MSF	1G1L,21	37	23.21		29.00
260	300 HP bulldozer	MSF	1G1L,22	78	15.75		19.70
	300' maximum haul						
265	150 HP bulldozer	MSF	1G1L,21	24	35.78		44.70
270	300 HP bulldozer	MSF	1G1L,22	53	23.18		29.00
	500' maximum haul						
275	300 HP bulldozer	MSF	1G1L,22	36	34.13		42.70
280	10 CY towed scraper	MSF	1A1L,30	27	36.22		45.30
285	15 CY towed scraper	MSF	1A1L,31	55	17.96		22.50
290	20 CY towed scraper	MSF	1A1L,32	61	22.75		28.40
	1000' maximum haul						
295	10 CY towed scraper	MSF	1A1L,30	22	44.45		56.00
300	15 CY towed scraper	MSF	1A1L,31	42	23.52		29.40
305	20 CY towed scraper	MSF	1A1L,32	47	29.53		36.90
310	15 CY motor scraper, 1/4 push dozer	MSF	1A1G1L,22,33	55	31.73		39.70
315	10 CY elevating scraper	MSF	1A1L,34	46	21.04		26.30
320	20 CY elevating scraper	MSF	1A1L,35	66	22.69		28.40

EARTHWORK

KEY	DESCRIPTION	UNIT	CREW AND EQUIPMENT	PER DAY	INSTALLATION COST	MATERIALS COST	TOTAL + 25%
	From stockpile spread topsoil 6" deep						
	50' maximum haul						
325	by hand	SY	2L	51	8.00		10.00
330	1/2 CY wheel loader	MSF	1G,10	5	96.94		121.00
335	50 HP bulldozer	MSF	1G,20	22	20.21		25.30
	150' maximum haul						
340	by hand	SY	2L	41	9.95		12.40
345	1/2 CY wheel loader	MSF	1G,10	3.4	142.56		178.00
350	50 HP bulldozer	MSF	1G,20	9	49.41		62.00
355	150 HP bulldozer	MSF	1G1L,21	29	29.61		37.00
360	300 HP bulldozer	MSF	1G1L,22	63	19.50		24.40
	300' maximum haul						
365	150 HP bulldozer	MSF	1G1L,21	18	47.71		60.00
370	300 HP bulldozer	MSF	1G1L,22	40	30.72		38.40
	500' maximum haul						
375	300 HP bulldozer	MSF	1G1L,22	24	51.20		64.00
380	10 CY towed scraper	MSF	1A1L,30	23	42.52		53.00
385	15 CY towed scraper	MSF	1A1L,31	44	22.45		28.10
390	20 CY towed scraper	MSF	1A1L,32	50	27.76		34.70
	1000' maximum haul						
395	10 CY towed scraper	MSF	1A1L,30	17	57.52		72.00
400	15 CY towed scraper	MSF	1A1L,31	33	29.94		37.40
405	20 CY towed scraper	MSF	1A1L,32	37	37.51		46.90
410	15 CY motor scraper, 1/5 push dozer	MSF	1A1G1L,22,33	45	37.92		47.40
415	10 CY elevating scraper	MSF	1A1L,34	36	26.89		33.60
420	20 CY elevating scraper	MSF	1A1L,35	55	27.23		34.00
	From stockpile spread topsoil 8" deep						
	50' maximum haul						
425	by hand	SY	2L	39	10.46		13.10
430	1/2 CY wheel loader	MSF	1G,10	4.2	115.41		144.00
435	50 HP bulldozer	MSF	1G,20	18	24.71		30.90
	150' maximum haul						
440	by hand	SY	2L	31	13.16		16.50
445	1/2 CY wheel loader	MSF	1G,10	2.6	186.43		233.00
450	50 HP bulldozer	MSF	1G,20	7	63.53		79.00
455	150 HP bulldozer	MSF	1G1L,21	24	35.78		44.70
460	300 HP bulldozer	MSF	1G1L,22	53	23.18		29.00
	300' maximum haul						
465	150 HP bulldozer	MSF	1G1L,21	14	61.34		77.00
470	300 HP bulldozer	MSF	1G1L,22	32	38.40		48.00
	500' maximum haul						
475	300 HP bulldozer	MSF	1G1L,22	21	58.51		73.00
480	10 CY towed scraper	MSF	1A1L,30	19	51.47		64.00
485	15 CY towed scraper	MSF	1A1L,31	38	26.00		32.50
490	20 CY towed scraper	MSF	1A1L,32	43	32.28		40.30
	1000' maximum haul						
495	10 CY towed scraper	MSF	1A1L,30	14	69.85		87.00
500	15 CY towed scraper	MSF	1A1L,31	27	36.59		45.70
505	20 CY towed scraper	MSF	1A1L,32	30	46.26		58.00
510	15 CY motor scraper, 1/6 push dozer	MSF	1A1G1L,22,33	37	45.43		57.00
515	10 CY elevating scraper	MSF	1A1L,34	29	33.37		41.70
520	20 CY elevating scraper	MSF	1A1L,35	47	31.87		39.80
55	**FINE GRADING**						
	Fine grade site						
	level site (0-4 percent)						
100	by hand	SY	1L	80	2.55		3.19
110	small motor grader	SY	1G1L,36	680	1.01		1.27
120	large motor grader	SY	1G1L,37	1700	0.45		0.57

EARTHWORK

02210 Grading — 1994

KEY	DESCRIPTION	UNIT	CREW AND EQUIPMENT	PER DAY	INSTALLATION COST	MATERIALS COST	TOTAL + 25%
	sloped site (5 percent or greater)						
130	by hand	SY	1L	60	3.40		4.25
140	small motor grader	SY	1G1L,36	540	1.28		1.59
150	large motor grader	SY	1G1L,37	1350	0.57		0.71
	Fine grade pavement subgrade						
160	by hand	SY	1L	65	3.14		3.92
170	small motor grader	SY	1G1L,36	680	1.01		1.27
180	large motor grader	SY	1G1L,37	1700	0.45		0.57

02220 Excavating, Backfilling & Compacting

KEY	DESCRIPTION	UNIT	CREW AND EQUIPMENT	PER DAY	INSTALLATION COST	MATERIALS COST	TOTAL + 25%
10	**STRUCTURE EXCAVATION**						
	Pits and piers to 6' deep						
	light or medium soil						
100	by hand	BCY	1L	6	34.01		42.50
110	small backhoe/loader	BCY	1G1L,13	100	5.64		7.00
	heavy soil						
120	by hand	BCY	1L	4	51.01		64.00
130	small backhoe/loader	BCY	1G1L,13	70	8.05		10.10
	Pits and piers to 12' deep						
	light or medium soil						
140	by hand	BCY	2L	7	58.29		73.00
150	small backhoe/loader	BCY	1G1L,13	80	7.05		8.80
	heavy soil						
160	by hand	BCY	1L	5	40.81		51.00
170	small backhoe/loader	BCY	1G1L,13	55	10.25		12.80
	Foundations						
	light or medium soil						
180	1/2 CY backhoe	BCY	1G1L,14	215	2.92		3.66
190	1 CY backhoe	BCY	1G1L,15	375	1.97		2.46
200	3/4 CY track loader	BCY	1G1L,16	300	2.13		2.66
210	1 CY track loader	BCY	1G1L,17	500	1.44		1.80
	heavy soil						
220	1/2 CY backhoe	BCY	1G1L,14	145	4.34		5.40
230	1 CY backhoe	BCY	1G1L,15	250	2.95		3.69
240	3/4 CY track loader	BCY	1G1L,16	200	3.19		3.99
250	1 CY track loader	BCY	1G1L,17	335	2.15		2.68
20	**TRENCHING**						
	Trench, 6" to 16" wide, up to 2' deep						
	light or medium soil						
100	by hand	BCY	1L	12	17.00		21.30
110	30 HP trencher	LF	1G,26	1000	0.32		0.41
	heavy soil						
120	by hand	BCY	1L	9	22.67		28.30
130	30 HP trencher	LF	1G,26	850	0.38		0.48
	Trench, 1 1/2' to 4' wide, to 4' deep						
	light or medium soil						
140	by hand	BCY	1L	8	25.50		31.90
150	small backhoe/loader	BCY	1G1L,13	150	3.76		4.70
	heavy soil						
160	by hand	BCY	1L	6	34.01		42.50
170	small backhoe/loader	BCY	1G1L,13	100	5.64		7.00
	Trench, 2' to 4' wide, to 6' deep						
	light or medium soil						
180	by hand	BCY	1L	7	29.15		36.40
190	1/2 CY backhoe	BCY	1G1L,14	225	2.79		3.49

31

EARTHWORK

KEY	DESCRIPTION	UNIT	CREW AND EQUIPMENT	PER DAY	INSTALLATION COST	MATERIALS COST	TOTAL + 25%
	heavy soil						
200	by hand	BCY	1L	4	51.01		64.00
210	1/2 CY backhoe	BCY	1G1L,14	150	4.19		5.20
	Square and grade trench bottom						
220	light or medium soil	SF	1L	150	1.36		1.70
230	heavy soil	SF	1L	100	2.04		2.55
30	**STRUCTURE EXCAVATION SHORING**						
	Shoring of pit and pier excavation to 4' wide, 6' deep						
100	wood bracing, no sheeting	SF	2C	280	1.81	1.15	3.70
	wood sheet piling and bracing						
110	no salvage	SF	2C	130	3.89	3.04	8.70
120	salvage	SF	2C	100	5.06	0.76	7.30
	Shoring of pit and pier excavation to 4' wide, 12' deep						
	wood sheet piling and bracing						
	by hand						
130	no salvage	SF	2C	100	5.06	3.04	10.10
140	salvage	SF	2C	80	6.32	0.76	8.90
	air hammer						
150	no salvage	SF	1G1L,86	220	2.38	3.04	6.80
160	salvage	SF	1G1L,86	160	3.27	0.76	5.00
	Trench excavation to 4' wide, 6' deep						
170	wood bracing, no sheeting	SF	2C	320	1.58	1.24	3.53
	wood sheet piling and bracing						
	by hand						
180	no salvage	SF	2C	150	3.37	3.04	8.00
190	salvage	SF	2C	115	4.40	0.76	6.40
	air hammer						
200	no salvage	SF	1G1L,86	300	1.75	3.04	6.00
210	salvage	SF	1G1L,86	230	2.28	0.76	3.80
40	**STRUCTURE BACKFILLING**						
	Backfill with excavated soil, small areas, compaction not included						
	light or medium soil						
100	by hand	CCY	2L	32	12.75		15.90
110	1 CY wheel loader	CCY	1G1L,11	300	2.51		3.14
	heavy soil						
120	by hand	CCY	2L	24	17.00		21.30
130	1 CY wheel loader	CCY	1G1L'11	240	3.14		3.93
	Backfill with granular material, small areas, compaction not included						
	crushed stone						
140	by hand	CCY	2L	24	17.00	15.80	41.00
150	1 CY wheel loader	CCY	1G1L,11	240	3.14	15.80	23.70
	bank gravel						
160	by hand	CCY	2L	24	17.00	15.10	40.10
170	1 CY wheel loader	CCY	1G1L,11	250	3.01	15.10	22.60
	bank sand						
180	by hand	CCY	2L	26	15.69	8.70	30.50
190	1 CY wheel loader	CCY	1G1L,11	300	2.51	8.70	14.00
50	**HAULING**						
	Material prices include 10 mile round trip haul and dumping with 6 CY dump truck in medium traffic. See Appendix I for additional or less distance.						
60	**STRUCTURE BACKFILL COMPACTION**						
	Compact backfill						
100	by hand, 6" layers	CCY	2L	26	15.69		19.60
110	rammer compactor	CCY	1L,45	36	6.50		8.10
120	vibratory compactor	CCY	1L,46	90	2.49		3.11

02220 Excavating, Backfilling & Compacting — 1994

KEY	DESCRIPTION	UNIT	CREW AND EQUIPMENT	PER DAY	INSTALLATION COST	MATERIALS COST	TOTAL + 25%
70	**PAVEMENT SUBGRADE EXCAVATION AND BACKFILL**						
	See Section 02210, "Site Grading"						
80	**PAVEMENT SUBGRADE COMPACTION**						
100	Rip subgrade	MSF	1G,21	490	1.34		1.67
	Compact subgrade, 6" lifts						
	pneumatic tire roller, towed						
110	4 passes per lift	CCY	1G,40	2640	0.19		0.23
120	8 passes per lift	CCY	1G,40	1320	0.37		0.47
130	12 passes per lift	CCY	1G,40	880	0.56		0.70
	sheepsfoot roller, towed						
140	4 passes per lift	CCY	1G,41	2100	0.23		0.28
150	8 passes per lift	CCY	1G,41	780	0.61		0.76
160	12 passes per lift	CCY	1G,41	520	0.91		1.14
	vibratory roller, towed						
170	4 passes per lift	CCY	1G,42	2260	0.26		0.32
180	8 passes per lift	CCY	1G,42	840	0.70		0.87
190	12 passes per lift	CCY	1G,42	560	1.04		1.31
200	10 ton steel roller	SY	1G,43	2000	0.23		0.28

02230 Base Course

KEY	DESCRIPTION	UNIT	CREW AND EQUIPMENT	PER DAY	INSTALLATION COST	MATERIALS COST	TOTAL + 25%
10	**STRUCTURE SUB-BASE**						
	Crushed stone (compaction not included)						
100	by hand	CCY	3L	35	17.49	15.80	41.60
110	3/4 CY track loader	CCY	1G1L,16	240	2.66	15.80	23.10
	Bank gravel (compaction not included)						
120	by hand	CCY	3L	35	17.49	15.10	40.70
130	3/4 CY track loader	CCY	1G1L,16	250	2.55	15.10	22.10
	Bank sand (compaction not included)						
140	by hand	CCY	3L	40	15.30	8.70	30.00
150	3/4 CY track loader	CCY	1G1L,16	300	2.13	8.70	13.50
20	**SLAB SUB-BASE**						
	Crushed stone (compaction not included)						
	4" thick						
100	by hand	SY	3L	225	2.72	1.76	5.60
110	3/4 CY track loader	SY	1G1L,16	500	1.28	1.76	3.80
	6" thick						
120	by hand	SY	3L	150	4.08	2.64	8.40
130	3/4 CY track loader	SY	1G1L,16	400	1.60	2.64	5.30
	8" thick						
140	by hand	SY	3L	110	5.56	3.51	11.30
150	3/4 CY track loader	SY	1G1L,16	300	2.13	3.51	7.00
	10" thick						
160	by hand	SY	3L	90	6.80	4.51	14.10
170	3/4 CY track loader	SY	1G1L,16	200	3.19	4.51	9.60
	Bank gravel (compaction not included)						
	4" thick						
180	by hand	SY	3L	285	2.15	1.68	4.78
190	3/4 CY track loader	SY	1G1L,16	600	1.06	1.68	3.43
	6" thick						
200	by hand	SY	3L	190	3.22	2.53	7.20
210	3/4 CY track loader	SY	1G1L,16	480	1.33	2.53	4.83
	8" thick						
220	by hand	SY	3L	145	4.22	3.37	9.50
230	3/4 CY track loader	SY	1G1L,16	360	1.77	3.37	6.40

EARTHWORK

KEY	DESCRIPTION	UNIT	CREW AND EQUIPMENT	PER DAY	INSTALLATION COST	MATERIALS COST	TOTAL + 25%
	10" thick						
240	by hand	SY	3L	115	5.32	4.32	12.10
250	3/4 CY track loader	SY	1G1L,16	240	2.66	4.32	8.70
	Bank sand (compaction not included)						
	4" thick						
260	by hand	SY	3L	255	2.40	0.97	4.21
270	3/4 CY track loader	SY	1G1L,16	800	0.80	0.97	2.21
	6" thick						
280	by hand	SY	3L	170	3.60	1.45	6.30
290	3/4 CY track loader	SY	1G1L,16	640	1.00	1.45	3.06
	8" thick						
300	by hand	SY	3L	130	4.71	1.93	8.30
310	3/4 CY track loader	SY	1G1L,16	480	1.33	1.93	4.08
	10" thick						
320	by hand	SY	3L	105	5.83	2.49	10.40
330	3/4 CY track loader	SY	1G1L,16	320	2.00	2.49	5.60
50	**GRANULAR PAVEMENT BASE**						
	Crushed stone base (compaction not included)						
	4" thick						
100	by hand	SY	2L	180	2.27	1.76	5.00
110	small motor grader	SY	1G2L,36	4200	0.23	1.76	2.49
	6" thick						
120	by hand	SY	2L	120	3.40	2.64	7.60
130	small motor grader	SY	1G2L,36	2800	0.35	2.64	3.73
	8" thick						
140	by hand	SY	2L	90	4.53	3.51	10.10
150	small motor grader	SY	1G2L,36	2070	0.47	3.51	4.97
	10" thick						
160	by hand	SY	2L	72	5.67	4.51	12.70
170	small motor grader	SY	1G2L,36	1680	0.58	4.51	6.40
	Bank gravel base (compaction not included)						
	4" thick						
180	by hand	SY	2L	180	2.27	1.68	4.93
190	small motor grader	SY	1G2L,36	4590	0.21	1.68	2.36
	6" thick						
200	by hand	SY	2L	120	3.40	2.53	7.40
210	small motor grader	SY	1G2L,36	3020	0.32	2.53	3.57
	8" thick						
220	by hand	SY	2L	90	4.53	3.37	9.90
230	small motor grader	SY	1G2L,36	2300	0.42	3.37	4.74
	10" thick						
240	by hand	SY	2L	70	5.83	4.32	12.70
250	small motor grader	SY	1G2L,36	1850	0.53	4.32	6.10
	Bank sand (compaction not included)						
	4" thick						
260	by hand	SY	2L	300	1.36	0.97	2.91
270	small motor grader	SY	1G2L,36	5740	0.17	0.97	1.42
	6" thick						
280	by hand	SY	2L	200	2.04	1.45	4.36
290	small motor grader	SY	1G2L,36	3780	0.26	1.45	2.13
	8" thick						
300	by hand	SY	2L	150	2.72	1.93	5.80
310	small motor grader	SY	1G2L,36	2880	0.34	1.93	2.83
	10" thick						
320	by hand	SY	2L	125	3.26	2.49	7.20
330	small motor grader	SY	1G2L,36	2300	0.42	2.49	3.64
60	**SOIL CEMENT BASE**						
	See Section 02240, "Soil Stabilization, Cement"						

02230 Base Course

KEY	DESCRIPTION	UNIT	CREW AND EQUIPMENT	PER DAY	INSTALLATION COST	MATERIALS COST	TOTAL + 25%
70	**STABILIZATION OF PAVEMENT BASE** See Section 02510, "Crushed Stone Paving"						
80	**HAULING** Material prices include 10 mile round trip haul and dumping with 6 CY dump truck in medium traffic. See Appendix I for additional or less distance.						
90	**COMPACTION**						
100	Compact granular base, small areas	CCY	1L,46	90	2.71		3.39
110	4 passes	SY	1L,46	900	0.27		0.34
120	8 passes	SY	1L,46	485	0.50		0.63
	Compact granular base 4 passes						
130	pneumatic roller	SY	1A1L,44	3000	0.17		0.21
140	pneumatic roller, towed	SY	1A1L,40	2800	0.25		0.31
	8 passes						
150	pneumatic roller	SY	1A1L,44	1500	0.34		0.42
160	pneumatic roller, towed	SY	1A1L,40	1400	0.50		0.62

02240 Soil Stabilization

KEY	DESCRIPTION	UNIT	CREW AND EQUIPMENT	PER DAY	INSTALLATION COST	MATERIALS COST	TOTAL + 25%
00	**COMPOSITE COSTS**						
	Soil-asphalt stabilization						
100	6" depth	MSF					550.00
110	8" depth	MSF					730.00
120	12" depth	MSF					1090.00
	Soil-cement stabilization						
130	6" depth	MSF					214.00
140	8" depth	MSF					271.00
150	12" depth	MSF					421.00
	Soil-lime stabilization						
160	6" depth	MSF					331.00
170	8" depth	MSF					435.00
180	12" depth	MSF					650.00
10	**ASPHALT**						
	Spread asphalt, mix with soil to 6" depth						
100	1/3 gal/SY/inch depth	MSF	1A,94	110	10.40	409.00	520.00
110	1/2 gal/SY/inch depth	MSF	1A,94	110	10.40	610.00	780.00
	to 8" depth						
120	1/3 gal/SY/inch depth	MSF	1A,94	85	13.46	550.00	700.00
130	1/2 gal/SY/inch depth	MSF	1A,94	85	13.46	820.00	1040.00
	to 12" depth						
140	1/3 gal/SY/inch depth	MSF	1A,94	66	17.33	820.00	1050.00
150	1/2 gal/SY/inch depth	MSF	1A,94	66	17.33	1240.00	1570.00
	Compact soil						
160	4 passes	MSF	1A,45	18	16.88		21.10
170	8 passes	MSF	1A,45	9	33.76		42.20
20	**CEMENT**						
	Spread cement for 6" depth						
100	6% by volume	MSF	1D1L,06	845	0.65	98.00	123.00
110	8% by volume	MSF	1D1L,06	845	0.65	131.00	165.00
120	10% by volume	MSF	1D1L,06	845	0.65	163.00	205.00
130	12% by volume	MSF	1D1L,06	845	0.65	197.00	247.00

EARTHWORK

02240 Soil Stabilization — 1994

KEY	DESCRIPTION	UNIT	CREW AND EQUIPMENT	PER DAY	INSTALLATION COST	MATERIALS COST	TOTAL + 25%
	for 8" depth						
140	6% by volume	MSF	1D1L,06	845	0.65	131.00	165.00
150	8% by volume	MSF	1D1L,06	845	0.65	174.00	218.00
160	10% by volume	MSF	1D1L,06	845	0.65	218.00	273.00
170	12% by volume	MSF	1D1L,06	845	0.65	262.00	328.00
	for 12" depth						
180	6% by volume	MSF	1D1L,06	845	0.65	197.00	247.00
190	8% by volume	MSF	1D1L,06	845	0.65	262.00	328.00
200	10% by volume	MSF	1D1L,06	845	0.65	326.00	408.00
210	12% by volume	MSF	1D1L,06	845	0.65	392.00	491.00
	Mix soil and cement						
220	6" depth	MSF	1A,94	110	10.40		13.00
230	8" depth	MSF	1A,94	85	13.46		16.80
240	12" depth	MSF	1A,94	66	17.33		21.70
	Compact soil						
250	4 passes	MSF	1A,44	18	27.99		35.00
260	8 passes	MSF	1A,44	9	55.98		70.00
30	**LIME**						
	Spread lime slurry						
	for 6" depth						
100	2% by weight	MSF	1D1L,09	845	0.67	119.00	150.00
110	4% by weight	MSF	1D1L,09	845	0.67	244.00	306.00
120	6% by weight	MSF	1D1L,09	845	0.67	357.00	447.00
	for 8" depth						
130	2% by weight	MSF	1D1L,09	845	0.67	158.00	198.00
140	4% by weight	MSF	1D1L,09	845	0.67	324.00	406.00
150	6% by weight	MSF	1D1L,09	845	0.67	476.00	600.00
	for 12" depth						
160	2% by weight	MSF	1D1L,09	845	0.67	236.00	296.00
170	4% by weight	MSF	1D1L,09	845	0.67	487.00	610.00
180	6% by weight	MSF	1D1L,09	845	0.67	710.00	890.00
	Mix soil and lime						
190	6" depth	MSF	1A,94	110	10.40		13.00
200	8" depth	MSF	1A,94	85	13.46		16.80
210	12" depth	MSF	1A,94	66	17.33		21.70
	Compact soil						
220	4 passes	MSF	1A1G,41,44	143	6.84		8.60
230	8 passes	MSF	1A1G,41,44	71	13.78		17.20

02270 Slope Protection and Erosion Control

KEY	DESCRIPTION	UNIT	CREW AND EQUIPMENT	PER DAY	INSTALLATION COST	MATERIALS COST	TOTAL + 25%
10	**EROSION CONTROL FABRIC AND MAT**						
100	Jute mesh	SY	2L	1600	0.26	0.81	1.33
	Excelsior blanket						
110	standard	SY	2L	1600	0.26	0.90	1.44
120	high velocity	SY	2L	1450	0.28	1.18	1.83
	Three dimensional, nondegradable nylon monofilament soil reinforcement mat						
130	9 mm thick	SY	2L	2000	0.20	5.80	7.50
140	18 mm thick	SY	2L	1600	0.26	8.30	10.70
150	Burlap, 1/4" x 1/4" weave	SY	2L	2000	0.20	0.68	1.11
	Polypropylene plastic mesh						
160	1/4" x 1/4" mesh	SY	2L	2400	0.17	0.42	0.73
170	3/4" x 3/4" mesh	SY	2L	2400	0.17	0.25	0.53
180	1" x 2" mesh	SY	2L	2400	0.17	0.21	0.47

02270 Slope Protection and Erosion Control

KEY	DESCRIPTION	UNIT	CREW AND EQUIPMENT	PER DAY	INSTALLATION COST	MATERIALS COST	TOTAL + 25%
	Polypropylene yarn and paper strip fabric						
200	11/16" x 11/16" mesh	SY	2L	2400	0.17	1.05	1.53
210	Twisted paper mesh, 1/4" x 1/4"	SY	2L	2400	0.17	1.02	1.49
220	Tobacco cloth, reclaimed	SY	2L	2400	0.17	0.40	0.72
20	**GABIONS**						
	Revetments, stone filled gabions						
	(does not include excavation)						
	galvanized						
100	1' high	SY	1A3L,95	240	5.44	4.03	11.80
110	1'-6" high	SY	1A3L,95	180	7.26	9.30	20.70
120	3' high	SY	1A3L,95	105	12.44	24.20	45.80
	PVC coated						
130	1' high	SY	1A3L,95	105	12.44	5.30	22.20
140	1'-6" high	SY	1A3L,95	105	12.44	9.30	27.20
150	3' high	SY	1A3L,95	240	5.44	27.40	41.10
	6" mattress						
160	galvanized	SY	1A3L,95	180	7.26	7.90	18.90
170	PVC coated	SY	1A3L,95	105	12.44	11.80	30.30
	9" mattress						
180	galvanized	SY	1A3L,95	105	12.44	8.90	26.70
190	PVC coated	SY	1A3L,95	105	12.44	14.40	33.50
	Retaining walls, stone filled gabions						
	(does not include excavation)						
	galvanized						
200	1' high	SY	1A3L,95	80	16.32	36.30	66.00
210	1'-6" high	SY	1A3L,95	90	14.51	43.60	73.00
220	3' high	SY	1A3L,95	105	12.44	73.00	107.00
	PVC coated						
230	1' high	SY	1A3L,95	80	16.32	48.40	81.00
240	1'-6" high	SY	1A3L,95	90	14.51	55.00	87.00
250	3' high	SY	1A3L,95	105	12.44	82.00	118.00

MARINE WORK

02488 Docks and Facilities 1994

KEY	DESCRIPTION	UNIT	CREW AND EQUIPMENT	PER DAY	INSTALLATION COST	MATERIALS COST	TOTAL + 25%
10	**FLOATING BOAT DOCKS**						
	Wood decking						
	Polystyrene foam floats						
100	6' x 10'	Ea	2L	4	102.02	1200.00	1630.00
110	8' x 12'	Ea	2L	4	102.02	1430.00	1920.00
	Urethane coated polystyrene						
120	6' x 10'	Ea	2L	4	102.02	1380.00	1850.00
130	8' x 12'	Ea	2L	4	102.02	1490.00	1990.00
	Polystyrene foam encased in polyethylene casing						
140	6' x 10'	Ea	2L	4	102.02	1420.00	1900.00
20	**DOCK BUMPER**						
100	8' long	Ea	1L	8	25.50	26.50	65.00
110	Corner bumper	Ea	1L	12	17.00	16.60	42.00
30	**ALUMINIUM DOCK LADDER**						
100	2 step	Ea	1L	8	25.50	134.00	199.00
110	3 step	Ea	1L	8	25.50	144.00	212.00
120	4 step	Ea	1L	8	25.50	157.00	228.00
130	5 step	Ea	1L	8	25.50	168.00	242.00
140	6 step	Ea	1L	8	25.50	313.00	423.00
150	7 step	Ea	1L	8	25.50	377.00	500.00
160	8 step	Ea	1L	8	25.50	400.00	530.00
170	9 step	Ea	1L	8	25.50	464.00	610.00
180	10 step	Ea	1L	8	25.50	510.00	670.00

02510 Walk, Road, and Parking Paving

KEY	DESCRIPTION	UNIT	CREW AND EQUIPMENT	PER DAY	INSTALLATION COST	MATERIALS COST	TOTAL + 25%
00	**COMPOSITE COSTS**						
	Asphaltic concrete paving						
	2" thick on primed compacted subgrade,						
100	1000 SF or less	SY					21.80
	3" thick on 4" primed granular base,						
	compacted subgrade						
110	1000 SF or less	SY					36.10
120	over 1000 SF	SY					16.60
130	over 10,000 SF	SY					13.40
	3" thick on 4" asphaltic base, primed						
	compacted subgrade						
140	1000 SF or less	SY					49.00
150	over 1000 SF	SY					26.10
160	over 10,000 SF						20.60
	Crushed limestone paving, compacted on compacted						
	subgrade (ripping and grading not included)						
	2" paving						
170	2000 SF or less	SY					10.20
180	over 2000 SF	SY					6.10
	4" paving						
190	2000 SF or less	SY					15.70
200	over 2000 SF	SY					10.60
	2" paving, 4" base						
210	2000 SF or less	SY					16.60
220	over 2000 SF	SY					9.30
	4" paving, 4" base						
230	2000 SF or less	SY					22.00
240	over 2000 SF	SY					13.80
	Portland cement concrete paving, broom finish, includes						
	expansion joints and fine grading						
250	4" non-reinforced	SY					40.40
	6" reinforced, 6" gravel base						
260	1000 SF or less	SY					60.00
270	over 1000 SF	SY					57.00
280	over 10,000 SF	SY					20.30
	8" reinforced, 6" gravel base						
290	1000 SF or less	SY					72.00
300	over 1000 SF	SY					67.00
310	over 10,000 SF	SY					25.80
	Patterned concrete paving, 4" thick with color and						
	pattern imprinted finish, finished subgrade						
320	small area	SF					7.30
330	large area	SF					5.30
10	**ASPHALT CONCRETE PAVING**						
	Granular base, see Section 02230 "Base Course"						
100	Prime coat, cutback asphalt (add to pavement base cost)	SY	1G1D,96	1600	0.55	0.26	1.01
	Asphaltic concrete base course						
	2" thick						
110	by hand	SY	3L,46	110	5.75	4.04	12.20
120	motor grader	SY	2G4L,36,44	800	2.23	3.63	7.30
130	asphalt paver	SY	2A7L,90,44	3000	0.82	3.10	4.90
	4" thick						
140	by hand	SY	3L,46	65	9.72	8.10	22.30
150	motor grader	SY	2G4L,36,44	700	2.55	7.20	12.20
160	asphalt paver	SY	2A7L,90,44	1700	1.44	6.20	9.60
190	Tack coat, asphalt emulsion	SY	1G1D,96	2000	0.44	0.27	0.89

PAVING AND SURFACING

KEY	DESCRIPTION	UNIT	CREW AND EQUIPMENT	PER DAY	INSTALLATION COST	MATERIALS COST	TOTAL + 25%
	Asphaltic concrete wearing course						
	1 1/2" thick						
200	by hand	SY	3L,46	90	7.02	3.96	13.70
210	motor grader	SY	2G4L,36,44	800	2.23	3.59	7.30
220	asphalt paver	SY	2A7L,90,44	3400	0.72	3.17	4.87
	2" thick						
230	by hand	SY	3L,46	70	9.03	5.20	17.80
240	motor grader	SY	2G4L,36,44	800	2.23	4.78	8.80
250	asphalt paver	SY	2A7L,90,44	2800	0.88	4.21	6.40
	3" thick						
260	by hand	SY	3L,46	55	11.49	7.90	24.20
270	motor grader	SY	2G4L,36,44	700	2.55	7.30	12.30
280	asphalt paver	SY	2A7L,90,44	1700	1.44	6.30	9.70
20	**CRUSHED STONE PAVING**						
	Crushed bluestone paving						
	2" thick						
100	by hand	SY	2L	145	2.81	3.23	7.60
110	small motor grader	SY	1G2L,36	2880	0.31	3.23	4.42
	4" thick						
120	by hand	SY	2L	110	3.71	6.50	12.80
130	small motor grader	SY	1G2L,36	2160	0.41	6.50	8.60
	Crushed granite paving						
	2" thick						
140	by hand	SY	2L	145	2.81	1.27	5.10
150	small motor grader	SY	1G2L,36	2880	0.31	1.27	1.97
	4" thick						
160	by hand	SY	2L	110	3.71	2.54	7.80
170	small motor grader	SY	1G2L,36	2160	0.41	2.54	3.69
	Crushed limestone paving						
	2" thick						
180	by hand	SY	2L	145	2.81	3.51	7.90
190	small motor grader	SY	1G2L,36	2880	0.31	3.51	4.77
	4" thick						
200	by hand	SY	2L	110	3.71	7.00	13.40
210	small motor grader	SY	1G2L,36	2160	0.41	7.00	9.30
	Crushed white marble						
	2" thick						
220	by hand	SY	2L	145	2.81	10.10	16.10
230	small motor grader	SY	1G2L,36	2880	0.31	10.10	13.00
	4" thick						
240	by hand	SY	2L	110	3.71	20.10	29.80
250	small motor grader	SY	1G2L,36	2160	0.41	20.10	25.60
260	Calcium chloride treatment	SY					0.25

Compaction, see Sections 02220 "Excavating,
Backfilling, & Compacting" and 02230 "Base Course"

Material costs include 10 mile round trip haul and
dumping with 6 CY dump truck in medium traffic.
See Appendix I for additional or less distance.

30 PORTLAND CEMENT CONCRETE PAVING

Forms and screeds, see Section 03110,
"Structural Cast-in-Place Concrete Formwork"

Reinforcing, see Sections 03210, "Reinforcing Steel",
and 03220, "Welded Wire Fabric"

KEY	DESCRIPTION	UNIT	CREW AND EQUIPMENT	PER DAY	INSTALLATION COST	MATERIALS COST	TOTAL + 25%
	Concrete paving						
100	4" thick by hand, ready mixed	SF	6L	1000	1.22	0.82	2.56
	6" thick						
110	by hand, ready mixed	SF	6L	780	1.57	1.22	3.49
120	paving machine	SY	1A5L,91	1200	1.66	6.80	10.60
	8" thick						
130	by hand, ready mixed	SF	6L	620	1.97	1.62	4.49
140	paving machine	SY	1A5L,91	1000	1.99	9.20	14.00
150	10" thick, paving machine	SY	1A5L,91	800	2.49	11.10	17.00
160	12" thick, paving machine	SY	1A5L,91	600	3.32	13.50	21.00
170	Strike off, consolidation and floating	SF	2F	645	0.75		0.94
	Color						
	dust-on color						
180	black or brown	SF	1F	1000	0.24	1.40	2.05
190	green or red	SF	1F	1000	0.24	0.53	0.97
	integral color, top 1"						
200	black, brown, or red	SF	1F	600	0.41	0.33	0.92
210	green or blue	SF	1F	600	0.41	1.00	1.76
	Finish						
220	belted finish, add	SF	2F	2500	0.19		0.24
230	broomed finish, add	SF	2F	1200	0.41		0.51
240	burlap dragged finish, add	SF	2F	2200	0.22		0.28
250	grooved finish, add	SF	2F	700	0.70		0.87
	Exposed aggregrate finish						
260	hand seeded, add	SF	2F	500	0.97	0.15	1.40
270	scrubbed, add	SF	2F	800	0.61	0.36	1.21
280	Control joint, tooled	LF	1F	400	0.61		0.76
290	Curing, resin, rubber, or wax base	SF	1L	1000	0.20	0.05	0.32
	See also Section 03345, "Concrete Finishing"						
	Expansion joint, premolded expansion joint filler						
	asphalt						
300	1/2" x 4"	LF	1L	400	0.51	0.51	1.28
310	1/2" x 6"	LF	1L	380	0.54	0.76	1.62
320	1/2" x 8"	LF	1L	350	0.58	1.01	1.99
	asphalt tongue & groove						
330	1/8" x 3 1/2"	LF	1L	400	0.51	0.44	1.19
340	1/8" x 5 1/2"	LF	1L	380	0.54	0.53	1.33
350	1/2" x 7 1/2"	LF	1L	350	0.58	0.64	1.53
	fibre, bituminous						
360	1/2" x 4"	LF	1L	400	0.51	0.28	0.99
370	1/2" x 6"	LF	1L	380	0.54	0.38	1.15
380	1/2" x 8"	LF	1L	350	0.58	0.49	1.34
	cork, bituminous						
390	1/2" x 4"	LF	1L	400	0.51	0.80	1.64
400	1/2" x 6"	LF	1L	380	0.54	0.89	1.78
410	1/2" x 8"	LF	1L	350	0.58	1.21	2.24
	Expansion joint sealer						
420	rubber-asphalt, hot applied	LF	1L	530	0.38	0.28	0.83
430	rubber compound, cold applied	LF	1L	625	0.33	0.52	1.06

PAVING AND SURFACING

KEY	DESCRIPTION	UNIT	CREW AND EQUIPMENT	PER DAY	INSTALLATION COST	MATERIALS COST	TOTAL + 25%
00	**COMPOSITE COSTS**						
	Brick pavers, 2 1/4" thick, finished subgrade						
	dry joints						
100	2" sand base	SF					8.00
	4" asphaltic concrete base						
110	with asphaltic tack coat	SF					10.10
	mortar joints and setting bed, 4" reinforced						
120	concrete base, with 4" gravel sub-base	SF					11.60
	Concrete pavers, interlocking, 2 3/8" thick,						
	dry joints, on finished subgrade						
130	on 2" sand base	SF					5.50
140	on 2" sand base, 4" gravel sub-base	SF					6.10
	Local random ashlar pavers, 2 1/2", includes fine grading						
150	dry joints, sand bed	SF					15.00
	mortar bed and joints						
160	4" concrete base	SF					17.10
	6" reinforced concrete base, with						
170	6" gravel sub-base	SF					19.40
	Granite block pavers, 4" x 4" x 3", includes fine grading						
180	dry joints, sand bed	SF					12.90
	mortar bed and joints						
190	4" concrete base	SF					16.00
	6" reinforced concrete base, with						
200	6" gravel sub-base	SF					18.20
	Limestone random ashlar pavers, 2 1/2", includes fine grading						
205	dry joints, sand bed	SF					14.30
	mortar bed and joints						
210	4" concrete base	SF					16.80
	6" reinforced concrete base, with						
220	6" gravel sub-base	SF					19.10
	Slate pavers						
	1 1/4" irregular fitted, dry joints,						
230	sand bed, includes fine grading	SF					15.70
	3/4" random ashlar on 4" concrete base,						
240	mortar bed and joints, includes fine grading	SF					16.40
10	**PAVEMENT BASE**						
	Granular base, see Section 02230, "Base Course"						
	Concrete or asphalt base, see Section 02510, "Walk, Road and Parking Paving"						
100	2" sand base	SF	1L	750	0.27	0.20	0.59
110	15 Lb felt underlayment	SF	1L	3000	0.07	0.11	0.22
120	Asphalt tack coat	SF	1L	1500	0.14	0.09	0.28
130	2% neoprene tack coat	SF	1L	1500	0.14	0.11	0.31
20	**BRICK PAVERS**						
	Brick pavers, extruded hard red, dry joints						
	laid flat						
	running bond						
100	4" x 8" x 2 1/4"	SF	2B1L	220	3.29	2.27	7.00
110	4" x 8" x 1 5/8"	SF	2B1L	225	3.22	2.14	6.70
120	3 5/8" x 7 5/8" x 2 1/4"	SF	2B1L	195	3.72	2.57	7.90
130	3 5/8" x 7 5/8" x 1 5/8"	SF	2B1L	200	3.62	2.38	7.50
	basket weave						
140	4" x 8" x 2 1/4"	SF	2B1L	190	3.81	2.27	7.60
150	4" x 8" x 1 5/8"	SF	2B1L	195	3.72	2.12	7.30

KEY	DESCRIPTION	UNIT	CREW AND EQUIPMENT	PER DAY	INSTALLATION COST	MATERIALS COST	TOTAL + 25%
	herringbone						
160	4" x 8" x 2 1/4"	SF	2B1L	170	4.26	2.27	8.20
170	4" x 8" x 1 5/8"	SF	2B1L	175	4.14	2.12	7.80
180	3 5/8" x 7 5/8" x 2 1/4"	SF	2B1L	150	4.83	2.57	9.30
190	3 5/8" x 7 5/8" x 1 5/8"	SF	2B1L	155	4.68	2.38	8.80
	laid on edge, running bond						
200	4" x 8" x 2 1/4"	SF	2B1L	100	7.25	4.04	14.10
210	3 5/8" x 7 5/8" x 2 1/4"	SF	2B1L	95	7.63	4.13	14.70
	Brick pavers, extruded hard red, mortar joints and setting bed						
	laid flat						
	running bond						
220	4" x 8" x 2 1/4"	SF	2B1L	200	3.62	2.36	7.50
230	4" x 8" x 1 5/8"	SF	2B1L	205	3.54	2.23	7.20
240	3 5/8" x 7 5/8" x 2 1/4"	SF	2B1L	175	4.14	2.67	8.50
250	3 5/8" x 7 5/8" x 1 5/8"	SF	2B1L	180	4.03	2.49	8.10
	basket weave						
260	3 3/4" x 8" x 2 1/4"	SF	2B1L	170	4.26	2.36	8.30
270	3 3/4" x 8" x 1 5/8"	SF	2B1L	175	4.14	2.21	7.90
280	3 5/8" x 7 5/8" x 2 1/4"	SF	2B1L	170	4.26	2.67	8.70
290	3 5/8" x 7 5/8" x 1 5/8"	SF	2B1L	175	4.14	2.67	8.50
	herringbone						
300	4" x 8" x 2 1/4"	SF	2B1L	155	4.68	2.36	8.80
310	4" x 8" x 1 5/8"	SF	2B1L	160	4.53	2.21	8.40
320	3 5/8" x 7 5/8" x 2 1/4"	SF	2B1L	145	5.00	2.67	9.60
330	3 5/8" x 7 5/8" x 1 5/8"	SF	2B1L	150	4.83	2.49	9.20
	laid on edge, running bond						
340	4" x 8" x 2 1/4"	SF	2B1L	90	8.05	4.20	15.30
350	3 5/8" x 7 5/8" x 2 1/4"	SF	2B1L	80	9.06	4.20	16.60
	Colored mortar - add						
360	red or yellow	SF					0.05
370	black or brown	SF					0.09
380	green	SF					0.26
30	**BRICK EDGING**						
	Brick, extruded hard red, 8" deep, set in concrete						
	dry joints						
	headers						
100	4" x 8" x 2 1/4"	LF	2B1L	170	4.26	2.16	8.00
110	3 5/8" x 7 5/8" x 2 1/4"	LF	2B1L	160	4.53	2.62	8.90
	rowlocks						
120	4" x 8" x 2 1/4"	LF	2B1L	95	7.63	3.92	14.40
130	3 5/8" x 7 5/8" x 2 1/4"	LF	2B1L	100	7.25	3.78	13.80
	mortar joints						
	headers						
140	4" x 8" x 2 1/4"	LF	2B1L	155	4.68	2.45	8.90
150	3 5/8" x 7 5/8" x 2 1/4"	LF	2B1L	145	5.00	2.57	9.50
	rowlocks						
160	4" x 8" x 2 1/4"	LF	2B1L	80	9.06	3.58	15.80
170	3 5/8" x 7 5/8" x 2 1/4"	LF	2B1L	85	8.53	3.58	15.10
40	**CONCRETE PAVERS**						
	Interlocking pavers, 9" x 4 1/2", dry joints						
	natural grey						
100	2 3/8" thick	SF	2B1L,46	450	1.65	1.77	4.28
110	3 1/8" thick	SF	2B1L,46	400	1.86	2.05	4.89
	standard colors						
120	2 3/8" thick	SF	2B1L,46	450	1.65	2.25	4.88
130	3 1/8" thick	SF	2B1L,46	400	1.86	2.53	5.50
	custom colors						
140	2 3/8" thick	SF	2B1L,46	450	1.65	2.45	5.10
150	3 1/8" thick	SF	2B1L,46	400	1.86	2.74	5.80

PAVING AND SURFACING

02515 Unit Pavers   1994

KEY	DESCRIPTION	UNIT	CREW AND EQUIPMENT	PER DAY	INSTALLATION COST	MATERIALS COST	TOTAL + 25%
	Patio blocks, 8" x 16" x 2", dry joints						
160	natural grey	SF	2B1L,46	500	1.49	1.27	3.45
170	standard colors	SF	2B1L,46	500	1.49	1.48	3.71
50	**STONE PAVERS**						
	Local flagstone paving						
	sand bed, dry joints						
100	random ashlar, 1 1/4"	SF	1L2M	130	5.61	2.48	10.10
110	random ashlar, 2 1/2"	SF	1L2M	110	6.63	4.97	14.50
120	irregular fitted, 1 1/4"	SF	1L2M	120	6.07	2.12	10.20
130	irregular fitted, 2 1/2"	SF	1L2M	100	7.29	3.28	13.20
	mortar bed and joints						
140	random ashlar, 1 1/4"	SF	1L2M	120	6.07	2.59	10.80
150	random ashlar, 2 1/2"	SF	1L2M	100	7.29	3.95	14.00
160	irregular fitted, 1 1/4"	SF	1L2M	110	6.63	2.24	11.10
170	irregular fitted, 2 1/2"	SF	1L2M	90	8.10	3.43	14.40
	Granite paving, modular						
	sand bed, dry joints						
180	4" x 4" x 3"	SF	1L2M	140	5.21	4.66	12.30
190	12" x 12" x 3"	SF	1L2M	120	6.07	4.78	13.60
	mortar bed and joints						
200	4" x 4" x 3"	SF	1L2M	130	5.61	4.72	12.90
210	12" x 12" x 3"	SF	1L2M	110	6.63	4.90	14.40
	Limestone flag paving						
	sand bed, dry joints						
220	random ashlar, 1 1/4"	SF	1L2M	130	5.61	2.30	9.90
230	random ashlar, 2 1/2"	SF	1L2M	110	6.63	4.39	13.80
240	irregular fitted, 1 1/2"	SF	1L2M	120	6.07	2.14	10.30
250	irregular fitted, 2 1/2"	SF	1L2M	100	7.29	3.66	13.70
	mortar bed and joints						
260	random ashlar, 1"	SF	1L2M	120	6.07	2.03	10.10
270	random ashlar, 2 1/2"	SF	1L2M	100	7.29	4.51	14.70
280	irregular fitted, 1 1/4"	SF	1L2M	110	6.63	1.79	10.50
290	irregular fitted, 1"	SF	1L2M	90	8.10	3.39	14.40
	Slate flag paving, natural cleft						
	sand bed, dry joints						
300	random ashlar, 1 1/4"	SF	1L2M	145	5.03	7.10	15.20
310	irregular fitted, 1 1/4"	SF	1L2M	130	5.61	6.60	15.30
	mortar bed and joints						
320	random ashlar, 3/4"	SF	1L2M	145	5.03	5.60	13.30
330	random ashlar, 1"	SF	1L2M	120	6.07	6.60	15.80
340	irregular fitted, 3/4"	SF	1L2M	130	5.61	5.10	13.40
350	irregular fitted, 1"	SF	1L2M	110	6.63	6.10	15.90
360	sand rubbed, add	SF				1.12	1.40

02525 Curbs — 1994

KEY	DESCRIPTION	UNIT	CREW AND EQUIPMENT	PER DAY	INSTALLATION COST	MATERIALS COST	TOTAL + 25%
00	**COMPOSITE COSTS**						
	Vertical concrete curb, 6" x 12", cast-in-place, includes excavation and backfill						
100	straight curb ***	LF					11.50
110	curved curb ***	LF					13.10
	Rolled concrete curb and gutter, cast-in-place, 18" x 6" roll, 6" gravel base, includes excavation and backfill						
120	straight curb ***	LF					18.80
130	curved curb ***	LF					21.50
10	**ASPHALT CONCRETE CURBS**						
	Straight asphalt concrete curb						
	8" x 6"						
100	by hand ***	LF	3L	100	6.12	1.45	9.50
110	machine extruded ***	LF	1G3L,93	320	3.10	1.13	5.30
	8" x 8"						
120	by hand	LF	3L	100	6.12	1.92	10.10
130	machine extruded	LF	1G3L,93	320	3.10	1.54	5.80
	Curved asphalt concrete curb						
	8" x 6"						
140	by hand ***	LF	3L	80	7.65	1.45	11.40
150	machine extruded ***	LF	1G3L,93	260	3.81	1.13	6.20
	8" x 8"						
160	by hand	LF	3L	80	7.65	1.92	12.00
170	machine extruded	LF	1G3L,93	260	3.81	1.48	6.60
20	**CONCRETE CURBS**						
	Formwork, see Section 03110, "Structural Cast-in-Place Concrete Formwork"						
	Vertical curb, cast-in-place						
	6" x 12"						
100	straight curb ***	LF	1F2L	130	5.01	2.51	9.40
110	curved curb ***	LF	1F2L	95	6.86	2.51	11.70
	6" x 18"						
120	straight curb	LF	1F2L	120	5.43	3.72	11.40
130	curved curb	LF	1F2L	85	7.66	3.72	14.20
	6" x 24"						
140	straight curb	LF	1F2L	115	5.66	4.94	13.30
150	curved curb	LF	1F2L	80	8.14	4.94	16.40
	Rolled curb and gutter, 6" roll, cast-in-place						
	18" x 6" base						
160	straight curb ***	LF	1F2L	100	6.51	4.94	14.30
170	curved curb ***	LF	1F2L	75	8.69	4.94	17.00
	24" x 6" base						
180	straight curb	LF	1F2L	85	7.66	6.20	17.30
190	curved curb	LF	1F2L	60	10.86	6.20	21.30
	Reinforcing, see Section 02310, "Reinforcing Steel"						

PAVING AND SURFACING

KEY	DESCRIPTION	UNIT	CREW AND EQUIPMENT	PER DAY	INSTALLATION COST	MATERIALS COST	TOTAL + 25%
00	**COMPOSITE COSTS**						
	Asphaltic concrete athletic paving, on finished subgrade, with surface finish						
100	acrylic emulsion color finish	SY					14.50
110	acrylic emulsion texture coat and acrylic emulsion color finish	SY					17.20
120	rubber/acrylic compound cushion coat, acrylic emulsion texture coat and acrylic emulsion color finish	SY					23.50
	Portland cement concrete athletic paving on finished subgrade						
130	with acrylic emulsion texture coat and acrylic emulsion color finish	SY					24.50
140	with rubber/acrylic compound cushion coat, acrylic emulsion texture coat and color coat	SY					30.90
10	**PAVING**						
	Asphaltic concrete and Portland cement Concrete paving see Section 02510, "Walk, Road and Parking Paving"						
20	**SURFACE PREPARATION**						
100	Acid etch concrete surface	SY	3L	1600	0.38	0.09	0.59
	Primer						
110	on asphalt	SY	3L	3200	0.19	0.16	0.44
120	on concrete	SY	3L	3200	0.19	0.27	0.58
	Filler, per coat						
130	asphalt emulsion, 1 coat	SY	3L	2400	0.26	0.20	0.57
140	acrylic	SY	3L	2400	0.26	0.48	0.92
30	**ACRYLIC ATHLETIC SURFACING**						
100	Rubber/acrylic compound cushion coat, per coat	SY	3L	1600	0.38	1.31	2.12
	Acrylic emulsion texture coat, per coat						
110	sand filled	SY	3L	3200	0.19	0.66	1.06
120	rubber filled	SY	3L	3200	0.19	0.86	1.31
	Acrylic emulsion surface color coat, per coat						
130	tan, brown, or red	SY	3L	3200	0.19	0.25	0.55
140	greens	SY	3L	3200	0.19	0.27	0.58
150	blue	SY	3L	3200	0.19	0.32	0.64
40	**STRIPING**						
100	Stripe tennis court with white striping paint	Ea	1L	4	51.01	10.90	77.00
50	**PLAYGROUND SURFACING**						
100	Rubber cushioned concrete pavers, 18" x 18", dry joints	SF	2B1L	600	1.21	10.00	14.00

02580 Pavement Marking — 1994

KEY	DESCRIPTION	UNIT	CREW AND EQUIPMENT	PER DAY	INSTALLATION COST	MATERIALS COST	TOTAL + 25%
10	**PAINTING**						
	White or color marking						
	lines						
100	3" wide	LF	1L,97	3000	0.07	0.05	0.15
110	4" wide	LF	1L,97	3000	0.07	0.07	0.18
120	letters, symbols, shapes	LF	1L,97	500	0.44	0.31	0.94
	Reflectorized white or yellow marking lines						
130	4" wide	LF	1L,97	3000	0.07	0.16	0.29
140	8" wide	LF	1L,97	2000	0.11	0.26	0.46
150	letters, symbols, shapes	SF	1L,97	500	0.44	0.51	1.19
20	**THERMOPLASTIC TAPE**						
	Reflectorized thermoplastic tape lines						
100	4" wide	LF	1L,97	1000	0.22	0.25	0.59
110	6" wide	LF	1L,97	800	0.28	0.38	0.82
120	letters, symbols, shapes	SF	1L,97	200	1.10	1.12	2.78

SEWERAGE AND DRAINAGE

KEY	DESCRIPTION	UNIT	CREW AND EQUIPMENT	PER DAY	INSTALLATION COST	MATERIALS COST	TOTAL + 25%
10	**EXCAVATION AND BACKFILL**						
	See Sec. 02220 "Excavating, Backfilling, & Compacting"						
20	**DRAINAGE TUBING**						
	Corrugated plastic tubing, plain or perforated, with snap fittings, does not include excavation and backfill						
	tubing						
100	3" tubing	LF	1G2L,50	3000	0.23	0.26	0.62
110	4" tubing	LF	1G2L,50	2550	0.28	0.29	0.71
120	5" tubing	LF	1G2L,50	2250	0.31	0.48	0.99
130	6" tubing	LF	1G2L,50	2000	0.35	0.77	1.40
140	8" tubing	LF	1G2L,50	1650	0.43	1.31	2.17
	tee fitting						
150	3" tee	Ea	1L	300	0.68	2.56	4.05
160	4" tee	Ea	1L	300	0.68	2.89	4.46
170	5" tee	Ea	1L	300	0.68	4.34	6.30
180	6" tee	Ea	1L	300	0.68	5.10	7.20
	ell fitting						
190	3" ell	Ea	1L	500	0.41	2.43	3.55
200	4" ell	Ea	1L	500	0.41	2.82	4.04
210	5" ell	Ea	1L	500	0.41	4.25	5.80
220	6" ell	Ea	1L	500	0.41	4.70	6.40
30	**DRAINAGE TILE**						
	Vitrified clay drainage tile, does not include excavation and backfill						
	covered joints						
100	4" tile	LF	1L	80	2.55	1.34	4.86
110	6" tile	LF	1L	64	3.19	3.28	8.10
120	8" tile	LF	1L	53	3.85	3.04	8.60
130	10" tile	LF	1L	46	4.44	3.68	10.10
	open joints						
140	4" tile	LF	1L	130	1.57	1.30	3.59
150	6" tile	LF	1L	105	1.94	1.55	4.37
160	8" tile	LF	1L	89	2.29	2.95	6.60
170	10" tile	LF	1L	76	2.68	3.68	8.00
	tee or ell fitting, add						
180	4" tile	Ea				3.28	4.10
190	6" tile	Ea				6.00	7.50
200	8" tile	Ea				9.70	12.10
210	10" tile	Ea				12.40	15.50

KEY	DESCRIPTION	UNIT	CREW AND EQUIPMENT	PER DAY	INSTALLATION COST	MATERIALS COST	TOTAL + 25%
00	**COMPOSITE COSTS**						
	Catch basin including 20" diameter grate and frame, 6" concrete top and base, excavation and backfill. Sheet piling not included.						
	precast concrete, 4' diameter						
100	4' deep ***	Ea					2060.00
110	6' deep ***	Ea					2580.00
120	8' deep ***	Ea					3150.00
	concrete block radial, 4' diameter						
130	4' deep ***	Ea					2170.00
140	6' deep ***	Ea					2770.00
150	8' deep ***	Ea					3550.00

02720 Storm Sewage Systems — 1994

KEY	DESCRIPTION	UNIT	CREW AND EQUIPMENT	PER DAY	INSTALLATION COST	MATERIALS COST	TOTAL + 25%
10	**EXCAVATION AND BACKFILL**						
	See Sec. 02220, "Excavating, Backfilling, & Compacting"						
20	**CATCH BASIN GRATES AND FRAMES**						
	Light duty grate, gray iron, asphalt coated						
	grate on pipe bell						
100	6" diameter, 13 Lb	Ea	1I	30	9.43	12.80	27.80
110	8" diameter, 25 Lb	Ea	1I	25	11.31	33.70	56.00
	frame and grate						
120	8" diameter, 55 Lb	Ea	2I	29	19.50	73.00	116.00
130	17" diameter, 135 Lb	Ea	2I	15	37.70	174.00	265.00
	Medium duty frame and grate						
140	11" diameter, 70 Lb	Ea	2I	28	20.20	91.00	139.00
150	15" diameter, 120 Lb	Ea	2I	16	35.35	163.00	248.00
160	radial grate, 20" dia., 140 Lb ***	Ea	1D2I,07	12	77.29	184.00	327.00
	Heavy duty frame and grate						
	flat grate						
170	11 1/2" diameter, 85 Lb	Ea	2I	23	24.59	117.00	177.00
180	20" diameter, 235 Lb ***	Ea	1D2I,07	10	92.75	303.00	495.00
190	21" diameter, 315 Lb	Ea	1D2I,07	8	115.94	386.00	630.00
200	24" diameter, 350 Lb	Ea	1D2I,07	8	115.94	433.00	690.00
210	30" diameter, 555 Lb	Ea	1D2I,07	5	185.50	630.00	1020.00
	convex or concave grate						
220	20" diameter, 200 Lb ***	Ea	1D2I,07	11	84.32	222.00	383.00
230	20" diameter, 325 Lb	Ea	1D2I,07	8	115.94	380.00	620.00
	Beehive grate and frame						
240	11" diameter, 80 Lb	Ea	2I	25	22.62	167.00	237.00
250	15" diameter, 120 Lb	Ea	1D2I,07	11	84.32	157.00	302.00
260	21" diameter, 285 Lb	Ea	1D2I,07	8	115.94	324.00	550.00
270	24" diameter, 375 Lb	Ea	1D2I,07	7	132.50	442.00	720.00
30	**CULVERT PIPES**						
	Corrugated galvanized metal pipe, bituminous coated, and paved invert						
	round 20' to 30' long						
100	8" diameter	LF	2L	230	1.77	4.68	8.10
110	10" diameter	LF	2L	190	2.15	6.00	10.20
120	12" diameter	LF	1D3L,07	260	3.75	7.80	14.40
130	15" diameter	LF	1D3L,07	240	4.06	9.70	17.20
140	18" diameter	LF	1D3L,07	220	4.43	11.60	20.00
150	21" diameter	LF	1D3L,07	200	4.87	13.30	22.70
160	24" diameter	LF	1A4L,95	250	6.04	15.00	26.30
170	30" diameter	LF	1A4L,95	240	6.29	21.70	35.00
180	36" diameter	LF	1A4L,95	220	6.86	29.30	45.20
	oval, 20' to 30' long						
190	18" x 11"	LF	1D3L,07	250	3.90	10.50	18.00
200	22" x 13"	LF	1D3L,07	200	4.87	13.60	23.10
210	29" x 18"	LF	1D3L,07	150	6.49	16.60	28.90
220	36" x 22"	LF	1A4L,95	250	6.04	23.00	36.30
230	43" x 27"	LF	1A4L,95	200	7.55	36.60	55.00
	flared end sections for oval pipe						
240	18" x 11"	Ea	1D3L,07	20	48.70	40.80	112.00
250	22" x 13"	Ea	1D3L,07	19	51.27	52.00	129.00
260	29" x 18"	Ea	1D3L,07	18	54.11	97.00	189.00
270	36" x 22"	Ea	1A4L,95	24	62.91	132.00	244.00
280	43" x 27"	Ea	1A4L,95	20	28.00	160.00	235.00
	Reinforced concrete pipe, class 4 span arch (deformed round, 8' long)						
290	18" dia., 22" span, 13" rise	LF	1A4L,95	140	10.79	34.70	57.00
300	24" dia., 29" span, 18" rise	LF	1A4L,95	120	12.58	42.60	69.00
310	30" dia., 36" span, 22" rise	LF	1A4L,95	100	15.10	49.00	80.00

SEWERAGE AND DRAINAGE

KEY	DESCRIPTION	UNIT	CREW AND EQUIPMENT	PER DAY	INSTALLATION COST	MATERIALS COST	TOTAL + 25%
	Corrugated polyethylene culvert pipe, heavy duty, 10' and 20' lengths						
350	8" diameter	LF	2L	400	1.02	1.51	3.16
360	10" diameter	LF	2L	360	1.13	2.40	4.42
370	12" diameter	LF	2L	270	1.51	3.39	6.10
380	15" diameter	LF	2L	140	2.91	5.40	10.40
390	18" diameter	LF	2L	125	3.26	10.90	17.70
400	24" diameter	LF	2L	100	4.08	15.40	24.40
40	**CURB INLETS**						
	Gray iron, asphalt coated, heavy duty frame, grate and curb box						
100	20" x 11", 260 Lb	Ea	1D2I,07	11	84.32	304.00	485.00
110	20" x 16.5", 300 Lb	Ea	1D2I,07	10	92.75	333.00	530.00
120	20" x 17", 400 Lb	Ea	1D2I,07	7	132.50	422.00	690.00
130	19" x 18", 500 Lb	Ea	1D2I,07	6	154.58	500.00	820.00
140	30" x 17", 600 Lb	Ea	1D2I,07	5	185.50	550.00	920.00
50	**GUTTER INLETS**						
	Gray iron, asphalt coated, heavy duty frame and grate						
100	8" x 11.5", 85 Lb	Ea	2I	28	20.20	102.00	153.00
110	22" x 17", 260 Lb, concave	Ea	1D2I,07	11	84.32	289.00	467.00
120	22.3" x 22.3", 475 Lb	Ea	1D2I,07	7	132.50	317.00	560.00
130	two 29.8" x 17.8", 750 LB	Ea	1D2I,07	6	154.58	481.00	790.00
60	**TRENCH INLETS**						
100	Ductile iron, light duty frame and grate for pedestrian traffic, 53.5" x 8.3", 100 Lb	Ea	2I	25	22.62	111.00	167.00
	Gray iron, asphalt coated frame and grate or solid cover light cover						
110	8" wide grate	LF	2I	50	11.31	42.40	67.00
120	12" wide grate	LF	2I	45	12.57	59.00	89.00
130	8" wide solid cover	LF	2I	50	11.31	46.90	73.00
140	12" side solid cover	LF	2I	45	12.57	68.00	101.00
	heavy duty, 1 3/4"						
150	8" wide grate	LF	2I	45	12.57	46.90	74.00
160	12" wide grate	LF	2I	40	14.14	69.00	104.00
170	8" wide solid cover	LF	2I	45	12.57	53.00	82.00
180	12" side solid cover	LF	2I	40	14.14	74.00	110.00
70	**DRAINAGE PIPE**						
	Corrugated galvanized metal, bituminous coated, with bands and gaskets						
100	8" diameter	LF	2L	350	1.17	4.59	7.20
110	10" diameter	LF	2L	280	1.46	5.70	8.90
120	12" diameter	LF	1D3L,07	325	3.00	7.00	12.50
130	15" diameter	LF	1D3L,07	300	3.25	8.70	14.90
140	18" diameter	LF	1D3L,07	250	3.90	10.30	17.70
150	21" diameter	LF	1D3L,07	200	4.87	14.70	24.50
160	24" diameter	LF	1A4L,95	300	5.03	16.50	26.90
170	30" diameter	LF	1A4L,95	285	5.30	19.70	31.20
180	36" diameter	LF	1A4L,95	270	5.59	30.30	44.90
	Reinforced concrete with rubber gaskets						
190	12" diameter	LF	1A3L,07	220	4.73	8.20	16.20
200	15" diameter	LF	1A3L,07	200	5.20	11.10	20.40
210	18" diameter	LF	1A4L,95	250	6.04	12.50	23.20
220	21" diameter	LF	1A4L,95	190	7.95	14.10	27.60

KEY	DESCRIPTION	UNIT	CREW AND EQUIPMENT	PER DAY	INSTALLATION COST	MATERIALS COST	TOTAL + 25%
230	24" diameter	LF	1A4L,95	140	10.79	19.20	37.50
240	30" diameter	LF	1A4L,95	110	13.73	24.10	47.30
250	36" diameter	LF	1A4L,95	90	16.78	34.10	64.00
	Corrugated plastic pipe						
260	4" diameter	LF	2L	1800	0.23	0.53	0.95
270	6" diameter	LF	2L	1500	0.27	1.04	1.64
280	8" diameter	LF	2L	1200	0.34	1.50	2.30
80	**MANHOLES**						
	Manhole top and base, cast-in-place concrete, see Sections 03110, 03210, and 03311						
	Manhole and cone, precast concrete, 4' inside diameter						
100	4' deep ***	Ea	1D2L,07	4	192.50	252.00	560.00
110	6' deep	Ea	1D2L,07	2.5	308.00	379.00	860.00
120	8' deep	Ea	1D2L,07	1.8	427.78	500.00	1160.00
130	10' deep	Ea	1D2L,07	1.3	592.32	570.00	1450.00
140	depths over 10'	LF	1D2L,07	13	59.23	70.00	162.00
150	top slab, 6" thick	Ea	1D2L,07	8	96.25	145.00	302.00
160	base slab, 6" thick	Ea	1D2L,07	6	128.33	145.00	342.00
	Concrete block radial, 4' inside diameter						
170	4' deep ***	Ea	1B1L	2	232.19	305.00	670.00
180	6' deep	Ea	1B1L	1.2	386.98	453.00	1050.00
190	8' deep	Ea	1B1L	0.8	580.47	670.00	1560.00
200	10' deep	Ea	1B1L	0.6	773.96	780.00	1940.00
210	depths over 10'	LF	1B1L	7	66.34	85.00	189.00
220	2' depth cone block for 30" grate	LF	1B1L	3	154.79	129.00	355.00
230	2'-6' depth cone block for 24" grate	LF	1B1L	2.5	185.75	171.00	446.00
	Manhole steps, cast iron, heavy type, asphalt coated						
240	7" x 9"	Ea	1B	36	7.23	8.90	20.20
250	8" x 9"	Ea	1B	36	7.23	13.20	25.50
90	**MANHOLE FRAMES AND SOLID COVERS**						
	Gray iron, asphalt coated, standard sizes						
	light duty frame and lid						
100	15" diameter, 65 Lb	Ea	2I	28	20.20	73.00	116.00
110	22" diameter, 140 Lb	Ea	2I	13	43.50	154.00	247.00
	medium duty frame and lid						
120	11" diameter, 75 Lb	Ea	1D2I,07	20	46.37	216.00	328.00
130	20" diameter, 185 Lb	Ea	1D2I,07	10	92.75	198.00	363.00
	heavy duty frame and lid						
140	17" diameter, 135 Lb	Ea	1D2I,07	12	77.29	147.00	280.00
150	21" diameter, 315 Lb	Ea	1D2I,07	8	115.94	330.00	560.00
160	24" diameter, 375 Lb	Ea	1D2I,07	7	132.50	385.00	650.00

02810 Irrigation Systems · 1994

KEY	DESCRIPTION	UNIT	CREW AND EQUIPMENT	PER DAY	INSTALLATION COST	MATERIALS COST	TOTAL + 35%
00	**COMPOSITE COSTS**						
	Non-freezing areas						
	residential or small commercial						
100	high	MSF					500.00
110	low	MSF					325.00
	medium commercial (parks, schools)						
120	high	MSF					425.00
130	low	MSF					275.00
	large systems (parks, golf courses)						
140	high	Ac					6300.00
150	low	Ac					3750.00
	Freezing areas						
	residential or small commercial						
160	high	MSF					500.00
170	low	MSF					300.00
	medium commercial (parks, schools)						
180	high	MSF					400.00
190	low	MSF					250.00
	large systems (parks, golf courses)						
200	high	Ac					6300.00
210	low	Ac					3750.00
05	**TRENCHING**						
	Trenching						
	main lines						
100	12" deep	LF	1G,26	800	0.41		0.55
110	18" deep	LF	1G,26	600	0.54		0.73
120	24" deep	LF	1G,26	400	0.81		1.10
	lateral lines - trencher						
130	8" deep	LF	1G,26	800	0.41		0.55
140	12" deep	LF	1G,26	800	0.41		0.55
	lateral lines - pulled						
150	8" deep	LF	1G1L,25	2000	0.26		0.35
160	12" deep	LF	1G1L,25	1000	0.52		0.71
	add for shelf, rockfield, or hardpan				20%		20%
	add for existing turf				5%		5%
10	**BORING**						
	Boring under pavement						
100	to 8' wide	LF	1L,80	30	7.63		10.30
110	over 8' wide	LF	1L,80	20	11.45		15.50
15	**POINTS OF CONNECTION**						
	Non-freezing area						
	residential or small commercial						
100	tap	Ea	1L	2	102.02	15.00	158.00
110	stub	Ea	1L	3	68.01	11.00	107.00
120	medium commercial, stub	Ea	1L	2	102.02	30.00	178.00
	Freezing area						
	residential or small commercial						
130	tap	Ea	1L	2	102.02	19.00	163.00
140	stub	Ea	1L	3	68.01	14.00	111.00
150	medium commercial, stub	Ea	1L	2	102.02	35.00	185.00
20	**BACKFLOW PREVENTION**						
	Atmospheric vacuum breaker, brass, with shut off						
100	3/4"-1"	Ea	1L	4	51.01	17.42	92.00
110	1 1/4"-2"	Ea	1L	4	51.01	29.90	109.00
115	add for union	Ea				6.50	8.80
	Pressure type vacuum breaker, with two valves						
120	1"-1 1/4"	Ea	1L	2	102.02	185.90	389.00
130	1 1/2"-2"	Ea	1L	2	102.02	252.20	478.00

02810 Irrigation Systems

KEY	DESCRIPTION	UNIT	CREW AND EQUIPMENT	PER DAY	INSTALLATION COST	MATERIALS COST	TOTAL + 35%
	Double check valve assembly						
140	1 1/2", with two gates	Ea	1L	2	102.02	224.90	441.00
150	2", with two gates	Ea	2L	2	204.03	267.80	640.00
160	3", with two gates	Ea	2L	2	204.03	442.00	870.00
170	4", with two gates	Ea	2L	2	204.03	708.50	1230.00
	Reduced pressure backflow preventer, with gate valves						
175	1"	Ea	1L	4	51.01	281.45	449.00
180	1 1/2"	Ea	1L	4	51.01	452.40	680.00
185	2"	Ea	1L	3	68.01	566.15	860.00
190	3" flanged	Ea	2L	3	136.02	780.00	1240.00
200	4" flanged	Ea	2L	2	204.03	1820.00	2730.00
210	6" flanged	Ea	2L	1	408.06	3120.00	4760.00
25	**AUTOMATIC VALVES**						
	Brass electric solenoid, with flow control						
100	3/4"-1"	Ea	1L	8	25.50	74.75	135.00
110	1 1/4"-1 1/2"	Ea	1L	8	25.50	104.00	175.00
120	2"	Ea	1L	8	25.50	123.50	201.00
130	2 1/2"	Ea	1L	6	34.01	230.75	357.00
140	3"	Ea	1L	4	51.01	259.35	419.00
	Plastic electric solenoid, with flow control						
150	3/4"-1"	Ea	1L	8	25.50	28.60	73.00
160	1 1/4"-1 1/2"	Ea	1L	8	25.50	50.05	102.00
170	2"	Ea	1L	6	34.01	74.10	146.00
190	3"	Ea	2L	6	68.01	129.35	266.00
	Brass hydraulic, with flow control						
200	3/4"-1"	Ea	1L	8	25.50	61.75	118.00
210	1 1/4"-1 1/2"	Ea	1L	8	25.50	93.60	161.00
220	2"	Ea	1L	6	34.01	105.30	188.00
230	2 1/2"	Ea	1L	6	34.01	221.00	344.00
240	3"	Ea	2L	6	68.01	248.95	428.00
	Plastic hydraulic, with flow control						
250	3/4"-1"	Ea	1L	8	25.50	14.63	54.00
260	1 1/4"-1 1/2"	Ea	1L	8	25.50	45.50	96.00
270	2"	Ea	1L	6	34.01	70.85	142.00
30	**VALVE BOXES**						
	Plastic valve box, with lid						
100	8" round	Ea	1L	12	17.00	3.90	28.20
110	10" round	Ea	1L	12	17.00	8.45	34.40
120	10"x16" rectangular	Ea	1L	12	17.00	14.30	42.30
130	6" rectangular extension	Ea	1L	12	17.00	7.80	33.50
140	jumbo rectangular	Ea	1L	8	25.50	24.48	67.00
150	add for security bolt	Ea	1L	200	1.02	5.85	9.30
35	**AUTOMATIC CONTROLLERS**						
	Mechanical - electrical controller						
	indoor mount						
100	4 station	Ea	1L	3	68.01	97.50	223.00
110	6 station	Ea	1L	3	68.01	117.00	250.00
120	7-8 station	Ea	1L	2	102.02	162.50	357.00
130	10-12 station	Ea	1L	6	34.01	138.00	232.00
	outdoor mount						
150	4 station	Ea	1E	3	92.99	175.50	362.00
160	6 station	Ea	1E	3	92.99	211.25	411.00
170	7-8 station	Ea	1E	2	139.48	243.75	520.00
180	10-12 station	Ea	1E	2	139.48	325.00	630.00

SITE IMPROVEMENTS

			CREW AND	PER	INSTALLATION	MATERIALS	
KEY	DESCRIPTION	UNIT	EQUIPMENT	DAY	COST	COST	TOTAL + 35%
190	16-18 station	Ea	1E	1	278.96	845.00	1520.00
200	20-24 station	Ea	1E	1	278.96	975.00	1690.00
	Solid-state controller, electronic						
	indoor mount, dual program						
220	4 station	Ea	1E	3	92.99	58.50	205.00
230	6 station	Ea	1E	3	92.99	78.00	231.00
240	8 station	Ea	1E	2	139.48	117.00	346.00
	outdoor mount, dual program						
250	4 station	Ea	1E	3	92.99	97.50	257.00
260	6 station	Ea	1E	3	92.99	117.00	283.00
270	8 station	Ea	1E	3	92.99	156.00	336.00
280	10-12 station	Ea	1E	2	139.48	208.00	469.00
290	16-18 station	Ea	1E	1	278.96	455.00	990.00
300	20-24 station	Ea	1E	1	278.96	650.00	1250.00
	Adjustment factor						
310	outdoor controller pedestal	Ea	1L	2	102.02	130.00	313.00
	add for dual program	Ea			5%		
40	**UNDERGROUND FEEDER WIRE**						
	Includes waterproof connectors						
	in trench						
100	14 gauge	LF	1L	2000	0.10	0.05	0.21
110	12 gauge	LF	1L	2000	0.10	0.08	0.25
120	10 gauge	LF	1L	1400	0.15	0.10	0.33
130	8 gauge	LF	1L	1000	0.20	0.17	0.50
	pulled (large system)						
140	14 gauge	LF	1L1G,25	5000	0.10	0.05	0.21
150	12 gauge	LF	1L1G,25	4000	0.13	0.08	0.28
160	10 gauge	LF	1L1G,25	3000	0.17	0.10	0.37
170	8 gauge	LF	1L1G,25	2000	0.26	0.17	0.58
	1/4" polyethylene, includes fittings						
180	in trench	LF	1L	2000	0.10	0.05	0.21
190	pulled (large systems)	LF	1L1G,25	5000	0.10	0.05	0.21
45	**PIPE**						
	PVC, solvent weld, includes fittings						
	Class 160						
100	1" diameter	LF	2L	1000	0.41	0.13	0.73
110	1 1/4" diameter	LF	2L	1000	0.41	0.27	0.92
120	1 1/2" diameter	LF	2L	800	0.51	0.34	1.15
130	2" diameter	LF	2L	800	0.51	0.52	1.39
	Class 200						
140	3/4" diameter	LF	2L	1000	0.41	0.14	0.74
150	1" diameter	LF	2L	1000	0.41	0.18	0.79
160	1 1/4" diameter	LF	2L	1000	0.41	0.28	0.93
170	1 1/2" diameter	LF	2L	800	0.51	0.36	1.17
180	2" diameter	LF	2L	800	0.51	0.56	1.44
	Class 315						
190	1/2" diameter	LF	2L	1000	0.41	0.26	0.90
200	3/4" diameter	LF	2L	1000	0.41	0.27	0.92
210	1" diameter	LF	2L	1000	0.41	0.26	0.90
220	1 1/4" diameter	LF	2L	1000	0.41	0.56	1.31
230	1 1/2" diameter	LF	2L	800	0.51	0.72	1.66
240	2" diameter	LF	2L	800	0.51	1.12	2.20
	Schedule 40, includes fittings						
250	1/2" diameter	LF	2L	1000	0.41	0.18	0.79
260	3/4" diameter	LF	2L	1000	0.41	0.25	0.89
270	1" diameter	LF	2L	1000	0.41	0.20	0.82
280	1 1/4" diameter	LF	2L	1000	0.41	0.32	0.98
290	1 1/2" diameter	LF	2L	800	0.51	0.51	1.38
300	2" diameter	LF	2L	800	0.51	0.71	1.65

KEY	DESCRIPTION	UNIT	CREW AND EQUIPMENT	PER DAY	INSTALLATION COST	MATERIALS COST	TOTAL + 35%
	PVC - bell - spigot, Class 160, includes fittings						
310	1 1/2" diameter	LF	2L	1000	0.41	0.33	1.00
320	2" diameter	LF	2L	800	0.51	0.53	1.40
330	2 1/2" diameter	LF	2L	700	0.58	0.73	1.77
340	3" diameter	LF	2L	500	0.82	1.08	2.56
350	4" diameter	LF	3L	300	2.04	1.77	5.10
360	6" diameter	LF	3L	200	3.06	3.71	9.10
370	8" diameter	LF	3L	100	6.12	5.94	16.30
380	10" diameter	LF	3L	100	6.12	9.82	21.50
	Polyethylene, 100#, includes fittings						
390	3/4" diameter	LF	2L	1000	0.41	0.18	0.79
400	1" diameter	LF	2L	1000	0.41	0.25	0.89
410	1 1/4" diameter	LF	2L	800	0.51	0.44	1.28
420	1 1/2" diameter	LF	2L	600	0.68	0.61	1.74
430	2" diameter	LF	2L	500	0.82	1.00	2.45
	Polyethylene, 80#, includes fittings						
440	3/4" diameter	LF	2L	1000	0.41	0.12	0.71
450	1" diameter	LF	2L	1000	0.41	0.18	0.79
460	1 1/4" diameter	LF	2L	800	0.51	0.38	1.20
470	1 1/2" diameter	LF	2L	600	0.68	0.51	1.61
480	2" diameter	LF	2L	500	0.82	0.81	2.20
50	**SHRUB SPRINKLERS AND BUBBLERS**						
	All head costs include riser						
100	Bubbler, plastic (5' spacing, 12" riser)	Ea	1L	24	8.50	1.17	13.10
110	flex riser	Ea	1L	24	8.50	1.82	13.90
120	double swing joint	Ea	1L	12	17.00	5.23	30.00
130	triple swing joint	Ea	1L	12	17.00	6.92	32.30
140	Shrub spray, plastic (8'-18' spacing, 12" riser)	Ea	1L	20	10.20	2.89	17.70
150	flex riser	Ea	1L	20	10.20	5.92	21.80
160	double swing joint	Ea	1L	12	17.00	7.61	33.20
170	triple swing joint	Ea	1L	12	17.00	8.61	34.60
	Stream spray (12'-22' spacing, 12" riser)						
180	plastic	Ea	1L	20	10.20	2.89	17.70
190	flex riser	Ea	1L	20	10.20	5.92	21.80
200	double swing joint	Ea	1L	12	17.00	7.61	33.20
210	triple swing joint	Ea	1L	12	17.00	8.61	34.60
220	metal, pressure compensating	Ea	1L	20	10.20	5.95	21.80
230	flex riser	Ea	1L	20	10.20	8.55	25.30
240	double swing joint	Ea	1L	12	17.00	10.67	37.40
250	triple swing joint	Ea	1L	12	17.00	11.66	38.70
	Rotary head (20'-40' spacing, 12" riser)						
260	plastic	Ea	1L	20	10.20	9.72	26.90
270	flex riser	Ea	1L	20	10.20	12.32	30.40
280	double swing joint	Ea	1L	12	17.00	14.44	42.40
290	triple swing joint	Ea	1L	12	17.00	15.43	43.80
300	plastic impact	Ea	1L	20	10.20	6.92	23.10
310	flex riser	Ea	1L	20	10.20	9.52	26.60
320	double swing joint	Ea	1L	12	17.00	11.64	38.70
330	triple swing joint	Ea	1L	12	17.00	12.64	40.00
340	metal	Ea	1L	20	10.20	13.00	31.30
350	flex riser	Ea	1L	20	10.20	15.60	34.80
360	double swing joint	Ea	1L	12	17.00	17.72	46.90
370	triple swing joint	Ea	1L	12	17.00	18.71	48.20

SITE IMPROVEMENTS

KEY	DESCRIPTION	UNIT	CREW AND EQUIPMENT	PER DAY	INSTALLATION COST	MATERIALS COST	TOTAL + 35%
380	metal impact	Ea	1L	20	10.20	13.00	31.30
390	flex riser	Ea	1L	20	10.20	15.60	34.80
400	double swing joint	Ea	1L	12	17.00	17.72	46.90
410	triple swing joint	Ea	1L	12	17.00	18.71	48.20
420	Hi-pop spray, 6" pop-up (6" riser)	Ea	1L	20	10.20	6.27	22.20
430	flex riser	Ea	1L	20	10.20	8.22	24.90
440	double swing joint	Ea	1L	12	17.00	10.33	36.90
450	triple swing joint	Ea	1L	12	17.00	11.45	38.40
460	Hi-pop spray, 10"-12" pop-up (6" riser)	Ea	1L	15	13.60	8.21	29.40
470	flex riser	Ea	1L	15	13.60	10.81	33.00
480	double swing joint	Ea	1L	10	20.40	12.93	45.00
490	triple swing joint	Ea	1L	10	20.40	13.92	46.30
500	Rotary, hi-pop, 10"-12" pop-up (6" riser)	Ea	1L	15	13.60	24.02	51.00
510	flex riser	Ea	1L	15	13.60	26.62	54.00
520	double swing joint	Ea	1L	10	20.40	28.09	65.00
530	triple swing joint	Ea	1L	10	20.40	29.74	68.00
	For shrub sprinklers and bubblers to be installed in existing shrub and flower beds, add	LF			50%		
55	**LAWN SPRINKLERS**						
	All head costs include riser						
	1" pop-up spray (10'-12' spacing)						
	regular						
100	plastic	Ea	1L	170	1.20	1.79	4.04
110	metal	Ea	1L	170	1.20	2.83	5.40
	double swing joint						
120	plastic	Ea	1L	161	1.27	2.54	5.10
130	metal	Ea	1L	161	1.27	3.61	6.60
	triple swing joint						
140	plastic	Ea	1L	158	1.29	2.93	5.70
150	metal	Ea	1L	158	1.29	4.00	7.10
	2" pop-up spray (10'-12' spacing)						
	regular						
160	plastic	Ea	1L	20	10.20	2.28	16.90
170	metal	Ea	1L	20	10.20	3.80	18.90
	double swing joint						
180	plastic	Ea	1L	12	17.00	7.06	32.50
190	metal	Ea	1L	12	17.00	9.52	35.80
	triple swing joint						
200	plastic	Ea	1L	12	17.00	8.36	34.20
210	metal	Ea	1L	12	17.00	10.95	37.70
	Rotary pop-up, plastic (20'-30' spacing)						
220	regular	Ea	1L	20	10.20	13.62	32.20
230	double swing joint	Ea	1L	10	20.40	18.34	52.00
240	triple swing joint	Ea	1L	10	20.40	19.33	54.00
	Rotary pop-up, plastic (30'-50' spacing)						
250	regular	Ea	1L	20	10.20	14.27	33.00
260	double swing joint	Ea	1L	10	20.40	18.99	53.00
270	triple swing joint	Ea	1L	10	20.40	19.98	55.00
60	**TURF SPRINKLERS**						
	Rotary head (50'-70' spacing)						
100	full circle	Ea	1L	8	25.50	78.00	140.00
110	w/integral check valve	Ea	1L	8	25.50	78.00	140.00
120	w/integral auto electric valve	Ea	1L	8	25.50	94.25	162.00

KEY	DESCRIPTION	UNIT	CREW AND EQUIPMENT	PER DAY	INSTALLATION COST	MATERIALS COST	TOTAL + 35%
130	part circle	Ea	2L	105	3.89	76.00	108.00
140	w/integral check valve	Ea	2L	105	3.89	95.00	133.00
150	w/integral auto electric valve	Ea	2L	100	4.08	98.00	138.00
	Rotary head (70'-80' spacing)						
160	full circle	Ea	2L	100	4.08	88.00	124.00
170	w/integral check valve	Ea	2L	100	4.08	107.00	150.00
180	w/integral auto electric valve	Ea	2L	95	4.30	110.00	154.00
190	part circle	Ea	2L	90	4.53	90.00	128.00
200	w/integral check valve	Ea	2L	90	4.53	109.00	153.00
210	w/integral auto electric valve	Ea	2L	85	4.80	112.00	158.00
220	Rotary head metal cover	Ea				5.50	7.40
65	**GATE VALVES**						
	Gate valve						
100	3/4"	Ea	1L	40	5.10	8.00	17.70
110	1"	Ea	1L	35	5.83	9.60	20.80
120	1 1/4"	Ea	1L	30	6.80	14.20	28.40
130	1 1/2"	Ea	1L	30	6.80	17.00	32.10
140	2"	Ea	1L	25	8.16	25.00	44.80
150	2 1/2"	Ea	2L	40	10.20	44.00	73.00
160	3"	Ea	2L	35	11.66	64.00	102.00
170	4" cast iron	Ea	2L	30	13.60	142.80	211.00
180	6" cast iron	Ea	2L	15	27.20	188.00	291.00
190	8" cast iron	Ea	2L	8	51.01	357.00	550.00
70	**QUICK COUPLING VALVES**						
	Quick coupling valve, with cover						
	3/4" brass						
100	regular	Ea	1L	85	2.40	16.10	25.00
110	2-piece	Ea	1L	85	2.40	18.80	28.60
120	double swing joint, add	Ea	1L	81	2.52	1.50	5.40
130	triple swing joint, add	Ea	1L	79	2.58	2.00	6.20
	1" brass						
140	regular	Ea	1L	80	2.55	23.00	34.50
150	2-piece	Ea	1L	80	2.55	27.60	40.70
160	double swing joint, add	Ea	1L	76	2.68	2.00	6.30
170	triple swing joint, add	Ea	1L	74	2.76	3.00	7.80
	1 1/4" brass						
180	regular	Ea	1L	70	2.91	29.00	43.10
190	double swing joint, add	Ea	1L	66	3.09	3.00	8.20
200	triple swing joint, add	Ea	1L	65	3.14	5.00	11.00
	1 1/2" brass						
210	regular	Ea	1L	60	3.40	35.00	52.00
220	double swing joint, add	Ea	1L	57	3.58	3.50	9.60
230	triple swing joint, add	Ea	1L	56	3.64	5.50	12.30
240	Locking, vinyl cover, add	Ea				7.80	10.50
250	Hose bib, 3/4" on 12" galvanized riser	Ea	1L	180	1.13	8.00	12.30
75	**BACKFILL TRENCHES AND COMPACTION**						
100	Backfill mains to 24" deep	LF	1L,45	1000	0.23		0.32
110	Backfill laterals to 12" deep	LF	1L,45	1500	0.16		0.21
80	**RESTORE TURF**						
100	Replacing and rolling sod	SY	1L	400	0.51		0.69
110	Re-seeding and rolling	MSF	1L	70	2.91		3.93

SITE IMPROVEMENTS

02820 Fountains | 1994

KEY	DESCRIPTION	UNIT	CREW AND EQUIPMENT	PER DAY	INSTALLATION COST	MATERIALS COST	TOTAL + 35%
00	**COMPOSITE COSTS**						
	Institutional and public fountains includes jets, pumps, drain and overflow system, water supply system, underwater electrical box, automatic control panel and wind controls (pool not included)						
100	high (950 gallons in motion)	Ea					11100.00
110	low (75 gallons in motion)	Ea					8000.00
	Residential fountains including jet, pump, drain and overflow system, water supply system, underwater lights and electrical work (pool not included)						
120	high (950 gallons in motion)	Ea					13500.00
130	low (75 gallons in motion)	Ea					1660.00
05	**JETS, SMOOTH BORE TAPERED**						
	Fixed jet						
	Pipe Size / GPM / Feet Head / Spray Height						
100	1" 12-24 14-53 10'-40'	Ea	1U	20	14.70	47.30	84.00
110	1 1/2" 30-66 14-53 10'-40'	Ea	1U	13	22.61	49.70	98.00
120	2" 52-135 14-66 10'-50'	Ea	1U	11	26.72	72.00	133.00
	Swivel jet						
	Pipe Size / GPM / Feet Head / Spray Height						
160	1" 12-24 14-53 10'-40'	Ea	1U	20	14.70	85.00	135.00
170	1 1/2" 30-66 14-53 10'-40'	Ea	1U	13	22.61	98.00	163.00
180	2" 52-135 14-66 10'-50'	Ea	1U	11	26.72	164.00	257.00
	Fixed jets on spray ring						
	Pipe Size / GPM / Feet Head / Spray Height						
	12" ring, 24 jets						
200	1" 7.5-14 4-10 2'-6'	Ea	1L1U	3	165.98	600.00	1030.00
	36" ring, 56 jets						
210	1 1/4" 18-63 4-26 2'-16'	Ea	1L1U	1.5	331.96	1090.00	1920.00
	48" ring, 83 jets						
220	1 1/4" 24-85 4-26 2'-16'	Ea	1L1U	1	497.94	1300.00	2430.00
	72" ring, 124 jets						
230	1 1/2" 31-100 4-26 2'-16'	Ea	1L1U	0.7	711.34	1720.00	3280.00
	Swivel jets on spray ring, 6-30 FH, 2'-10' spray height						
	1" pipe						
240	12" ring, 16 jets, 6.4-17.6 GPM	Ea	1L1U	3	165.98	580.00	1010.00
250	24" ring, 22 jets, 8.8-24.2 GPM	Ea	1L1U	2	248.97	870.00	1510.00
	2" pipe						
260	36" ring, 47 jets, 18.8-51.7 GPM	Ea	1L1U	1.5	331.96	1110.00	1950.00
270	48" ring, 50 jets, 20-55 GPM	Ea	1L1U	1	497.94	1290.00	2410.00
10	**JETS, AERATING**						
	Aerating jet						
	Pipe Size / GPM / Feet Head / Spray Height						
100	1/2" 3.5-8 15-55 2'-10'	Ea	1U	14	20.99	109.00	175.00
110	3/4" 4.5-10 15-44 2'-10'	Ea	1U	14	20.99	117.00	186.00
120	1" 9.5-15 24-58 4'-12'	Ea	1U	13	22.61	143.00	224.00
130	1 1/4" 10-21 15-59 4'-12'	Ea	1U	11	26.72	164.00	257.00
140	1 1/2" 21-80 18-100 5'-35'	Ea	1U	10	29.39	211.00	325.00
150	2" 22-85 24-104 5'-40'	Ea	1U	10	29.39	322.00	474.00
160	2 1/2" 28-100 28-101 6'-40'	Ea	1L1U	11	45.27	416.00	620.00

KEY	DESCRIPTION	UNIT	CREW AND EQUIPMENT	PER DAY	INSTALLATION COST	MATERIALS COST	TOTAL + 35%
	Cascade jet						
	Pipe Size / GPM / Feet Head / Spray Height						
180	1/2" / 10-15.7 / 42-72 / 2'-5'	Ea	1U	20	14.70	30.70	61.00
190	3/4" / 17.5-30 / 30-77 / 2'-8'	Ea	1U	15	19.59	34.70	73.00
200	1 1/2" / 27.8-67 / 15-83 / 2'-15'	Ea	1U	12	24.49	68.00	125.00
210	2" / 71-129 / 21-90 / 4'-20'	Ea	1U	10	29.39	109.00	187.00
	Calyx jet						
	Jet Height / Pipe Size / GPM / Feet Head / Spray Height						
230	8" / 1 1/2" / 0.7 / 1.0 / 20"	Ea	1U	13	22.61	177.00	269.00
240	9" / 2" / 1.0 / 1.0 / 21"	Ea	1U	11	26.72	207.00	316.00
	Calyx, hollow stream, 1.5'-20' spray height						
	Jet Height / Pipe Size / GPM / Feet Head						
280	8" / 2" / 21-135 / 3-40	Ea	1L1U	11	45.27	380.00	570.00
290	10.5" / 3" / 46-260 / 3-40	Ea	1L1U	8	62.24	770.00	1120.00
	Bubbler, under water						
320	1 1/2" pipe, 50 GPM, 10 FH	Ea	1U	7	41.99	122.00	221.00
330	3" pipe, 125 GPM, 25 FH	Ea	1L1U	8	62.24	195.00	347.00
15	**JETS, FORMED**						
	Bell form jet						
	1/2" pipe, 2-8 GPM, 3-4 FH, 1'-2.5' spray diameter						
100	6" jet height	Ea	1U	5	58.78	80.00	187.00
110	9" jet height	Ea	1U	5	58.78	99.00	213.00
120	12" jet height	Ea	1U	4	73.48	107.00	244.00
	1" pipe, 5-12 GPM, 4-8 FH, 2'-4' spray diameter						
130	12" jet height	Ea	1L1U	5	99.59	142.00	326.00
140	18" jet height	Ea	1L1U	5	99.59	156.00	345.00
150	24" jet height	Ea	1L1U	5	99.59	181.00	379.00
	Mushroom form jet						
	Jet Height / Pipe Size / GPM / Feet Head / Spray Diameter						
160	4.5" / 3/4" / 2-6 / 1-3 / 6"-16"	Ea	1U	5	58.78	116.00	236.00
170	5.6" / 1" / 3-10 / 1-4 / 10"-30"	Ea	1U	5	58.78	113.00	232.00
180	6" / 1 1/2" / 18-35 / / 12"-24"	Ea	1U	4	73.48	136.00	283.00
190	8" / 2" / 35-60 / / 2'-7'	Ea	1U	4	73.48	153.00	306.00
200	12" / 3" / 100-170 / / 5'-10'	Ea	1L1U	5	99.59	207.00	414.00
	Exploding (bursting) jet						
	Jet Height / Pipe Size / GPM / Feet Head / Spray Height						
230	4.5" / 3/4" / 2-6 / 1-3 / 6"-16"	Ea	1U	5	58.78	50.00	147.00
240	5.6" / 1" / 3-10 / 1-4 / 10"-13"	Ea	1U	5	58.78	66.00	168.00
250	11" / 1" / 10-16 / 13-19 / 5'-8'	Ea	1U	4	73.48	89.00	219.00
	Fan form jet, swivel						
	Pipe Size / GPM / Feet Head / Spray Height						
260	1/2" / 3-7 / 4-17 / 2'-19'	Ea	1U	5	58.78	94.00	206.00
270	3/4" / 5-25 / 4-32 / 5'-25'	Ea	1U	5	58.78	118.00	239.00
280	1" / 2-7 / 2-9 / 2"-12"	Ea	1U	5	58.78	94.00	206.00
290	1" / 10-55 / 4-35 / 7'-28'	Ea	1U	5	58.78	177.00	318.00
300	1 1/4" / 4-20 / 2-15 / 2'-16.4'	Ea	1U	5	58.78	177.00	318.00

SITE IMPROVEMENTS

KEY	DESCRIPTION				UNIT	CREW AND EQUIPMENT	PER DAY	INSTALLATION COST	MATERIALS COST	TOTAL + 35%
310	1 1/2"	7-26	2-15	1.7'-19.7'	Ea	1U	5	58.78	201.00	351.00
320	2"	11-31	2-14	1'-19.7'	Ea	1L1U	5	99.59	212.00	421.00
330	3"	22-119	2-14	4'-21.3'	Ea	1L1U	4	124.48	236.00	487.00
20	**JETS, SPRAY HEAD**									
	Crown									
	Pipe Size	GPM	Feet Head	Spray Height						
100	1/4"	1-2	4-11	2'-5'	Ea	1U	30	9.80	62.00	97.00
110	3/4"	9-22	6-16	4'-10'	Ea	1U	25	11.76	79.00	123.00
	High spray and crown									
	Pipe Size	GPM	Feet Head	Spray Height						
120	1/4"	0.5-2	7-20.7	2'-6'	Ea	1U	30	9.80	62.00	97.00
130	1/4"	2-3.5	5-11	2'-5'	Ea	1U	30	9.80	62.00	97.00
	High spray and double crown									
	Pipe Size	GPM	Feet Head	Spray Height						
140	1/4"	1.6-2.7	5-11	2'-5'	Ea	1U	30	9.80	62.00	97.00
150	1/4"	2.7-4.5	6-12	2'-5'	Ea	1U	30	9.80	70.00	108.00
160	1/2"	3.5-8.5	6-13	2'-6'	Ea	1U	25	11.76	79.00	123.00
170	3/4"	9-24	6-11	2'-8'	Ea	1U	25	11.76	94.00	143.00
180	1 1/4"	19-35	7-26	4'-12'	Ea	1U	20	14.70	115.00	175.00
190	1 1/4"	27-46	8-37	4'-12'	Ea	1U	20	14.70	123.00	186.00
25	**JETS, MULTI-JET HEADS**									
	2.75" diameter head with small fixed jets, 3/4" pipe, 1'-10' spray height									
100	13 jets, 3-17 GPM, 2.5-22 FH				Ea	1U	12	24.49	131.00	210.00
110	22 jets, 7-19 GPM, 5-25 FH				Ea	1U	12	24.49	145.00	229.00
	5" diameter head, 26 small fixed jets, 1" pipe, 16-38 GPM, 5-17 FH, 3'-10' spray height									
120					Ea	1U	12	24.49	196.00	298.00
	7" wide fan head, 27 small fixed jets, 25-40 GPM, 5-15 FH, 2'-6' spray height									
130	fixed head, 1" pipe				Ea	1U	11	26.72	171.00	267.00
140	swivel head, 1 1/4" pipe				Ea	1U	10	29.39	203.00	314.00
150	10" diameter head, one 2" swivel jet, six 1.5" swivel jets, 4" pipe, 182-310 GPM, 44-88 FH, 10'-30' spray ht.				Ea	1L1U	1	497.94	1980.00	3350.00
160	18" diameter head, seven 2.75" swivel jets, 6" pipe, 483-1260 GPM, 46-115 FH, 10'-50' spray height				Ea	1L1U	0.7	711.34	4020.00	6400.00
30	**PUMPS**									
	Submersible, small, epoxy encapsulated, brass screen									
100	1/35 HP, 5-3.3 GPM at 1-6 FH				Ea	1L1U	5	99.59	115.00	290.00
110	1/20 HP, 8.5-3 GPM at 1-12 FH				Ea	1L1U	5	99.59	206.00	413.00
120	1/12 HP, 12.5-3.3 GPM at 1-18 FH				Ea	1L1U	5	99.59	277.00	510.00
130	1/8 HP, 16.7-5.7 GPM at 1-24 FH				Ea	1L1U	5	99.59	320.00	570.00
	Submersible, heavy duty, bronze and brass									
140	1/3 HP, 73-5 GPM at 10-35 FH				Ea	1L1U	1	497.94	1510.00	2710.00
150	1/2 HP, 87-5 GPM at 10-39 FH				Ea	1L1U	1	497.94	1530.00	2740.00
160	3/4 HP, 102-5 GPM at 10-49 FH				Ea	1L1U	0.7	711.34	1640.00	3170.00
170	1 HP, 112-5 GPM at 10-57 FH				Ea	1L1U	0.7	711.34	1810.00	3400.00
	Dry type pump									
180	1/2 HP, 80-5 GPM at 18-49 FH				Ea	1L1U	0.7	711.34	1640.00	3170.00
190	3/4 HP, 118-40 GPM at 16-36 FH				Ea	1L1U	0.7	711.34	1670.00	3210.00
200	1 HP, 133-50 GPM at 22-41 FH				Ea	1L1U	0.7	711.34	1630.00	3160.00

KEY	DESCRIPTION	UNIT	CREW AND EQUIPMENT	PER DAY	INSTALLATION COST	MATERIALS COST	TOTAL + 35%
	02820 Fountains						**1994**
210	1 1/2 HP, 150-50 GPM at 29-52 FH	Ea	1L1U	0.7	711.34	2420.00	4230.00
220	2 HP, 155-55 GPM at 34-58 FH	Ea	1L1U	0.6	829.89	2550.00	4560.00
	Motor starter and control for 3 phase						
270	and/or 3 HP to 10 HP pumps	Ea	1E	8	34.87	52.00	117.00
	Pump strainer, in-line type, cast iron with brass basket						
280	1 1/2" NPS screwed connection	Ea	1L1U	15	33.20	263.00	400.00
290	2" NPS screwed connection	Ea	1L1U	15	33.20	263.00	400.00
300	2 1/2" NPS screwed connection	Ea	1L1U	15	33.20	317.00	473.00
310	3" NPS screwed connection	Ea	1L1U	14	35.57	317.00	476.00
	Residential scale pump, submersible						
360	1/200 HP, 140-35 GPH at 1-5 FH	Ea	1U	5	58.78	49.50	146.00
370	1/40 HP, 300-55 GPH at 1-11 FH	Ea	1U	5	58.78	67.00	170.00
380	1/15 HP, 500-163 GPH at 1-13 FH	Ea	1U	5	58.78	109.00	227.00
390	1-12 HP, 810-80 GPH at 1-22 FH	Ea	1U	5	58.78	153.00	286.00
35	**DRAIN AND OVERFLOW SYSTEMS**						
	Overflow standpipe, dome top, 18" depth						
100	2" NPS drain connection	Ea	1U	4	73.48	275.00	470.00
110	3" NPS drain connection	Ea	1U	3.5	83.97	291.00	510.00
120	4" NPS drain connection	Ea	1U	2.5	117.56	374.00	660.00
	Anti-vortex plate						
130	8" wide, 200 GPM	Ea	1U	10	29.39	57.00	117.00
140	12" wide, 440 GPM	Ea	1U	10	29.39	243.00	368.00
150	20" wide, 950 GPM	Ea	1U	10	29.39	510.00	730.00
	Anti-vortex plate and sump, 8" wide and 7" deep with						
160	2" NPS side outlet	Ea	1U	5	58.78	96.00	209.00
40	**WATER SUPPLY SYSTEMS**						
	Filters, fine screen, sand media, including pump, electrical and plumbing						
100	24" diameter and less	Ea	1U	3	97.97	3730.00	5200.00
110	24" to 36" diameter	Ea	1U	2.5	117.56	7900.00	10800.00
120	automatic backwash, add residential scale	Ea	1U	5	58.78	1320.00	1860.00
130	17" diameter	Ea	1U	8	36.74	313.00	472.00
140	20" diameter	Ea	1U	8	36.74	350.00	520.00
150	24" diameter	Ea	1U	7	41.99	410.00	610.00
	Surface skimmers						
	pool edge type, automatic check valve,						
170	basket and vacuum hose connection	Ea	1U	8	36.74	180.00	293.00
180	floating type, 1 1/2" vacuum fitting	Ea	1U	8	36.74	238.00	371.00
	Filtration fittings						
	adjustable inlet						
190	1 1/2" pipe	Ea	1U	20	14.70	34.40	66.00
200	2" pipe	Ea	1U	20	14.70	52.00	90.00
210	vacuum fitting, 1 1/2" pipe	Ea	1U	20	14.70	31.00	62.00
220	eyeball inlet fitting, 1 1/2" pipe	Ea	1U	20	14.70	59.00	99.00
	suction screen						
230	100 GPM, 2" pipe	Ea	1L1U	10	49.79	156.00	278.00
240	200 GPM, 2" or 3" pipe	Ea	1L1U	7	71.13	206.00	374.00
250	300 GPM, 3" or 4" pipe	Ea	1L1U	5	99.59	342.00	600.00
260	500 GPM, 4" or 5" pipe	Ea	1L1U	3	165.98	462.00	850.00
270	600 GPM, 5" or 6" pipe	Ea	1L1U	2	248.97	690.00	1270.00

SITE IMPROVEMENTS

02820 Fountains

KEY	DESCRIPTION	UNIT	CREW AND EQUIPMENT	PER DAY	INSTALLATION COST	MATERIALS COST	TOTAL + 35%
45	**PIPE AND PIPE FITTINGS**						
	Brass pipe, plain ends for field cutting, threading, flanging, or soldering						
	regular weight						
100	1/8" NPS	LF	1U	85	3.46	209.00	287.00
105	1/4" NPS	LF	1U	84	3.50	3.09	8.90
110	1/2" NPS	LF	1U	83	3.54	5.30	11.90
115	1" NPS	LF	1U	82	3.58	7.80	15.40
120	1 1/2" NPS	LF	1U	80	3.67	18.10	29.40
125	2" NPS	LF	1U	78	3.77	24.90	38.70
145	extra heavy weight, 2" NPS	LF	1U	74	3.97	37.20	56.00
	Brass fitting, including field cutting, threading, flanging, or soldering of pipe ends						
	elbow						
165	1/8" NPS	Ea	1U	30	9.80	2.32	16.40
170	1/4" NPS	Ea	1U	30	9.80	2.32	16.40
175	1/2" NPS	Ea	1U	29	10.13	10.80	28.30
180	1" NPS	Ea	1U	27	10.89	7.30	24.60
185	1 1/2" NPS	Ea	1U	24	12.25	15.00	36.80
190	2" NPS	Ea	1U	22	13.36	25.00	52.00
	tee						
210	1/8" NPS	Ea	1U	25	11.76	3.23	20.20
215	1/4" NPS	Ea	1U	25	11.76	3.23	20.20
220	1/2" NPS	Ea	1U	24	12.25	3.23	20.90
225	1" NPS	Ea	1U	23	12.78	10.70	31.70
230	1 1/2" NPS	Ea	1U	20	14.70	20.20	47.10
235	2" NPS	Ea	1U	18	16.33	33.10	67.00
	coupling						
255	1/8" NPS	Ea	1U	33	8.91	2.32	15.20
260	1/4" NPS	Ea	1U	33	8.91	2.32	15.20
265	1/2" NPS	Ea	1U	32	9.18	2.90	16.30
270	1" NPS	Ea	1U	30	9.80	5.80	21.10
275	1 1/2" NPS	Ea	1U	27	10.89	12.60	31.70
280	2" NPS	Ea	1U	24	12.25	20.50	44.20
	companion flange coupling						
300	1/2" NPS	Pr	1U	21	13.9955102	36.5	68.00
305	1" NPS	Pr	1U	20	14.70	50.00	87.00
310	1 1/2" NPS	Pr	1U	18	16.33	71.00	118.00
315	2" NPS	Pr	1U	16	18.37	96.00	154.00
	Copper pipe, plain ends for field cutting, threading flanging, or soldering type M, soft copper						
335	1/8" NPS	LF	1U	85	3.46	0.31	5.10
340	1/4" NPS	LF	1U	84	3.50	0.31	5.10
345	1/2" NPS	LF	1U	83	3.54	0.57	5.50
350	1" NPS	LF	1U	82	3.58	1.32	6.60
355	1 1/2" NPS	LF	1U	80	3.67	2.70	8.60
360	2" NPS	LF	1U	78	3.77	4.25	10.80
	type K, hard copper, high strength						
380	2" NPS	LF	1U	74	3.97	5.70	13.10
	Copper fitting, including field cutting, threading, flanging, or soldering of pipe ends						
	elbow						
400	1/8" NPS	Ea	1U	30	9.80	1.09	14.70
405	1/4" NPS	Ea	1U	30	9.80	1.09	14.70
410	1/2" NPS	Ea	1U	29	10.13	0.42	14.20

KEY	DESCRIPTION	UNIT	CREW AND EQUIPMENT	PER DAY	INSTALLATION COST	MATERIALS COST	TOTAL + 35%
415	1" NPS	Ea	1U	27	10.89	1.41	16.60
420	1 1/2" NPS	Ea	1U	24	12.25	2.53	19.90
425	2" NPS	Ea	1U	22	13.36	4.23	23.70
	tee						
445	1/8" NPS	Ea	1U	25	11.76	1.32	17.70
450	1/4" NPS	Ea	1U	25	11.76	1.32	17.70
455	1/2" NPS	Ea	1U	24	12.25	1.25	18.20
460	1" NPS	Ea	1U	23	12.78	2.38	20.50
465	1 1/2" NPS	Ea	1U	20	14.70	4.01	25.30
470	2" NPS	Ea	1U	18	16.33	6.62	31.00
	coupling						
490	1/8" NPS	Ea	1U	33	8.91	0.07	12.10
495	1/4" NPS	Ea	1U	33	8.91	0.07	12.10
500	1/2" NPS	Ea	1U	32	9.18	0.13	12.60
505	1" NPS	Ea	1U	30	9.80	1.00	14.60
510	1 1/2" NPS	Ea	1U	27	10.89	1.55	16.80
515	2" NPS	Ea	1U	24	12.25	2.30	19.60
	companion flange coupling						
535	1/2" NPS	Pr	1U	21	14.00	3.18	23.20
540	1" NPS	Pr	1U	20	14.70	7.10	29.40
545	1 1/2" NPS	Pr	1U	18	16.33	13.90	40.80
550	2" NPS	Pr	1U	16	18.37	23.90	57.00
	Stainless steel pipe, plain ends for field cutting, threading, flanging, or soldering AISI 303, Schedule 40						
570	1/8" NPS	LF	1U	85	3.46	2.56	8.10
575	1/4" NPS	LF	1U	84	3.50	2.58	8.20
580	1/2" NPS	LF	1U	83	3.54	3.60	9.60
585	1" NPS	LF	1U	82	3.58	5.30	12.00
590	1 1/2" NPS	LF	1U	80	3.67	7.50	15.10
595	2" NPS	LF	1U	78	3.77	9.80	18.30
610	AISI 303, Schedule 80, 2" NPS	LF	1U	74	3.97	17.20	28.60
	Stainless steel fittings, including field cutting, threading, or flanging of pipe elbow						
	elbow						
625	1/8" NPS	Ea	1U	30	9.80	3.21	17.60
630	1/4" NPS	Ea	1U	30	9.80	3.21	17.60
635	1/2" NPS	Ea	1U	29	10.13	4.79	20.10
640	1" NPS	Ea	1U	27	10.89	8.60	26.30
645	1 1/2" NPS	Ea	1U	24	12.25	14.30	35.80
650	2" NPS	Ea	1U	22	13.36	21.70	47.30
	tee						
665	1/8" NPS	Ea	1U	25	11.76	4.11	21.40
670	1/4" NPS	Ea	1U	25	11.76	4.11	21.40
675	1/2" NPS	Ea	1U	24	12.25	7.20	26.30
680	1" NPS	Ea	1U	23	12.78	11.10	32.20
685	1 1/2" NPS	Ea	1U	20	14.70	20.80	47.90
690	2" NPS	Ea	1U	18	16.33	29.70	62.00
	coupling						
705	1/8" NPS	Ea	1U	33	8.91	1.14	13.60
710	1/4" NPS	Ea	1U	33	8.91	1.14	13.60
715	1/2" NPS	Ea	1U	32	9.18	2.23	15.40
720	1" NPS	Ea	1U	30	9.80	5.20	20.20
725	1 1/2" NPS	Ea	1U	27	10.89	10.70	29.10
730	2" NPS	Ea	1U	24	12.25	14.00	35.40
	companion flange coupling						
745	1/2" NPS	Pr	1U	21	14.00	23.50	51.00
750	1" NPS	Pr	1U	20	14.70	33.50	65.00

KEY	DESCRIPTION	UNIT	CREW AND EQUIPMENT	PER DAY	INSTALLATION COST	MATERIALS COST	TOTAL + 35%
755	1 1/2" NPS	Pr	1U	18	16.33	47.20	86.00
760	2" NPS	Pr	1U	16	18.37	55.00	99.00
	PVC pipe and fittings, solvent cement joints						
	regular						
775	1/4" NPS	LF	1U	90	3.27	1.00	5.80
780	1/2" NPS	LF	1U	85	3.46	1.22	6.30
785	1" NPS	LF	1U	80	3.67	1.73	7.30
790	1 1/2" NPS	LF	1U	70	4.20	2.40	8.90
795	2" NPS	LF	1U	60	4.90	2.59	10.10
815	high strength, 2" NPS	LF	1U	55	5.34	9.00	19.40
50	**BACKFLOW PREVENTION**						
	Vacuum breakers, check & gate valves, pressure back-flow preventers, see Section 02810, "Irrigation Systems"						
	Backwater valve in sewer pipe, gate and flapper valve						
100	3" pipe	Ea	1U	4	73.48	272.00	466.00
110	4" pipe	Ea	1U	3	97.97	436.00	720.00
55	**CONTROL SYSTEMS**						
	Automatic solenoid valve, cast iron and bronze trim						
100	1" pipe	Ea	1E1U	3	190.95	231.00	570.00
110	1 1/4" pipe	Ea	1E1U	3	190.95	260.00	610.00
120	1 1/2" pipe	Ea	1E1U	2.5	229.15	261.00	660.00
130	2" pipe	Ea	1E1U	2.5	229.15	346.00	780.00
	Water level control, float and valve assembly						
170	1/2" valve, 1/2" NPS	Ea	1U	10	29.39	54.00	113.00
180	3/4" valve, 3/4" NPS	Ea	1U	10	29.39	67.00	130.00
190	1" valve, 1" NPS	Ea	1U	10	29.39	94.00	167.00
	Wall recessed float valve, slotted face,						
200	3/4" valve and drain connection	Ea	1U	5	58.78	286.00	465.00
	Recycling timers, 115V, 1800W						
210	1 circuits	Ea	1E	3	92.99	272.00	493.00
220	2 circuits	Ea	1E	3	92.99	380.00	640.00
230	3 circuits	Ea	1E	2.5	111.58	493.00	820.00
240	4 circuits	Ea	1E	2	139.48	610.00	1010.00
250	5 circuits	Ea	1E	2	139.48	710.00	1150.00
	Wind control unit						
260	single stage	Ea	1E	3	92.99	1320.00	1910.00
270	dual stage	Ea	1E	3	92.99	1550.00	2220.00
280	motor starter control	Ea	1E	10	27.90	23.10	69.00
	Automatic time switches						
290	standard	Ea	1E	8	34.87	99.00	181.00
	astronomic						
300	SPST & DPST	Ea	1E	6	46.49	249.00	399.00
310	4PST	Ea	1E	5	55.79	434.00	660.00
60	**ELECTRICAL COMPONENTS**						
	See Division 16 sections for electrical components						
	Submersible junction boxes, cast bronze and stainless steel fastening and ground connections, 3/4" bottom outlet, 1/2" side outlets						
100	2 side outlets	Ea	1E	8	34.87	73.00	146.00
110	4 side outlets	Ea	1E	8	34.87	98.00	179.00
120	8 side outlets	Ea	1E	7	39.85	162.00	272.00
130	16 side outlets	Ea	1E	7	39.85	222.00	353.00
140	20 side outlets	Ea	1E	6	46.49	302.00	470.00

KEY	DESCRIPTION	UNIT	CREW AND EQUIPMENT	PER DAY	INSTALLATION COST	MATERIALS COST	TOTAL + 35%
	Transformer boxes, cast bronze						
150	230 cubic inches	Ea	1E	1	278.96	334.00	830.00
160	420 cubic inches	Ea	1E	0.7	398.51	670.00	1440.00
170	1944 cubic inches	Ea	1E	0.4	697.39	1930.00	3550.00
65	**FOUNTAIN LIGHTING**						
	Underwater luminaires, cast bronze and stainless steel construction, heat resistant glass, colored lenses, rock guard and stand						
100	150 watt	Ea	1E	8	34.87	331.00	494.00
110	300 watt	Ea	1E	8	34.87	450.00	650.00
120	500 watt	Ea	1E	8	34.87	590.00	840.00
	See Section 16530, "Site Lighting" for low voltage lighting and other lighting						
70	**FOUNTAIN KITS**						
100	Single aerating jet, 5 GPM, submersible pump, 1 underwater light, no plumbing	Ea	1E	1	278.96	1080.00	1830.00
110	Mushroom jet, 40 GPM, submersible pump, 3 underwater lights, no plumbing	Ea	1E	1	278.96	2310.00	3500.00
120	Aerating center jet, 30" diameter spray ring, total 40 GPM, submersible pump, 5 underwater lights, no plumbing	Ea	1E	0.7	398.51	3560.00	5300.00
75	**EXCAVATION**						
	Excavation and trenching, see Section 02220, "Excavation, Backfilling, & Compacting"						
	Boring under pavement, see Section 02810, "Irrigation Systems"						
80	**POOLS**						
	For construction and finishes, see Divisions 3 (Concrete) and 4 (Masonry)						
	Fiberglass bowls, round, 10" depth						
100	36" diameter, 20 gallon	Ea	1L	5	40.81	111.00	205.00
110	48" diameter, 30 gallon	Ea	1L	4	51.01	176.00	306.00
120	72" diameter, 50 gallon	Ea	1L	3	68.01	830.00	1210.00
	Fiberglass garden pools free form						
130	80 gallon, 8" depth	Ea	1L	3	68.01	392.00	620.00
140	280 gallon, 8" depth	Ea	1L	2	102.02	720.00	1110.00
150	490 gallon, 16" depth	Ea	1L	1	204.03	780.00	1330.00
	8' diameter						
160	200 gallon, 8" depth	Ea	1L	2	102.02	590.00	930.00
170	400 gallon, 16" depth	Ea	1L	1	204.03	670.00	1180.00

SITE IMPROVEMENTS

KEY	DESCRIPTION	UNIT	CREW AND EQUIPMENT	PER DAY	INSTALLATION COST	MATERIALS COST	TOTAL + 25%
10	**CHAIN LINK FENCES**						
	Galvanized posts and top rail, galvanized, aluminized, or bonded vinyl coated fabric						
	9 ga fabric						
	C-section posts						
100	4' high	LF	2I,80	300	1.90	5.50	9.30
105	5' high	LF	2I,80	250	2.28	6.60	11.10
110	6' high	LF	2I,80	155	3.68	7.20	13.60
115	7' high	LF	2I,80	140	4.08	8.20	15.30
120	8' high	LF	2I,80	125	4.57	9.00	17.00
125	10' high	LF	2I,80	100	5.71	11.30	21.30
130	12' high	LF	2I,80	95	6.01	13.00	23.80
	schedule 40 posts						
135	4' high	LF	2I,80	300	1.90	7.10	11.30
140	5' high	LF	2I,80	250	2.28	7.60	12.40
145	6' high	LF	2I,80	155	3.68	8.40	15.10
150	7' high	LF	2I,80	140	4.08	9.20	16.60
155	8' high	LF	2I,80	125	4.57	10.30	18.60
160	10' high	LF	2I,80	100	5.71	12.60	22.90
165	12' high	LF	2I,80	95	6.01	14.60	25.80
	6 ga fabric						
	c-section posts						
170	6' high	LF	2I,80	140	4.08	11.40	19.30
175	7' high	LF	2I,80	125	4.57	12.80	21.70
180	8' high	LF	2I,80	110	5.19	14.20	24.20
185	10' high	LF	2I,80	90	6.34	17.40	29.70
190	12' high	LF	2I,80	85	6.71	20.50	34.00
	schedule 40 posts						
195	6' high	LF	2I,80	140	4.08	12.00	20.10
200	7' high	LF	2I,80	125	4.57	13.70	22.80
205	8' high	LF	2I,80	110	5.19	15.40	25.70
210	10' high	LF	2I,80	90	6.34	18.60	31.20
215	12' high	LF	2I,80	85	6.71	21.50	35.30
	11 ga x 1 3/4" fabric (tennis court)						
220	10' high	LF	2I,80	100	5.71	11.80	21.90
225	12' high (w/middle rail)	LF	2I,80	85	6.71	15.30	27.50
	Bonded vinyl coated posts and top rail, bonded vinyl coated fabric						
	9 ga fabric						
	C-section posts						
230	4' high	LF	2I,80	300	1.90	7.10	11.30
235	5' high	LF	2I,80	250	2.28	8.20	13.10
240	6' high	LF	2I,80	155	3.68	9.00	15.90
245	7' high	LF	2I,80	140	4.08	10.00	17.60
250	8' high	LF	2I,80	125	4.57	11.20	19.70
255	10' high	LF	2I,80	100	5.71	13.90	24.50
260	12' high	LF	2I,80	95	6.01	15.90	27.40
	schedule 40 posts						
265	4' high	LF	2I,80	300	1.90	8.80	13.40
270	5' high	LF	2I,80	250	2.28	9.40	14.60
275	6' high	LF	2I,80	155	3.68	10.00	17.10
280	7' high	LF	2I,80	140	4.08	11.30	19.20
285	8' high	LF	2I,80	125	4.57	12.30	21.10
290	10' high	LF	2I,80	100	5.71	14.50	25.30
295	12' high	LF	2I,80	95	6.01	17.90	29.90
	6 ga fabric						
	c-section posts						
300	6' high	LF	2I,80	140	4.08	13.30	21.70
305	7' high	LF	2I,80	125	4.57	15.00	24.50
310	8' high	LF	2I,80	110	5.19	16.40	27.00
315	10' high	LF	2I,80	90	6.34	19.80	32.70
320	12' high	LF	2I,80	85	6.71	22.90	37.00

KEY	DESCRIPTION	UNIT	CREW AND EQUIPMENT	PER DAY	INSTALLATION COST	MATERIALS COST	TOTAL + 25%
	schedule 40 posts						
325	6' high	LF	2l,80	140	4.08	13.60	22.10
330	7' high	LF	2l,80	125	4.57	15.30	24.80
335	8' high	LF	2l,80	110	5.19	16.90	27.60
340	10' high	LF	2l,80	90	6.34	20.70	33.80
345	12' high	LF	2l,80	85	6.71	24.00	38.40
	11 ga x 1 3/4" fabric (tennis court)						
350	10' high	LF	2l,80	100	5.71	13.50	24.00
355	12' high (w/middle rail)	LF	2l,80	85	6.71	17.30	30.00
	Bottom rail with fittings						
360	galvanized	LF	2l	3450	0.16	1.52	2.10
365	bonded vinyl coated	LF	2l	3450	0.16	2.27	3.04
	Tension wire						
370	galvanized, 7 ga	LF	2l	15000	0.04	0.13	0.21
375	bonded vinyl coated, 6 ga	LF	2l	16000	0.04	0.13	0.21
	Barbed wire on diagonal support arm galvanized						
380	3 strands, one side	LF	2l	5750	0.10	0.76	1.07
385	6 strands, two sides	LF	2l	2875	0.20	1.54	2.17
	bonded vinyl coated						
390	3 strands, one side	LF	2l	5750	0.10	1.00	1.37
395	6 strands, two sides	LF	2l	2875	0.20	1.69	2.36
	Corner post galvanized square						
400	4' high	Ea	2l,80	65	8.78	54.00	78.00
405	5' high	Ea	2l,80	65	8.78	54.00	78.00
410	6' high with bracing	Ea	2l,80	35	16.31	98.00	143.00
415	7' high with bracing	Ea	2l,80	35	16.31	103.00	149.00
420	8' high with bracing	Ea	2l,80	35	16.31	108.00	155.00
425	10' high with bracing	Ea	2l,80	25	22.83	118.00	176.00
430	12' high with bracing	Ea	2l,80	25	22.83	127.00	187.00
	schedule 40 pipe						
435	4' high	Ea	2l,80	65	8.78	57.00	82.00
440	5' high	Ea	2l,80	65	8.78	57.00	82.00
445	6' high with bracing	Ea	2l,80	35	16.31	106.00	153.00
450	7' high with bracing	Ea	2l,80	35	16.31	111.00	159.00
455	8' high with bracing	Ea	2l,80	35	16.31	118.00	168.00
460	10' high with bracing	Ea	2l,80	25	22.83	131.00	192.00
465	12' high with bracing	Ea	2l,80	25	22.83	163.00	232.00
	bonded vinyl coated square						
470	4' high	Ea	2l,80	65	8.78	79.00	110.00
475	5' high	Ea	2l,80	65	8.78	79.00	110.00
480	6' high with bracing	Ea	2l,80	35	16.31	141.00	197.00
485	7' high with bracing	Ea	2l,80	35	16.31	152.00	210.00
490	8' high with bracing	Ea	2l,80	35	16.31	158.00	218.00
495	10' high with bracing	Ea	2l,80	25	22.83	172.00	244.00
500	12' high with bracing	Ea	2l,80	25	22.83	188.00	264.00
	schedule 40 pipe						
505	4' high	Ea	2l,80	65	8.78	80.00	111.00
510	5' high	Ea	2l,80	65	8.78	83.00	115.00
515	6' high with bracing	Ea	2l,80	35	16.31	163.00	224.00
520	7' high with bracing	Ea	2l,80	35	16.31	167.00	229.00
525	8' high with bracing	Ea	2l,80	35	16.31	173.00	237.00
530	10' high with bracing	Ea	2l,80	25	22.83	203.00	282.00
535	12' high with bracing	Ea	2l,80	25	22.83	232.00	319.00

KEY	DESCRIPTION	UNIT	CREW AND EQUIPMENT	PER DAY	INSTALLATION COST	MATERIALS COST	TOTAL + 25%
20	**CHAIN LINK GATES**						
	3' wide gate, includes 2 gate posts						
	galvanized schedule 40 frame						
100	4' high	Ea	2l,80	55	10.38	277.00	359.00
110	5' high	Ea	2l,80	55	10.38	288.00	373.00
120	6' high	Ea	2l,80	30	19.02	317.00	420.00
130	7' high	Ea	2l,80	30	19.02	342.00	451.00
140	8' high	Ea	2l,80	30	19.02	376.00	494.00
	vinyl coated square steel frame						
150	4' high	Ea	2l,80	55	10.38	420.00	540.00
160	5' high	Ea	2l,80	55	10.38	421.00	540.00
170	6' high	Ea	2l,80	30	19.02	530.00	690.00
180	7' high	Ea	2l,80	30	19.02	560.00	720.00
190	8' high	Ea	2l,80	30	19.02	610.00	790.00
200	Wide swing gate, 6' to 8' high (add gate posts, below)	LF	2l	170	3.33	61.00	80.00
	Cantilever slide gate, aluminum frame (add gate posts, below)						
210	up to 30' single (3 posts)	LF	2l	115	4.92	122.00	159.00
220	up to 60' souble (4 posts)	LF	2l	115	4.92	122.00	159.00
230	over 30' single (6 posts)	LF	2l	60	9.43	319.00	411.00
240	over 60' double (6 posts)	LF	2l	60	9.43	319.00	411.00
	Gate post, 4" O.D., with brace assembly						
	galvanized						
250	4' high	Ea	2l,80	65	8.78	89.00	122.00
260	5' high	Ea	2l,80	65	8.78	89.00	122.00
270	6' high	Ea	2l,80	35	16.31	113.00	162.00
280	7' high	Ea	2l,80	35	16.31	118.00	168.00
290	8' high	Ea	2l,80	35	16.31	126.00	178.00
	vinyl coated						
300	4' high	Ea	2l,80	65	8.78	116.00	156.00
310	5' high	Ea	2l,80	65	8.78	117.00	157.00
320	6' high	Ea	2l,80	35	16.31	159.00	219.00
330	7' high	Ea	2l,80	35	16.31	163.00	224.00
340	8' high	Ea	2l,80	35	16.31	173.00	237.00
30	**WOOD FENCES**						
	Picket fence, 1" x 2" pickets, 2" x 4" rails, 4" x 4" posts						
	fir, pine or spruce, preservative treated						
100	3' high, 2 rail	LF	2C,80,81	135	3.89	10.30	17.70
110	5' high, 3 rail	LF	2C,80,81	125	4.20	16.00	25.30
	western cedar, #2 grade						
120	3' high, 2 rail	LF	2C,80,81	135	3.89	10.00	17.40
130	5' high, 3 rail	LF	2C,80,81	125	4.20	15.90	25.10
	redwood, clear heart grade						
140	3' high, 2 rail	LF	2C,80,81	135	3.89	10.80	18.40
150	5' high, 3 rail	LF	2C,80,81	125	4.20	16.90	26.40
	Board fence, 1" x 6" boards, 2" x 4" rails, 4" x 4" posts						
	fir, pine or spruce, preservative treated						
160	3' high, 2 rail	LF	2C,80,81	130	4.04	15.70	24.70
170	4' high, 3 rail	LF	2C,80,81	127	4.14	14.70	23.50
180	6' high, 3 rail	LF	2C,80,81	120	4.38	19.10	29.30
	western cedar, #2 grade						
190	3' high, 2 rail	LF	2C,80,81	130	4.04	11.50	19.40
200	4' high, 3 rail	LF	2C,80,81	127	4.14	14.60	23.40
210	6' high, 3 rail	LF	2C,80,81	120	4.38	18.90	29.10

02830 Fences and Gates

KEY	DESCRIPTION	UNIT	CREW AND EQUIPMENT	PER DAY	INSTALLATION COST	MATERIALS COST	TOTAL + 25%
	redwood, clear heart grade						
220	3' high, 2 rail	LF	2C,80,81	130	4.04	11.20	19.10
230	4' high, 3 rail	LF	2C,80,81	127	4.14	16.40	25.70
240	6' high, 3 rail	LF	2C,80,81	120	4.38	21.40	32.20
	Board and batten fence, 1" x 6" boards, 1" x 2" battens, 2" x 4" rails, 4" x 4" posts						
	fir, pine or spruce, preservative treated						
250	3' high, 2 rail	LF	2C,80,81	120	4.38	14.40	23.50
260	4' high, 3 rail	LF	2C,80,81	115	4.57	19.70	30.30
270	6' high, 3 rail	LF	2C,80,81	110	4.78	26.50	39.10
	western cedar, #2 grade						
280	3' high, 2 rail	LF	2C,80,81	120	4.38	14.20	23.20
290	4' high, 3 rail	LF	2C,80,81	115	4.57	19.30	29.80
300	6' high, 3 rail	LF	2C,80,81	110	4.78	26.00	38.50
	redwood, clear heart grade						
310	3' high, 2 rail	LF	2C,80,81	120	4.38	15.10	24.30
320	4' high, 3 rail	LF	2C,80,81	115	4.57	21.60	32.70
330	6' high, 3 rail	LF	2C,80,81	110	4.78	29.10	42.30
	Basketweave fence, redwood, clear heart grade, 1" x 6" boards, 2" x 4" stringers or spreaders, 4" x 4" posts						
	wide-span						
340	4' high	LF	2C,80,81	155	3.39	10.30	17.10
350	6' high	LF	2C,80,81	150	3.50	15.30	23.50
	tight-weave						
360	4' high	LF	2C,80,81	155	3.39	13.10	20.60
370	6' high	LF	2C,80,81	150	3.50	18.40	27.40
380	vertical weave, 6' high	LF	2C,80,81	155	3.39	18.30	27.10
	Open rail fence						
	split cedar rails, 2" x 4"						
390	3' high, 2 rail	LF	2C,80,81	150	3.50	4.38	9.90
400	4' high, 3 rail	LF	2C,80,81	140	3.75	5.80	11.90
	rustic cedar rails, 4" round						
410	3' high, 2 rail	LF	2C,80,81	150	3.50	4.97	10.60
420	4' high, 3 rail	LF	2C,80,81	140	3.75	6.40	12.70
	Cedar stockade fence						
	halved poles						
430	6' high	LF	2C,80,81	155	3.39	12.40	19.70
440	8' high	LF	2C,80,81	145	3.62	16.10	24.70
	whole round posts						
450	6' high	LF	2C,80,81	155	3.39	19.10	28.10
460	8' high	LF	2C,80,81	145	3.62	25.00	35.80
40	**FOOTINGS**						
100	Concrete footing, 8" diameter, 3' deep	Ea	2L	100	3.79	3.59	9.20
50	**WOOD GATES**						
	Picket gate, 3' wide, 1" x 2" pickets, 2" x 4" frame, 4" x 4" post						
	fir, pine or spruce, preservative treated						
100	3' high	Ea	2C,80,81	23	22.84	41.70	81.00
110	4' high	Ea	2C,80,81	22	23.88	52.00	95.00
120	5' high	Ea	2C,80,81	20	26.27	63.00	112.00
	western cedar, #2 grade						
130	3' high	Ea	2C,80,81	23	22.84	44.40	84.00
140	4' high	Ea	2C,80,81	22	23.88	55.00	99.00
150	5' high	Ea	2C,80,81	20	26.27	67.00	117.00
	redwood, clear heart grade						
160	3' high	Ea	2C,80,81	23	22.84	38.30	76.00
170	4' high	Ea	2C,80,81	22	23.88	47.50	89.00
180	5' high	Ea	2C,80,81	20	26.27	58.00	105.00

SITE IMPROVEMENTS

02830 Fences and Gates   1994

KEY	DESCRIPTION	UNIT	CREW AND EQUIPMENT	PER DAY	INSTALLATION COST	MATERIALS COST	TOTAL + 25%
	Board gate, 3' wide, 1" x 6" boards, 2" x 4" frame, 4" x 4" post						
	fir, pine or wpruce, preservative treated						
190	3' high	Ea	2C,80,81	22	23.88	47.10	89.00
200	4' high	Ea	2C,80,81	21	25.02	57.00	103.00
210	5' high	Ea	2C,80,81	19	27.65	65.00	116.00
220	6' high	Ea	2C,80,81	17	30.91	84.00	144.00
	western cedar, #2 grade						
230	3' high	Ea	2C,80,81	22	23.88	49.40	92.00
240	4' high	Ea	2C,80,81	21	25.02	60.00	106.00
250	5' high	Ea	2C,80,81	19	27.65	75.00	128.00
260	6' high	Ea	2C,80,81	17	30.91	87.00	147.00
	redwood, clear heart grade						
270	3' high	Ea	2C,80,81	22	23.88	49.00	91.00
280	4' high	Ea	2C,80,81	21	25.02	60.00	106.00
290	5' high	Ea	2C,80,81	19	27.65	74.00	127.00
300	6' high	Ea	2C,80,81	17	30.91	85.00	145.00
60	**GATE HARDWARE**						
	Latches						
100	standard	Ea				4.36	3.43
110	heavy duty	Ea				14.40	8.00
	Hinges						
120	standard	Pr				3.31	7.00
130	heavy duty	Pr				16.60	17.40
140	No-sag cable kit	Ea				9.70	10.30
150	Self closing spring	Ea				8.50	9.00
70	**WOOD FENCE FINISHING**						
	Paint or stain fence, 2 coats						
100	3' high	LF	1P	55	4.77	0.67	6.80
110	4' high	LF	1P	45	5.83	0.83	8.30
120	5' high	LF	1P	40	6.56	0.99	9.40
130	6' high	LF	1P	30	8.75	1.16	12.40
	Paint or stain gate, 2 coats						
140	3' or 4' high	LF	1P	50	5.25	1.78	8.80
150	5' or 6' high	LF	1P	35	7.50	2.73	12.80

02840 Walk, Road, and Parking Appurtenances

KEY	DESCRIPTION	UNIT	CREW AND EQUIPMENT	PER DAY	INSTALLATION COST	MATERIALS COST	TOTAL + 25%
10	**BICYCLE RACKS**						
	Galvanized pipe rack, embedded or surface mounted						
	double entry						
100	5' long, 7 bikes	Ea	2L,80	4.3	100.71	258.00	448.00
110	10' long, 14 bikes	Ea	2L,80	4.3	100.71	361.00	580.00
120	20' long, 28 bikes	Ea	2L,80	2.9	149.33	640.00	990.00
130	30' long, 42 bikes	Ea	2L,80	2.2	196.85	910.00	1380.00
	single side entry						
140	5' long, 4 bikes	Ea	2L,80	5.9	73.40	225.00	373.00
150	10' long, 8 bikes	Ea	2L,80	5.9	73.40	262.00	419.00
160	20' long, 16 bikes	Ea	2L,80	4	108.27	560.00	840.00
	Wood and metal rack, embedded or surface mounted						
	double entry						
170	10' long, 14 bikes	Ea	2L,80	4.3	100.71	426.00	660.00
	single entry						
190	10' long, 8 bikes	Ea	2L,80	5.9	73.40	333.00	510.00

02840 Walk, Road, and Parking Appurtenances — 1994

KEY	DESCRIPTION	UNIT	CREW AND EQUIPMENT	PER DAY	INSTALLATION COST	MATERIALS COST	TOTAL + 25%
	Recycled plastic rack, embedded or surface mounted						
210	double entry, 10' long, 18 bikes	Ea	2L,80	4.3	100.71	428.00	660.00
215	single entry, 10' long, 8 bikes	Ea	2L,80	5.9	73.40	319.00	491.00
225	Single bike loop, steel with plastic coating, embedded	Ea	2L	4	102.02	52.00	193.00
	Single tube galvanized steel, looped wave pattern, 30" high, surface mounted						
230	3' long, 5 bikes	Ea	2L	4	102.02	324.00	530.00
235	5' long, 7 bikes	Ea	2L	4	102.02	370.00	590.00
240	7' long, 9 bikes	Ea	2L	3	136.02	468.00	760.00
250	9' long, 11 bikes	Ea	2L	3	136.02	790.00	1160.00
260	bonded color, add	Ea				45.00	94.00
270	embedded mounting, add	Ea	2L,80	8	54.13	17.00	89.00
20	**BOLLARDS**						
	Concrete bollard, exposed aggregrate, surface mounted						
100	square, 12" x 12" x 30" high	Ea	1D2L,07,81	7	150.23	179.00	412.00
110	round, 12" diameter x 30" high	Ea	1D2L,07,81	7	150.23	159.00	387.00
	Granite bollard, dowelled to concrete foundation or slab (foundation not included) square cross section smooth matt finish, flat top						
150	16" x 16" x 30", 756 lbs	Ea	1D2L,07	7	149.29	488.00	800.00
160	16" x 16" x 54", 1320 lbs	Ea	1D2L,07	6	174.17	740.00	1140.00
	rough cross section, smooth matt						
170	12" x 12" x 24", 330 lbs	Ea	1D2L,07	9	116.11	385.00	630.00
	round cross section, smooth matt finish,						
180	flat top, 12" diam, 18" ht	Ea	1D2L,07	7	149.29	510.00	820.00
	octagonal cross section, smooth matt finish,						
190	flat top, 24" x 24" x 20", 740 lbs	Ea	1D2L,07	7	149.29	1000.00	1440.00
	Wood bollard, pressure treated timber 8" x 8"						
210	30" high	Ea	2L,80	7	61.87	115.00	221.00
220	36" high	Ea	2L,80	7	61.87	121.00	229.00
230	42" high	Ea	2L,80	7	61.87	127.00	236.00
	12" x 12"						
240	24" high	Ea	2L,80	7	61.87	236.00	372.00
250	36" high	Ea	2L,80	7	61.87	259.00	401.00
260	42" high	Ea	2L,80	7	61.87	282.00	430.00
	footing						
270	concrete, add	Ea	2L	28	14.57	13.30	34.80
280	removable bollard footing, add	Ea	2L	28	14.57	83.00	122.00
290	45 degree angle top, add	Ea				30.00	81.00
300	single or double grooved sides, add	Ea				15.00	6.30
310	triple grooved sides, add	Ea				15.00	12.50
320	radiused top edges, add	Ea				20.00	3.75
330	chamfered top edges, add	Ea				4.00	5.00

02860 Playfields and Equipment

KEY	DESCRIPTION	UNIT	CREW AND EQUIPMENT	PER DAY	INSTALLATION COST	MATERIALS COST	TOTAL + 25%
00	**COMPOSITE COSTS**						
	Play structures						
	Slide tower with climber ladder, dimensional wood, galvanized pipe ladder rungs, 12' x 18'						
100	stainless steel slide	Ea					3490.00

SITE IMPROVEMENTS

02860 Playfields and Equipment

KEY	DESCRIPTION	UNIT	CREW AND EQUIPMENT	PER DAY	INSTALLATION COST	MATERIALS COST	TOTAL + 25%
110	Fire pole tower with tire swing, dimensional wood, galvanized pipe fire pole, chain ladder	Ea					3070.00
120	All component structure, two 4' high and two 6' platforms, beam and suspension bridges, 12' x 18" slide, horizontal ladder, fire pole, tire and belt swings, ladders, balance beam, chain ladder	Ea					17200.00
	Baseball field, includes rough and fine grading and backstop						
130	seeded	Ea					17300.00
140	sodded	Ea					40600.00
	Football field, includes rough and fine grading and goal posts						
150	seeded	Ea					14600.00
160	sodded	Ea					37200.00
	Softball field, includes rough and fine grading and backstop						
170	seeded	Ea					12500.00
180	sodded	Ea					27700.00
	Tennis courts, asphaltic concrete, includes rough and fine grading, fencing net and posts						
	color finished surface						
190	single court	Ea					23500.00
200	2 court battery	Ea					36500.00
210	4 court battery	Ea					58500.00
	texture and color finished surface						
220	single court	Ea					26100.00
230	2 court battery	Ea					40300.00
240	4 court battery	Ea					65600.00
	Basketball court, asphaltic concrete, includes rough and fine grading and goals						
250	plain surface	Ea					16100.00
260	color finished surface	Ea					17100.00
	18 hole golf course (the following costs are reprinted courtesy of the National Golf Foundation)						
	construction of 18 hole course						
270	high						3500000.00
280	low						1500000.00
	irrigation system (including pump station)						
290	high						800000.00
300	low						200000.00
	golf course maintenance equipment						
350	high						400000.00
360	low						150000.00
	maintenance building						
370	high						250000.00
380	low						100000.00
	total golf course development costs						
390	high						4950000.00
400	low						1950000.00
05	**PLAYGROUND EQUIPMENT**						
	Balance beams						
	12" beam, 12" high, concrete footings						
100	metal	Ea	2L,80	16	34.37	280.00	393.00
110	wood	Ea	2L,80	16	34.37	259.00	367.00
120	Multi-level wood beam, three 12' sections, 0' to 2' high, concrete footings	Ea	2L,80	5.3	103.76	690.00	990.00

KEY	DESCRIPTION	UNIT	CREW AND EQUIPMENT	PER DAY	INSTALLATION COST	MATERIALS COST	TOTAL + 25%
	Climber						
	geodesic dome, galvanized pipe, concrete footings						
130	8' diameter, 4' high	Ea	2L	1.3	403.81	540.00	1180.00
140	13' diameter, 5' high	Ea	2L	1.3	403.81	1300.00	2130.00
150	16' diameter, 6' high	Ea	2L	1.1	477.23	1250.00	2160.00
160	17' diameter. 7' high	Ea	2L	1.1	477.23	1250.00	2160.00
	Horizontal ladder						
	galvanized pipe, concrete footings						
220	12' long, 6.5' high	Ea	2L,80	8	68.74	530.00	750.00
230	16' long, 7.5' high	Ea	2L,80	8	68.74	580.00	810.00
	dimensional wood legs, galvanized pipe rungs						
240	8' long	Ea	2L,80	16	34.37	1100.00	1420.00
250	10' long	Ea	2L,80	16	34.37	810.00	1060.00
	Pull-up bars						
	galvanized pipe, concrete footings						
260	2 bars at 2 heights	Ea	2L,80	16	34.37	268.00	378.00
270	3 bars at 3 heights	Ea	2L,80	11	50.00	290.00	425.00
	dimensional wood posts, galvanized pipe rungs, footings						
280	2 bars at 2 heights	Ea	2L,80	16	34.37	495.00	660.00
290	3 bars at 3 heights	Ea	2L,80	11	50.00	620.00	840.00
	Sandbox, prefabricated						
	dimensional wood, 10" high, concrete footings, includes sand						
300	6' x 6'	Ea	2L	5.2	100.95	810.00	1140.00
310	8' x 8'	Ea	2L	4.4	119.31	720.00	1050.00
	painted galvanized steel, 12" high, pine seats, includes sand						
340	6' x 6'	Ea	2L	6.4	82.02	366.00	560.00
350	12' x 12'	Ea	2L	5.3	99.05	520.00	770.00
	Seesaw						
	galvanized pipe frame, wood, metal or plastic seats, concrete footings						
360	1 unit, 2 seater	Ea	2L,80	4.6	119.56	343.00	580.00
370	2 units, 4 seater	Ea	2L,80	3.7	148.64	760.00	1140.00
380	4 units, 8 seater	Ea	2L,80	2.9	189.64	1490.00	2100.00
390	6 units, 12 seater	Ea	2L,80	2.3	239.11	1530.00	2210.00
400	dimensional wood frame, wood seats, concrete footings, 1 unit, 2 seater	Ea	2C,80	5.3	100.15	620.00	900.00
	Slide, 18" stainless steel bed, galvanized pipe frame, concrete footings						
410	8' long	Ea	2L,80	3.3	166.65	910.00	1350.00
420	10' long	Ea	2L,80	3	183.32	1060.00	1550.00
430	12' long	Ea	2L,80	2.7	203.69	1200.00	1750.00
440	16' long	Ea	2L,80	2	274.98	1330.00	2010.00
	Swing, two leg ends, belt seats, galvanized pipe frame, concrete footings						
	8' high						
460	2 seater	Ea	2L,80	2.5	219.98	415.00	790.00
470	4 seater	Ea	2L,80	2	274.98	710.00	1230.00
480	6 seater	Ea	2L,80	1.7	323.50	1000.00	1650.00
490	8 seater	Ea	2L,80	1.4	392.82	1180.00	1970.00

SITE IMPROVEMENTS

| | 02860 Playfields and Equipment | | | | | | 1994 |

KEY	DESCRIPTION	UNIT	CREW AND EQUIPMENT	PER DAY	INSTALLATION COST	MATERIALS COST	TOTAL + 25%
	10' high						
500	2 seater	Ea	2L,80	2.2	249.98	560.00	1010.00
510	4 seater	Ea	2L,80	1.6	343.72	840.00	1480.00
520	6 seater	Ea	2L,80	1.5	366.64	1210.00	1970.00
530	8 seater	Ea	2L,80	1.3	423.04	1500.00	2400.00
	Swing, three leg ends, belt seats, galvanized pipe frame, concrete footings						
	10' high						
540	3 seater	Ea	2L,80	2	274.98	810.00	1360.00
550	6 seater	Ea	2L,80	1.7	323.50	1320.00	2050.00
560	9 seater	Ea	2L,80	1.4	392.82	1830.00	2780.00
	12' high						
570	3 seater	Ea	2L,80	1.8	305.53	840.00	1430.00
580	6 seater	Ea	2L,80	1.5	366.64	1630.00	2500.00
590	9 seater	Ea	2L,80	1.3	423.04	1910.00	2920.00
595	Wheelchair swing platform	Ea	2L	4	131.24	750.00	1100.00
	Swing, T-bar galvanized pipe frame, belt seats, concrete footings						
600	2 seater	Ea	2L	1.6	328.10	590.00	1150.00
610	3 seater	Ea	2L	1.5	349.97	960.00	1640.00
620	4 seater	Ea	2L	1.4	374.97	770.00	1430.00
630	Tether ball set, galvanized pipe post, nylon rope, ball, concrete footing, ground sleeve	Ea	2L	16	32.81	153.00	232.00
	Whirl, painted galvanized steel, concrete footing						
640	6' diameter	Ea	2L	2.8	187.48	940.00	1410.00
650	8' diameter	Ea	2L	2	262.48	1450.00	2140.00
660	10' diameter	Ea	2L	1.2	437.46	1980.00	3020.00
10	PLAY STRUCTURE COMPONENTS						
	Platform, 4' x 4', dimensional wood, two side walls or railings						
100	4' high	Ea	2C,80	3.2	165.87	2380.00	3180.00
110	6' high	Ea	2C,80	3.2	165.87	1340.00	1880.00
	Bridge, dimensional wood, galvanized chain railings						
130	suspension	Ea	2C,80	5.3	100.15	1720.00	2280.00
	Slide, stainless steel bed, railings						
	18" wide						
140	8' long	Ea	2C,80	8	66.35	800.00	1080.00
150	12' long	Ea	2C,80	8	66.35	1020.00	1360.00
160	16' long	Ea	2C,80	8	66.35	1360.00	1780.00
	36" wide						
170	5' long	Ea	2C,80	8	66.35	860.00	1160.00
180	8' long	Ea	2C,80	8	66.35	860.00	1160.00
190	12' long	Ea	2C,80	8	66.35	1100.00	1460.00
200	Horizontal ladder, 8' to 10' long, galvanized pipe rungs, dimensional wood uprights	Ea	2C,80	16	33.17	960.00	1240.00
210	Fire pole, 8' to 10' high, galvanized pipe	Ea	2C,80	8	66.35	137.00	254.00
220	Tire swing, dimensional wood frame, auto tire seat	Ea	2C,80	8	66.35	880.00	1180.00
230	Belt seat swing, dimensional wood frame, 2 seater	Ea	2C,80	8	66.35	770.00	1050.00
240	Ladder, 6' high, galvanized pipe rungs	Ea	2C,80	32	16.59	550.00	710.00

02860 Playfields and Equipments						1994
KEY	DESCRIPTION	UNIT	CREW AND EQUIPMENT	PER DAY	INSTALLATION COST	MATERIALS COST	TOTAL + 25%

KEY	DESCRIPTION	UNIT	CREW AND EQUIPMENT	PER DAY	INSTALLATION COST	MATERIALS COST	TOTAL + 25%
260	Balance beam, 12' long, dimensional wood	Ea	2C,80	16	33.17	383.00	520.00
270	Seesaw, dimensional wood, 2 seater, concrete footings	Ea	2C,80	5.3	100.15	790.00	1110.00
15	**FITNESS TRAILS**						
100	10 stations, 5 structures, 11 signs	Ea	2C,80	0.5	1061.59	5800.00	8600.00
110	15 stations, 7 structures, 16 signs	Ea	2C,80	0.4	1326.99	8700.00	12500.00
120	20 stations, 10 structures, 21 signs	Ea	2C,80	0.3	1769.32	11600.00	16700.00
20	**FOOTBALL GOALS**						
	Regulation goal, galvanized steel pipe						
100	single support	Pr	2L	1	524.95	2080.00	3260.00
110	double support	Pr	2L	1	524.95	2020.00	3180.00
120	Combination football/soccer goal, regulation, galvanized steel pipe, double support	Pr	2L	1.5	349.97	1990.00	2920.00
25	**SOCCER GOALS**						
100	Regulation goal, galvanized steel pipe frame, net	Pr	2L	8	65.62	1780.00	2310.00
30	**BASKETBALL GOALS**						
	Basketball goals, steel fan backboard, hoop and net						
	single support						
100	up to 1" backboard extension	Pr	2L	1.5	349.97	2290.00	3300.00
110	4' to 6' backboard extension	Pr	2L	1.4	374.97	1920.00	2870.00
	double support						
120	up to 1" backboard extension	Pr	2L	1	524.95	2250.00	3470.00
130	4' to 7' backboard extension	Pr	2L	0.9	583.28	2200.00	3480.00
140	double back to back	Ea	2L	0.9	583.28	1580.00	2700.00
35	**VOLLEYBALL**						
100	Galvanized posts, net, ground sleeves, concrete footings	Ea	2L	8	65.62	301.00	458.00
40	**ATHLETIC BENCHES**						
	Backed athletic bench, galvanized pipe frame, embedded						
	aluminum seat and back						
100	6' long	Ea	2L,80	10	55.00	289.00	430.00
110	8' long	Ea	2L,80	8	68.74	318.00	483.00
120	15' long	Ea	2L,80	7.1	77.46	476.00	690.00
	fiberglass seat and back						
130	10' long	Ea	2L,80	10	55.00	362.00	520.00
140	12' long	Ea	2L,80	8	68.74	425.00	620.00
150	16' long	Ea	2L,80	7.1	77.46	570.00	810.00
	galvanized steel seat and back						
160	15' long	Ea	2L,80	7.1	77.46	340.00	520.00
	Backless athletic bench, galvanized pipe frame, embedde						
	aluminum seat						
170	6' long	Ea	2L,80	12	45.83	173.00	274.00
180	8' long	Ea	2L,80	12	45.83	194.00	300.00
190	15' long	Ea	2L,80	11	50.00	313.00	454.00
	wood seat						
200	6' long	Ea	2L,80	12	45.83	146.00	240.00
210	8' long	Ea	2L,80	12	45.83	153.00	249.00
220	15' long	Ea	2L,80	11	50.00	283.00	416.00
45	**TENNIS EQUIPMENT**						
	Net posts, reel						
	galvanized steel						
100	3 1/2" diameter	Pr	2L,80	3	183.32	288.00	590.00
110	4 1/2" diameter	Pr	2L,80	3	183.32	423.00	760.00
	galvanized steel with ground sleeves						
120	3 1/2" diameter	Pr	2L,80	2.5	219.98	550.00	960.00
130	4 1/2" diameter	Pr	2L,80	2.5	219.98	790.00	1260.00

SITE IMPROVEMENTS

KEY	DESCRIPTION	UNIT	CREW AND EQUIPMENT	PER DAY	INSTALLATION COST	MATERIALS COST	TOTAL + 25%
	Tennis nets						
150	cloth	Ea	2L	10	52.50	155.00	259.00
160	poly	Ea	2L	10	52.50	207.00	324.00
170	nylon	Ea	2L	10	52.50	220.00	341.00
180	steel	Ea	2L	7.5	69.99	438.00	630.00
	Windbreak, 9' high, closed mesh polypropylene, lashed to chain link fence						
200		LF	2L	2880	0.18	3.70	4.85

02870 Site and Street Furnishings

KEY	DESCRIPTION	UNIT	CREW AND EQUIPMENT	PER DAY	INSTALLATION COST	MATERIALS COST	TOTAL + 25%
05	**PREFABRICATED PLANTERS**						
	Dimensional redwood planter, fiberglass lined (does not include soil)						
	square						
100	24" square, 20" high	Ea	2L	16	25.50	1220.00	1560.00
	36" square						
105	20" high	Ea	2L	15	27.20	1600.00	2030.00
110	30" high	Ea	2L	14	29.15	1120.00	1440.00
	48" square						
115	20" high	Ea	2L	13	31.39	940.00	1210.00
120	30" high	Ea	2L	12	34.01	1480.00	1890.00
	60" square						
125	20" high	Ea	2L	10	40.81	1310.00	1690.00
130	30" high	Ea	2L	8	51.01	1600.00	2060.00
	cylindrical						
	30" diameter						
135	20" high	Ea	2L	16	25.50	1220.00	1560.00
140	30" high	Ea	2L	15	27.20	640.00	830.00
	36" diameter						
145	20" high	Ea	2L	15	27.20	1400.00	1780.00
150	30" high	Ea	2L	15	27.20	710.00	920.00
	48" diameter						
155	20" high	Ea	2L	14	29.15	810.00	1050.00
160	30" high	Ea	2L	13	31.39	990.00	1280.00
	60" diameter						
165	20" high	Ea	2L	13	31.39	1040.00	1340.00
170	30" high	Ea	2L	10	40.81	1120.00	1450.00
	rectangular						
	36" x 24"						
175	20" high	Ea	2L	15	27.20	600.00	780.00
180	30" high	Ea	2L	15	27.20	990.00	1270.00
	48" x 30"						
185	20" high	Ea	2L	15	27.20	2070.00	2620.00
190	30" high	Ea	2L	14	29.15	890.00	1150.00
	60" x 30"						
195	20" high	Ea	2L	14	29.15	2660.00	3360.00
200	30" high	Ea	2L	13	31.39	1020.00	1310.00
	Fiberglass planter (does not include soil)						
	square						
	24" square						
205	21" high	Ea	2L	21	19.43	580.00	750.00
210	27" high	Ea	2L	20	20.40	630.00	810.00
215	30" square, 21" high	Ea	2L	20	20.40	810.00	1040.00

02870 Site and Street Furnishings

KEY	DESCRIPTION	UNIT	CREW AND EQUIPMENT	PER DAY	INSTALLATION COST	MATERIALS COST	TOTAL + 25%
	36" square						
220	21" high	Ea	2L	19	21.48	950.00	1210.00
225	30" high	Ea	2L	18	22.67	1140.00	1450.00
230	36" high	Ea	2L	17	24.00	1330.00	1690.00
	48" square						
235	21" high	Ea	2L	17	24.00	1330.00	1690.00
240	30" high	Ea	2L	15	27.20	1660.00	2110.00
245	36" high	Ea	2L	14	29.15	1860.00	2360.00
	60" square						
250	30" high	Ea	2L	11	37.10	1070.00	1380.00
255	36" high	Ea	2L	10	40.81	1200.00	1550.00
	cylindrical						
	24" diameter						
275	21" high	Ea	2L	21	19.43	550.00	710.00
280	27" high	Ea	2L	21	19.43	660.00	850.00
285	30" diameter, 21" high	Ea	2L	20	20.40	690.00	890.00
	36" diameter						
290	21" high	Ea	2L	20	20.40	850.00	1090.00
295	30" high	Ea	2L	19	21.48	990.00	1260.00
300	36" high	Ea	2L	18	22.67	1140.00	1450.00
	48" diameter						
305	21" high	Ea	2L	18	22.67	1220.00	1550.00
310	30" high	Ea	2L	16	25.50	1450.00	1840.00
315	36" high	Ea	2L	15	27.20	1620.00	2060.00
	60" diameter						
320	30" high	Ea	2L	13	31.39	970.00	1250.00
325	36" high	Ea	2L	12	34.01	1060.00	1370.00
330	72" diameter, 30" high	Ea	2L	11	37.10	1260.00	1620.00
	rectangular						
345	36" x 20", 21" high	Ea	2L	20	20.40	299.00	399.00
350	48" x 24", 27" high	Ea	2L	19	21.48	890.00	1140.00
	72" x 24"						
355	21" high	Ea	2L	18	22.67	1450.00	1840.00
360	27" high	Ea	2L	17	24.00	1620.00	2060.00
	Precast concrete planter, exposed aggregate finish, does not include soil (includes transport & placement on site)						
	square						
365	18" x 18" x 24"	Ea	2L	22	18.55	173.00	239.00
370	30" x 30" x 30"	Ea	2L	16	25.50	403.00	540.00
380	36" x 36" x 30"	Ea	2L	12	34.01	481.00	640.00
385	48" x 48" x 30"	Ea	2L	10	40.81	590.00	790.00
390	60" x 60" x 36"	Ea	2L	8	51.01	790.00	1050.00
	round						
395	18" diameter x 24"	Ea	2L	22	18.55	170.00	236.00
400	30" diameter x 17"	Ea	2L	16	25.50	291.00	396.00
405	30" diameter x 30"	Ea	2L	16	25.50	374.00	499.00
410	36" diameter x 24"	Ea	2L	22	18.55	385.00	500.00
415	36" diameter x 30"	Ea	2L	15	27.20	446.00	590.00
420	48" diameter x 24"	Ea	2L	22	18.55	550.00	710.00
425	48" diameter x 30"	Ea	2L	10	40.81	580.00	780.00
430	60" diameter x 17"	Ea	2L	8	51.01	550.00	750.00
435	60" diameter x 36"	Ea	2L	8	51.01	750.00	1000.00
10	**PREFABRICATED SHELTERS**						
	Metal shelter						
	rectangular, flat roof, surface mounted on concrete slab						
100	150 square feet	Ea	2C,80	2	256.20	1810.00	2580.00
110	180 square feet	Ea	2C,80	1.8	284.66	2610.00	3620.00
120	300 square feet	Ea	3C2L,80	1.5	782.24	2660.00	4300.00

KEY	DESCRIPTION	UNIT	CREW AND EQUIPMENT	PER DAY	INSTALLATION COST	MATERIALS COST	TOTAL + 25%
130	360 square feet rectangular, pitched roof, footings, slab not included	Ea	3C2L,80	1.3	902.58	3770.00	5800.00
160	500 square feet	Ea	3C2L,80	1	1173.35	4230.00	6800.00
180	1000 square feet	Ea	3C2L,80	0.6	1955.59	8200.00	12700.00
190	1500 square feet	Ea	3C2L,80	0.3	3911.18	12000.00	19900.00
	Wood shelter rectangular, pitched asphalt shingled roof, slab not included						
200	250 square feet	Ea	2C,80,07	1.9	496.00	4470.00	6200.00
210	500 square feet	Ea	2C,80,07	1	942.40	5900.00	8600.00
220	750 square feet	Ea	3C2L,80,07	1	1603.35	7500.00	11400.00
230	1000 square feet	Ea	3C2L,80,07	0.7	2290.50	9200.00	14400.00
240	1500 square feet	Ea	3C2L,80,07	0.5	3206.71	14300.00	21900.00
	hexagonal, pitched asphalt shingled roof, slab not included						
250	20' diameter	Ea	3C2L,80,07	1.9	843.87	7900.00	10900.00
260	32' diameter	Ea	3C2L,80,07	1	1603.35	10500.00	15100.00
270	40' diameter	Ea	3C2L,80,07	0.6	2672.26	13400.00	20100.00
12	**GARDEN FURNITURE**						
	Garden arm chairs coated wire grid mesh & tubular steel						
100	gangable, 23" x 26" x 31"	Ea	1L	50	4.08	219.00	279.00
110	ganging clamps (per additional seat)	Ea	1L	50	4.08	69.00	91.00
120	ornamental drawn steel, "ice cream" style, 22" x 22" x 34"	Ea	1L	50	4.08	351.00	444.00
130	Chaise lounge, coated wire grid mesh & tubular steel, stackable, 28" x 72" x 18"	Ea	1L	50	4.08	620.00	780.00
140	Security chain, matching	LF	1L	300	0.68	5.80	8.10
15	**CONTOUR BACKED BENCHES**						
	Redwood or cedar bench square tube steel pedestal embedded						
100	6' long	Ea	2C,80	5.3	96.68	720.00	1020.00
110	8' long	Ea	2C,80	4.6	111.39	1260.00	1710.00
	surface mounted						
120	6' long	Ea	2C,81	6.4	79.84	930.00	1260.00
130	8' long	Ea	2C,81	6.4	79.84	1240.00	1650.00
	ornamental cast iron frame, surface mounted						
140	4' long	Ea	2C,81	6.4	79.84	570.00	810.00
150	6' long	Ea	2C,81	6.4	79.84	690.00	960.00
160	8' long	Ea	2C,81	6.4	79.84	920.00	1250.00
	Purpleheart bench square tube steel pedestal embedded						
170	6' long	Ea	2C,80	5.3	96.68	1080.00	1470.00
180	8' long	Ea	2C,80	4.6	111.39	1300.00	1760.00
	surface mounted						
190	6' long	Ea	2C,81	6.4	79.84	1360.00	1800.00
200	8' long	Ea	2C,81	6.4	79.84	1590.00	2090.00
	Pine or fir bench square tube steel pedestal embedded						
210	6' long	Ea	2C,80	5.3	96.68	640.00	920.00
220	8' long	Ea	2C,80	4.6	111.39	720.00	1040.00

KEY	DESCRIPTION	UNIT	CREW AND EQUIPMENT	PER DAY	INSTALLATION COST	MATERIALS COST	TOTAL + 25%
	surface mounted						
230	6' long	Ea	2C,81	6.4	79.84	640.00	900.00
240	8' long	Ea	2C,81	6.4	79.84	720.00	1000.00
	Coated wire grid mesh bench, gangable, coated tube steel pedestal, embedded, surface mounted, or wall mounted.						
250	straight, 4' long, 2 seats	Ea	2C,81	5	102.20	1400.00	1880.00
260	curved, 6' radius, 60 degrees	Ea	2C,81	4.5	113.55	2440.00	3190.00
20	**STRAIGHT BACKED BENCHES**						
	Redwood or cedar bench						
	square tube steel pedestal, embedded						
100	6' long	Ea	2C,80	6.4	80.06	840.00	1150.00
110	8' long	Ea	2C,80	6.4	80.06	980.00	1330.00
	square tube or flat steel pedestal, surface mounted						
120	6' long	Ea	2C,81	11	46.45	1060.00	1380.00
130	8' long	Ea	2C,81	11	46.45	1220.00	1580.00
	steel pipe pedestal						
	embedded						
140	6' long	Ea	2C,80	6.4	80.06	253.00	416.00
145	8' long	Ea	2C,80	6.4	80.06	324.00	510.00
	surface mounted						
150	6' long	Ea	2C,81	11	46.45	210.00	321.00
155	8' long	Ea	2C,81	11	46.45	289.00	419.00
	Pine or fir bench						
	steel pipe pedestal, embedded						
200	6' long	Ea	2C,80	6.4	80.06	197.00	346.00
210	8' long	Ea	2C,80	6.4	80.06	241.00	401.00
	wood pedestal, surface mounted						
220	6' long	Ea	2C,81	11	46.45	870.00	1150.00
230	8' long	Ea	2C,81	11	46.45	1130.00	1470.00
	Fiberglass bench, steel pipe pedestal, embedded						
240	6' long	Ea	2C,80	6.4	80.06	325.00	510.00
250	8' long	Ea	2C,80	6.4	80.06	432.00	640.00
	Painted steel bench, steel pipe pedestal, embedded						
260	6' long	Ea	2C,80	6.4	80.06	320.00	500.00
270	8' long	Ea	2C,80	6.4	80.06	399.00	600.00
	Aluminum, steel pipe pedestal, embedded						
280	6' long	Ea	2C,80	6.4	80.06	320.00	500.00
290	8' long	Ea	2C,80	6.4	80.06	362.00	550.00
	Recycled plastic, steel pipe						
	embedded						
300	6' long	Ea	2C,80	6.4	80.06	440.00	650.00
310	8' long	Ea	2C,80	6.4	80.06	600.00	850.00
	surface mounted						
320	6' long	Ea	2C,81	11	46.45	386.00	540.00
330	8' long	Ea	2C,81	11	46.45	540.00	730.00
25	**BACKLESS BENCHES**						
	Redwood or cedar bench						
	square tube steel pedestal, embedded						
100	6' long	Ea	2C,80	8	64.05	620.00	860.00
110	8' long	Ea	2C,80	8	64.05	850.00	1140.00
	square tube or flat steel pedestal, surface mounted						
120	6' long	Ea	2C,81	16	31.94	820.00	1060.00
130	8' long	Ea	2C,81	16	31.94	940.00	1210.00
	wood pedestal, surface mounted						
140	6' long	Ea	2C,81	16	31.94	660.00	860.00
150	8' long	Ea	2C,81	16	31.94	720.00	940.00

SITE IMPROVEMENTS

KEY	DESCRIPTION	UNIT	CREW AND EQUIPMENT	PER DAY	INSTALLATION COST	MATERIALS COST	TOTAL + 25%
	steel pipe pedestal, embedded						
160	6' long	Ea	2C,80	8	64.05	456.00	650.00
170	8' long	Ea	2C,80	8	64.05	640.00	880.00
	ornamental cast iron frame, surface mounted						
180	4' long	Ea	2C,81	16	31.94	344.00	470.00
190	6' long	Ea	2C,81	16	31.94	344.00	470.00
200	8' long	Ea	2C,81	16	31.94	690.00	900.00
	Pine or fir bench						
	square tube steel pedestal, embedded						
270	6' long	Ea	2C,80	8	64.05	297.00	451.00
280	8' long	Ea	2C,80	8	64.05	333.00	496.00
	steel pipe pedestal, embedded						
290	6' long	Ea	2C,80	8	64.05	378.00	550.00
300	8' long	Ea	2C,80	8	64.05	560.00	780.00
	Coated wire grid mesh bench, gangable, coated tube steel pedestal						
	2 seat, embedded, surface, or wall mounted						
310	straight, 4' long	Ea	2C,81	10	51.10	830.00	1100.00
320	curved, 5' radius, 30 degrees	Ea	2C,81	10	51.10	590.00	800.00
330	1 seat, wall mounted, 15" x 15"	Ea	2C,81	20	25.55	213.00	298.00
	Recycled plastic						
	embedded						
340	6' long	Ea	2C,80	8	64.05	338.00	500.00
350	8' long	Ea	2C,80	8	64.05	399.00	580.00
30	**SQUARE BACKLESS BENCHES**						
	Redwood or cedar bench, square tube steel pedestal						
	embedded						
100	3' x 3'	Ea	2C,80	11	46.58	780.00	1030.00
110	4' x 4'	Ea	2C,80	11	46.58	650.00	870.00
	surface mounted						
120	3' x 3'	Ea	2C,81	16	31.94	750.00	980.00
130	4' x 4'	Ea	2C,81	16	31.94	620.00	810.00
	Purpleheart bench, square tube steel pedestal						
	embedded						
140	3' x 3'	Ea	2C,80	11	46.58	1080.00	1410.00
150	4' x 4'	Ea	2C,80	11	46.58	850.00	1120.00
	surface mounted						
160	3' x 3'	Ea	2C,81	16	31.94	1410.00	1800.00
170	4' x 4'	Ea	2C	16	31.61	820.00	1060.00
	Pine or fir bench, square tube steel pedestal, embedded						
180	3' x 3'	Ea	2C,80	11	46.58	467.00	640.00
190	4' x 4'	Ea	2C,80	11	46.58	740.00	980.00
35	**PICNIC TABLES**						
	Redwood or cedar seats, top, and frame						
	embedded						
100	6' long	Ea	2L,80	4	103.67	950.00	1320.00
110	8' long	Ea	2L,80	4	103.67	1180.00	1600.00
	portable						
120	6' long	Ea	2L	32	12.75	485.00	620.00
130	8' long	Ea	2L	32	12.75	430.00	550.00

KEY	DESCRIPTION	UNIT	CREW AND EQUIPMENT	PER DAY	INSTALLATION COST	MATERIALS COST	TOTAL + 25%
	Pine seats and top, galvanized pipe frame						
	embedded						
140	6' long	Ea	2L,80	4	103.67	447.00	690.00
150	8' long	Ea	2L,80	4	103.67	470.00	720.00
	portable						
160	6' long	Ea	2L	32	12.75	239.00	315.00
170	8' long	Ea	2L	32	12.75	280.00	366.00
	wheelchair accessible, portable						
180	6' long	Ea	2L	32	12.75	301.00	392.00
190	8' long	Ea	2L	32	12.75	262.00	343.00
	wheelchair accessible,embedded						
200	8' long	Ea	2L,80	4	103.67	220.00	405.00
	Aluminum seats and top, galvanized pipe frame						
	portable						
220	6' long	Ea	2L	32	12.75	486.00	620.00
230	8' long	Ea	2L	32	12.75	590.00	750.00
	wheelchair accessible						
240	6' long	Ea	2L	32	12.75	540.00	690.00
250	8' long	Ea	2L,80	4	103.67	600.00	880.00
	Fiberglass seats and top, galanized pipe frame, portable						
260	6' long	Ea	2L	32	12.75	470.00	600.00
270	8' long	Ea	2L	32	12.75	640.00	820.00
280	Concrete seats and top, 7' long	Ea	2L1D,07	16	65.31	580.00	810.00
	Recycled plastic, steel pipe frame						
290	portable, 6' long	Ea	2L	32	12.75	406.00	520.00
37	**TABLES**						
	Pedestal cafe table, fiberglassed, 39" diameter or 27 1/2" square						
100	standard	Ea	1L	40	5.10	420.00	530.00
110	umbrella type	Ea	1L	40	5.10	660.00	830.00
	Umbrella, 78" diameter						
120	Ultralite	Ea	1L	40	5.10	500.00	630.00
130	canvas or Acrylan	Ea	1L	40	5.10	454.00	570.00
140	Base for portable umbrella	Ea	1L	40	5.10	144.00	186.00
150	Permanent installation clamps, add for each table	Ea	1L	20	10.20	34.50	56.00
40	**PERMANENT WASTE RECEPTACLES**						
	Painted metal basket, no liner, pole or wall mounted						
100	10 gallon	Ea	1L	16	12.75	113.00	157.00
110	22 gallon	Ea	1L	14	14.57	149.00	204.00
120	34 gallon	Ea	1L	12	17.00	138.00	194.00
	Wood slat basket						
	pole or wall mounted						
	no liner						
130	10 gallon	Ea	1L	16	12.75	162.00	218.00
140	15 gallon	Ea	1L	14	14.57	248.00	328.00
	with plastic liner						
150	10 gallon	Ea	1L	15	13.60	195.00	261.00
160	15 gallon	Ea	1L	13	15.69	288.00	380.00
	embedded or surface mounted, with plastic liner						
170	10 gallon	Ea	1L	10	20.4030357	185.00	257.00
180	22 gallon	Ea	1L	8	25.50	221.00	308.00
45	**PORTABLE WASTE RECEPTACLES**						
	Painted metal receptacle with cover and liner						
	square						
100	10 gallon	Ea	1L	32	6.38	159.00	207.00
110	24 gallon	Ea	1L	32	6.38	204.00	263.00
120	48 gallon	Ea	1L	23	8.87	380.00	486.00

KEY	DESCRIPTION	UNIT	CREW AND EQUIPMENT	PER DAY	INSTALLATION COST	MATERIALS COST	TOTAL + 25%
	cylindrical						
130	10 gallon	Ea	1L	32	6.38	142.00	185.00
140	24 gallon	Ea	1L	32	6.38	204.00	263.00
	Redwood or aggregate covered shell, metal drum receptacle, covered						
150	30 gallon	Ea	2L	10	40.81	444.00	610.00
160	55 gallon	Ea	2L	10	40.81	580.00	780.00
180	push doors, add	Ea				48.00	60.00
195	plastic liner, add	Ea				54.00	68.00
	Dimensional redwood, covered, with liner						
200	24 gallon	Ea	2L	8	51.01	477.00	660.00
210	30 gallon	Ea	2L	8	51.01	540.00	740.00
	Exposed aggregate concrete receptacle, covered, with liner						
	square						
220	43 gallon	Ea	3L	15	40.81	680.00	900.00
	cylindrical						
230	32 gallon	Ea	3L	12	51.01	510.00	700.00
50	**GARBAGE CAN HOLDERS**						
	Galvanized metal can holder, 20-32 gallon, 12" ground clearance, concrete footing						
100	single can	Ea	2L	12	34.01	129.00	204.00
110	two cans	Ea	2L	12	34.01	185.00	274.00
	Timber can holder, 30-32 gallon, 12" ground clearance						
120	single can	Ea	2L	12	34.01	113.00	184.00
130	two cans	Ea	2L	12	34.01	144.00	223.00
55	**CAMP FIRE PITS**						
	Anchor embedment, 7" high, steel, with grate						
100	30" diameter	Ea	2L	32	12.75	121.00	167.00
110	Anchor embedment, adjustable grill height	Ea	2L	32	12.75	127.00	175.00
60	**RAISED PICNIC GRILLS**						
	Cast iron firebox, 272 square inch, adjustable grate, embedded steel post	Ea	2L	8	51.01	168.00	274.00
100							
	Welded galvanized steel firebox, 280 square inch, adjustable grate, embedded steel post	Ea	2L	8	51.01	115.00	208.00
110							
65	**TREE GRATES**						
	Tree grate, light duty, gray iron, asphalt painted (includes slab opening)						
	without light access holes						
	square, 2 sections						
100	36" x 36", 120 lb	Ea	3C3L	25	54.83	147.00	252.00
110	48" x 48", 240 lb	Ea	3C3L	13	105.44	274.00	474.00
120	60" x 60", 400 lb	Ea	3C1D3L,07	16	125.48	389.00	640.00
130	72" x 72", 570 lb	Ea	3C1D3L,07	13	154.44	500.00	820.00
	square, 4 sections						
140	45" x 45", 300 lb	Ea	3C3L	10	137.08	371.00	640.00
150	51" x 51", 510 lb	Ea	3C3L	6	228.46	580.00	1010.00
160	108" x 108", 1300 lb	Ea	3C1D3L,07	6	334.62	1050.00	1730.00
	round, 2 sections						
170	32" diameter, 105 lb	Ea	3C3L	17	80.63	130.00	263.00
180	56" diameter, 280 lb	Ea	3C1D3L,07	17	118.10	297.00	520.00
190	66" diameter, 595 lb	Ea	3C1D3L,07	13	154.44	530.00	860.00

KEY	DESCRIPTION	UNIT	CREW AND EQUIPMENT	PER DAY	INSTALLATION COST	MATERIALS COST	TOTAL + 25%
	round, 4 sections						
200	78" diameter, 610 lb	Ea	3C3L	13	105.44	590.00	870.00
210	88" diameter, 810 lb	Ea	3C1D3L,07	10	200.77	750.00	1190.00
	with light access holes						
	square, 2 sections						
220	60" x 60", 470 lb	Ea	3C1D3L,07	16	125.48	415.00	680.00
230	72" x 72", 600 lb	Ea	3C1D3L,07	13	154.44	530.00	860.00
	round, 2 sections						
240	56" diameter, 310 lb	Ea	3C1D3L,07	17	118.10	330.00	560.00
250	72" diameter, 515 lb	Ea	3C1D3L,07	13	154.44	457.00	760.00
	round, 4 sections						
260	119" diameter, 2050 lb	Ea	3C1D3L,07	4	501.93	1670.00	2710.00
	Tree grate, heavy duty, gray iron asphaltic painted (includes slab opening)						
	without light access holes						
	square, 2 sections						
270	56" x 56", 560 lb	Ea	3C1D3L,07	14	143.41	423.00	710.00
280	72" x 72", 1305 lb	Ea	3C1D3L,07	6	334.62	987.00	1650.00
	square, 4 sections						
290	96" x 96", 1600 lb	Ea	3C1D3L,07	5	401.55	1100.00	1880.00
	with light access holes						
	square, 4 sections						
300	72" x 72", 1575 lb	Ea	3C1D3L,07	5	401.55	1160.00	1950.00
70	**FRAMES FOR TREE GRATES**						
	Frame, gray iron, asphaltic painted, cast into surrounding concrte						
	for light duty grate						
100	36" x 36", 1" seat	Ea	1l	9	31.42	99.00	163.00
110	48" x 48", 1 1/4" seat	Ea	1l	8	35.35	138.00	217.00
120	60" x 60", 1 1/2" seat	Ea	1l	7	43.50	185.00	286.00
130	72" x 72", 3 1/4" seat	Ea	1l	5	56.55	297.00	442.00
140	45" x 45", 1 1/4" seat	Ea	1l	8	35.35	130.00	207.00
150	51" x 51", 1 1/2" seat	Ea	1l	7	40.40	148.00	235.00
160	108" x 108", 1 3/4" seat	Ea	1l	5	62.84	318.00	476.00
170	32" diameter, 1 1/2" seat	Ea	1l	10	29.77	84.00	142.00
180	56" diameter, 1 1/2" seat	Ea	1l	8	35.35	137.00	215.00
190	60" diameter, 1 1/4" seat	Ea	1l	8	37.70	145.00	228.00
200	66" diameter, 3" seat	Ea	1l	6	47.13	217.00	330.00
210	72" diameter, 1 1/2" seat	Ea	1l	7	40.40	169.00	262.00
220	72" diameter, 2 1/4" seat	Ea	1l	5	56.55	201.00	322.00
230	88" diameter, 3" seat	Ea	1l	7	43.50	244.00	359.00
240	119" diameter, 1 1/4" seat	Ea	1l	5	62.84	364.00	530.00
	for heavy duty grate						
250	56" x 56", 3" seat	Ea	1l	6	47.13	236.00	354.00
260	72" x 72", 2 1/4" seat	Ea	1l	6	51.41	249.00	376.00
270	72" x 72", 3" seat	Ea	1l	3	113.11	277.00	488.00
280	96" x 96", 3 1/4" seat	Ea	1l	4	70.69	381.00	560.00

SITE IMPROVEMENTS

02890 Footbridges

1994

KEY	DESCRIPTION	UNIT	CREW AND EQUIPMENT	PER DAY	INSTALLATION COST	MATERIALS COST	TOTAL + 25%
10	**PEDESTRIAN AND SPECIAL USE BRIDGES**						
	Self weathering steel, clear span arch type bridge, treated wood deck (does not include foundations)						
	4' wide, 2000-5000 lb vehicle load						
100	20' span	Ea	1D2L,07	2	522.50	5500.00	7500.00
110	30' span	Ea	1D2L,07	2	522.50	6800.00	9200.00
120	40' span	Ea	1D2L,07	2	522.50	8200.00	10900.00
130	60' span	Ea	1A2L,95	1.5	1034.60	11800.00	16000.00
140	80' span	Ea	1A3L,95	1.5	1170.62	15300.00	20600.00
	6' wide, 2000-5000 lb vehicle load						
150	20' span	Ea	1D2L,07	2	522.50	5700.00	7800.00
160	30' span	Ea	1D2L,07	2	522.50	7100.00	9500.00
170	40' span	Ea	1A2L,95	1.5	1034.60	8600.00	12000.00
180	60' span	Ea	1A3L,95	1.5	1170.62	12000.00	16500.00
190	80' span	Ea	1A3L,95	1	1755.93	19000.00	25900.00
	8' wide, 10,000 lb vehicle load						
200	20' span	Ea	1D2L,07	2	522.50	7000.00	9400.00
210	30' span	Ea	1A2L,95	1.5	1034.60	8500.00	11900.00
220	40' span	Ea	1A3L,95	1.5	1170.62	10400.00	14500.00
230	60' span	Ea	1A3L,95	1	1755.93	15800.00	21900.00
240	80' span	Ea	1A3L,95	1	1755.93	25200.00	33700.00
	10' wide, 10,000 lb vehicle load						
250	30' span	Ea	1A3L,95	1.5	1170.62	9800.00	13700.00
260	40' span	Ea	1A3L,95	1	1755.93	11900.00	17100.00
270	50' span	Ea	1A3L,95	1	1755.93	14400.00	20200.00

02920 Soil Preparation

KEY	DESCRIPTION	UNIT	CREW AND EQUIPMENT	PER DAY	INSTALLATION COST	MATERIALS COST	TOTAL + 35%
00	**COMPOSITE COSTS**						
	Apply complete fertilizer, till and level						
100	1000 SF or less	SY					8.90
110	over 1000 SF	SY					1.16
120	over 1 acre	MSF					5.60
	Apply complete fertilizer and ground limestone, till and level						
130	1000 SF or less	SY					9.00
140	over 1000 SF	SY					1.20
150	over 1 acre	MSF					8.40
	Mix planting soil of composted manure, peat moss, and on-site topsoil						
160	1 CY or less	CCY					4.20
170	over 1 CY	CCY					3.12
	Mix planting soil of composted manure, peat moss, and purchased screened loam						
180	1 CY or less	CCY					4.71
190	over 1 CY	CCY					3.63
10	**TOPSOIL**						
	Loam topsoil, delivered to site						
100	natural	CCY				13.16	17.80
110		LCY				7.35	9.90
120	screened	CCY				16.92	22.80
130		LCY				9.45	12.80
	Load, haul, and dump topsoil on site, see Appendix I, "Hauling"						
20	**SOIL CONDITIONERS**						
	Spread granular or powdered soil conditioners (add material cost)						
100	by hand	MSF	1J	18	14.58		19.70
110	hand broadcast spreader	MSF	1J	70	3.75		5.10
120	push gravity spreader	MSF	1J	25	10.50		14.20
130	push broadcast spreader	MSF	1J	160	1.64		2.21
140	tractor drawn broadcast spreader	MSF	1G,50	695	0.42		0.57
	Spread organic soil conditioners (add material cost)						
150	by hand	MSF	1J	8	32.81		44.30
160	push gravity spreader	MSF	1J	22	11.93		16.10
170	manure spreader	MSF	1G,50	275	1.07		1.45
	Agricultural fertilizer						
190	0-20-20	Lb				0.12	0.16
200	3-9-9	Lb				0.12	0.16
210	3-9-18	Lb				0.09	0.12
220	4-8-12	Lb				0.12	0.16
230	5-10-10	Lb				0.09	0.12
240	5-10-15	Lb				0.09	0.12
250	5-20-20	Lb				0.12	0.16
260	6-6-6	Lb				0.11	0.15
270	6-12-12	Lb				0.11	0.15
280	6-24-24	Lb				0.13	0.18
290	8-24-24	Lb				0.13	0.18
300	8-32-16	Lb				0.14	0.19
310	10-10-10	Lb				0.11	0.15
320	10-15-15	Lb				0.13	0.18
330	10-20-10	Lb				0.12	0.16

PLANTING

KEY	DESCRIPTION	UNIT	CREW AND EQUIPMENT	PER DAY	INSTALLATION COST	MATERIALS COST	TOTAL + 35%
340	10-20-20	Lb				0.13	0.18
350	10-34-0	Lb				0.14	0.19
355	11-52-0	Lb				0.16	0.22
360	12-12-12	Lb				0.12	0.16
370	13-13-13	Lb				0.12	0.16
380	15-15-15	Lb				0.13	0.18
390	16-20-0	Lb				0.14	0.19
400	18-46-0	Lb				0.14	0.19
410	19-9-0	Lb				0.19	0.26
	Lawn and garden fertilizer						
430	5-10-5	Lb				0.99	1.34
440	Aluminum sulfate	Lb				0.46	0.62
450	Ammonium nitrate	Lb				0.10	0.14
460	Ammonium sulfate	Lb				0.11	0.15
464	Anhydrous ammonia	Lb				0.12	0.16
466	Aqua ammonia	Lb				0.13	0.18
470	Calcium nitrate	Lb				0.26	0.35
480	Magnesium sulfate	Lb				0.53	0.72
490	Muriate of potash	Lb				0.07	0.09
500	Potassium nitrate	Lb				0.38	0.51
510	Sodium nitrate	Lb				0.10	0.14
520	Super phosphate	Lb				0.11	0.15
530	Urea	Lb				0.11	0.15
540	Prilled slow release fertilizer, 16-7-12	Lb				3.09	4.17
	Limestone, ground						
550	regular	Ton				71.00	96.00
560	dolomitic	Ton				78.00	105.00
570	Hydrated lime	Lb				0.12	0.16
590	Peat moss	LCF				2.05	2.77
595		CCF				3.49	4.71
600	Peat humus	Lb				0.70	0.95
610	Composted manure	LCF				3.20	4.32
615		Lb				0.04	0.05
620	Sand	LCF				0.36	0.49
630	Perlite	LCF				1.89	2.55
640	Vermiculite	LCF				1.72	2.32
30	**TILLING**						
	Till soil						
	light soil						
	2" deep						
100	by hand	SY	1J	95	2.76		3.73
110	26" tiller	SY	1J,71	1225	0.24		0.32
120	6' disk	MSF	1G,50	460	0.64		0.86
130	12' disk	MSF	1G,51	860	0.40		0.54
	4" deep						
140	by hand	SY	1J	75	3.50		4.72
150	26" tiller	SY	1J,71	980	0.30		0.40
160	6' disk	MSF	1G,50	370	0.80		1.08
170	12' disk	MSF	1G,51	690	0.50		0.67

02920 Soil Preparation   1994

KEY	DESCRIPTION	UNIT	CREW AND EQUIPMENT	PER DAY	INSTALLATION COST	MATERIALS COST	TOTAL + 35%
	6" deep						
180	by hand	SY	1J	56	4.69		6.30
190	26" tiller	SY	1J,71	735	0.40		0.54
200	6' disk	MSF	1G,50	275	1.07		1.45
210	12' disk	MSF	1G,51	550	0.63		0.85
	8" deep						
220	26" tiller	SY	1J,71	490	0.60		0.81
230	6' disk	MSF	1G,50	185	1.59		2.15
240	12' disk	MSF	1G,51	345	1.00		1.35
	medium soil						
	2" deep						
250	by hand	SY	1J	75	3.50		4.72
260	26" tiller	SY	1J,71	890	0.33		0.44
270	6' disk	MSF	1G,50	395	0.75		1.01
280	12' disk	MSF	1G,51	730	0.47		0.64
	4" deep						
290	by hand	SY	1J	60	4.37		5.90
300	26" tiller	SY	1J,71	710	0.41		0.56
310	6' disk	MSF	1G,50	315	0.94		1.26
320	12' disk	MSF	1G,51	535	0.64		0.87
	6" deep						
330	by hand	SY	1J	45	5.83		7.90
340	26" tiller	SY	1J,71	535	0.55		0.74
350	6' disk	MSF	1G,50	235	1.25		1.69
360	12' disk	MSF	1G,51	440	0.78		1.06
	8" deep						
370	26" tiller	SY	1J,71	355	0.82		1.11
380	6' disk	MSF	1G,50	160	1.84		2.49
390	12' disk	MSF	1G,51	290	1.19		1.60
	heavy soil						
	2" deep						
400	by hand	SY	1J	60	4.37		5.90
410	26" tiller	SY	1J,71	550	0.53		0.72
420	6' disk	MSF	1G,50	325	0.91		1.22
430	12' disk	MSF	1G,51	605	0.57		0.77
	4" deep						
440	by hand	SY	1J	45	5.83		7.90
450	26" tiller	SY	1J,71	440	0.66		0.90
460	6' disk	MSF	1G,50	260	1.13		1.53
470	12' disk	MSF	1G,51	485	0.71		0.96
	6" deep						
480	by hand	SY	1J	35	7.50		10.10
490	26" tiller	SY	1J,71	330	0.89		1.20
500	6' disk	MSF	1G,50	195	1.51		2.04
510	12' disk	MSF	1G,51	365	0.94		1.27
	8" deep						
520	26" tiller	SY	1J,71	220	1.33		1.79
530	6' disk	MSF	1G,50	130	2.27		3.06
540	12' disk	MSF	1G,51	240	1.44		1.94
	Level surface						
550	by hand	SY	1J	890	0.29		0.40
560	6' drag harrow	MSF	1G,50	490	0.60		0.81
570	12' drag harrow	MSF	1G,51	915	0.38		0.51
40	**MIXING**						
	Mix planting soil mix						
100	by hand	CCF	1J	215	1.22		1.65
110	1/2 CY wheel loader	CCF	1G,10	1545	0.31		0.42
120	soil shredder	CCF	1J1G,64	2430	0.28		0.38

PLANTING

KEY	DESCRIPTION	UNIT	CREW AND EQUIPMENT	PER DAY	INSTALLATION COST	MATERIALS COST	TOTAL + 35%
00	**COMPOSITE COSTS**						
	Sow lawn grass seed, cover, water, and mulch						
100	1000 SF or less	SY					0.53
110	over 1000 SF	SY					0.38
120	over 1 acre	MSF					27.80
	Lay lawn grass sod, roll, water						
130	north	SY					3.10
140	west	SY					3.22
150	south	SY					4.87
	Sprig lawn grass stolons, water, and mulch						
160	1000 SF or less	SY					0.76
170	over 1000 SF	SY					0.42
180	over 1 acre	MSF					32.50
	Broadcast lawn grass stolons, cover, water and mulch						
190	1000 SF or less	SY					0.99
200	over 1000 SF	SY					0.44
210	over 1 acre	MSF					34.70
220	Set lawn grass plugs, water	SY					1.15
	Hydroseed lawn grass seed, fertilizer, and mulch						
230	congested	MSF					87.00
240	open area	MSF					77.00
10	**SEEDING**						
	Sow seed (add seed cost)						
100	hand broadcast spreader	MSF	1J	70	2.71		3.66
105	push broadcast spreader	MSF	1J	160	1.18		1.60
110	broadcast spreader, tractor drawn	MSF	1G,50	695	0.42		0.57
115	6' seed drill	MSF	1G,50	495	0.60		0.80
120	12' seed drill	MSF	1G,51	915	0.38		0.51
	800 gallon hydraulic planter						
125	congested area	MSF	1J1D,60	627	0.91		1.23
130	open area	MSF	1J1D,60	1255	0.46		0.61
	1500 gallon hydraulic planter						
135	congested area	MSF	1J1D,61	810	0.80		1.08
140	open area	MSF	1J1D,61	1620	0.40		0.54
	Kentucky bluegrass seed						
	Certified Blue Tag (add $0.05 for Gold Tag, deduct $0.05 for uncertified)						
145	A-34	Lb				2.71	3.66
150	Adelphi	Lb				2.63	3.55
155	Baron	Lb				1.75	2.36
175	Eclipse	Lb				2.70	3.65
180	Fylking	Lb				2.00	2.70
185	Glade	Lb				2.36	3.19
190	Julia	Lb				2.04	2.75
195	Merion	Lb				2.55	3.44
205	Midnight	Lb				2.35	3.17
215	Nassau	Lb				1.81	2.44
220	Newport	Lb				0.76	1.03
225	Nugget	Lb				2.90	3.92
235	Park	Lb				0.78	1.05
245	Ram I	Lb				2.31	3.12
260	S-21	Lb				0.80	1.08
	uncertified						
280	Common 85-80	Lb				0.54	0.73
285	Common 98/85	Lb				0.59	0.80
290	Poa trivialis	Lb				2.30	3.11

KEY	DESCRIPTION	UNIT	CREW AND EQUIPMENT	PER DAY	INSTALLATION COST	MATERIALS COST	TOTAL + 35%
	Fescue seed						
295	chewings fescue	Lb				0.93	1.26
300	Atlanta chewings	Lb				1.55	2.09
305	Jamestown chewings	Lb				1.28	1.73
310	Koket	Lb				1.55	2.09
315	Shadow	Lb				1.10	1.49
320	creeping red fescue	Lb				0.70	0.95
325	Dawson creeping red	Lb				1.52	2.05
330	Pennlawn creeping red	Lb				0.76	1.03
335	Ruby creeping red	Lb				1.45	1.96
	hard fescue						
340	Biljart	Lb				1.22	1.65
345	Reliant hard	Lb				1.71	2.31
350	Scaldis hard	Lb				1.66	2.24
	tall fescue						
355	Adventure tall	Lb				1.85	2.50
360	Brookstone tall	Lb				1.63	2.20
365	Falcon tall	Lb				1.65	2.23
370	Galway tall	Lb				1.43	1.93
375	Kentucky 31 tall	Lb				0.76	1.03
380	Mustang tall	Lb				1.52	2.05
385	Olympic tall	Lb				1.52	2.05
390	Rebel tall	Lb				1.25	1.69
395	Triathalawn tall	Lb				1.65	2.23
	Ryegrass seed						
400	annual ryegrass	Lb				0.30	0.41
405	perennial ryegrass	Lb				0.75	1.01
410	All star perennial	Lb				0.81	1.09
415	Barry perennial	Lb				0.81	1.09
420	Cowboy perennial	Lb				0.95	1.28
425	Derby perennial	Lb				0.88	1.19
430	Fiesta perennial	Lb				0.86	1.16
435	Goalie perennial	Lb				0.89	1.20
440	Manhattan perennial, uncertified	Lb				0.96	1.30
445	Manhattan II perennial	Lb				1.00	1.35
450	Palmer perennial	Lb				0.98	1.32
455	Pennant perennial	Lb				0.89	1.20
460	Pennfine perennial	Lb				0.98	1.32
465	Prelude perennial	Lb				0.98	1.32
470	Premier perennial	Lb				0.80	1.08
475	Regal perennial	Lb				0.85	1.15
480	Repell perennial	Lb				1.00	1.35
485	Tara perennial	Lb				1.02	1.38
490	Yorktown II perennial	Lb				0.97	1.31
	Bentgrass seed, Certified, Blue Tag						
500	Astoria	Lb				6.60	8.90
505	Emerald	Lb				7.10	9.60
510	Highland colonial	Lb				3.30	4.46
515	Penncross	Lb				7.80	10.50
520	Penneagle	Lb				7.30	9.90
525	Seaside	Lb				4.30	5.80
	Bermudagrass seed						
540	common hulled	Lb				2.20	2.97
545	unhulled	Lb				1.50	2.03

PLANTING

KEY	DESCRIPTION	UNIT	CREW AND EQUIPMENT	PER DAY	INSTALLATION COST	MATERIALS COST	TOTAL + 35%
550	Redtop seed	Lb				1.82	2.46
555	Timothy seed	Lb				1.32	1.78
560	Orchardgrass	Lb				1.55	2.09
563	Alfalfa, common	Lb				1.81	2.44
565	White clover seed	Lb				2.12	2.86
568	Red clover seed	Lb				1.43	1.93
570	Ladies white clover seed	Lb				2.94	3.97
575	Birdsfoot trefoil seed	Lb				2.70	3.65
580	Crownvetch seed, Penngift	Lb				12.90	17.40
585	"Fults" Puccinellia distans	Lb				2.75	3.71
	Native grass seed, PLS						
590	Big bluestem, certified	Lb				11.00	14.90
595	Blue grama	Lb				10.20	13.80
600	Buffalograss	Lb				15.10	20.40
605	Indiangrass, certified	Lb				9.10	12.30
610	Little bluestem, certified	Lb				13.80	18.60
620	Sand bluestem	Lb				11.20	15.10
630	Sideoats grama, certified	Lb				7.00	9.50
635	Switchgrass, certified	Lb				6.10	8.20
640	Western wheatgrass, Baron	Lb				7.10	9.60
645	Western wheatgrass, South Dakota	Lb				6.10	8.20
20	**SPRIGGING**						
	Sprig stolons, (add stolon cost)						
	in rows						
	by hand						
100	6" spacing	SY	1J	445	0.43		0.58
110	9" spacing	SY	1J	835	0.23		0.31
120	12" spacing	SY	1J	1185	0.16		0.22
130	walk behind sprig planter	MSF	1J,76	80	2.93		3.96
140	small towed sprig planter	MSF	1G,50	495	0.60		0.80
150	large towed sprig planter	MSF	1G,51	915	0.38		0.51
	spot, by hand						
160	6" O.C.	SY	1J	445	0.43		0.58
170	9" O.C.	SY	1J	835	0.23		0.31
180	12" O.C.	SY	1J	1185	0.16		0.22
	Broadcast stolons (add stolon cost)						
	by hand						
190	2 Bu per MSF	SY	1J	1780	0.11		0.14
200	4 Bu per MSF	SY	1J	1185	0.16		0.22
210	6 Bu per MSF	SY	1J	890	0.21		0.29
220	manure spreader	MSF	1G,50	195	1.51		2.04
	800 gallon hydraulic planter						
230	congested area	MSF	1J1D,60	50	11.43		15.40
240	open area	MSF	1J1D,60	100	5.72		7.70
	1500 gallon hydraulic planter						
250	congested area	MSF	1J1D,61	75	8.62		11.60
260	open area	MSF	1J1D,61	150	4.31		5.80
270	Hybrid Bermudagrass stolons	Bu				2.10	2.84
30	**SODDING**						
	Place sod (add sod cost)						
100	on level ground	SY	2J	400	0.95		1.28
110	on slope with stakes	SY	2J	320	1.18	0.09	1.72
	Set plugs (add sod cost)						
120	6" O.C.	SY	1J	180	1.05		1.42
130	9" O.C.	SY	1J	370	0.51		0.69
140	12" O.C.	SY	1J	595	0.32		0.43

PLANTING

02930 Lawns and Grass

1994

KEY	DESCRIPTION	UNIT	CREW AND EQUIPMENT	PER DAY	INSTALLATION COST	MATERIALS COST	TOTAL + 35%
	Sod (site delivery not included)						
	in Northwest and Midwest						
150	Kentucky bluegrass blend or mix	SY				1.21	1.63
160	bentgrass	SY				2.54	3.43
	in Great Plains and West						
170	Kentucky bluegrass blend or mix	SY				1.30	1.76
180	bentgrass	SY				2.75	3.71
	in South						
210	Bermudagrass, hybrid	SY				2.52	3.40
220	St. Augustine grass	SY				3.95	5.30
230	Zoysiagrass	SY				3.10	4.19
240	Centipede grass	SY				2.20	2.97
250	bluegrass blend	SY				1.63	2.20
260	bluegrass/ryegrass mix	SY				1.72	2.32
	Sod site delivery, add						
270	under 10 miles	SY				0.20	0.27
280	10 to 30 miles	SY				0.33	0.45
290	35 to 60 miles	SY				0.41	0.55
300	65 to 90 miles	SY				0.47	0.63
40	**COVERING**						
	Work seed into soil						
100	by hand	SY	1J	1780	0.11		0.14
110	6' drag harrow	MSF	1G,50	460	0.64		0.86
120	12' drag harrow	MSF	1G,51	860	0.40		0.54
	Work stolons into soil						
130	by hand	SY	1J	800	0.24		0.32
140	6' disk	MSF	1G,50	345	0.85		1.15
150	12' disk	MSF	1G,51	645	0.53		0.72
	Topdress over seed or stolons (add material cost)						
160	by hand	SY	1J	535	0.35		0.48
170	manure spreader	MSF	1G,50	295	1.00		1.35
50	**ROLLING**						
	Roll sod or soil surface						
100	push roller	SY	1J	3555	0.05		0.07
110	roller, tractor drawn	MSF	1G,50	210	1.40		1.89
60	**MULCHING**						
	Spread straw or hay (add material cost)						
100	by hand	Lb	1J	1280	0.15		0.20
110	small power mulcher	Ton	1D2J,62	27	28.00		37.80
120	large power mulcher	Ton	1D4J,63	80	15.13		20.40
130	Straw	Ton				87.00	117.00
140	Hay	Ton				68.40	92.00
150	Asphalt emulsion, applied simultaneously with hay or straw from power mulcher, add to above costs	Gal				1.49	2.01
	Wood cellulose fiber mulch						
	800 gallon hydraulic mulcher						
160	congested area	Lb	1D1J,60	2250	0.25	0.20	0.61
170	open area	Lb	1D1J,60	4500	0.13	0.20	0.44
	1500 gallon hydraulic mulcher						
180	congested area	Lb	1D1J,61	3410	0.19	0.20	0.53
190	open area	Lb	1D1J,61	6820	0.09	0.20	0.40

PLANTING

02930 Lawns and Grass   1994

KEY	DESCRIPTION	UNIT	CREW AND EQUIPMENT	PER DAY	INSTALLATION COST	MATERIALS COST	TOTAL + 35%
	Wood cellulose fiber mulch with soil stabilizer or mulch tack added						
	800 gallon hydraulic mulcher						
200	congested area	Lb	1D1J,60			0.65	0.88
210	open area	Lb	1D1J,60			0.65	0.88
	1500 gallon hydraulic mulcher						
220	congested area	Lb	1D1J,61			0.65	0.88
230	open area	Lb	1D1J,61			0.65	0.88
	For seeding and/or fertilizing simultaeously with wood cellulose fiber mulch application, add seed and fertilizer material costs to above mulching costs.						

02950 Trees, Plants, and Ground Covers

KEY	DESCRIPTION	UNIT	CREW AND EQUIPMENT	PER DAY	INSTALLATION COST	MATERIALS COST	TOTAL + 35%
00	**COMPOSITE COSTS**						
	Shade tree, balled and burlapped, plant, prune, mulch, wrap, and guy (includes plant material cost as indicated)						
	on site topsoil backfill						
100	1 1/4" caliper (@ $64)	Ea					148.00
110	2" caliper (@ $146)	Ea					292.00
120	3" caliper (@ $257)	Ea					520.00
130	4" caliper (@ $400)	Ea					820.00
140	5" caliper (@ $590)	Ea					1210.00
	prepared mix backfill						
150	1 1/4" caliper (@ $64)	Ea					166.00
160	2" caliper (@ $146)	Ea					318.00
170	3" caliper (@ $257)	Ea					600.00
180	4" caliper (@ $400)	Ea					1010.00
190	5" caliper (@ $590)	Ea					1530.00
	Small tree, balled and burlapped, plant, prune, mulch, and wrap (includes plant material cost as indicated)						
	on site topsoil backfill						
200	3' height (@ $30)	Ea					70.00
210	4' height (@ $42)	Ea					94.00
220	5' height (@ $53)	Ea					120.00
230	6' height (@ $72)	Ea					162.00
240	8' height (@ $118)	Ea					265.00
	prepared mix backfill						
250	3' height (@ $30)	Ea					82.00
260	4' height (@ $42)	Ea					109.00
270	5' height (@ $53)	Ea					137.00
280	6' height (@ $72)	Ea					186.00
290	8' height (@ $118)	Ea					319.00
	Coniferous evergreen tree, balled and burlapped, plant, prune, mulch, and guy (includes plant material cost as indicated)						
	on site topsoil backfill						
300	3' height (@ $46)	Ea					110.00
310	4' height (@ $74)	Ea					139.00
320	5' height (@ $101)	Ea					188.00
330	6' height (@ $135)	Ea					273.00
340	8' height (@ $212)	Ea					405.00
350	10' height (@ $280)	Ea					510.00
	prepared mix backfill						
360	3' height (@ $46)	Ea					124.00
370	4' height (@ $74)	Ea					157.00
380	5' height (@ $101)	Ea					212.00

02950 Trees, Plants, and Ground Covers — 1994

KEY	DESCRIPTION	UNIT	CREW AND EQUIPMENT	PER DAY	INSTALLATION COST	MATERIALS COST	TOTAL + 35%
390	6' height (@ $135)	Ea					323.00
400	8' height (@ $212)	Ea					474.00
410	10' height (@ $280)	Ea					710.00
	Deciduous shrub, balled and burlapped, plant, prune, and mulch (plant material cost included as indicated) on site topsoil						
420	15" height (@ $14)	Ea					38.70
430	18" height (@ $16)	Ea					42.50
440	2' height (@ $16)	Ea					45.50
450	3' height (@ $21)	Ea					59.00
460	4' height (@ $29)	Ea					68.00
	prepared mix backfill						
470	15" height (@ $14)	Ea					64.00
480	18" height (@ $16)	Ea					49.90
490	2' height (@ $16)	Ea					58.00
500	3' height (@ $21)	Ea					69.00
510	4' height (@ $29)	Ea					82.00
	Evergreen shrub, balled and burlapped, plant, prune, and mulch (plant material cost included) on site topsoil backfill						
520	18" ht or spread (@ $28)	Ea					55.00
530	2' ht or spread (@ $34)	Ea					67.00
540	2 1/2' ht or spread (@ $41)	Ea					81.00
550	3' ht or spread (@ $61)	Ea					105.00
560	3 1/2' ht or spread (@ $94)	Ea					139.00
	prepared mix backfill						
570	18" ht or spread (@ $28)	Ea					64.00
580	2' ht or spread (@ $34)	Ea					79.00
590	2 1/2' ht or spread (@ $41)	Ea					96.00
600	3' ht or spread (@ $61)	Ea					123.00
610	3 1/2' ht or spread (@ $94)	Ea					161.00
	Ground covers, planted 1' O.C. in prepared bed, mulch (includes plant material cost as indicated)						
620	bare root, 2 yr (@ $4.10)	SY					44.90
630	2" - 3" peat pots (@ $1.72 Ea)	SY					13.40
640	Ground cover or vine, 1 gallon container in prepared bed, mulch (includes plant material cost @ $4.95)	Ea					10.10
	Stone mulch						
	mulch bed 2" deep						
650	volcanic rock	SY					12.40
660	marble chips	SY					8.40
670	washed gravel	SY					6.60
	place polyethylene film and mulch bed 2" deep						
680	volcanic rock	SY					13.00
690	marble chips	SY					8.90
700	washed gravel	SY					7.20
	place filter fabric and mulch bed 2" deep						
710	volcanic rock	SY					14.00
720	marble chips	SY					9.90
730	washed gravel	SY					8.20
	Organic mulch						
	construct earth rim around plant, mulch with wood chips 3" deep						
740	2' diameter	Ea					3.28
750	4' diameter	Ea					7.80
760	6' diameter	Ea					15.40

PLANTING

KEY	DESCRIPTION	UNIT	CREW AND EQUIPMENT	PER DAY	INSTALLATION COST	MATERIALS COST	TOTAL + 35%
	mulch shrub bed 3" deep						
770	wood chips	SY					3.28
780	ground redwood bark	SY					6.30
	mulch ground cover bed 1 1/2" deep						
790	wood chips	SY					1.64
800	ground redwood bark	SY					3.17
10	**PLANTING TREES AND SHRUBS**						
100	Stake out tree locations	Ea	2J	200	1.90		2.56
110	Stake out shrub locations	Ea	2J	300	1.26		1.71
	Dig planting pit for shrub or tree (see Appendix N, "Planting Pit Volumes")						
	light soil						
120	by hand	BCF	1J	160	1.18		1.60
130	1/4 CY backhoe	BCF	1G1J,13	2700	0.20		0.27
140	earth auger	Ea	1G1J,51	100	5.34		7.20
	medium soil						
150	by hand	BCF	1J	110	1.72		2.33
160	1/4 CY backhoe	BCF	1G1J,13	2700	0.20		0.27
170	earth auger	Ea	1G1J,51	100	5.34		7.20
	heavy soil						
180	by hand	BCF	1J	95	2.00		2.69
190	1/4 CY backhoe	BCF	1G1J,13	1890	0.29		0.39
200	earth auger	Ea	1G1J,51	80	6.68		9.00
	hardpan or rocky soil						
210	air tools	BCF	1G2L,86	110	6.62		8.90
220	1/4 CY backhoe	BCF	1G1J,13	1510	0.36		0.49
230	earth auger	Ea	1G1J,51	50	10.69		14.40
	Place shrub or tree (see Appendix M for ball weights) (add plant material cost)						
	by hand						
240	to 50 Lb or bareroot	Ea	1J	150	1.26		1.71
250	50-100 Lb	Ea	1J	100	1.90		2.56
260	100-200 Lb	Ea	2J	100	3.79		5.10
270	200-300 Lb	Ea	3J	50	11.37		15.40
280	300-400 Lb	Ea	4J	35	21.66		29.20
290	400-500 Lb	Ea	5J	25	37.91		51.00
	1-2 CY wheel loader						
300	100-500 Lb	Ea	1G2J,10	75	11.52		15.50
310	500-1000 Lb	Ea	1G2J,10	50	17.28		23.30
	boom truck						
320	500-2000 Lb	Ea	1D2J,07	50	20.32		27.40
330	over 2000 Lb	Ea	1D2J,07	25	40.64		55.00
	Backfill planting pit (see Appendix O, "Backfill Volumes") (add material cost)						
340	light soil	CCF	1J	270	0.70		0.95
350	medium soil	CCF	1J	230	0.82		1.11
360	heavy soil	CCF	1J	175	1.08		1.46
	Fertilizer tablet						
370	10 gram	Ea				0.06	0.08
380	21 gram	Ea				0.11	0.15
20	**PRUNING**						
	Prune tree of dead and injured wood						
100	to 7' height or 1" caliper	Ea	1J	95	2.00		2.69
110	to 12' height or 2" caliper	Ea	1J	50	3.79		5.10
120	over 2" caliper	Ea	2J	50	7.58		10.20

02950 Trees, Plants, and Ground Covers

KEY	DESCRIPTION	UNIT	CREW AND EQUIPMENT	PER DAY	INSTALLATION COST	MATERIALS COST	TOTAL + 35%
	Prune tree of dead and injured wood, and 1/4 to 1/2 of live wood						
130	to 7' height or 1" caliper	Ea	1J	35	5.42		7.30
140	to 12' height or 2" caliper	Ea	1J	20	9.48		12.80
150	over 2" caliper	Ea	2J	20	18.96		25.60
	Prune shrub of dead and injured wood						
160	under 3' height	Ea	1J	195	0.97		1.31
170	3' - 6' height	Ea	1J	95	2.00		2.69
180	over 6' height	Ea	1J	50	3.79		5.10
	Prune shrub of dead and injured wood, and 1/4 to 1/2 of live wood						
190	under 3' height	Ea	1J	70	2.71		3.66
200	3' - 6' height	Ea	1J	35	5.42		7.30
210	over 6' height	Ea	1J	18	10.53		14.20
30	**WRAPPING AND GUYING**						
	Apply tree wrap to first branches of tree and tie						
	duplex paper						
100	to 8" height	Ea	1J	150	1.26	0.21	1.99
110	1" - 1 3/4" caliper	Ea	1J	95	2.00	0.52	3.40
120	2" - 3 1/2" caliper	Ea	1J	50	3.79	1.34	6.90
130	4" - 6" caliper	Ea	1J	35	5.42	2.87	11.20
	burlap						
140	to 8" height	Ea	1J	150	1.26	0.08	1.81
150	1" - 1 3/4" caliper	Ea	1J	95	2.00	0.19	2.95
160	2" - 3 1/2" caliper	Ea	1J	50	3.79	0.46	5.70
170	4" - 6" caliper	Ea	1J	35	5.42	0.97	8.60
	Tree guard						
	preformed plastic						
180	24" height	Ea	1J	250	0.76	0.53	1.74
185	36" height	Ea	1J	250	0.76	0.79	2.09
190	wire mesh	Ea	1J	95	2.00	1.53	4.76
	Guy tree, under 3" caliper, hose covered wire						
200	1 stake, 7' x 2 1/2" diameter	Ea	1J	45	4.21	1.10	7.20
210	2 stakes, 8' x 3" diameter	Ea	1J	25	7.58	4.61	16.50
220	3 stakes, 3' x 2" x 4"	Ea	2J	25	15.16	3.94	25.80
230	3 earth anchors, 18"	Ea	2J	21	18.05	8.20	35.40
	Guy tree, 3" - 6" caliper						
	hose-covered wire						
240	3 earth anchors, 24"	Ea	2J	19	19.95	20.70	55.00
250	3 deadmen	Ea	2J	14	27.08	11.80	52.00
	cable						
260	3 earth anchors, 24"	Ea	2J	19	19.95	26.00	62.00
270	3 deadmen	Ea	2J	14	27.08	16.50	59.00
	cable, turnbuckles						
280	3 earth anchors, 24"	Ea	2J	14	27.08	53.00	108.00
290	3 deadmen	Ea	2J	11	34.46	43.90	106.00
	Guy tree, over 6" caliper						
	cable						
300	3 earth anchors, 24"	Ea	2J	14	27.08	31.90	80.00
310	3 deadmen	Ea	2J	11	34.46	25.80	81.00
	cable, turnbuckles						
320	3 earth anchors, 24"	Ea	2J	11	34.46	66.00	136.00
330	3 deadmen	Ea	2J	9	42.12	59.00	137.00
40	**GROUND COVERS AND VINES**						
	Plant bare root plant (add plant material cost)						
100	1 year	Ea	1J	400	0.47		0.64
110	2 year	Ea	1J	280	0.68		0.91

PLANTING

KEY	DESCRIPTION	UNIT	CREW AND EQUIPMENT	PER DAY	INSTALLATION COST	MATERIALS COST	TOTAL + 35%
	Plant peat potted plant (add plant material cost)						
120	2 1/4" pot	Ea	1J	600	0.32		0.43
130	3" pot	Ea	1J	400	0.47		0.64
140	4" pot	Ea	1J	280	0.68		0.91
	Plant container plant (add plant material cost)						
150	1 quart	Ea	1J	100	1.90		2.56
160	1 gallon	Ea	1J	60	3.16		4.26
170	2 gallon	Ea	1J	45	4.21		5.70
180	3 gallon	Ea	1J	35	5.42		7.30
190	5 gallon	Ea	1J	25	7.58		10.20
	Fertilizer tablet						
200	5 gram	Ea				0.03	0.04
210	10 gram	Ea				0.05	0.07
50	**BED EDGING**						
	Painted steel edging, staked						
110	4" x 1/8"	LF	1J	400	0.47	1.87	3.16
120	4" x 3/16"	LF	1J	300	0.63	2.19	3.81
130	5" x 1/4"	LF	1J	240	0.79	2.78	4.82
	Aluminum edging, staked plain						
140	4" x 1/8"	LF	1J	750	0.25	1.73	2.68
150	4" x 3/16"	LF	1J	550	0.34	2.51	3.85
152	5 1/2" x 1/8"			680	0.19	2.51	3.39
155	5 1/2" x 3/16"			530	0.25	3.36	4.54
	black anodized						
160	4" x 1/8"	LF	1J	750	0.25	2.31	3.46
170	4" x 3/16"	LF	1J	550	0.34	3.36	5.00
172	5 1/2" x 1/8"			680	0.19	3.36	4.54
175	5 1/2" x 3/16"			530	0.25	4.49	6.10
	Polyethylene edging, tubular top, anchor hook bottom, staked						
180	5" x 1/8"	LF	1J	400	0.47	0.49	1.30
190	corner, tee, or vee connector	Ea	1J	240	0.79	1.60	3.23
	Polyethylene edging, common, staked						
200	4 5/8" x 5/32"	LF	1J	400	0.47	0.52	1.40
210	4 5/8" x 1/4"	LF	1J	370	0.51	0.83	1.81
230	90 degree angle	Ea	1J	240	0.79	1.60	3.23
	Redwood, cedar or cypress						
	straight						
310	1" x 4"	LF	1J	320	0.59	0.86	1.96
320	1" x 6"	LF	1J	240	0.79	0.66	1.96
330	2" x 4"	LF	1J	240	0.79	0.84	2.20
340	2" x 6"	LF	1J	200	0.95	0.96	2.58
	curved						
350	1" x 4"	LF	1J	200	0.95	0.65	2.16
360	1" x 6"	LF	1J	160	1.18	0.81	2.69
60	**EARTH RIM**						
	Construct earth rim around plant for watering basin						
100	2' diameter	Ea	1J	120	1.58		2.13
110	3' diameter	Ea	1J	95	2.00		2.69
120	4' diameter	Ea	1J	80	2.37		3.20
130	5' diameter	Ea	1J	65	2.92		3.94
140	6' diameter	Ea	1J	50	3.79		5.10
70	**WEED BARRIER FILM**						
	Black polyethylene film						
100	1.5 mil	SY	1J	800	0.24	0.08	0.43
110	4 mil	SY	1J	800	0.24	0.19	0.58
120	6 mil	SY	1J	800	0.24	0.28	0.70
130	Filter fabric, spun bonded polyurethane	SY	1J	800	0.24	0.93	1.58

02950 Trees, Plants, and Ground Covers

KEY	DESCRIPTION	UNIT	CREW AND EQUIPMENT	PER DAY	INSTALLATION COST	MATERIALS COST	TOTAL + 35%
80	**STONE MULCH**						
100	Volcanic rock, red or black, 3/4" - 1 1/2"	CF	1J	350	0.54	5.60	8.30
110	White marble chips	CF	1J	300	0.63	3.50	5.60
115	White crushed stone	CF	1J	300	0.63	2.00	3.55
120	Granite chips	CF	1J	300	0.63	2.15	3.76
130	River rock	CF	1J	300	0.63	2.65	4.43
90	**ORGANIC MULCH**						
100	Wood chips, clean	LCF	1J	500	0.38	0.70	1.46
110	Shredded cypress	LCF	1J	500	0.38	1.55	2.60
	Decorative redwood bark						
120	nuggets	LCF	1J	500	0.38	1.71	2.82
125	chunks	LCF	1J	500	0.38	1.71	2.82
130	Ground or shredded hardwood bark	LCF	1J	500	0.38	1.10	2.00
160	Peat moss	LCF	1J	350	0.54	1.89	3.28
170	Straw	LCF	1J	350	0.54	0.08	0.84
180	Hay	LCF	1J	350	0.54	0.06	0.81

PLANTING

DESCRIPTION	HIGH	LOW	AVG.
These costs for plant materials are derived from a national survey of wholesale plant costs. The costs shown here are those wholesale costs plus 50% for overhead and profit.			
200 Acer campestre			
balled and burlapped			
1 1/2" cal	120.00	96.00	106.00
1 3/4" cal	158.00	98.00	133.00
2" cal	195.00	128.00	168.00
2 1/2" cal	251.00	150.00	218.00
3" cal	291.00	225.00	269.00
bare root			
1 1/2" cal	77.00	65.00	68.00
202 Acer circinatum			
container			
15 gal	83.00	56.00	67.00
24" box	248.00	225.00	236.00
204 Acer ginnala			
balled and burlapped			
1 1/2" cal	120.00	59.00	88.00
1 3/4" cal	195.00	83.00	124.00
2" cal	240.00	98.00	154.00
2 1/2" cal	241.00	173.00	198.00
3' ht	60.00	22.50	38.00
4' ht	81.00	22.90	51.00
5' ht	105.00	24.40	69.00
6' ht	134.00	28.90	91.00
8' ht	203.00	39.40	106.00
206 Acer ginnala 'Flame'			
balled and burlapped			
1 3/4" cal	158.00	90.00	129.00
2" cal	203.00	114.00	167.00
2 1/2" cal	260.00	143.00	211.00
4' ht	81.00	22.50	59.00
5' ht	105.00	37.50	79.00
6' ht	134.00	39.80	89.00
208 Acer ginnala, multi-stem			
balled and burlapped			
3' ht	69.00	31.50	44.70
4' ht	99.00	18.40	56.00
5' ht	173.00	24.40	85.00
6' ht	210.00	26.60	114.00
8' ht	228.00	36.40	173.00
210 Acer griseum			
balled and burlapped			
1 3/4" cal	255.00	204.00	234.00
6' ht	204.00	155.00	177.00
container			
5 gal	74.00	29.30	45.20
212 Acer negundo 'Variegatum'			
bare root			
5' ht	13.90	13.00	13.40
6' ht	15.20	14.90	15.10

See pages 91 and 92 for more generic plant
material costs and composite planting costs.

DESCRIPTION	HIGH	LOW	AVG.
214 Acer nigrum			
balled and burlapped			
2" cal	270.00	225.00	215.00
2 1/2" cal	337.00	195.00	267.00
216 Acer palmatum			
balled and burlapped			
1 1/2" cal	161.00	96.00	133.00
2" cal	225.00	134.00	186.00
2 1/2" cal	270.00	162.00	228.00
5' ht	113.00	38.20	84.00
6' ht	143.00	46.80	106.00
container			
1 gal	8.90	4.73	5.80
5 gal	45.00	15.40	23.80
15 gal	71.00	54.00	63.00
24" box	338.00	225.00	254.00
36" box	610.00	600.00	600.00
218 Acer palmatum 'Atropurpureum'			
balled and burlapped			
3' ht	135.00	36.40	74.00
4' ht	165.00	44.90	106.00
5' ht	225.00	58.00	132.00
6' ht	338.00	72.00	192.00
8' ht	339.00	227.00	275.00
container			
2 gal	34.50	18.80	26.30
3 gal	35.30	18.90	27.00
5 gal	68.00	19.50	34.50
15 gal	83.00	60.00	74.00
24" box	255.00	225.00	242.00
220 Acer palmatum 'Bloodgood'			
balled and burlapped			
1 1/2" cal	263.00	180.00	214.00
2" cal	59.00	32.40	45.30
2 1/2" cal	78.00	39.50	61.00
3' ht	143.00	54.00	93.00
4' ht	174.00	64.00	120.00
5' ht	276.00	75.00	185.00
6' ht	329.00	91.00	208.00
7' ht	441.00	198.00	305.00
8' ht	570.00	272.00	443.00
container			
5 gal	53.00	21.80	38.50
15 gal	98.00	60.00	77.00
222 Acer palmatum 'Dissectum'			
balled and burlapped			
2" cal	225.00	48.00	113.00
3' ht	216.00	91.00	148.00
224 Acer platanoides			
balled and burlapped			
1 1/4" cal	80.00	45.00	66.00
1 1/2" cal	105.00	66.00	92.00
1 3/4" cal	152.00	84.00	113.00
2" cal	195.00	105.00	142.00
2 1/2" cal	240.00	140.00	183.00
3" cal	372.00	173.00	249.00
3 1/2" cal	375.00	210.00	297.00
4" cal	488.00	263.00	372.00
4 1/2" cal	500.00	413.00	453.00
5" cal	680.00	477.00	590.00

02950 Trees, Shade and Flowering

DESCRIPTION	HIGH	LOW	AVG.
bare root			
1" cal	23.90	16.50	20.10
1 1/4" cal	54.00	19.40	28.70
1 1/2" cal	65.00	25.20	41.10
1 3/4" cal	83.00	35.70	57.00
2" cal	98.00	46.10	76.00
6' ht	22.10	12.20	17.10
226 Acer platanoides 'Cleveland'			
balled and burlapped			
1 1/2" cal	107.00	89.00	98.00
1 3/4" cal	152.00	104.00	125.00
2" cal	186.00	123.00	149.00
2 1/2" cal	221.00	164.00	191.00
3" cal	300.00	195.00	259.00
3 1/2" cal	368.00	258.00	327.00
4" cal	488.00	332.00	422.00
bare root			
1 1/4" cal	54.00	25.80	35.30
1 1/2" cal	65.00	35.20	48.00
1 3/4" cal	83.00	42.00	60.00
2" cal	98.00	47.30	66.00
6' ht	22.10	20.00	21.00
228 Acer platanoides 'Columnare'			
balled and burlapped			
1 1/2" cal	117.00	89.00	102.00
1 3/4" cal	164.00	104.00	127.00
2" cal	198.00	123.00	155.00
2 1/2" cal	233.00	164.00	194.00
3" cal	326.00	203.00	261.00
3 1/2" cal	386.00	233.00	319.00
4" cal	580.00	332.00	431.00
4 1/2" cal	920.00	398.00	610.00
5" cal	1280.00	473.00	800.00
bare root			
1 1/4" cal	54.00	27.80	36.60
1 1/2" cal	68.00	35.60	52.00
1 3/4" cal	83.00	56.00	72.00
2" cal	107.00	63.00	89.00
230 Acer platanoides 'Crimson King'			
balled and burlapped			
1 1/4" cal	94.00	57.00	76.00
1 1/2" cal	145.00	77.00	108.00
1 3/4" cal	195.00	83.00	128.00
2" cal	272.00	98.00	171.00
2 1/2" cal	318.00	128.00	220.00
3" cal	393.00	165.00	281.00
3 1/2" cal	435.00	263.00	357.00
4" cal	550.00	338.00	414.00
bare root			
1" cal	37.50	26.80	31.30
1 1/4" cal	60.00	31.10	43.40
1 1/2" cal	77.00	35.70	55.00
1 3/4" cal	96.00	48.20	69.00
2" cal	120.00	73.00	101.00
6' ht	30.80	22.00	26.10
232 Acer platanoides 'Emerald Queen'			
balled and burlapped			
1 1/2" cal	155.00	83.00	108.00
1 3/4" cal	156.00	84.00	115.00
2" cal	237.00	105.00	154.00
2 1/2" cal	308.00	143.00	197.00
3" cal	398.00	173.00	262.00

DESCRIPTION	HIGH	LOW	AVG.
3 1/2" cal	431.00	210.00	329.00
4" cal	570.00	263.00	433.00
4 1/2" cal	790.00	398.00	570.00
5" cal	1040.00	473.00	720.00
bare root			
1" cal	33.00	21.50	25.30
1 1/4" cal	54.00	22.90	31.50
1 1/2" cal	68.00	28.40	45.20
1 3/4" cal	83.00	37.30	59.00
2" cal	107.00	47.30	74.00
6' ht	25.90	17.00	21.20
234 Acer platanoides 'Jade Glen'			
balled and burlapped			
1 3/4" cal	152.00	111.00	129.00
2" cal	186.00	146.00	164.00
2 1/2" cal	221.00	191.00	204.00
236 Acer platanoides 'Royal Red'			
balled and burlapped			
1 1/2" cal	191.00	77.00	117.00
1 3/4" cal	195.00	95.00	136.00
2" cal	285.00	116.00	183.00
2 1/2" cal	306.00	149.00	219.00
3" cal	393.00	219.00	283.00
3 1/2" cal	495.00	281.00	356.00
bare root			
1" cal	30.50	26.80	29.20
1 1/4" cal	46.50	31.10	38.10
1 1/2" cal	77.00	40.80	55.00
1 3/4" cal	96.00	48.20	66.00
6' ht	31.70	23.40	27.60
238 Acer platanoides 'Schwedleri'			
balled and burlapped			
1 1/2" cal	112.00	77.00	96.00
1 3/4" cal	181.00	90.00	128.00
2" cal	263.00	113.00	170.00
2 1/2" cal	333.00	149.00	214.00
3" cal	401.00	182.00	288.00
3 1/2" cal	467.00	263.00	382.00
4" cal	530.00	338.00	444.00
240 Acer platanoides 'Summer Shade'			
balled and burlapped			
1 1/2" cal	117.00	89.00	106.00
1 3/4" cal	143.00	111.00	128.00
2" cal	174.00	128.00	155.00
2 1/2" cal	210.00	143.00	191.00
3" cal	297.00	188.00	251.00
3 1/2" cal	386.00	285.00	333.00
4" cal	476.00	338.00	432.00
242 Acer platanoides 'Superform'			
balled and burlapped			
1 1/2" cal	110.00	83.00	98.00
1 3/4" cal	152.00	84.00	119.00
2" cal	218.00	134.00	162.00
2 1/2" cal	332.00	173.00	215.00
3" cal	398.00	239.00	287.00
3 1/2" cal	461.00	284.00	349.00
4" cal	530.00	435.00	471.00
bare root			
1 1/4" cal	54.00	25.80	35.30
1 1/2" cal	68.00	35.20	52.00
1 3/4" cal	83.00	42.00	65.00

PLANTING

DESCRIPTION	HIGH	LOW	AVG.
2" cal	107.00	63.00	89.00
6' ht	22.10	20.00	21.00
244 Acer rubrum			
balled and burlapped			
1" cal	83.00	33.80	59.00
1 1/4" cal	84.00	34.50	60.00
1 1/2" cal	120.00	37.50	86.00
1 3/4" cal	164.00	45.00	112.00
2" cal	244.00	68.00	145.00
2 1/2" cal	289.00	90.00	182.00
3" cal	334.00	180.00	253.00
3 1/2" cal	402.00	228.00	329.00
4" cal	560.00	263.00	397.00
4 1/2" cal	730.00	413.00	530.00
5" cal	770.00	520.00	660.00
bare root			
1" cal	31.90	14.30	23.50
1 1/4" cal	59.00	16.80	30.70
1 1/2" cal	72.00	21.30	49.30
1 3/4" cal	90.00	45.30	73.00
2" cal	113.00	77.00	99.00
5' ht	24.00	10.50	15.30
6' ht	28.10	12.20	18.40
container			
5 gal	22.50	18.00	20.30
15 gal	69.00	53.00	63.00
246 Acer rubrum 'Armstrong'			
balled and burlapped			
1 1/4" cal	84.00	31.40	57.00
1 1/2" cal	120.00	77.00	101.00
1 3/4" cal	164.00	108.00	130.00
2" cal	198.00	135.00	160.00
2 1/2" cal	248.00	171.00	204.00
3" cal	360.00	203.00	268.00
3 1/2" cal	428.00	248.00	349.00
4" cal	480.00	368.00	423.00
4 1/2" cal	560.00	465.00	500.00
bare root			
1" cal	39.40	28.10	32.80
1 1/4" cal	59.00	33.80	43.10
1 1/2" cal	77.00	45.50	64.00
1 3/4" cal	96.00	55.00	80.00
2" cal	120.00	62.00	97.00
6' ht	33.00	22.50	26.80
248 Acer rubrum 'Autumn Flame'			
balled and burlapped			
1 1/2" cal	152.00	77.00	113.00
1 3/4" cal	164.00	108.00	139.00
2" cal	247.00	135.00	184.00
2 1/2" cal	248.00	173.00	216.00
3" cal	334.00	218.00	285.00
3 1/2" cal	390.00	375.00	380.00
4" cal	510.00	423.00	457.00
250 Acer rubrum 'Bowhall'			
balled and burlapped			
1 1/2" cal	116.00	105.00	110.00
1 3/4" cal	137.00	113.00	128.00
2" cal	180.00	138.00	158.00
2 1/2" cal	240.00	179.00	210.00
3" cal	330.00	234.00	273.00
3 1/2" cal	447.00	305.00	364.00
4" cal	510.00	368.00	426.00

DESCRIPTION	HIGH	LOW	AVG.
bare root			
1" cal	39.40	34.10	36.80
6' ht	36.40	27.80	31.50
252 Acer rubrum 'October Glory'			
balled and burlapped			
1 1/4" cal	102.00	57.00	80.00
1 1/2" cal	132.00	67.00	104.00
1 3/4" cal	191.00	107.00	140.00
2" cal	222.00	108.00	161.00
2 1/2" cal	290.00	135.00	210.00
3" cal	348.00	195.00	278.00
3 1/2" cal	425.00	248.00	371.00
4" cal	580.00	315.00	473.00
bare root			
1" cal	39.40	37.40	38.60
1 1/4" cal	59.00	44.00	48.90
1 1/2" cal	77.00	60.00	68.00
1 3/4" cal	96.00	73.00	88.00
2" cal	120.00	86.00	105.00
5' ht	28.10	20.90	23.60
6' ht	36.40	29.80	32.20
254 Acer rubrum 'Red Sunset'			
balled and burlapped			
1 1/4" cal	102.00	57.00	82.00
1 1/2" cal	159.00	77.00	111.00
1 3/4" cal	180.00	87.00	138.00
2" cal	263.00	105.00	171.00
2 1/2" cal	330.00	135.00	222.00
3" cal	430.00	203.00	309.00
3 1/2" cal	500.00	248.00	388.00
4" cal	630.00	315.00	496.00
4 1/2" cal	760.00	690.00	720.00
bare root			
1 1/4" cal	60.00	44.30	53.00
1 1/2" cal	77.00	60.00	68.00
1 3/4" cal	96.00	73.00	86.00
2" cal	120.00	86.00	101.00
6' ht	36.40	30.10	33.20
container			
15 gal	114.00	60.00	82.00
24" box	263.00	225.00	244.00
256 Acer rubrum 'Scarlet Sentinel'			
balled and burlapped			
1 1/2" cal	135.00	98.00	115.00
2" cal	178.00	150.00	157.00
2 1/2" cal	240.00	195.00	213.00
3" cal	330.00	255.00	292.00
bare root			
1 1/4" cal	59.00	40.10	47.60
6' ht	36.40	27.10	31.20
258 Acer rubrum 'Schlesingeri'			
balled and burlapped			
1 1/2" cal	107.00	107.00	107.00
1 3/4" cal	164.00	126.00	145.00
2" cal	198.00	158.00	178.00
2 1/2" cal	233.00	194.00	213.00
bare root			
1" cal	34.10	30.20	32.00
1 1/4" cal	40.20	36.30	38.10

02950 Trees, Shade and Flowering

DESCRIPTION	HIGH	LOW	AVG.
260 Acer saccharinum			
balled and burlapped			
1 1/2" cal	98.00	22.50	64.00
1 3/4" cal	122.00	30.00	90.00
2" cal	173.00	45.00	112.00
2 1/2" cal	195.00	51.00	130.00
3" cal	255.00	60.00	177.00
3 1/2" cal	263.00	198.00	236.00
4" cal	338.00	203.00	275.00
4 1/2" cal	413.00	292.00	342.00
5' ht	680.00	325.00	473.00
6' ht	1130.00	520.00	720.00
bare root			
1 1/4" cal	46.50	14.20	24.20
1 1/2" cal	59.00	17.70	30.30
4' ht	8.90	5.90	7.60
5' ht	10.70	7.80	9.70
6' ht	13.10	10.40	11.80
8' ht	14.40	11.90	13.50
container			
5 gal	22.50	19.30	20.40
15 gal	68.00	60.00	63.00
24" box	240.00	225.00	235.00
36" box	610.00	600.00	600.00
262 Acer saccharinum 'Silver Queen'			
balled and burlapped			
1 3/4" cal	93.00	74.00	85.00
2" cal	120.00	98.00	107.00
2 1/2" cal	156.00	128.00	140.00
3" cal	225.00	158.00	187.00
3 1/2" cal	254.00	195.00	222.00
4" cal	317.00	260.00	286.00
bare root			
1 1/4" cal	23.50	15.80	20.80
1 1/2" cal	28.10	24.00	26.70
264 Acer saccharum			
balled and burlapped			
1 1/4" cal	90.00	37.50	68.00
1 1/2" cal	194.00	48.80	101.00
1 3/4" cal	194.00	60.00	115.00
2" cal	248.00	83.00	157.00
2 1/2" cal	296.00	113.00	199.00
3" cal	401.00	165.00	271.00
3 1/2" cal	467.00	225.00	337.00
4" cal	570.00	288.00	418.00
4 1/2" cal	760.00	413.00	530.00
5" cal	770.00	488.00	630.00
6" cal	1130.00	1040.00	1070.00
bare root			
1" cal	39.80	26.30	32.50
1 1/4" cal	54.00	32.00	42.00
1 1/2" cal	68.00	46.80	60.00
5' ht	27.00	19.60	22.40
6' ht	35.60	22.70	29.00
266 Acer saccharum 'Green Mountain'			
balled and burlapped			
1 1/4" cal	129.00	57.00	90.00
1 1/2" cal	180.00	77.00	113.00
1 3/4" cal	182.00	87.00	132.00
2" cal	227.00	105.00	167.00
2 1/2" cal	390.00	135.00	227.00
3" cal	470.00	203.00	306.00
3 1/2" cal	550.00	293.00	404.00

DESCRIPTION	HIGH	LOW	AVG.
4" cal	600.00	353.00	478.00
4 1/2" cal	760.00	480.00	650.00
bare root			
1" cal	44.30	37.40	40.50
1 1/4" cal	59.00	49.90	53.00
1 1/2" cal	72.00	62.00	68.00
1 3/4" cal	90.00	87.00	88.00
2" cal	113.00	97.00	106.00
6' ht	37.50	30.50	33.80
268 Acer tataricum			
balled and burlapped			
1 3/4" cal	159.00	150.00	153.00
2" cal	188.00	180.00	184.00
270 Aesculus glabra			
balled and burlapped			
2" cal	242.00	158.00	190.00
2 1/2" cal	302.00	203.00	251.00
272 Aesculus hippocastanum			
balled and burlapped			
2" cal	180.00	150.00	170.00
2 1/2" cal	225.00	192.00	212.00
274 Albizia julibrissin			
container			
5 gal	22.50	16.50	19.80
15 gal	69.00	60.00	63.00
24" box	240.00	218.00	231.00
36" box	610.00	600.00	600.00
276 Albizia julibrissin, multi-stem			
container			
15 gal	71.00	60.00	67.00
24" box	248.00	225.00	236.00
36" box	610.00	600.00	600.00
278 Amelanchier canadensis			
balled and burlapped			
2" cal	204.00	119.00	149.00
2 1/2" cal	262.00	149.00	188.00
3' ht	39.40	18.80	29.70
4' ht	110.00	30.00	61.00
5' ht	140.00	45.00	83.00
6' ht	195.00	83.00	120.00
8' ht	221.00	117.00	169.00
container			
5 gal	18.80	14.20	16.80
280 Betula maximowicziana			
balled and burlapped			
3" cal	225.00	180.00	202.00
282 Betula nigra			
balled and burlapped			
1 1/4" cal	63.00	26.30	41.80
1 1/2" cal	77.00	37.10	61.00
2" cal	132.00	44.30	96.00
2 1/2" cal	173.00	55.00	130.00
3" cal	225.00	124.00	183.00
3 1/2" cal	282.00	143.00	231.00
4" cal	377.00	270.00	315.00
4 1/2" cal	510.00	315.00	392.00
5" cal	690.00	360.00	448.00

PLANTING

DESCRIPTION	HIGH	LOW	AVG.		DESCRIPTION	HIGH	LOW	AVG.
container					bare root			
15 gal	66.00	45.80	57.00		4' ht	13.40	13.30	13.40
					5' ht	15.20	13.40	14.60
284 Betula nigra, multi-stem					6' ht	18.00	17.00	17.50
balled and burlapped					7' ht	19.50	19.20	19.30
5' ht	113.00	26.30	62.00		8' ht	0.00	21.50	22.00
6' ht	152.00	30.00	87.00					
8' ht	242.00	43.10	127.00		**294 Betula pendula 'Youngii'**			
10' ht	300.00	48.00	158.00		balled and burlapped			
12' ht	302.00	119.00	211.00		1 1/4" cal	94.00	62.00	79.00
14'ht	338.00	158.00	263.00		1 1/2" cal	165.00	77.00	114.00
					1 3/4" cal	182.00	101.00	134.00
286 Betula papyrifera					2" cal	219.00	105.00	159.00
balled and burlapped					2 1/2" cal	288.00	156.00	218.00
1 3/4" cal	98.00	75.00	87.00		3" cal	350.00	195.00	278.00
2" cal	177.00	98.00	120.00		3 1/2" cal	428.00	233.00	344.00
2 1/2" cal	179.00	120.00	134.00					
bare root					**296 Betula pendula, multi-stem**			
1" cal	17.60	16.10	17.00		balled and burlapped			
1 1/4" cal	23.00	20.10	21.10		5' ht	53.00	27.00	42.50
1 1/2" cal	29.90	28.00	28.80		6' ht	105.00	30.00	59.00
6' ht	15.10	14.20	14.60		8' ht	128.00	42.00	91.00
					10' ht	152.00	88.00	124.00
288 Betula papyrifera, multi-stem					12' ht	188.00	134.00	166.00
balled and burlapped					bare root			
5' ht	84.00	48.00	70.00		4' ht	13.40	12.50	13.10
6' ht	98.00	59.00	83.00		5' ht	16.90	15.20	16.20
8' ht	131.00	69.00	109.00		6' ht	19.70	17.40	18.80
10' ht	188.00	88.00	141.00		7' ht	22.40	20.40	21.40
12' ht	240.00	134.00	188.00		8' ht	25.40	20.50	23.40
14' ht	270.00	225.00	252.00		container			
bare root					5 gal	32.30	17.60	21.70
5' ht	45.00	17.70	26.90		15 gal	68.00	56.00	64.00
6' ht	60.00	20.30	33.50		24" box	263.00	225.00	239.00
8' ht	71.00	25.80	40.70		36" box	630.00	600.00	610.00
290 Betula pendula					**298 Carpinus betulus 'Fastigiata'**			
balled and burlapped					balled and burlapped			
1 3/4" cal	99.00	44.30	79.00		1 1/4" cal	210.00	63.00	115.00
2" cal	130.00	45.00	98.00		1 1/2" cal	252.00	99.00	151.00
2 1/2" cal	158.00	51.00	125.00		2" cal	335.00	134.00	205.00
3" cal	204.00	69.00	157.00		2 1/2" cal	362.00	176.00	255.00
3 1/2" cal	248.00	203.00	219.00		3" cal	363.00	230.00	306.00
4" cal	324.00	225.00	280.00					
bare root					**300 Carpinus caroliniana**			
1" cal	15.20	14.30	14.90		balled and burlapped			
1 1/4" cal	19.70	16.80	18.50		1 1/2" cal	219.00	59.00	126.00
1 1/2" cal	26.30	21.30	23.90		2" cal	276.00	128.00	187.00
1 3/4" cal	32.30	27.60	30.20		2 1/2" cal	378.00	171.00	242.00
4' ht	8.90	7.40	8.00					
5' ht	10.50	9.00	9.80		**302 Catalpa speciosa**			
6' ht	12.80	11.90	12.30		balled and burlapped			
container					1 3/4" cal	150.00	83.00	105.00
5 gal	28.50	16.50	19.90		2" cal	180.00	98.00	127.00
15 gal	68.00	38.30	58.00		2 1/2" cal	225.00	128.00	162.00
24" box	248.00	218.00	233.00		3" cal	285.00	158.00	202.00
36" box	630.00	600.00	610.00					
					304 Celtis occidentalis			
292 Betula pendula 'Gracilis Laciniata'					balled and burlapped			
balled and burlapped					1 1/2" cal	135.00	72.00	96.00
1 1/2" cal	113.00	77.00	88.00		1 3/4" cal	173.00	83.00	114.00
1 3/4" cal	140.00	90.00	105.00		2" cal	218.00	98.00	144.00
2" cal	225.00	92.00	142.00		2 1/2" cal	327.00	122.00	195.00
2 1/2" cal	261.00	113.00	169.00		3" cal	392.00	165.00	261.00
3" cal	326.00	188.00	241.00		3 1/2" cal	456.00	228.00	314.00
					4" cal	570.00	263.00	382.00

02950 Trees, Shade and Flowering

DESCRIPTION	HIGH	LOW	AVG.
4 1/2" cal	790.00	369.00	510.00
5" cal	1040.00	375.00	580.00
bare root			
6' ht	21.40	19.10	20.50
306 Cercidiphyllum japonicum			
balled and burlapped			
1 1/2" cal	135.00	65.00	108.00
1 3/4" cal	164.00	90.00	132.00
2" cal	203.00	105.00	164.00
2 1/2" cal	264.00	143.00	213.00
3" cal	351.00	173.00	261.00
3 1/2" cal	426.00	210.00	313.00
4" cal	620.00	263.00	411.00
bare root			
1" cal	36.50	27.10	32.60
6' ht	33.70	23.90	28.40
308 Cercis canadensis			
balled and burlapped			
1 1/4" cal	86.00	33.80	62.00
1 1/2" cal	203.00	45.00	111.00
2" cal	248.00	60.00	146.00
2 1/2" cal	285.00	143.00	187.00
3" cal	330.00	180.00	236.00
3 1/2" cal	332.00	228.00	267.00
4' ht	113.00	17.30	56.00
5' ht	194.00	20.60	77.00
6' ht	233.00	25.10	93.00
8' ht	281.00	60.00	129.00
bare root			
4' ht	15.10	12.40	13.60
5' ht	20.50	13.50	18.10
6' ht	29.30	19.70	25.50
container			
5 gal	22.50	12.80	17.70
7 gal	39.00	33.80	35.60
15 gal	69.00	60.00	64.00
30 gal	135.00	105.00	122.00
24" box	240.00	218.00	231.00
310 Cercis canadensis, multi-stem			
balled and burlapped			
4' ht	98.00	19.40	61.00
5' ht	128.00	23.90	74.00
6' ht	187.00	32.30	105.00
8' ht	281.00	64.00	158.00
container			
15 gal	75.00	68.00	70.00
24" box	293.00	225.00	252.00
312 Cladrastis lutea			
balled and burlapped			
1 1/2" cal	135.00	99.00	111.00
1 3/4" cal	170.00	113.00	144.00
2" cal	203.00	150.00	173.00
2 1/2" cal	252.00	215.00	230.00
314 Cornus alternifolia			
balled and burlapped			
3' ht	53.00	26.60	41.30
4' ht	96.00	33.80	65.00
5' ht	156.00	42.40	94.00
6' ht	188.00	78.00	127.00
7' ht	219.00	111.00	166.00
8' ht	270.00	113.00	190.00

DESCRIPTION	HIGH	LOW	AVG.
316 Cornus florida			
balled and burlapped			
1 1/4" cal	86.00	63.00	71.00
1 1/2" cal	110.00	65.00	82.00
1 3/4" cal	143.00	90.00	123.00
2" cal	225.00	59.00	152.00
3" cal	249.00	210.00	228.00
3' ht	68.00	16.50	27.40
4' ht	101.00	18.00	35.80
5' ht	135.00	22.50	54.00
6' ht	165.00	30.00	69.00
8' ht	174.00	41.30	127.00
container			
1 gal	6.80	4.50	5.30
5 gal	30.00	12.80	18.90
15 gal	89.00	60.00	75.00
24" box	263.00	225.00	244.00
318 Cornus florida 'Cherokee Chief'			
balled and burlapped			
1 3/4" cal	225.00	75.00	140.00
2" cal	293.00	90.00	182.00
3' ht	36.00	26.30	32.00
4' ht	44.50	31.50	39.30
5' ht	85.00	34.50	55.00
6' ht	113.00	68.00	96.00
320 Cornus florida 'Cherokee Princess'			
balled and burlapped			
2" cal	169.00	90.00	126.00
2 1/2" cal	225.00	113.00	164.00
3' ht	36.00	26.30	32.30
4' ht	43.10	31.50	38.90
5' ht	85.00	34.50	58.00
6' ht	96.00	63.00	83.00
322 Cornus florida 'Rubra'			
balled and burlapped			
1 1/2" cal	188.00	95.00	132.00
1 3/4" cal	192.00	122.00	149.00
2" cal	281.00	165.00	214.00
3' ht	39.00	26.30	32.80
4' ht	71.00	31.50	46.30
5' ht	89.00	34.50	61.00
6' ht	113.00	45.00	90.00
7' ht	150.00	113.00	127.00
container			
5 gal	30.00	17.30	23.60
324 Cornus kousa			
balled and burlapped			
3' ht	62.00	22.50	35.00
4' ht	123.00	27.00	56.00
5' ht	126.00	33.00	69.00
6' ht	113.00	54.00	84.00
7' ht	143.00	64.00	116.00
326 Cornus kousa chinensis			
balled and burlapped			
3' ht	93.00	18.80	42.20
4' ht	124.00	24.00	52.00
5' ht	155.00	33.00	70.00
6' ht	186.00	53.00	101.00

PLANTING

DESCRIPTION	HIGH	LOW	AVG.
328 Crataegus x Lavallei			
balled and burlapped			
1 3/4" cal	140.00	78.00	110.00
2" cal	177.00	102.00	138.00
2 1/2" cal	237.00	132.00	174.00
3" cal	360.00	172.00	246.00
3 1/2" cal	426.00	215.00	298.00
330 Crataegus crus-galli			
balled and burlapped			
3' ht	53.00	22.50	39.50
4' ht	70.00	30.00	54.00
5' ht	95.00	40.50	74.00
6' ht	195.00	59.00	116.00
8' ht	182.00	90.00	147.00
332 Crataegus crus-galli inermis			
balled and burlapped			
1 1/4" cal	101.00	45.00	74.00
1 1/2" cal	173.00	64.00	113.00
2 " cal	252.00	105.00	165.00
2 1/2" cal	255.00	155.00	194.00
3" cal	327.00	206.00	251.00
3 1/2" cal	344.00	246.00	280.00
4" cal	420.00	317.00	358.00
bare root			
6' ht	24.80	18.00	20.30
7' ht	27.00	20.10	22.80
334 Crataegus laevigata 'Paulii'			
balled and burlapped			
1 3/4" cal	135.00	101.00	118.00
2" cal	173.00	123.00	156.00
bare root			
6' ht	15.20	15.00	15.10
7' ht	17.60	17.00	17.30
container			
15 gal	72.00	47.30	60.00
336 Crataegus laevigata 'Superba'			
balled and burlapped			
1 1/2" cal	149.00	110.00	126.00
1 3/4" cal	162.00	113.00	138.00
2" cal	203.00	138.00	168.00
2 1/2" cal	251.00	204.00	230.00
3" cal	360.00	249.00	312.00
338 Crataegus phaenopyrum			
balled and burlapped			
1 1/4" cal	80.00	37.50	59.00
1 1/2" cal	135.00	45.00	95.00
1 3/4" cal	143.00	90.00	111.00
2" cal	218.00	113.00	154.00
2 1/2" cal	237.00	147.00	193.00
3" cal	360.00	180.00	245.00
3 1/2" cal	371.00	204.00	296.00
4" cal	396.00	233.00	322.00
4 1/2" cal	530.00	334.00	424.00
4' ht	38.30	22.40	32.20
5' ht	90.00	22.50	46.70
6' ht	105.00	30.00	68.00
7' ht	165.00	40.10	105.00
8' ht	166.00	92.00	122.00
container			
5 gal	22.50	14.90	19.40

DESCRIPTION	HIGH	LOW	AVG.
15 gal	72.00	60.00	66.00
24" box	240.00	225.00	233.00
340 Crataegus phaenopyrum, multi-stem			
balled and burlapped			
5' ht	98.00	59.00	77.00
6' ht	128.00	69.00	95.00
7' ht	143.00	86.00	108.00
8' ht	203.00	96.00	147.00
10' ht	285.00	132.00	197.00
12' ht	338.00	173.00	261.00
342 Crataegus toba			
balled and burlapped			
1 3/4" cal			
2" cal			
344 Crataegus viridis 'Winter King'			
balled and burlapped			
1 1/4" cal	86.00	47.30	74.00
1 1/2" cal	149.00	65.00	110.00
1 3/4" cal	162.00	99.00	129.00
2" cal	203.00	126.00	164.00
2 1/2" cal	251.00	173.00	206.00
3" cal	327.00	237.00	264.00
bare root			
1" cal	31.50	23.00	26.10
6' ht	24.80	17.00	19.90
7' ht	27.00	20.10	22.40
346 Elaeagnus angustifolia			
balled and burlapped			
2" cal	203.00	117.00	160.00
2 1/2" cal	255.00	147.00	201.00
3" cal	263.00	180.00	221.00
container			
5 gal	16.70	15.00	15.90
348 Fagus sylvatica			
balled and burlapped			
1 1/2" cal	146.00	67.00	108.00
1 3/4" cal	173.00	96.00	146.00
2" cal	231.00	124.00	185.00
2 1/2" cal	435.00	172.00	260.00
3" cal	600.00	220.00	371.00
3 1/2" cal	750.00	338.00	496.00
4" cal	1130.00	428.00	710.00
4 1/2" cal	1010.00	690.00	870.00
5" cal	1500.00	930.00	1210.00
350 Fagus sylvatica 'Pendula'			
balled and burlapped			
1 3/4" cal	225.00	135.00	183.00
2" cal	413.00	165.00	272.00
2 1/2" cal	520.00	215.00	335.00
3" cal	700.00	281.00	437.00
3 1/2" cal	840.00	366.00	580.00
352 Fagus sylvatica 'Riversii'			
balled and burlapped			
1 3/4" cal	263.00	135.00	198.00
2" cal	375.00	165.00	272.00
2 1/2" cal	560.00	215.00	377.00
3" cal	600.00	281.00	448.00
3 1/2" cal	740.00	366.00	550.00

02950 Trees, Shade and Flowering

DESCRIPTION	HIGH	LOW	AVG.
354 Fraxinus americana			
balled and burlapped			
1 1/2" cal	96.00	72.00	85.00
1 3/4" cal	132.00	90.00	106.00
2" cal	198.00	113.00	150.00
2 1/2" cal	233.00	150.00	190.00
3" cal	270.00	192.00	234.00
4" cal	360.00	338.00	345.00
356 Fraxinus americana 'Autumn Applause'			
balled and burlapped			
1 1/4" cal	99.00	78.00	85.00
1 1/2" cal	129.00	105.00	115.00
1 3/4" cal			
2" cal	238.00	143.00	173.00
2 1/2" cal	323.00	173.00	229.00
3" cal	434.00	240.00	306.00
3 1/2" cal	510.00	278.00	393.00
4" cal	580.00	468.00	530.00
bare root			
6' ht	35.90	27.50	30.40
358 Fraxinus americana 'Autumn Purple'			
balled and burlapped			
1 1/4" cal	84.00	45.00	72.00
1 1/2" cal	125.00	64.00	98.00
1 3/4" cal	142.00	90.00	123.00
2" cal	255.00	95.00	171.00
2 1/2" cal	345.00	168.00	237.00
3" cal	449.00	170.00	310.00
3 1/2" cal	560.00	266.00	369.00
4" cal	680.00	329.00	463.00
4 1/2" cal	750.00	465.00	620.00
bare root			
1" cal	34.60	14.90	27.80
1 1/4" cal	59.00	17.50	39.70
1 1/2" cal	71.00	22.30	50.00
5' ht	21.00	11.30	17.70
6' ht	35.90	13.00	25.60
360 Fraxinus americana 'Rosehill'			
balled and burlapped			
1 1/4" cal	99.00	78.00	85.00
1 1/2" cal	129.00	90.00	110.00
1 3/4" cal	158.00	98.00	131.00
2" cal	238.00	113.00	174.00
2 1/2" cal	323.00	143.00	234.00
3" cal	434.00	240.00	332.00
3 1/2" cal	560.00	278.00	417.00
4" cal	680.00	456.00	530.00
4 1/2" cal	750.00	570.00	660.00
bare root			
1 1/4" cal	59.00	16.80	40.60
1 1/2" cal	71.00	21.30	51.00
1 3/4" cal	89.00	55.00	73.00
6' ht	35.90	12.20	25.30
362 Fraxinus americana 'Skyline'			
balled and burlapped			
1 1/2" cal	125.00	105.00	116.00
1 3/4" cal	135.00	128.00	131.00
2" cal	173.00	160.00	166.00
2 1/2" cal	233.00	203.00	220.00
3" cal	315.00	263.00	290.00

DESCRIPTION	HIGH	LOW	AVG.
364 Fraxinus pennsylvanica lanceolata			
balled and burlapped			
1 1/2" cal	33.80	27.00	30.00
1 3/4" cal	140.00	41.30	107.00
2" cal	174.00	45.00	121.00
2 1/2" cal	230.00	58.00	163.00
3" cal	279.00	74.00	212.00
3 1/2" cal	360.00	263.00	295.00
bare root			
1" cal	36.00	14.70	20.80
1 1/4" cal	43.90	16.10	25.50
1 1/2" cal	59.00	22.10	36.70
6' ht	28.10	9.80	15.10
366 Fraxinus pennsylvanica lanceolata 'Marshall's'			
balled and burlapped			
1 1/4" cal	80.00	33.80	64.00
1 1/2" cal	129.00	41.30	88.00
1 3/4" cal	158.00	90.00	111.00
2" cal	192.00	63.00	135.00
2 1/2" cal	285.00	8.30	182.00
3" cal	375.00	84.00	244.00
3 1/2" cal	455.00	210.00	304.00
4" cal	550.00	263.00	381.00
4 1/2" cal	570.00	338.00	430.00
5" cal	680.00	375.00	530.00
6" cal	990.00	450.00	720.00
bare root			
1" cal	21.50	14.30	19.50
1 1/4" cal	46.50	16.80	28.40
1 1/2" cal	59.00	21.30	38.00
1 3/4" cal	74.00	47.20	58.00
2" cal	95.00	55.00	70.00
5" cal	15.50	10.50	12.80
6" cal	30.40	12.20	19.30
container			
15 gal	75.00	44.30	62.00
368 Fraxinus pennsylvanica lanceolata 'Summit'			
balled and burlapped			
1 1/4" cal	83.00	45.00	69.00
1 1/2" cal	117.00	64.00	91.00
1 3/4" cal	158.00	90.00	117.00
2" cal	186.00	98.00	145.00
2 1/2" cal	255.00	113.00	189.00
3" cal	383.00	158.00	248.00
3 1/2" cal	455.00	210.00	305.00
4" cal	530.00	263.00	379.00
4 1/2" cal	570.00	338.00	448.00
5" cal	630.00	413.00	540.00
6" cal	990.00	640.00	810.00
bare root			
1" cal	36.00	14.30	22.50
1 1/4" cal	47.30	16.80	32.40
1 1/2" cal	59.00	21.30	44.50
1 3/4" cal	75.00	47.20	63.00
2" cal	96.00	57.00	77.00
5' ht	15.50	10.50	12.80
6' ht	30.40	12.20	20.20
container			
5 gal	15.50	10.50	12.80
10 gal	30.40	12.20	20.20
370 Fraxinus velutina			
container			
15 gal	68.00	57.00	61.00

PLANTING

DESCRIPTION	HIGH	LOW	AVG.
24" box	240.00	225.00	230.00
36" box	610.00	600.00	600.00
372 Fraxinus velutina glabra 'Modesto'			
container			
5 gal	28.50	19.50	24.00
15 gal	68.00	59.00	62.00
24" box	240.00	225.00	233.00
36" box	610.00	600.00	600.00
374 Ginko biloba			
balled and burlapped			
1 1/2" cal	138.00	53.00	99.00
1 3/4" cal	165.00	98.00	130.00
2" cal	215.00	128.00	172.00
2 1/2" cal	389.00	150.00	239.00
3" cal	464.00	189.00	300.00
3 1/2" cal	540.00	300.00	386.00
container			
5 gal	18.00	12.80	15.80
15 gal	68.00	60.00	64.00
24" box	240.00	225.00	233.00
36" box	610.00	600.00	600.00
376 Gleditsia triacanthos inermis			
balled and burlapped			
1 1/2" cal	120.00	33.00	73.00
1 3/4" cal	152.00	53.00	93.00
2" cal	186.00	68.00	119.00
2 1/2" cal	221.00	83.00	162.00
3" cal	291.00	180.00	237.00
3 1/2" cal	450.00	204.00	307.00
4" cal	383.00	233.00	324.00
4 1/2" cal	384.00	413.00	419.00
bare root			
1" cal	19.50	14.90	17.70
1 1/4" cal	23.90	17.30	20.10
1 1/2" cal	30.40	22.30	27.00
5' ht	11.70	9.10	10.90
6' ht	15.50	11.90	13.90
378 Gleditsia triacanthos inermis 'Imperial'			
balled and burlapped			
1 1/2" cal	117.00	74.00	101.00
1 3/4" cal	152.00	96.00	124.00
2" cal	225.00	113.00	166.00
2 1/2" cal	263.00	143.00	208.00
3" cal	353.00	218.00	270.00
4" cal	360.00	315.00	339.00
4 1/2" cal	449.00	375.00	412.00
5" cal	499.00	450.00	471.00
bare root			
1 1/4" cal	51.00	39.60	43.40
1 1/2" cal	68.00	46.50	55.00
380 Gleditsia triacanthos inermis 'Moraine'			
balled and burlapped			
2" cal	201.00	125.00	163.00
2 1/2" cal	245.00	215.00	228.00
3" cal	330.00	279.00	309.00
bare root			
1" cal	31.80	14.90	25.00
6' ht	27.20	13.00	21.50
container			
15 gal	68.00	60.00	63.00

DESCRIPTION	HIGH	LOW	AVG.
24" box	240.00	225.00	230.00
36" box	600.00	600.00	600.00
382 Gleditsia triacanthos inermis 'Shademaster'			
balled and burlapped			
1 1/4" cal	101.00	67.00	80.00
1 1/2" cal	123.00	71.00	98.00
1 3/4" cal	135.00	90.00	118.00
2" cal	225.00	91.00	154.00
2 1/2" cal	263.00	131.00	202.00
3" cal	375.00	210.00	278.00
3 1/2" cal	431.00	248.00	335.00
4" cal	570.00	315.00	418.00
5" cal	680.00	450.00	550.00
bare root			
1" cal	37.10	14.90	28.80
1 1/4" cal	54.00	17.50	38.30
1 1/2" cal	65.00	22.30	48.60
5' ht	20.80	11.30	17.60
6' ht	32.90	13.00	26.00
container			
15 gal	69.00	60.00	65.00
24" box	240.00	225.00	234.00
384 Gleditsia triacanthos inermis 'Skyline'			
balled and burlapped			
1 1/4" cal	101.00	67.00	81.00
1 1/2" cal	123.00	71.00	100.00
1 3/4" cal	152.00	75.00	119.00
2" cal	203.00	77.00	151.00
2 1/2" cal	263.00	78.00	195.00
3" cal	375.00	203.00	269.00
3 1/2" cal	450.00	248.00	338.00
4" cal	570.00	315.00	429.00
4 1/2" cal	630.00	375.00	494.00
5" cal	740.00	450.00	580.00
6" cal	1060.00	750.00	900.00
bare root			
1" cal	37.10	31.80	33.60
1 1/4" cal	54.00	36.00	44.20
1 1/2" cal	71.00	46.50	57.00
1 3/4" cal	83.00	59.00	67.00
6' ht	32.90	27.10	29.40
386 Gleditsia triacanthos inermis 'Sunburst'			
balled and burlapped			
1 1/4" cal	101.00	67.00	79.00
1 1/2" cal	123.00	81.00	100.00
1 3/4" cal	164.00	90.00	126.00
2" cal	206.00	105.00	154.00
2 1/2" cal	263.00	143.00	200.00
3" cal	375.00	218.00	275.00
3 1/2" cal	393.00	263.00	327.00
4" cal	480.00	315.00	413.00
4 1/2" cal	540.00	494.00	520.00
5" cal	680.00	550.00	610.00
6" cal	1060.00	660.00	820.00
bare root			
1 1/4" cal	55.00	36.00	45.40
1 1/2" cal	72.00	51.00	62.00
1 3/4" cal	90.00	63.00	78.00
6' ht	32.90	27.10	29.00
container			
5 gal	31.50	19.50	24.50
15 gal	68.00	64.00	66.00

02950 Trees, Shade and Flowering

	DESCRIPTION	HIGH	LOW	AVG.
388	**Gymnocladus dioica**			
	balled and burlapped			
	1 1/2" cal	195.00	81.00	126.00
	1 3/4" cal	225.00	105.00	143.00
	2" cal	278.00	132.00	182.00
	2 1/2" cal	338.00	173.00	238.00
	3" cal	398.00	210.00	297.00
	3 1/2" cal	465.00	285.00	360.00
	4" cal	560.00	345.00	437.00
390	**Juglans nigra**			
	balled and burlapped			
	2" cal	299.00	113.00	207.00
	4" cal	479.00	300.00	399.00
	5" cal	600.00	450.00	520.00
392	**Koelreuteria bipinnata**			
	balled and burlapped			
	2 1/2" cal	188.00	102.00	148.00
	3" cal	263.00	128.00	200.00
	container			
	15 gal	68.00	59.00	61.00
	24" box	240.00	225.00	233.00
	36" box	630.00	600.00	610.00
394	**Koelreuteria paniculata**			
	balled and burlapped			
	1 1/2" cal	165.00	48.00	90.00
	1 3/4" cal	194.00	60.00	110.00
	2" cal	195.00	83.00	126.00
	2 1/2" cal	242.00	135.00	175.00
	3" cal	339.00	209.00	257.00
	5' ht	95.00	21.00	52.00
	6' ht	114.00	26.30	59.00
	8' ht	155.00	108.00	130.00
	bare root			
	1" cal	25.40	14.90	21.70
	1 1/4" cal	30.30	17.50	25.60
	container			
	1 gal	5.60	4.65	5.00
	5 gal	20.90	15.40	18.30
	15 gal	69.00	56.00	63.00
	24" box	240.00	225.00	235.00
	36" box	610.00	600.00	600.00
396	**Laburnum x watereri 'Vossii'**			
	balled and burlapped			
	2" cal	183.00	105.00	153.00
	6' ht	158.00	48.00	93.00
398	**Laurus nobilis**			
	container			
	1 gal	5.60	4.05	4.85
	5 gal	18.90	13.70	16.80
	15 gal	72.00	53.00	63.00
	24" box	248.00	225.00	240.00
400	**Liquidambar styraciflua**			
	balled and burlapped			
	1 1/4" cal	63.00	30.00	44.70
	1 1/2" cal	152.00	45.00	88.00
	1 3/4" cal	153.00	53.00	110.00
	2" cal	210.00	59.00	135.00
	2 1/2" cal	246.00	74.00	176.00
	3" cal	327.00	86.00	240.00
	3 1/2" cal	428.00	228.00	317.00

	DESCRIPTION	HIGH	LOW	AVG.
	4" cal	560.00	263.00	375.00
	4 1/2" cal	560.00	413.00	473.00
	container			
	1 gal	5.60	4.73	5.10
	5 gal	20.90	14.90	17.10
	15 gal	69.00	58.00	62.00
	24" box	285.00	218.00	240.00
	36" box	630.00	488.00	580.00
	48" box	1280.00	1280.00	1280.00
402	**Liquidambar styraciflua 'Burgandy'**			
	container			
	5 gal	24.00	19.50	22.40
	15 gal	72.00	60.00	65.00
	24" box	255.00	225.00	239.00
	36" box	630.00	590.00	610.00
404	**Liquidambar styraciflua 'Palo Alto'**			
	container			
	5 gal	24.00	19.50	22.40
	15 gal	72.00	60.00	65.00
	24" box	255.00	225.00	239.00
	30" box	435.00	428.00	431.00
	36" box	630.00	590.00	610.00
406	**Liriodendron tulipifera**			
	balled and burlapped			
	1 1/4" cal	42.00	30.00	37.20
	1 1/2" cal	135.00	37.50	87.00
	1 3/4" cal	163.00	53.00	115.00
	2" cal	200.00	75.00	139.00
	2 1/2" cal	252.00	90.00	172.00
	3" cal	317.00	105.00	221.00
	3 1/2" cal	396.00	195.00	297.00
	4" cal	413.00	248.00	320.00
	container			
	1 gal	5.60	4.80	5.10
	5 gal	20.90	15.40	18.00
	15 gal	69.00	58.00	62.00
	24" box	255.00	225.00	239.00
	30" box	458.00	413.00	435.00
	36" box	670.00	600.00	620.00
	42" box	1000.00	890.00	950.00
	48" box	1280.00	1280.00	1280.00
408	**Magnolia grandiflora**			
	balled and burlapped			
	5' ht	86.00	48.80	66.00
	6' ht	112.00	60.00	85.00
	8' ht	165.00	87.00	115.00
	container			
	1 gal	5.60	4.13	4.89
	5 gal	20.60	15.40	18.30
	15 gal	72.00	59.00	63.00
	24" box	270.00	218.00	236.00
	36" box	600.00	488.00	580.00
	48" box	1280.00	1280.00	1280.00
410	**Magnolia loebneri 'Merrill'**			
	balled and burlapped			
	3' ht	86.00	22.40	42.40
	4' ht	113.00	30.00	54.00
	5' ht	146.00	37.20	72.00
	6' ht	177.00	49.50	100.00
	container			
	5 gal	30.30	21.00	23.70

PLANTING

	DESCRIPTION	HIGH	LOW	AVG.
412	**Magnolia soulangiana**			
	balled and burlapped			
	3' ht	36.40	22.40	29.10
	4' ht	125.00	24.80	50.00
	5' ht	173.00	28.90	82.00
	6' ht	210.00	53.00	111.00
	7' ht	255.00	113.00	175.00
	8' ht	300.00	128.00	182.00
	container			
	1 gal	5.90	4.80	5.20
	5 gal	36.00	15.40	21.20
	15 gal	72.00	59.00	65.00
	24" box	240.00	225.00	230.00
	36" box	610.00	600.00	600.00
414	**Magnolia soulangiana 'Alexandrina'**			
	balled and burlapped			
	5' ht	126.00	37.20	76.00
	6' ht	162.00	55.00	101.00
416	**Magnolia stellata**			
	balled and burlapped			
	3' ht	78.00	30.00	56.00
	4' ht	98.00	37.50	69.00
	5' ht	135.00	60.00	93.00
418	**Malus x American Beauty**			
	balled and burlapped			
	1 1/2" cal	98.00	68.00	83.00
	2" cal	128.00	98.00	117.00
420	**Malus x atrosanguinea**			
	balled and burlapped			
	2" cal	150.00	126.00	139.00
	2 1/2" cal	195.00	159.00	177.00
	3" cal	225.00	161.00	202.00
	3 1/2" cal	258.00	191.00	230.00
	4" cal	282.00	228.00	261.00
	8' ht	273.00	113.00	198.00
422	**Malus x Beverly**			
	balled and burlapped			
	1 1/2" cal	164.00	75.00	106.00
	2" cal	166.00	105.00	129.00
	2 1/2" cal	168.00	135.00	149.00
	3" cal	228.00	158.00	191.00
	3 1/2" cal	284.00	210.00	232.00
	4" cal	324.00	245.00	280.00
	6' ht	134.00	120.00	124.00
	8' ht	240.00	180.00	203.00
424	**Malus dolgo**			
	balled and burlapped			
	1 1/2" cal	116.00	68.00	80.00
	1 3/4" cal	158.00	81.00	102.00
	2" cal	203.00	98.00	120.00
	2 1/2" cal	240.00	117.00	159.00
	3" cal	242.00	140.00	190.00
	5' ht	111.00	42.00	66.00
	6' ht	134.00	53.00	87.00
426	**Malus floribunda**			
	balled and burlapped			
	1 1/4" cal	83.00	57.00	73.00
	1 1/2" cal	114.00	57.00	88.00
	1 3/4" cal	128.00	68.00	103.00

	DESCRIPTION	HIGH	LOW	AVG.
	2" cal	162.00	83.00	125.00
	2 1/2" cal	182.00	98.00	149.00
	3" cal	233.00	152.00	195.00
	3 1/2" cal	318.00	204.00	244.00
	4" cal	414.00	231.00	291.00
	5' ht	105.00	42.00	67.00
	6' ht	120.00	53.00	86.00
	bare root			
	1" cal	25.40	14.40	20.20
	1 1/4" cal	46.50	23.30	32.40
	4' ht	16.50	9.30	12.60
	5' ht	17.60	10.80	13.40
	6' ht	21.00	13.10	15.60
	7' ht	23.30	15.40	18.90
	container			
	15 gal	69.00	60.00	66.00
	24" box	240.00	210.00	225.00
	36" box	610.00	600.00	600.00
428	**Malus x hopa**			
	balled and burlapped			
	1 1/2" cal	75.00	68.00	72.00
	2" cal	116.00	98.00	106.00
	2 1/2" cal	149.00	135.00	142.00
430	**Malus ioensis 'Improved Bechtels'**			
	balled and burlapped			
	1 1/2" cal	84.00	75.00	81.00
	1 3/4" cal	102.00	87.00	92.00
	2" cal	233.00	104.00	137.00
	2 1/2" cal	288.00	151.00	200.00
	bare root			
	1" cal	19.10	14.40	17.10
	5' ht	13.70	10.80	11.90
	6' ht	15.20	13.10	13.90
432	**Malus x pink perfection**			
	balled and burlapped			
	1 1/2" cal	98.00	75.00	86.00
434	**Malus x purpurea 'Eleyi'**			
	balled and burlapped			
	5' ht	45.00	18.80	35.30
	6' ht	75.00	26.30	51.00
436	**Malus x radiant**			
	balled and burlapped			
	1" cal	59.00	26.30	41.10
	1 1/4" cal	83.00	34.50	58.00
	1 1/2" cal	105.00	47.60	80.00
	1 3/4" cal	128.00	59.00	93.00
	2" cal	203.00	59.00	110.00
	2 1/2" cal	263.00	81.00	145.00
	3" cal	338.00	98.00	194.00
	4" cal	341.00	140.00	234.00
	5' ht	101.00	19.50	49.90
	6' ht	115.00	25.50	53.00
	8' ht	180.00	37.50	92.00
	bare root			
	1" cal	23.40	14.40	18.60
	1 1/4" cal	46.50	21.60	31.90
	4' ht	15.80	4.13	10.10
	5' ht	16.50	10.80	13.20
	6' ht	33.80	13.50	18.80

02950 Trees, Shade and Flowering

DESCRIPTION	HIGH	LOW	AVG.
438 Malus x red jade			
balled and burlapped			
1 1/4" cal	83.00	75.00	78.00
1 1/2" cal	140.00	78.00	103.00
1 3/4" cal	164.00	83.00	114.00
2" cal	186.00	98.00	138.00
2 1/2" cal	225.00	113.00	167.00
3" cal	249.00	173.00	211.00
3 1/2" cal	366.00	243.00	300.00
6' ht	135.00	68.00	105.00
bare root			
#2	21.80	21.70	21.70
#1 light	24.10	24.10	24.10
#1	25.20	25.00	25.10
hvy sel	26.90	26.90	26.90
440 Malus x red splendor			
balled and burlapped			
1 1/2" cal	105.00	71.00	91.00
1 3/4" cal	128.00	81.00	99.00
2" cal	155.00	98.00	126.00
2 1/2" cal	186.00	128.00	153.00
3" cal	233.00	152.00	198.00
3 1/2" cal	318.00	225.00	256.00
442 Malus x royalty			
balled and burlapped			
1 1/4" cal	83.00	51.00	70.00
1 1/2" cal	105.00	60.00	86.00
1 3/4" cal	128.00	68.00	99.00
2" cal	155.00	90.00	119.00
2 1/2" cal	188.00	113.00	150.00
3" cal	233.00	153.00	194.00
3 1/2" cal	318.00	183.00	230.00
4" cal	414.00	219.00	290.00
5' ht	45.00	19.90	35.60
6' ht	180.00	25.90	79.00
bare root			
1" cal	25.50	18.00	20.50
4' ht	12.80	10.40	11.80
5' ht	14.50	13.00	14.00
444 Malus x sargentii			
balled and burlapped			
1" cal	84.00	53.00	68.00
1 1/4" cal	90.00	72.00	82.00
1 1/2" cal	141.00	75.00	104.00
1 3/4" cal	143.00	98.00	120.00
2" cal	195.00	104.00	143.00
2 1/2" cal	233.00	143.00	183.00
3" cal	279.00	210.00	235.00
3 1/2" cal	326.00	248.00	286.00
4" cal	414.00	300.00	356.00
3' ht	105.00	41.30	77.00
4' ht	117.00	42.00	88.00
5' ht	143.00	42.00	90.00
6' ht	186.00	53.00	117.00
bare root			
1" cal	26.30	17.80	23.10
4' ht	16.50	12.20	14.90
5' ht	17.60	12.80	15.20
446 Malus x snowcloud			
balled and burlapped			
1 1/2" cal	105.00	68.00	84.00

DESCRIPTION	HIGH	LOW	AVG.
2" cal	128.00	98.00	116.00
2 1/2" cal	152.00	117.00	138.00
448 Malus x snowdrift			
balled and burlapped			
1 1/4" cal	83.00	39.00	66.00
1 1/2" cal	105.00	47.60	83.00
1 3/4" cal	128.00	72.00	98.00
2" cal	162.00	53.00	117.00
2 1/2" cal	203.00	114.00	152.00
3" cal	245.00	165.00	196.00
3 1/2" cal	318.00	206.00	239.00
4" cal	414.00	241.00	278.00
6' ht	134.00	25.90	68.00
8' ht	189.00	37.50	135.00
bare root			
1" cal	25.40	17.80	20.80
1 1/4" cal	47.30	23.30	35.30
1 1/2" cal	59.00	28.60	48.50
5' ht	17.60	11.30	14.30
6' ht	33.80	13.10	19.70
450 Malus x spring snow			
balled and burlapped			
1 1/4" cal	110.00	36.00	72.00
1 1/2" cal	111.00	59.00	87.00
1 3/4" cal	180.00	72.00	107.00
2" cal	225.00	105.00	132.00
2 1/2" cal	285.00	128.00	160.00
3" cal	315.00	171.00	206.00
3 1/2" cal	318.00	206.00	240.00
4" cal	414.00	246.00	298.00
bare root			
1 1/4" cal	47.30	27.10	40.30
1 1/2" cal	59.00	31.70	49.60
5' ht	17.60	14.40	15.80
452 Malus x Van Eseltine			
balled and burlapped			
1 3/4" cal	105.00	75.00	87.00
2" cal	128.00	105.00	116.00
2 1/2" cal	152.00	135.00	145.00
3" cal	218.00	173.00	192.00
454 Malus x zumi			
balled and burlapped			
1 3/4" cal	99.00	81.00	87.00
2" cal	135.00	105.00	119.00
2 1/2" cal	165.00	128.00	145.00
3" cal	218.00	152.00	190.00
3 1/2" cal	249.00	225.00	234.00
5' ht	98.00	39.00	69.00
456 Malus x zumi calocarpa			
balled and burlapped			
1 1/4" cal	83.00	39.00	60.00
1 1/2" cal	105.00	68.00	86.00
1 3/4" cal	128.00	81.00	103.00
2" cal	162.00	83.00	117.00
2 1/2" cal	203.00	113.00	150.00
3" cal	233.00	152.00	189.00
3 1/2" cal	278.00	191.00	239.00
4" cal	315.00	228.00	271.00
5' ht	111.00	21.00	63.00
6' ht	135.00	33.00	91.00
8' ht	192.00	113.00	168.00

PLANTING

DESCRIPTION	HIGH	LOW	AVG.
bare root			
1" cal	25.40	21.50	23.40
1 1/4" cal	47.30	27.60	40.40
1 1/2" cal	59.00	32.30	49.80
4' ht	12.80	9.80	11.70
5' ht	17.60	14.50	15.50
6' ht	21.00	16.10	17.80
7' ht	23.30	19.10	20.50
458 Morus alba, fruitless			
container			
5 gal	28.50	18.90	22.50
15 gal	69.00	68.00	68.00
460 Nyssa sylvatica			
balled and burlapped			
1 1/2" cal	113.00	90.00	102.00
2" cal	198.00	113.00	156.00
container			
5 gal	20.90	16.50	18.90
15 gal	72.00	60.00	66.00
24" box	240.00	225.00	233.00
462 Ostrya virginiana			
balled and burlapped			
3" cal	328.00	287.00	310.00
464 Oxydendron arboreum			
balled and burlapped			
3' ht	53.00	31.10	38.40
4' ht	72.00	36.00	49.30
5' ht	95.00	36.30	67.00
6' ht	119.00	54.00	87.00
container			
5 gal	24.80	20.30	22.30
466 Phellodendron amurense			
balled and burlapped			
1 3/4" cal	127.00	98.00	116.00
2" cal	180.00	105.00	142.00
2 1/2" cal	236.00	135.00	183.00
3" cal	326.00	210.00	256.00
3 1/2" cal	396.00	248.00	302.00
4" cal	400.00	285.00	326.00
468 Platanus x acerifolia			
balled and burlapped			
1 3/4" cal	132.00	90.00	104.00
2" cal	165.00	113.00	132.00
2 1/2" cal	206.00	143.00	172.00
3" cal	311.00	225.00	261.00
3 1/2" cal	373.00	263.00	322.00
4" cal	447.00	338.00	392.00
container			
5 gal	31.50	18.80	23.60
15 gal	68.00	59.00	63.00
24" box	240.00	225.00	233.00
470 Platanus x acerifolia 'Bloodgood'			
balled and burlapped			
1 1/2" cal	113.00	72.00	94.00
1 3/4" cal	131.00	83.00	105.00
2" cal	182.00	98.00	139.00
2 1/2" cal	222.00	128.00	182.00
3" cal	293.00	158.00	230.00
3 1/2" cal	384.00	188.00	278.00

DESCRIPTION	HIGH	LOW	AVG.
4" cal	480.00	218.00	334.00
4 1/2" cal	510.00	270.00	404.00
bare root			
1" cal	28.10	14.90	22.20
1 1/4" cal	46.50	17.50	32.80
1 1/2" cal	59.00	22.30	44.30
1 3/4" cal	74.00	43.90	60.00
2" cal	95.00	49.40	73.00
6' ht	23.10	13.00	19.10
container			
5 gal	20.30	19.50	19.70
15 gal	89.00	50.00	65.00
24" box	248.00	225.00	236.00
30" box	435.00	413.00	424.00
36" box	630.00	560.00	600.00
42" box	950.00	890.00	920.00
48" box	1280.00	1280.00	1280.00
472 Platanus occidentalis			
balled and burlapped			
2" cal	168.00	75.00	114.00
2 1/2" cal	201.00	150.00	168.00
3" cal	293.00	152.00	210.00
4" cal	375.00	285.00	317.00
474 Populus alba			
balled and burlapped			
2" cal	128.00	83.00	101.00
2 1/2" cal	165.00	113.00	131.00
3" cal	225.00	143.00	187.00
476 Populus nigra 'Italica' (Lombardy)			
container			
5 gal	22.50	15.90	18.60
15 gal	68.00	59.00	62.00
24" box	240.00	225.00	83.00
36" box	610.00	600.00	600.00
478 Populus tremuloides			
balled and burlapped			
1 1/2" cal	135.00	81.00	101.00
2" cal	225.00	83.00	132.00
2 1/2" cal	278.00	105.00	172.00
3" cal	351.00	135.00	237.00
container			
5 gal	18.00	16.50	17.10
15 gal	68.00	47.30	57.00
480 Prunus x blireiana			
bare root			
1" cal	21.90	14.00	17.80
1 1/4" cal	23.70	16.50	20.00
6' ht	16.30	12.90	14.10
7' ht	18.90	15.00	16.80
container			
15 gal	69.00	60.00	63.00
24" box	240.00	225.00	231.00
36" box	610.00	600.00	600.00
482 Prunus cerasifera 'Krauter Vesuvius'			
container			
5 gal	28.50	17.40	20.90
15 gal	69.00	59.00	63.00
24" box	248.00	225.00	234.00
30" box	435.00	413.00	424.00
36" box	630.00	600.00	610.00

PLANTING

02950 Trees, Shade and Flowering

DESCRIPTION	HIGH	LOW	AVG.
484 Prunus cerasifera 'Newportii'			
balled and burlapped			
1 1/2" cal	113.00	39.80	78.00
1 3/4" cal	122.00	75.00	93.00
2" cal	155.00	75.00	110.00
2 1/2" cal	275.00	105.00	155.00
3" cal	335.00	143.00	196.00
3 1/2" cal	368.00	173.00	228.00
4" cal	480.00	203.00	292.00
6' ht	49.50	25.90	36.10
bare root			
1" cal	19.10	17.50	18.50
1 1/4" cal	46.50	20.00	27.50
1 1/2" cal	59.00	21.20	33.80
1 3/4" cal	74.00	29.90	47.00
2" cal	95.00	33.50	59.00
6' ht	14.00	13.10	13.70
7' ht	16.00	15.00	15.60
486 Prunus cerasifera 'Thundercloud'			
balled and burlapped			
1 1/2" cal	98.00	74.00	89.00
1 3/4" cal	122.00	67.00	100.00
2" cal	158.00	90.00	122.00
2 1/2" cal	225.00	113.00	163.00
3" cal	255.00	147.00	204.00
3 1/2" cal	263.00	210.00	227.00
5' ht	60.00	22.50	40.00
6' ht	80.00	30.00	58.00
bare root			
1" cal	20.60	14.00	17.80
1 1/4" cal	23.50	16.50	20.00
4' ht	11.00	9.20	10.30
5' ht	12.10	10.40	11.50
6' ht	14.00	12.90	13.30
7' ht	16.50	15.00	15.80
container			
5 gal	22.50	14.90	19.40
7 gal	42.00	27.00	36.00
10 gal	53.00	34.10	41.40
15 gal	69.00	60.00	65.00
24" box	248.00	225.00	237.00
36" box	630.00	600.00	620.00
488 Prunus sargentii			
balled and burlapped			
1 1/2" cal	143.00	89.00	113.00
1 3/4" cal	144.00	116.00	130.00
2" cal	196.00	98.00	156.00
2 1/2" cal	245.00	128.00	189.00
490 Prunus serrulata 'Amanogawa'			
balled and burlapped			
2" cal	203.00	114.00	163.00
bare root			
1" cal	34.90	22.90	27.30
4' ht	22.50	14.70	18.70
5' ht	25.40	16.50	20.30
6' ht	28.10	18.90	22.40
7' ht	32.40	21.30	24.80
492 Prunus serrulata 'Kwanzan'			
balled and burlapped			
1 1/2" cal	105.00	59.00	85.00
1 3/4" cal	128.00	83.00	107.00
2" cal	162.00	90.00	127.00

DESCRIPTION	HIGH	LOW	AVG.
2 1/2" cal	210.00	113.00	166.00
3" cal	338.00	135.00	220.00
3 1/2" cal	413.00	218.00	283.00
4" cal	480.00	263.00	336.00
5' ht	53.00	24.80	38.30
6' ht	90.00	26.30	55.00
8' ht	120.00	81.00	104.00
bare root			
1" cal	31.50	21.80	24.70
1 1/4" cal	46.50	24.20	32.30
1 1/2" cal	59.00	28.50	41.50
1 3/4" cal	74.00	31.50	49.50
4' ht	19.80	13.90	16.40
5' ht	20.90	15.90	18.40
6' ht	27.00	18.00	21.20
7' ht	29.30	20.00	23.00
container			
10 gal	60.00	30.00	43.70
15 gal	122.00	56.00	78.00
24" box	240.00	225.00	233.00
494 Prunus serrulata 'Shiro-fungen'			
balled and burlapped			
1 3/4" cal	135.00	90.00	107.00
2" cal	173.00	105.00	131.00
2 1/2" cal	210.00	137.00	158.00
bare root			
1" cal	24.10	21.90	22.90
1 1/4" cal	27.50	24.20	25.80
496 Prunus serrulata 'Shirotae' (Mt. Fuji)			
balled and burlapped			
1 3/4" cal	135.00	90.00	108.00
2" cal	173.00	98.00	125.00
2 1/2" cal	210.00	128.00	160.00
3" cal	225.00	165.00	194.00
3 1/2" cal	242.00	218.00	231.00
4" cal	312.00	263.00	291.00
bare root			
1" cal	29.30	21.90	24.20
1 1/4" cal	32.00	24.20	27.90
5' ht	20.60	16.50	18.80
6' ht	22.70	18.90	20.70
7' ht	24.70	20.90	22.60
container			
15 gal	75.00	56.00	66.00
498 Prunus subhirtella 'Autumnalis'			
balled and burlapped			
1 1/2" cal	110.00	59.00	82.00
1 3/4" cal	135.00	83.00	105.00
2" cal	165.00	90.00	122.00
2 1/2" cal	167.00	113.00	140.00
bare root			
1" cal	26.30	21.90	23.80
5' ht	20.60	16.50	18.20
6' ht	22.40	18.90	20.40
7' ht	23.60	21.30	22.20
500 Prunus subhirtella 'Pendula'			
balled and burlapped			
1 1/2" cal	150.00	77.00	104.00
1 3/4" cal	173.00	96.00	127.00
2" cal	174.00	114.00	144.00
2 1/2" cal	210.00	135.00	174.00

111

PLANTING

	DESCRIPTION	HIGH	LOW	AVG.
	3" cal	315.00	188.00	248.00
	3 1/2" cal	371.00	218.00	311.00
	bare root			
	#2	26.30	22.50	24.40
	#1 light	30.10	26.20	28.10
	#1	33.60	29.10	31.30
	hvy sel	37.90	31.60	34.70
	1 1/4" cal	54.00	24.20	37.70
	container			
	15 gal	83.00	71.00	77.00
502	**Prunus virginiana 'Shubert' (Canada Red)**			
	balled and burlapped			
	1 1/4" cal	72.00	42.00	59.00
	1 1/2" cal	104.00	59.00	82.00
	1 3/4" cal	122.00	79.00	100.00
	2" cal	225.00	80.00	135.00
	2 1/2" cal	270.00	128.00	173.00
	3" cal	276.00	158.00	194.00
	3 1/2" cal	293.00	203.00	258.00
	4" cal	330.00	240.00	300.00
	6' ht	90.00	35.60	67.00
504	**Prunus yedoensis**			
	balled and burlapped			
	1 1/2" cal	90.00	59.00	75.00
	1 3/4" cal	128.00	83.00	105.00
	2" cal	162.00	90.00	127.00
	2 1/2" cal	203.00	113.00	160.00
	3" cal	300.00	135.00	208.00
	3 1/2" cal	305.00	218.00	246.00
	4" cal	390.00	263.00	316.00
	5' ht	45.00	24.80	32.00
	6' ht	90.00	28.50	46.30
	8' ht	113.00	34.50	76.00
	bare root			
	1" cal	27.20	21.90	24.90
	7' ht	24.90	21.80	23.40
	container			
	15 gal	104.00	68.00	86.00
506	**Pyrus calleryana 'Aristocrat'**			
	balled and burlapped			
	1 1/4" cal	80.00	48.80	69.00
	1 1/2" cal	127.00	43.90	86.00
	1 3/4" cal	140.00	59.00	111.00
	2" cal	233.00	66.00	135.00
	2 1/2" cal	234.00	98.00	177.00
	3" cal	317.00	128.00	229.00
	3 1/2" cal	399.00	204.00	316.00
	4" cal	530.00	233.00	383.00
	4 1/2" cal	710.00	270.00	470.00
	5" cal	950.00	294.00	560.00
	6' ht	48.00	36.80	41.70
	bare root			
	1" cal	39.40	20.40	31.30
	1 1/4" cal	54.00	24.50	41.60
	1 1/2" cal	65.00	28.80	51.00
	4' ht	19.10	13.20	16.10
	5' ht	23.40	15.20	18.80
	6' ht	34.80	20.90	25.90
	container			
	5 gal	27.80	19.50	23.10
	7 gal	58.00	33.80	44.60
	15 gal	69.00	60.00	63.00
	24" box	248.00	218.00	235.00

	DESCRIPTION	HIGH	LOW	AVG.
	36" box	630.00	488.00	590.00
	48" box	1280.00	1280.00	1280.00
508	**Pyrus calleryana 'Bradford'**			
	balled and burlapped			
	1 1/4" cal	83.00	33.80	63.00
	1 1/2" cal	127.00	37.50	82.00
	1 3/4" cal			
	2" cal	173.00	45.00	124.00
	2 1/5" cal	234.00	68.00	165.00
	3" cal	300.00	90.00	219.00
	3 1/2" cal	399.00	204.00	309.00
	4" cal	530.00	233.00	388.00
	4 1/2" cal	710.00	270.00	495.00
	5" cal	950.00	294.00	600.00
	6" cal	1060.00	750.00	950.00
	5' ht	45.00	22.50	31.30
	6' ht	90.00	30.00	46.90
	8' ht	150.00	63.00	90.00
	bare root			
	6' ht	34.80	17.40	26.10
	container			
	5 gal	28.50	19.50	24.20
	7 gal	41.30	33.80	36.40
	15 gal	75.00	60.00	65.00
	24" box	248.00	218.00	235.00
	30" box	435.00	413.00	424.00
	36" box	630.00	488.00	590.00
	42" box	950.00	890.00	920.00
	48" box	1280.00	1280.00	1280.00
510	**Pyrus calleryana 'Redspire'**			
	balled and burlapped			
	1 1/4" cal	83.00	48.80	72.00
	1 1/2" cal	127.00	56.00	98.00
	1 3/4" cal	140.00	71.00	115.00
	2" cal	168.00	90.00	139.00
	2 1/2" cal	225.00	129.00	182.00
	3" cal	300.00	180.00	230.00
	3 1/2" cal	390.00	257.00	313.00
	4" cal	530.00	300.00	408.00
	4 1/2" cal	710.00	353.00	520.00
	5" cal	950.00	413.00	650.00
	bare root			
	1" cal	39.40	20.40	31.60
	1 1/4" cal	54.00	24.50	42.90
	1 1/2" cal	65.00	28.80	51.00
	5' ht	23.60	15.20	19.50
	6' ht	34.80	17.40	26.90
	container			
	5 gal	27.80	19.50	23.20
	15 gal	69.00	60.00	64.00
	24" box	248.00	225.00	237.00
512	**Quercus acutissima**			
	balled and burlapped			
	1 1/2" cal	129.00	60.00	87.00
	1 3/4" cal	195.00	90.00	138.00
	2" cal	245.00	75.00	153.00
	2 1/2" cal	306.00	90.00	199.00
	3" cal	433.00	113.00	267.00
	3 1/2" cal	389.00	248.00	370.00
	4" cal	680.00	288.00	428.00
	4 1/2" cal	920.00	413.00	590.00
	5" cal	730.00	600.00	670.00

DESCRIPTION	HIGH	LOW	AVG.
6" cal	1130.00	750.00	930.00
7" cal	1680.00	1160.00	1450.00
514 Quercus alba			
balled and burlapped			
1 1/2" cal	225.00	83.00	137.00
2" cal	284.00	135.00	201.00
2 1/2" cal	306.00	188.00	222.00
3" cal	393.00	240.00	284.00
3 1/2" cal	491.00	278.00	356.00
4" cal	620.00	315.00	438.00
516 Quercus bicolor			
balled and burlapped			
1 1/2" cal	187.00	99.00	143.00
1 3/4" cal	188.00	132.00	154.00
2" cal	248.00	143.00	190.00
2 1/2" cal	368.00	195.00	249.00
3" cal	465.00	240.00	328.00
3 1/2" cal	590.00	278.00	440.00
4" cal	680.00	315.00	540.00
5" cal	860.00	800.00	840.00
bare root			
1" cal	39.40	32.00	34.60
5' ht	30.40	20.30	24.40
6' ht	33.80	27.10	29.60
518 Quercus coccinea			
balled and burlapped			
1 3/4" cal	156.00	83.00	122.00
2" cal	228.00	105.00	165.00
2 1/2" cal	314.00	135.00	219.00
3" cal	377.00	198.00	281.00
3 1/2" cal	449.00	254.00	345.00
4" cal	600.00	308.00	429.00
4 1/2" cal	710.00	375.00	550.00
5" cal	830.00	428.00	640.00
container			
5 gal	24.90	16.50	20.70
15 gal	83.00	60.00	70.00
24" box	263.00	225.00	242.00
520 Quercus macrocarpa			
balled and burlapped			
1 1/2" cal	230.00	59.00	140.00
2" cal	291.00	113.00	207.00
2 1/2" cal	324.00	150.00	230.00
3" cal	429.00	225.00	305.00
3 1/2" cal	510.00	263.00	354.00
4" cal	630.00	315.00	429.00
522 Quercus nigra			
balled and burlapped			
2" cal	143.00	48.80	89.00
2 1/2" cal	195.00	75.00	122.00
524 Quercus palustris			
balled and burlapped			
1 1/4" cal	80.00	30.00	54.00
1 1/2" cal	149.00	37.50	93.00
1 3/4" cal	179.00	53.00	118.00
2" cal	252.00	68.00	146.00
2 1/2" cal	297.00	83.00	182.00
3" cal	338.00	113.00	242.00
3 1/2" cal	449.00	165.00	320.00
4" cal	640.00	270.00	431.00

DESCRIPTION	HIGH	LOW	AVG.
4 1/2" cal	790.00	375.00	540.00
5" cal	1040.00	377.00	660.00
6" cal	1160.00	630.00	910.00
7" cal	1500.00	880.00	1140.00
8" cal	2250.00	1080.00	1570.00
bare root			
1" cal	33.40	31.00	32.80
1 1/4" cal	54.00	32.60	41.20
1 1/2" cal	65.00	43.40	54.00
1 3/4" cal	83.00	56.00	65.00
2" cal	98.00	57.00	72.00
5' ht	20.60	16.40	18.80
6' ht	27.50	17.00	23.40
container			
1 gal	5.90	4.58	5.30
5 gal	31.50	16.50	20.60
15 gal	78.00	60.00	69.00
24" box	248.00	240.00	242.00
526 Quercus phellos			
balled and burlapped			
1 1/4" cal	83.00	37.50	56.00
1 1/2" cal	116.00	45.00	83.00
1 3/4" cal	143.00	53.00	106.00
2" cal	216.00	68.00	140.00
2 1/2" cal	237.00	83.00	175.00
3" cal	326.00	225.00	272.00
3 1/2" cal	426.00	225.00	339.00
4" cal	620.00	285.00	451.00
4 1/2" cal	650.00	413.00	550.00
5" cal	790.00	488.00	700.00
6" cal	1050.00	980.00	1020.00
7" cal	1320.00	1200.00	1270.00
528 Quercus robur			
balled and burlapped			
1 1/2" cal	148.00	81.00	110.00
1 3/4" cal	149.00	105.00	126.00
2" cal	263.00	132.00	175.00
2 1/2" cal	330.00	173.00	224.00
3" cal	435.00	210.00	302.00
3 1/2" cal	488.00	248.00	351.00
4" cal	550.00	288.00	423.00
bare root			
1" cal	39.60	27.20	31.90
1 1/4" cal	54.00	31.70	40.40
5' ht	24.80	20.60	21.90
6' ht	31.10	24.00	26.80
530 Quercus robur 'Fastigiata'			
balled and burlapped			
1 1/4" cal	84.00	42.00	66.00
1 1/2" cal	135.00	59.00	86.00
1 3/4" cal	176.00	98.00	123.00
2" cal	263.00	87.00	158.00
2 1/2" cal	263.00	102.00	190.00
3" cal	326.00	203.00	252.00
3 1/2" cal	449.00	240.00	306.00
4" cal	530.00	288.00	373.00
bare root			
1" cal	39.40	24.90	32.20
1 1/4" cal	59.00	32.60	41.20
1 1/2" cal	71.00	44.60	54.00
5' ht	27.40	15.80	22.80
6' ht	32.90	19.70	27.60

PLANTING

	DESCRIPTION	HIGH	LOW	AVG.
532	**Quercus rubra (borealis)**			
	balled and burlapped			
	1 3/4" cal	188.00	48.00	137.00
	2" cal	285.00	48.80	179.00
	2 1/2" cal	386.00	75.00	233.00
	3" cal	465.00	108.00	302.00
	3 1/2" cal	540.00	143.00	363.00
	4" cal	680.00	195.00	457.00
	4 1/2" cal	740.00	240.00	540.00
	5" cal	930.00	450.00	760.00
	6" cal	1500.00	940.00	1260.00
	7" cal	2250.00	1130.00	1680.00
	8" cal	3000.00	1310.00	2130.00
	bare root			
	1" cal	39.40	24.50	31.10
	1 1/4" cal	59.00	30.80	40.60
	1 1/2" cal	71.00	35.00	50.00
	6' ht	31.50	20.90	26.10
	container			
	5 gal	24.00	16.50	20.30
	15 gal	72.00	57.00	64.00
	24" box	263.00	225.00	242.00
	36" box	600.00	590.00	600.00
534	**Quercus shumardii**			
	balled and burlapped			
	1 1/2" cal	72.00	48.80	58.00
	2" cal	240.00	60.00	138.00
	2 1/2" cal	312.00	83.00	179.00
	3" cal	405.00	143.00	256.00
	3 1/2" cal	510.00	248.00	320.00
	4" cal	630.00	293.00	408.00
	4 1/2" cal	790.00	560.00	620.00
	5" cal	990.00	640.00	780.00
	6" cal	1550.00	940.00	1120.00
	bare root			
	6' ht	29.40	24.60	27.30
	container			
	15 gal	75.00	68.00	71.00
536	**Quercus virginiana**			
	container			
	5 gal	20.30	16.50	18.30
	15 gal	75.00	60.00	65.00
	24" box	255.00	218.00	233.00
	36" box	670.00	488.00	590.00
	48" box	1430.00	1280.00	1330.00
538	**Salix alba 'Tristis'**			
	balled and burlapped			
	1 1/2" cal	120.00	66.00	93.00
	2" cal	221.00	78.00	131.00
	2 1/2" cal	221.00	113.00	154.00
	3" cal	252.00	150.00	198.00
	3 1/2" cal	254.00	188.00	211.00
	4" cal	337.00	236.00	288.00
	4 1/2" cal	396.00	281.00	364.00
	5" cal	495.00	315.00	412.00
	6" cal	900.00	413.00	680.00
540	**Salix babylonica**			
	balled and burlapped			
	1 1/2" cal	83.00	30.00	59.00
	2" cal	179.00	45.00	107.00
	2 1/2" cal	200.00	57.00	135.00
	3" cal	291.00	87.00	170.00

	DESCRIPTION	HIGH	LOW	AVG.
	container			
	5 gal	28.50	15.90	20.00
	15 gal	69.00	59.00	63.00
	24" box	240.00	225.00	233.00
	36" box	630.00	600.00	610.00
542	**Salix matsudana 'Tortuosa'**			
	container			
	5 gal	22.50	15.90	19.20
	15 gal	69.00	63.00	66.00
544	**Sophora japonica**			
	balled and burlapped			
	1 3/4" cal	143.00	98.00	113.00
	2" cal	218.00	113.00	158.00
	2 1/2" cal	225.00	147.00	172.00
	3" cal	226.00	198.00	209.00
	3 1/2" cal	375.00	228.00	288.00
	4" cal	450.00	263.00	362.00
546	**Sophora japonica 'Regent'**			
	balled and burlapped			
	1 3/4" cal	164.00	132.00	144.00
	2" cal	203.00	135.00	169.00
	2 1/2" cal	263.00	188.00	224.00
	3" cal	353.00	233.00	296.00
	3 1/2" cal	426.00	300.00	366.00
	container			
	15 gal	72.00	60.00	66.00
	24" box	248.00	225.00	236.00
548	**Sorbus aucuparia**			
	balled and burlapped			
	1 1/2" cal	113.00	75.00	92.00
	1 3/4" cal	128.00	76.00	104.00
	2" cal	162.00	99.00	123.00
	2 1/2" cal	255.00	132.00	170.00
	3" cal	258.00	165.00	202.00
	3 1/2" cal	285.00	203.00	236.00
	bare root			
	1 1/4" cal	54.00	19.70	29.90
	1 1/2" cal	65.00	26.00	37.10
	1 3/4" cal	83.00	33.10	49.50
	2" cal	98.00	38.20	60.00
	container			
	15 gal	69.00	46.50	61.00
550	**Sorbus aucuparia 'Cardinal Royal'**			
	balled and burlapped			
	1 3/4" cal	146.00	116.00	130.00
	2" cal	177.00	117.00	148.00
	2 1/2" cal	218.00	135.00	186.00
	3" cal	258.00	180.00	230.00
552	**Syringa reticulata**			
	balled and burlapped			
	1 1/2" cal	154.00	84.00	121.00
	1 3/4" cal	164.00	105.00	136.00
	2" cal	263.00	125.00	190.00
	2 1/2" cal	264.00	158.00	236.00
	3" cal	354.00	300.00	335.00
	4' ht	93.00	18.00	53.00
	5' ht	120.00	22.50	66.00
	6' ht	180.00	28.50	105.00
	7' ht	209.00	104.00	147.00
	8' ht	270.00	134.00	195.00

DESCRIPTION	HIGH	LOW	AVG.
554 Tilia americana			
balled and burlapped			
2" cal	264.00	113.00	176.00
2 1/2" cal	294.00	158.00	217.00
3" cal	356.00	165.00	248.00
3 1/2" cal	407.00	263.00	320.00
4" cal	465.00	338.00	385.00
556 Tilia cordata			
balled and burlapped			
1 1/2" cal	131.00	81.00	105.00
1 3/4" cal	135.00	90.00	106.00
2" cal	216.00	111.00	147.00
2 1/2" cal	248.00	150.00	192.00
3" cal	315.00	153.00	244.00
3 1/2" cal	405.00	248.00	329.00
4" cal	480.00	278.00	378.00
4 1/2" cal	520.00	315.00	416.00
5" cal	680.00	435.00	560.00
6" cal	1130.00	530.00	780.00
7" cal	1500.00	600.00	970.00
bare root			
6' ht	33.50	17.50	23.90
558 Tilia cordata 'Glenleven'			
balled and burlapped			
1 1/2" cal	116.00	81.00	97.00
1 3/4" cal	152.00	105.00	125.00
2" cal	233.00	132.00	167.00
2 1/2" cal	294.00	173.00	211.00
3" cal	357.00	210.00	272.00
3 1/2" cal	420.00	248.00	329.00
4" cal	495.00	338.00	435.00
bare root			
1 1/2" cal	65.00	40.20	50.00
1 3/4" cal	83.00	41.90	61.00
560 Tilia cordata 'Greenspire'			
balled and burlapped			
1 1/4" cal	80.00	60.00	72.00
1 1/2" cal	135.00	75.00	106.00
1 3/4" cal	188.00	90.00	126.00
2" cal	233.00	113.00	164.00
2 1/2" cal	294.00	158.00	213.00
3" cal	374.00	159.00	278.00
3 1/2" cal	495.00	248.00	348.00
4" cal	600.00	335.00	452.00
4 1/2" cal	790.00	398.00	560.00
5" cal	1040.00	450.00	710.00
6" cal	1160.00	690.00	920.00
bare root			
1" cal	34.70	32.90	33.60
1 1/4" cal	54.00	37.00	44.40
1 1/2" cal	72.00	46.50	58.00
1 3/4" cal	90.00	62.00	72.00
2" cal	113.00	73.00	89.00
6' ht	27.60	25.90	27.00
562 Tilia x euchlora			
balled and burlapped			
1 3/4" cal	138.00	90.00	123.00
2" cal	216.00	113.00	168.00
2 1/2" cal	249.00	149.00	229.00
3" cal	338.00	150.00	289.00
3 1/2" cal	425.00	263.00	359.00
4" cal	435.00	338.00	399.00

DESCRIPTION	HIGH	LOW	AVG.
bare root			
1 1/4" cal	59.00	34.80	44.20
564 Tilia x euchlora 'Redmond'			
balled and burlapped			
1 1/2" cal	135.00	81.00	103.00
1 3/4" cal	152.00	90.00	115.00
2" cal	225.00	105.00	154.00
2 1/2" cal	293.00	143.00	204.00
3" cal	400.00	173.00	264.00
3 1/2" cal	495.00	210.00	314.00
4" cal	600.00	263.00	398.00
4 1/2" cal	680.00	398.00	530.00
5" cal	750.00	450.00	610.00
bare root			
1" cal	25.80	24.50	25.30
1 1/4" cal	54.00	27.60	33.60
1 1/2" cal	65.00	37.00	45.10
1 3/4" cal	83.00	43.10	62.00
2" cal	98.00	46.30	72.00
6' ht	33.50	19.60	24.10
566 Ulmus parvifolia			
balled and burlapped			
2" cal	195.00	83.00	138.00
2 1/2" cal	249.00	113.00	188.00
3" cal	311.00	143.00	226.00
container			
36" box	600.00	590.00	600.00
568 Ulmus parvifolia 'Drake'			
container			
5 gal	18.00	15.40	16.60
15 gal	68.00	59.00	61.00
24" box	240.00	218.00	229.00
30" box	435.00	413.00	424.00
36" box	630.00	488.00	580.00
42" box	950.00	890.00	920.00
48" box	1280.00	1280.00	1280.00
570 Zelkova serrata			
balled and burlapped			
2 1/2" cal	233.00	150.00	195.00
3" cal	316.00	225.00	273.00
3 1/2" cal	395.00	263.00	339.00
4" cal	510.00	338.00	416.00
4 1/2" cal	660.00	413.00	530.00
5" cal	820.00	680.00	730.00
572 Zelkova serrata 'Green Vase'			
balled and burlapped			
1 1/2" cal	135.00	90.00	105.00
1 3/4" cal	158.00	108.00	130.00
2" cal	192.00	111.00	152.00
2 1/2" cal	249.00	143.00	197.00
3" cal	338.00	173.00	268.00
3 1/2" cal	425.00	203.00	342.00
4" cal	570.00	248.00	446.00
bare root			
1" cal	35.60	33.80	34.90
1 1/4" cal	54.00	40.30	45.70
6' ht	29.90	28.10	29.10
574 Zelkova serrata 'Village Green'			
balled and burlapped			
1 1/2" cal	135.00	105.00	119.00

PLANTING

DESCRIPTION	HIGH	LOW	AVG.
1 3/4" cal	158.00	108.00	133.00
2" cal	201.00	113.00	156.00
2 1/2" cal	249.00	128.00	193.00
3" cal	338.00	173.00	264.00
3 1/2" cal	425.00	248.00	344.00
4" cal	570.00	335.00	467.00
4 1/2" cal	790.00	383.00	640.00
bare root			
1" cal	35.60	14.90	29.90
1 1/4" cal	42.80	17.50	33.50
5' ht	23.00	11.30	18.80
6' ht	29.90	13.00	25.00

TREES, PALMS AND SUBTROPICAL

200 Acacia baileyana

DESCRIPTION	HIGH	LOW	AVG.
container			
1 gal	5.60	4.88	5.30
5 gal	18.00	15.40	16.60
15 gal	68.00	59.00	61.00
24" box	240.00	225.00	233.00

202 Acacia latifolia

DESCRIPTION	HIGH	LOW	AVG.
container			
1 gal	4.13	3.38	3.80
5 gal	13.10	12.00	12.80

204 Araucaria heterophylla

DESCRIPTION	HIGH	LOW	AVG.
container			
1 gal	5.40	4.88	5.10
2 gal	11.60	10.50	11.10

206 Archontophoenix cunninghamiana

DESCRIPTION	HIGH	LOW	AVG.
container			
1 gal	5.60	5.30	5.50
5 gal	19.50	15.40	17.50
15 gal	83.00	60.00	66.00
24" box	300.00	225.00	244.00
36" box	610.00	600.00	600.00
48" box	1280.00	1280.00	1280.00
54" box	1760.00	1580.00	1670.00
60" box	2120.00	2100.00	2110.00

208 Arecastrum ronamzoffianum

DESCRIPTION	HIGH	LOW	AVG.
container			
1 gal	5.90	5.60	5.80
5 gal	19.50	18.00	18.80
15 gal	83.00	59.00	66.00
24" box	248.00	225.00	234.00
30" box	435.00	413.00	425.00
36" box	630.00	600.00	610.00
42" box	950.00	890.00	920.00
48" box	1280.00	1280.00	1280.00

210 Bauhinia purpurea

DESCRIPTION	HIGH	LOW	AVG.
container			
1 gal	5.60	4.88	5.30
5 gal	18.00	15.40	16.60
15 gal	68.00	59.00	62.00
24" box	240.00	225.00	230.00
36" box	610.00	600.00	600.00

212 Brachychiton populneus

DESCRIPTION	HIGH	LOW	AVG.
container			
1 gal	5.60	4.88	5.30

DESCRIPTION	HIGH	LOW	AVG.
5 gal	18.00	15.40	16.60
15 gal	68.00	59.00	62.00
24" box	240.00	225.00	233.00
30" box	428.00	413.00	420.00
36" box	610.00	600.00	600.00
48" box	1280.00	1280.00	1280.00

214 Callistemon citrinus

DESCRIPTION	HIGH	LOW	AVG.
container			
1 gal	4.28	4.13	4.46
5 gal	16.50	13.50	15.10
15" gal	68.00	56.00	61.00
24" box	240.00	225.00	229.00
36" box	610.00	600.00	600.00

216 Ceratonia silique

DESCRIPTION	HIGH	LOW	AVG.
container			
1 gal	5.60	4.88	5.30
5 gal	18.90	15.40	17.20
15 gal	69.00	59.00	63.00
24" box	240.00	225.00	229.00
36" box	610.00	600.00	600.00

218 Chamaerops excelsa

DESCRIPTION	HIGH	LOW	AVG.
container			
1 gal	5.60	3.98	5.10
5 gal	18.80	15.40	16.80
15 gal	75.00	60.00	66.00
24" box	248.00	225.00	233.00
36" box	610.00	600.00	600.00

220 Chamaerops humilis

DESCRIPTION	HIGH	LOW	AVG.
container			
1 gal	6.40	5.90	6.20
5 gal	19.50	16.50	18.30
15 gal	83.00	60.00	67.00
24" box	300.00	225.00	246.00
30" box	428.00	413.00	420.00
36" box	610.00	600.00	600.00
48" box	1280.00	1280.00	1280.00
54" box	1760.00	1580.00	1670.00
60" box	2120.00	2100.00	2110.00

222 Cinnamomum camphora

DESCRIPTION	HIGH	LOW	AVG.
container			
1 gal	5.60	4.88	5.30
5 gal	18.90	15.40	17.20
15 gal	69.00	59.00	63.00
24" box	255.00	225.00	236.00
30" box	458.00	413.00	432.00
36" box	670.00	600.00	620.00
42" box	1000.00	890.00	950.00
48" box	1470.00	1280.00	1340.00
60" box	2120.00	2100.00	2110.00

224 Cordyline indivisa

DESCRIPTION	HIGH	LOW	AVG.
container			
1 gal	5.30	4.43	4.83

226 Cupaniopsis anacardiopsis

DESCRIPTION	HIGH	LOW	AVG.
container			
5 gal	16.50	15.40	15.90
15 gal	68.00	59.00	61.00
24" box	248.00	225.00	234.00
30" box	435.00	413.00	425.00
36" box	630.00	600.00	610.00

02950 Trees, Palms and Subtropical

DESCRIPTION	HIGH	LOW	AVG.
42" box	950.00	890.00	920.00
48" box	1430.00	1280.00	1330.00
60" box	2120.00	2100.00	2110.00
228 Cupaniopsis anacardiopsis, multi-stem			
container			
5 gal	18.00	16.90	17.40
15 gal	71.00	60.00	66.00
24" box	255.00	225.00	239.00
30" box	458.00	413.00	435.00
36" box	670.00	600.00	620.00
42" box	1000.00	890.00	950.00
48" box	1470.00	1280.00	1340.00
60" box	2120.00	2100.00	2110.00
230 Cycas revolta			
container			
1 gal	7.90	7.10	7.50
3 gal	37.50	22.50	29.00
5 gal	41.30	29.30	35.30
7 gal	57.00	53.00	55.00
15 gal	105.00	60.00	87.00
232 Eriobotrya deflexa (Photina deflexa)			
container			
5 gal	16.50	15.40	15.90
15 gal	68.00	59.00	61.00
24" box	248.00	225.00	236.00
30" box	435.00	413.00	424.00
36" box	630.00	600.00	610.00
234 Eriobotrya japonica			
container			
5 gal	16.50	12.80	14.90
15 gal	68.00	59.00	62.00
24" box	240.00	225.00	235.00
236 Eucalyptus camaldulensis (E. rostrata)			
container			
5 gal	16.50	15.40	15.90
15 gal	68.00	59.00	62.00
24" box	240.00	225.00	229.00
36" box	610.00	600.00	600.00
238 Eucalyptus cinerea			
container			
5 gal	19.50	15.40	17.40
15 gal	60.00	59.00	59.00
240 Eucalyptus citriodora			
container			
5 gal	18.00	15.40	16.60
15 gal	68.00	59.00	61.00
24" box	240.00	225.00	231.00
36" box	610.00	600.00	600.00
242 Eucalyptus ficifolia			
container			
5 gal	16.50	15.40	15.90
15 gal	68.00	59.00	61.00
24" box	248.00	225.00	233.00
36" box	610.00	600.00	600.00
244 Eucalyptus nicholii			
container			
5 gal	18.00	14.90	16.20

DESCRIPTION	HIGH	LOW	AVG.
15 gal	68.00	59.00	62.00
24" box	240.00	225.00	230.00
246 Eucalyptus polyanthemos			
container			
5 gal	18.00	14.90	16.20
15 gal	68.00	59.00	62.00
24" box	240.00	225.00	231.00
36" box	610.00	600.00	600.00
248 Eucalyptus rudis			
container			
5 gal	18.00	15.40	16.60
15 gal	68.00	59.00	62.00
24" box	240.00	225.00	229.00
36" box	610.00	600.00	600.00
250 Eucalyptus viminalis			
container			
5 gal	16.50	15.40	15.90
15 gal	68.00	59.00	63.00
24" box	240.00	225.00	233.00
252 Ficus benjamina			
container			
1 gal	6.50	5.90	6.30
5 gal	21.80	17.30	19.70
7 gal	59.00	42.80	51.00
15 gal	83.00	60.00	71.00
24" box	255.00	225.00	239.00
30" box	435.00	413.00	424.00
36" box	630.00	600.00	610.00
42" box	950.00	890.00	920.00
48" box	1430.00	1280.00	1330.00
54" box	1760.00	1580.00	1670.00
60" box	2120.00	2100.00	2110.00
254 Ficus benjamina, multi-stem			
container			
15 gal	79.00	68.00	73.00
24" box	255.00	225.00	242.00
36" box	670.00	600.00	630.00
54" box	1760.00	1580.00	1670.00
60" box	2120.00	2100.00	2110.00
256 Ficus microphylla			
container			
24" box	233.00	225.00	229.00
36" box	620.00	600.00	610.00
258 Ficus retus 'Nitida'			
container			
1 gal	5.60	4.80	5.20
5 gal	19.50	15.40	17.60
15 gal	83.00	59.00	66.00
24" box	248.00	225.00	233.00
30" box	435.00	880.00	431.00
36" box	630.00	600.00	610.00
42" box	950.00	890.00	920.00
48" box	1430.00	1280.00	1330.00
60" box	2120.00	2100.00	2110.00
260 Ficus retusa			
container			
5 gal	16.50	15.40	15.90
15 gal	71.00	59.00	63.00

PLANTING

02950 Trees, Palms and Subtropical					1994			
DESCRIPTION	HIGH	LOW	AVG.	DESCRIPTION	HIGH	LOW	AVG.
24" box	248.00	225.00	234.00	48" box	1280.00	1280.00	1280.00
30" box	435.00	413.00	424.00	60" box	2120.00	2100.00	2110.00
36" box	630.00	600.00	610.00	**274 Lagerstroemia indica, varieties**			
42" box	950.00	890.00	920.00	container			
262 Ficus rubiginosa (F. australis)				1 gal	5.90	3.60	4.68
container				3 gal	11.30	7.50	10.00
5 gal	16.50	15.40	15.90	5 gal	20.30	18.80	19.50
15 gal	71.00	59.00	62.00	15 gal	72.00	56.00	63.00
24" box	248.00	225.00	233.00	20 gal	105.00	98.00	101.00
36" box	630.00	600.00	610.00	24" box	270.00	218.00	238.00
42" box	950.00	890.00	920.00	30" box	435.00	413.00	424.00
48" box	1280.00	1280.00	1280.00	36" box	640.00	488.00	590.00
54" box	1760.00	1580.00	1670.00	42" box	950.00	890.00	920.00
60" box	2120.00	2100.00	2110.00	48" box	1280.00	1280.00	1280.00
264 Fraxinus uhdei				**276 Leptospermum laevigatum**			
container				container			
1 gal	5.60	4.88	5.30	1 gal	4.13	3.60	3.92
5 gal	19.90	15.40	17.40	5 gal	13.70	12.80	13.20
15 gal	69.00	59.00	63.00	15 gal	68.00	53.00	60.00
24" box	240.00	225.00	229.00	24" box	300.00	225.00	255.00
30" box	428.00	413.00	420.00	30" box	473.00	413.00	443.00
36" box	610.00	600.00	600.00	36" box	610.00	600.00	600.00
48" box	1280.00	1280.00	1280.00	**278 Myoporum laetum, varieties**			
266 Geijera parvifolia				container			
container				1 gal	4.88	3.90	4.38
1 gal	5.30	5.10	5.20	5 gal	18.00	15.40	16.60
5 gal	21.00	16.50	18.50	15 gal	68.00	56.00	60.00
15 gal	69.00	60.00	63.00	24" box	240.00	225.00	230.00
24" box	248.00	225.00	235.00				
30" box	435.00	413.00	424.00	4' ht	39.80	15.00	31.60
36" box	610.00	600.00	600.00	5' ht	57.00	22.50	40.80
42" box	890.00	890.00	890.00	6' ht	81.00	29.70	57.00
48" box	1280.00	1280.00	1280.00	7' ht	98.00	37.50	68.00
268 Grevillea robusta				8' ht	143.00	58.00	97.00
container				10' ht	242.00	101.00	164.00
1 gal	5.60	4.88	5.30	**280 Olea europaea, varieties**			
5 gal	18.00	15.40	16.60	container			
15 gal	68.00	59.00	62.00	1 gal	6.00	4.50	5.30
24" box	240.00	225.00	230.00	5 gal	26.30	14.90	17.90
36" box	610.00	600.00	600.00	15 gal	71.00	58.00	65.00
270 Jacaranda mimosifolia (J. ovalifolia)				24" box	255.00	225.00	242.00
container				**282 Olea europaea, varieties, multi-stem**			
1 gal	5.60	4.88	5.30	container			
5 gal	18.00	15.40	16.60	15 gal	68.00	60.00	65.00
15 gal	68.00	59.00	61.00	24" box	240.00	225.00	233.00
24" box	248.00	225.00	234.00	36" box	610.00	600.00	600.00
30" box	435.00	413.00	425.00	**284 Pistacia chinensis**			
36" box	630.00	600.00	610.00	balled and burlapped			
42" box	950.00	890.00	920.00	2" cal	128.00	114.00	121.00
48" box	1280.00	1280.00	1280.00	2 1/2" cal	173.00	171.00	172.00
54" box	1760.00	1760.00	1760.00	3" cal	231.00	225.00	228.00
60" box	2120.00	2100.00	2110.00	3 1/2" cal	312.00	300.00	306.00
272 Jacaranda mimosifolia, multi-stem				4" cal	422.00	375.00	398.00
container				container			
5 gal	18.00	17.60	17.80	1 gal	5.90	4.80	5.20
15 gal	68.00	60.00	65.00	5 gal	20.90	12.80	17.20
24" box	255.00	225.00	239.00	7 gal	51.00	34.10	42.60
30" box	458.00	413.00	432.00	15 gal	72.00	59.00	64.00
36" box	670.00	600.00	620.00	24" box	248.00	225.00	236.00
42" box	1000.00	890.00	950.00	30" box	435.00	413.00	424.00

02950 Trees, Palms and Subtropical — 1994

	DESCRIPTION	HIGH	LOW	AVG.
	36" box	630.00	590.00	600.00
	42" box	950.00	890.00	920.00
	48" box	1280.00	1280.00	1280.00
	60" box	2120.00	2100.00	2110.00
286	**Prunus caroliniana**			
	container			
	5 gal	75.00	59.00	65.00
	24" box	240.00	225.00	230.00
288	**Prunus caroliniana 'Compacta'**			
	container			
	1 gal	5.30	3.98	4.74
	5 gal	17.40	12.00	15.10
	15 gal	69.00	56.00	62.00
	24" box	300.00	225.00	263.00
290	**Pyrus kawakamii**			
	container			
	5 gal	24.00	19.50	21.50
	15 gal	83.00	60.00	66.00
	24" box	248.00	225.00	235.00
	30" box	428.00	413.00	420.00
	36" box	610.00	600.00	600.00
	42" box	890.00	890.00	890.00
	48" box	1280.00	1280.00	1280.00
	60" box	2120.00	2100.00	2110.00
292	**Pyrus kawakamii, multi-stem**			
	container			
	5 gal	19.50	13.70	16.60
294	**Quercus ilex**			
	container			
	5 gal	22.40	16.50	18.90
	15 gal	72.00	60.00	66.00
	24" box	240.00	225.00	235.00
	36" box	610.00	600.00	600.00
296	**Schinus molle**			
	container			
	1 gal	5.60	4.88	5.30
	5 gal	18.00	15.40	16.80
	15 gal	69.00	59.00	62.00
	24" box	248.00	225.00	234.00
	30" box	435.00	413.00	424.00
	36" box	630.00	600.00	610.00
	42" box	950.00	890.00	920.00
	48" box	1430.00	1280.00	1330.00
	60" box	2120.00	2100.00	2100.00
298	**Schinus terebinthifolius**			
	container			
	1 gal	5.60	4.88	5.30
	5 gal	18.00	15.40	16.60
	15 gal	68.00	59.00	62.00
	24" box	240.00	225.00	231.00
	30" box	435.00	413.00	424.00
	36" box	630.00	600.00	610.00
	42" box	950.00	890.00	920.00
	48" box	1280.00	1280.00	1280.00
	60" box	2120.00	2100.00	2110.00
300	**Strelitzia nicolai**			
	container			
	1 gal	5.60	4.88	5.20

	DESCRIPTION	HIGH	LOW	AVG.
	5 gal	18.00	13.50	16.00
	15 gal	90.00	60.00	72.00
	24" box	263.00	225.00	243.00
302	**Strelitzia reginae (S. parvifolia)**			
	container			
	1 gal	5.60	4.50	5.10
	5 gal	18.00	12.80	15.60
	15 gal	68.00	64.00	66.00
304	**Syzygium paniculatum (Eugenia myrtifolia)**			
	container			
	1 gal	5.60	3.60	4.70
	5 gal	18.00	12.80	15.40
	15 gal	68.00	59.00	62.00
306	**Tristania conferta**			
	container			
	5 gal	16.50	15.40	15.90
	15 gal	68.00	59.00	62.00
	24" box	248.00	225.00	234.00
	36" box	630.00	600.00	610.00
	48" box	1280.00	1280.00	1280.00
308	**Washingtonia robusta**			
	container			
	1 gal	4.73	3.98	4.25
	5 gal	16.50	13.90	15.30
	15 gal	68.00	59.00	63.00
	24" box	240.00	225.00	229.00
	36" box	610.00	600.00	600.00

CONIFERS

	DESCRIPTION	HIGH	LOW	AVG.
200	**Abies balsamea**			
	balled and burlapped			
	3' ht	71.00	53.00	62.00
	4' ht	87.00	65.00	76.00
202	**Abies balsamea 'Nana'**			
	container			
	1 gal	11.60	5.30	8.60
204	**Abies concolor**			
	balled and burlapped			
	4' ht	113.00	68.00	85.00
	5' ht	173.00	89.00	124.00
	6' ht	254.00	116.00	165.00
	7' ht	297.00	141.00	206.00
	8' ht	299.00	188.00	254.00
	10' ht	495.00	360.00	411.00
206	**Abies fraseri**			
	balled and burlapped			
	5' ht	102.00	59.00	81.00
	6' ht	165.00	92.00	124.00
	7' ht	195.00	123.00	155.00
208	**Cedrus atlantica 'Glauca'**			
	balled and burlapped			
	6' ht	174.00	75.00	120.00
	7' ht	188.00	128.00	158.00
	8' ht	375.00	135.00	228.00
	10' ht	450.00	188.00	293.00

PLANTING

DESCRIPTION	HIGH	LOW	AVG.
container			
5 gal	30.80	19.50	26.70
15 gal	79.00	60.00	71.00
24" box	263.00	225.00	242.00
36" box	680.00	600.00	630.00
42" box	980.00	890.00	940.00
210 Cedrus deodara			
container			
1 gal	5.60	4.88	5.30
5 gal	18.90	15.40	17.40
15 gal	71.00	60.00	65.00
24" box	263.00	225.00	239.00
36" box	610.00	600.00	600.00
48" box	1280.00	1280.00	1280.00
60" box	2120.00	2100.00	2110.00
212 Chamaecyparis obtusa 'Nana Gracili'			
container			
1 gal	16.90	13.50	15.10
2 gal	48.00	21.80	32.80
3 gal	53.00	39.00	46.10
214 Chamaecyparis pisifera 'Cyanovirid'			
balled and burlapped			
2' ht	26.30	17.30	21.80
3' ht	37.50	34.50	36.00
4' ht	53.00	49.50	51.00
5' ht	75.00	68.00	71.00
216 Cryptomeria japonica 'Lobbii'			
balled and burlapped			
8' ht	218.00	188.00	203.00
218 Cupressocyparis leylandii			
balled and burlapped			
4' ht	56.00	45.00	48.50
5' ht	74.00	59.00	65.00
container			
1 gal	5.30	4.50	5.00
5 gal	17.60	13.50	15.80
15 gal	83.00	59.00	66.00
24" box	240.00	225.00	229.00
36" box	610.00	600.00	600.00
220 Cupressus sempervirens			
container			
15 gal	68.00	60.00	64.00
24" box	233.00	225.00	229.00
222 Cupressus sempervirens 'Glauca'			
container			
1 gal	5.30	3.90	4.38
5 gal	16.50	13.10	14.80
15 gal	69.00	59.00	65.00
24" box	240.00	225.00	230.00
36" box	630.00	600.00	620.00
224 Juniperus chinensis 'Aureo-Pfitzer'			
balled and burlapped			
18" ht	23.30	15.00	19.10
2' ht	31.10	15.80	24.20
2 1/2' ht	33.00	21.80	26.40
3' ht	42.00	25.50	31.60
container			
1 gal	7.50	3.45	4.86

DESCRIPTION	HIGH	LOW	AVG.
2 gal	13.50	8.30	10.30
3 gal	18.80	11.30	14.70
5 gal	24.00	12.00	16.40
15 gal	56.00	50.00	53.00
15" ht	19.50	11.00	15.00
18" ht	19.80	14.10	17.00
226 Juniperus chinensis 'Blue Point'			
container			
1 gal	5.90	4.50	5.10
5 gal	20.30	13.50	16.70
15 gal	71.00	60.00	66.00
228 Juniperus chinensis 'Glauca Hetzii'			
balled and burlapped			
15" ht	14.60	12.00	13.10
18" ht	20.70	12.80	16.90
2' ht	25.90	13.50	20.00
2 1/2' ht	29.60	16.50	23.60
3' ht	42.00	21.00	30.10
container			
1 gal	4.65	3.45	4.08
2 gal	11.00	8.30	9.80
3 gal	13.20	11.30	11.90
5 gal	15.40	14.30	14.90
230 Juniperus chinensis 'Gold Coast'			
container			
3 gal	17.00	14.10	16.00
15" ht	19.80	14.30	16.80
18" ht	23.40	14.40	19.10
232 Juniperus chinensis 'Hetzii'			
balled and burlapped			
18" ht	21.80	18.80	19.80
2' ht	36.00	20.60	26.90
2 1/2' ht	42.00	20.60	30.50
container			
3 gal	16.50	11.60	13.40
15" ht	14.30	12.40	13.50
18" ht	19.50	12.80	16.10
234 Juniperus chinensis 'Keteleeri'			
balled and burlapped			
3' ht	42.00	37.50	40.50
4' ht	65.00	34.50	52.00
4 1/2' ht	75.00	57.00	63.00
5' ht	90.00	49.50	66.00
6' ht	120.00	60.00	82.00
236 Juniperus chinensis 'Mint Julep'			
container			
2 gal	11.60	10.10	10.90
3 gal	17.00	14.40	15.70
18" ht	28.50	14.40	22.10
238 Juniperus chinensis 'Old Gold'			
balled and burlapped			
15" ht	18.00	12.90	15.00
18" ht	22.50	17.60	19.80
container			
1 gal	8.30	3.45	5.20
2 gal	16.10	8.30	12.00
3 gal	21.00	11.30	14.60
5 gal	24.00	12.00	16.90
15 gal	56.00	50.00	53.00

02950 Conifers
1994

DESCRIPTION	HIGH	LOW	AVG.
15" ht	15.00	13.50	14.10
18" ht	19.50	16.50	17.50
240 Juniperus chinensis 'Pfitzerana'			
balled and burlapped			
15" ht	14.30	12.00	13.00
18" ht	19.50	12.00	15.80
2' ht	25.90	15.80	21.80
2 1/2' ht	33.00	18.80	26.40
3' ht	42.00	23.30	33.20
container			
1 gal	7.10	3.75	4.74
2 gal	16.10	8.30	11.40
3 gal	21.00	11.40	14.90
5 gal	22.50	12.00	15.90
15 gal	56.00	50.00	53.00
15" ht	14.30	11.00	12.90
18" ht	19.50	14.10	16.70
242 Juniperus chinensis 'Pfitzerana Armstrongii'			
container			
1 gal	6.80	3.45	4.61
2 gal	16.10	11.00	12.80
5 gal	22.50	12.00	16.10
15 gal	56.00	50.00	53.00
244 Juniperus chinensis 'Pfitzerana Compacta'			
balled and burlapped			
15" ht	20.60	12.00	14.10
18" ht	24.80	14.30	18.00
2' ht	33.00	16.50	22.80
2 1/2' ht	33.00	20.60	26.40
3' ht	60.00	25.50	39.40
container			
1 gal	7.10	3.45	4.61
2 gal	13.50	8.30	10.60
3 gal	17.60	11.30	13.80
5 gal	24.00	12.00	18.60
15" ht	16.50	12.20	14.00
18" ht	19.50	12.80	16.40
246 Juniperus chinensis 'Pfitzerana Glauca'			
container			
1 gal	6.80	3.45	4.37
2 gal	16.10	8.30	10.60
3 gal	21.00	11.30	14.30
5 gal	24.00	12.00	17.00
15 gal	58.00	56.00	57.00
18" ht	16.50	14.10	15.70
248 Juniperus chinensis 'San Jose'			
container			
1 gal	6.80	3.45	4.37
2 gal	16.10	8.30	10.60
3 gal	21.00	11.30	14.30
5 gal	24.00	12.00	17.00
15 gal	58.00	56.00	57.00
18" ht	16.50	14.10	15.70
250 Juniperus chinensis 'Torulosa'			
balled and burlapped			
3' ht	52.00	24.80	41.60
4' ht	93.00	30.00	64.00
5' ht	117.00	45.00	88.00
6' ht	173.00	96.00	131.00

DESCRIPTION	HIGH	LOW	AVG.
container			
1 gal	5.60	4.13	4.68
2 gal	13.10	9.80	11.40
5 gal	33.00	12.80	17.70
7 gal	42.80	30.00	36.20
15 gal	75.00	56.00	63.00
24" box	240.00	225.00	231.00
36" box	630.00	600.00	610.00
252 Juniperus chinensis procumbens			
container			
1 gal	7.10	3.75	5.20
3 gal	13.50	11.40	12.70
5 gal	18.00	15.40	16.70
12' ht	15.60	4.73	9.10
15' ht	21.60	11.00	15.60
18' ht	28.20	15.00	20.90
254 Juniperus chinensis procumbens 'Nana'			
container			
1 gal	8.60	4.13	5.40
2 gal	19.40	8.30	12.40
3 gal	19.50	11.30	14.70
5 gal	30.00	12.80	18.40
12" ht	19.20	7.10	13.20
15" ht	22.50	13.40	17.20
18" ht	28.20	14.40	20.70
256 Juniperus chinensis sargentii			
balled and burlapped			
18" ht	19.50	15.00	16.50
2' ht	24.80	17.90	21.70
2 1/2' ht	33.00	22.40	27.20
container			
1 gal	7.10	3.75	5.00
2 gal	18.00	8.30	12.00
3 gal	21.40	11.40	15.00
15" ht	18.00	10.90	13.90
18" ht	21.40	14.40	17.60
258 Juniperus chinensis sargentii 'Glauca'			
balled and burlapped			
2' ht	27.40	15.00	19.90
container			
1 gal	4.65	3.45	4.14
2 gal	12.30	8.30	10.40
3 gal	15.80	11.30	13.90
5 gal	16.10	14.30	14.90
12' ht	12.30	10.90	11.50
15' ht	16.50	11.00	14.10
18' ht	16.60	14.40	15.50
260 Juniperus communis 'Hibernica'			
balled and burlapped			
3' ht	18.80	13.50	16.20
4' ht	30.00	15.80	22.00
5' ht	45.00	21.80	30.00
6' ht	75.00	28.50	44.50
262 Juniperus conferta (Shore)			
container			
1 gal	8.30	3.45	4.83
2 gal	15.00	8.30	10.40

PLANTING

	DESCRIPTION	HIGH	LOW	AVG.
264	**Juniperus conferta 'Blue Pacific'**			
	container			
	1 gal	7.50	3.45	5.10
	2 gal	19.10	8.30	12.50
	3 gal	19.10	11.40	14.70
	5 gal	24.00	13.10	16.40
	12" ht	12.30	7.10	10.40
	15" ht	19.40	11.90	15.20
	18" ht	19.50	14.60	17.00
266	**Juniperus horizontalis 'Plumosa' (Andorra)**			
	balled and burlapped			
	15" ht	14.60	12.00	13.00
	18" ht	19.20	13.50	16.40
	container			
	5 gal	18.00	15.40	16.70
	18" ht	27.00	15.00	20.40
268	**Juniperus horizontalis 'Plumosa Compacta'**			
	balled and burlapped			
	15" ht	14.30	12.00	13.00
	18" ht	19.50	15.60	17.10
	2' ht	25.90	17.30	21.20
	2 1/2' ht	33.00	24.80	29.10
	container			
	1 gal	7.10	3.75	5.20
	2 gal	13.50	8.30	10.60
	3 gal	16.50	11.40	13.50
	12" ht	11.30	4.73	7.70
	15" ht	14.30	11.00	12.90
	18" ht	19.50	14.10	16.70
270	**Juniperus horizontalis 'Plumosa Compacta Ygstwn'**			
	balled and burlapped			
	15" ht	15.00	14.50	14.70
	18" ht	18.00	16.40	17.10
	2' ht	24.00	17.90	21.50
	2 1/2' ht	27.40	22.50	25.40
	3' ht	32.60	30.00	30.80
	container			
	1 gal	6.80	3.45	4.77
	2 gal	16.10	8.30	11.10
	3 gal	21.00	11.30	17.00
	5 gal	22.50	12.00	17.00
	15" ht	19.80	16.40	18.20
	18" ht	23.40	16.50	19.50
272	**Juniperus sabina 'Arcadia'**			
	container			
	1 gal	4.58	3.90	4.25
	5 gal	20.30	12.00	15.60
	15 gal	56.00	50.00	53.00
274	**Juniperus sabina 'Broadmoor'**			
	container			
	1 gal	6.80	3.90	4.80
	2 gal	16.10	10.10	12.10
	3 gal	21.00	12.60	16.20
	5 gal	24.00	12.80	17.10
	12" ht	15.00	11.00	12.80
	15" ht	19.80	13.50	16.20
	18" ht	23.40	14.40	17.50
276	**Juniperus sabina 'Buffalo'**			
	container			
	1 gal	6.80	3.90	4.80
	2 gal	16.10	10.10	12.60
	5 gal	22.50	12.00	16.20
	15" ht	19.80	14.30	17.10
	18" ht	23.40	14.40	17.80
278	**Juniperus sabina 'Skandia'**			
	container			
	1 gal	4.65	3.90	4.26
	2 gal	11.30	11.00	11.10
	5 gal	19.10	13.10	15.80
280	**Juniperus sabina 'Tamariscifolia' (Tam)**			
	container			
	1 gal	7.50	3.90	5.30
	2 gal	16.10	9.80	12.00
	3 gal	21.00	11.60	15.60
	5 gal	24.00	12.00	17.00
	15 gal	56.00	50.00	53.00
	15" ht	19.80	13.50	15.80
	18" ht	23.40	15.80	18.80
282	**Juniperus scopulorum 'Blue Haven'**			
	balled and burlapped			
	5' ht	90.00	53.00	70.00
	6' ht	98.00	60.00	79.00
284	**Juniperus scopulorum 'Welchii'**			
	balled and burlapped			
	3' ht	52.00	42.00	45.20
	4' ht	68.00	51.00	56.00
	4 1/2' ht	80.00	57.00	65.00
	5' ht	90.00	60.00	72.00
	6' ht	120.00	68.00	89.00
286	**Juniperus squamata 'Parsonii'**			
	container			
	1 gal	4.65	3.45	4.08
	2 gal	13.10	8.30	10.30
	3 gal	16.40	11.30	12.70
	5 gal	19.70	15.00	16.70
	15" ht	13.90	11.90	13.00
	18" ht	16.40	15.00	15.80
288	**Juniperus virginiana**			
	balled and burlapped			
	3' ht	42.00	22.50	29.70
	4' ht	53.00	25.90	38.00
	5' ht	68.00	41.30	53.00
	6' ht	90.00	53.00	72.00
	7' ht	120.00	68.00	100.00
	8' ht	150.00	105.00	135.00
	10' ht	188.00	150.00	175.00
290	**Juniperus virginiana 'Burkii'**			
	balled and burlapped			
	4' ht	56.00	23.60	43.20
	5' ht	74.00	33.40	56.00
292	**Juniperus virginiana 'Canaertii'**			
	balled and burlapped			
	4' ht	53.00	35.30	47.40
	5' ht	63.00	53.00	60.00
	6' ht	83.00	68.00	77.00

02950 Conifers

DESCRIPTION	HIGH	LOW	AVG.
294 Juniperus virginiana 'Cupressifoli' (Hillspire)			
container			
5 gal	30.30	12.00	21.60
7 gal	74.00	52.00	63.00
296 Juniperus virginiana 'Hillii' (Hill Dundee)			
balled and burlapped			
5' ht	86.00	33.00	60.00
298 Juniperus virginiana 'Skyrocket'			
balled and burlapped			
3' ht	42.00	34.50	37.70
4' ht	60.00	42.00	48.70
5' ht	90.00	47.30	68.00
6' ht	120.00	83.00	94.00
container			
1 gal	6.80	5.20	5.80
5 gal	20.30	12.00	17.90
7 gal	47.30	41.30	44.30
300 Metasequoia glyptostroboides			
balled and burlapped			
2" cal	173.00	108.00	131.00
2 1/2" cal	270.00	134.00	193.00
3" cal	315.00	158.00	247.00
5' ht	123.00	69.00	95.00
6' ht	153.00	71.00	116.00
8' ht	361.00	113.00	188.00
10' ht	444.00	134.00	249.00
container			
5 gal	24.90	16.50	20.30
302 Picea abies			
balled and burlapped			
2' ht	33.00	18.80	24.30
3' ht	78.00	21.00	39.10
4' ht	98.00	28.50	61.00
5' ht	180.00	45.00	88.00
6' ht	225.00	75.00	121.00
7' ht	270.00	105.00	156.00
8' ht	315.00	128.00	192.00
10' ht	315.00	188.00	244.00
12' ht	375.00	263.00	324.00
304 Picea abies 'Nidiformis'			
balled and burlapped			
18" ht	45.00	30.00	37.20
2' ht	87.00	45.00	59.00
3' ht	143.00	83.00	105.00
container			
1 gal	10.90	5.00	8.70
2 gal	33.80	12.00	20.50
3 gal	33.80	18.00	25.90
5 gal	41.30	18.10	29.30
15" ht	36.00	23.10	29.80
18" ht	41.30	34.50	37.70
306 Picea abies 'Pendula'			
balled and burlapped			
4' ht	132.00	98.00	116.00
5' ht	158.00	105.00	135.00
308 Picea glauca			
balled and burlapped			
3' ht	65.00	30.00	51.00
4' ht	87.00	52.00	71.00

DESCRIPTION	HIGH	LOW	AVG.
5' ht	116.00	68.00	86.00
6' ht	117.00	84.00	103.00
7' ht	263.00	119.00	185.00
8' ht	300.00	150.00	201.00
10' ht	375.00	210.00	270.00
310 Picea glauca 'Conica'			
balled and burlapped			
18" ht	29.90	20.30	25.70
2' ht	46.50	25.50	39.00
2 1/2' ht	92.00	34.50	62.00
3' ht	120.00	64.00	89.00
3 1/2' ht	155.00	72.00	108.00
4' ht	186.00	96.00	136.00
4 1/2' ht	230.00	122.00	162.00
container			
1 gal	11.30	6.20	8.60
2 gal	29.30	13.10	18.50
5 gal	41.30	21.00	30.40
12" ht	14.80	13.70	14.10
15" ht	23.10	17.10	19.30
18" ht	39.00	20.30	28.50
2' ht	60.00	27.00	39.20
2 1/2' ht	65.00	31.40	47.80
312 Picea glauca 'Densata'			
balled and burlapped			
2' ht	36.40	18.80	26.30
3' ht	59.00	30.00	44.20
4' ht	83.00	37.90	65.00
5' ht	158.00	60.00	96.00
6' ht	205.00	105.00	131.00
7' ht	270.00	126.00	175.00
8' ht	300.00	150.00	192.00
314 Picea omorika			
balled and burlapped			
3' ht	66.00	35.90	54.00
4' ht	87.00	54.00	73.00
5' ht	143.00	75.00	108.00
6' ht	186.00	111.00	148.00
7' ht	255.00	180.00	217.00
316 Picea pungens			
balled and burlapped			
2' ht	31.50	23.60	26.80
3' ht	84.00	25.50	49.90
4' ht	135.00	34.50	81.00
5' ht	186.00	45.00	113.00
6' ht	225.00	60.00	147.00
7' ht	263.00	119.00	194.00
10' ht	312.00	173.00	246.00
12' ht	390.00	210.00	324.00
318 Picea pungens 'Glauca'			
balled and burlapped			
3' ht	98.00	48.00	66.00
4' ht	146.00	49.50	92.00
5' ht	195.00	62.00	128.00
6' ht	270.00	95.00	172.00
7' ht	354.00	134.00	222.00
8' ht	433.00	162.00	278.00
10' ht	485.00	248.00	336.00

PLANTING

	DESCRIPTION	HIGH	LOW	AVG.
320	**Picea pungens 'Hoopsii'**			
	balled and burlapped			
	3' ht	114.00	60.00	87.00
	4' ht	165.00	83.00	124.00
	5' ht	249.00	120.00	162.00
	6' ht	311.00	173.00	240.00
	7' ht	389.00	210.00	295.00
	8' ht	530.00	263.00	367.00
322	**Pinus canariensis**			
	container			
	5 gal	17.40	13.70	15.40
	15 gal	69.00	59.00	62.00
	24" box	248.00	225.00	234.00
	30" box	435.00	413.00	425.00
	36" box	630.00	600.00	610.00
	42" box	950.00	890.00	920.00
	48" box	1280.00	1280.00	1280.00
	54" box	1760.00	1580.00	1670.00
	60" box	2120.00	2100.00	2110.00
324	**Pinus halepensis**			
	container			
	5 gal	17.40	13.70	15.80
	15 gal	69.00	59.00	63.00
	24" box	240.00	225.00	231.00
	30" box	435.00	413.00	424.00
	36" box	630.00	600.00	610.00
	42" box	950.00	890.00	920.00
	48" box	1280.00	1280.00	1280.00
326	**Pinus mugo**			
	balled and burlapped			
	12" ht	25.50	14.30	19.20
	15" ht	31.50	15.00	24.40
	18" ht	46.50	18.80	34.70
	2' ht	78.00	26.30	46.00
	container			
	1 gal	9.80	7.90	9.10
	2 gal	23.60	17.60	20.00
	3 gal	27.00	17.60	20.60
	12" ht	33.00	11.30	20.60
	15" ht	40.20	15.00	26.30
	18" ht	48.00	19.50	33.00
328	**Pinus mugo mugo**			
	balled and burlapped			
	15" ht	29.30	21.40	24.30
	18" ht	35.30	26.30	29.70
	container			
	1 gal	9.50	5.90	7.40
	2 gal	22.50	13.50	16.90
	15 gal	68.00	60.00	64.00
	12" ht	19.80	14.30	16.80
	15" ht	24.50	16.90	19.50
330	**Pinus nigra**			
	balled and burlapped			
	2' ht	30.40	22.50	25.80
	3' ht	87.00	26.60	47.40
	4' ht	143.00	33.40	75.00
	5' ht	188.00	47.60	105.00
	6' ht	270.00	95.00	147.00
	7' ht	334.00	120.00	189.00
	8' ht	363.00	150.00	237.00
	10' ht	550.00	210.00	332.00

	DESCRIPTION	HIGH	LOW	AVG.
	12' ht	660.00	248.00	422.00
	14" ht	660.00	375.00	478.00
	container			
	1 gal	5.30	4.65	4.98
	5 gal	17.40	16.50	16.80
	15 gal	71.00	69.00	70.00
332	**Pinus pinea**			
	container			
	1 gal	4.05	4.05	4.04
	5 gal	17.40	13.70	15.80
	15 gal	69.00	59.00	62.00
	24" box	248.00	225.00	234.00
	36" box	630.00	600.00	610.00
	48" box	1280.00	1280.00	1280.00
	60" box	2120.00	2100.00	2110.00
334	**Pinus ponderosa**			
	balled and burlapped			
	4' ht	84.00	60.00	72.00
	5' ht	107.00	83.00	96.00
	6' ht	122.00	113.00	118.00
	7' ht	144.00	135.00	140.00
	8' ht	401.00	150.00	230.00
	10' ht	500.00	210.00	324.00
336	**Pinus resinosa**			
	balled and burlapped			
	4' ht	72.00	46.50	59.00
	5' ht	120.00	60.00	90.00
	6' ht	120.00	83.00	110.00
	7' ht	173.00	137.00	153.00
	8' ht	207.00	138.00	167.00
	10' ht	300.00	153.00	246.00
	12' ht	372.00	224.00	308.00
338	**Pinus strobus**			
	balled and burlapped			
	2' ht	29.30	17.00	24.00
	3' ht	59.00	18.80	35.00
	4' ht	81.00	22.50	52.00
	5' ht	120.00	26.30	70.00
	6' ht	195.00	30.00	98.00
	7' ht	255.00	54.00	139.00
	8' ht	360.00	60.00	171.00
	10' ht	447.00	75.00	249.00
	12' ht	448.00	173.00	304.00
	14' ht	480.00	203.00	334.00
340	**Pinus strobus 'Nana'**			
	balled and burlapped			
	2' ht	150.00	75.00	105.00
	2 1/2' ht	135.00	105.00	118.00
342	**Pinus strobus 'Pendula'**			
	balled and burlapped			
	5' ht	177.00	120.00	144.00
	6' ht	240.00	128.00	188.00
	8' ht	338.00	216.00	278.00
344	**Pinus sylvestris**			
	balled and burlapped			
	3' ht	59.00	25.90	40.60
	4' ht	113.00	32.60	61.00
	5' ht	260.00	42.00	94.00
	6' ht	261.00	53.00	126.00

02950 Conifers

DESCRIPTION	HIGH	LOW	AVG.
7' ht	315.00	87.00	176.00
8' ht	390.00	89.00	211.00
10' ht	486.00	188.00	294.00
12' ht	492.00	248.00	363.00
346 Pinus taeda			
container			
1 gal	4.50	3.75	4.13
5 gal	19.70	12.00	15.80
10 gal	57.00	30.20	43.60
348 Pinus thunbergiana			
balled and burlapped			
2' ht	30.40	20.30	25.90
3' ht	53.00	26.30	39.80
4' ht	83.00	33.00	57.00
5' ht	120.00	49.50	83.00
6' ht	150.00	66.00	113.00
7' ht	188.00	90.00	140.00
8' ht	263.00	128.00	180.00
container			
1 gal	5.30	3.53	4.43
2 gal	11.00	7.50	9.40
3 gal	12.00	9.80	11.10
5 gal	17.40	13.50	15.10
7 gal	42.80	41.30	41.80
15 gal	75.00	59.00	65.00
24" box	248.00	225.00	234.00
30" box	435.00	413.00	424.00
36" box	630.00	600.00	610.00
350 Platycladus orientalis 'Berckmanni'			
container			
1 gal	4.65	3.38	4.08
2 gal	11.00	8.60	9.80
3 gal	11.60	11.60	11.60
5 gal	15.80	12.00	13.80
15 gal	59.00	56.00	57.00
352 Platycladus orientalis 'Blue Cone'			
container			
1 gal	4.65	3.45	4.07
5 gal	15.80	13.50	14.60
354 Podocarpus macrophyllus			
container			
1 gal	5.60	5.10	5.40
5 gal	18.00	16.10	16.90
15 gal	68.00	60.00	62.00
24" box	248.00	225.00	236.00
356 Podocarpus macrophyllus maki			
container			
1 gal	5.60	5.10	5.40
5 gal	18.90	16.10	17.40
15 gal	68.00	60.00	66.00
358 Pseudotsuga menziesii			
balled and burlapped			
3' ht	68.00	26.30	45.90
4' ht	94.00	45.00	66.00
5' ht	168.00	60.00	104.00
6' ht	270.00	83.00	142.00
7' ht	330.00	128.00	178.00
8' ht	362.00	150.00	210.00

DESCRIPTION	HIGH	LOW	AVG.
10' ht	550.00	188.00	310.00
12' ht	680.00	300.00	469.00
360 Sequoia sempervirens, varieties			
container			
5 gal	21.00	16.50	18.60
15 gal	69.00	59.00	62.00
24" box	240.00	225.00	231.00
30" box	435.00	413.00	420.00
36" box	630.00	600.00	610.00
42" box	950.00	890.00	920.00
48" box	1430.00	1280.00	1330.00
362 Taxodium distichum			
balled and burlapped			
1 1/2" cal	98.00	41.30	64.00
2" cal	188.00	60.00	118.00
2 1/2" cal	195.00	75.00	137.00
3" cal	300.00	90.00	203.00
3 1/2" cal	360.00	165.00	252.00
4" cal	413.00	225.00	300.00
4 1/2" cal	510.00	345.00	303.00
5" cal	690.00	300.00	462.00
5' ht	120.00	21.00	68.00
6' ht	164.00	28.50	96.00
7' ht	224.00	100.00	146.00
8' ht	269.00	102.00	168.00
10' ht	338.00	120.00	227.00
12' ht	339.00	225.00	286.00
14' ht	520.00	281.00	427.00
364 Taxus baccata 'Repandens'			
balled and burlapped			
15" ht	35.60	23.60	30.90
18" ht	57.00	26.60	41.50
2' ht	66.00	47.30	56.00
2 1/2' ht	81.00	62.00	72.00
366 Taxus cuspidata			
balled and burlapped			
15" ht	31.10	23.60	26.80
18" ht	68.00	24.00	39.90
2' ht	69.00	30.00	41.20
2 1/2' ht	87.00	50.00	64.00
368 Taxus cuspidata 'Capitata'			
balled and burlapped			
18" ht	45.00	22.50	30.20
2' ht	57.00	26.30	39.90
2 1/2' ht	83.00	30.00	51.00
3' ht	102.00	37.50	65.00
3 1/2' ht	126.00	51.00	79.00
4' ht	174.00	68.00	106.00
5' ht	175.00	102.00	130.00
370 Taxus x media 'Brownii'			
balled and burlapped			
15" ht	37.50	18.80	26.10
18" ht	51.00	21.00	31.40
2' ht	53.00	25.50	36.10
2 1/2' ht	64.00	33.80	51.00
372 Taxus x media 'Densiformis'			
balled and burlapped			
15" ht	39.00	18.00	26.60
18" ht	71.00	21.00	34.40

PLANTING

	DESCRIPTION	HIGH	LOW	AVG.
	2' ht	77.00	25.50	41.60
	2 1/2' ht	87.00	33.80	53.00
	3' ht	111.00	45.00	70.00
	4' ht	150.00	90.00	128.00
374	**Taxus x media 'Hatfieldii'**			
	balled and burlapped			
	15" ht	27.80	18.00	20.80
	18" ht	35.60	22.10	28.70
	2' ht	41.30	26.30	36.10
	2 1/2' ht	66.00	30.00	48.30
	3' ht	83.00	37.50	66.00
376	**Taxus x media 'Hicksii'**			
	balled and burlapped			
	15" ht	37.50	16.90	25.10
	18" ht	63.00	22.10	33.30
	2' ht	71.00	26.30	41.30
	2 1/2' ht	72.00	30.00	48.30
	3' ht	98.00	37.50	64.00
	3 1/2' ht	100.00	45.00	73.00
	4' ht	104.00	75.00	90.00
378	**Taxus x media 'Wardii'**			
	balled and burlapped			
	15" ht	40.50	21.40	28.90
	18" ht	43.50	26.30	33.30
	2' ht	47.90	30.00	39.30
	2 1/2' ht	53.00	37.50	43.00
380	**Thuja occidentalis 'Globosa'**			
	balled and burlapped			
	2' ht	21.00	14.30	16.70
	2 1/2' ht	26.30	18.80	21.80
	3' ht	37.50	22.50	29.70
382	**Thuja occidentalis 'Nigra'**			
	balled and burlapped			
	2' ht	24.80	12.40	19.60
	2 1/2' ht	31.50	16.50	24.10
	3' ht	53.00	16.50	28.40
	4' ht	74.00	22.50	40.60
	5' ht	125.00	33.80	57.00
	6' ht	158.00	45.00	83.00
	7' ht	203.00	60.00	124.00
384	**Thuja occidentalis 'Pyramidalis'**			
	balled and burlapped			
	2' ht	24.80	12.00	19.70
	2 1/2' ht	31.50	18.60	24.90
	3' ht	53.00	18.80	29.60
	4' ht	74.00	23.30	42.70
	5' ht	105.00	34.50	57.00
	6' ht	135.00	48.00	74.00
	7' ht	203.00	60.00	125.00
	container			
	1 gal	5.70	4.13	4.88
	5 gal	15.80	14.30	15.00
386	**Thuja occidentalis 'Techny'**			
	balled and burlapped			
	2 1/2' ht	45.80	25.60	32.80
	3' ht	62.00	25.90	36.50
	4' ht	90.00	36.40	52.00
	5' ht	125.00	48.80	76.00
	6' ht	158.00	75.00	112.00

	DESCRIPTION	HIGH	LOW	AVG.
388	**Thuja occidentalis 'Woodwardii'**			
	balled and burlapped			
	12" ht	13.10	9.90	11.50
	15" ht	16.10	11.20	14.20
	18" ht	24.40	12.10	18.40
	2' ht	28.10	15.80	22.50
	2 1/2' ht	32.60	21.00	29.80
	container			
	1 gal	5.70	4.13	5.00
	15 gal	15.80	12.00	13.50
390	**Tsuga canadensis**			
	balled and burlapped			
	2' ht	26.30	19.90	23.30
	2 1/2' ht	35.60	20.30	30.50
	3' ht	75.00	25.50	46.50
	4' ht	105.00	41.90	66.00
	5' ht	159.00	60.00	94.00
	6' ht	204.00	75.00	123.00
	7' ht	255.00	128.00	170.00
	8' ht	300.00	105.00	212.00

SHRUBS, TEMPERATE

	DESCRIPTION	HIGH	LOW	AVG.
200	**Abelia 'Edward Goucher'**			
	container			
	1 gal	6.80	3.38	4.22
	3 gal	13.50	11.70	12.40
	5 gal	24.00	12.00	16.00
	15 gal	66.00	56.00	61.00
202	**Abelia grandiflora**			
	balled and burlapped			
	18" ht	16.50	12.80	14.70
	2' ht	36.00	14.30	22.20
	3' ht	36.70	15.00	24.00
	container			
	1 gal	6.00	3.38	4.23
	3 gal	15.80	11.30	13.40
	5 gal	24.00	12.00	15.40
	15" ht	18.80	13.80	15.80
	18" ht	21.00	15.90	19.20
204	**Aronia arbutifolia 'Brilliantisma'**			
	balled and burlapped			
	2' ht	22.90	11.30	17.50
	2 1/2' ht	23.70	13.50	19.50
	3' ht	36.00	15.00	24.20
	4' ht	48.00	22.50	35.90
	bare root			
	18" ht	7.50	4.88	5.80
	2' ht	9.80	5.30	7.00
	container			
	18" ht	15.40	11.70	13.50
	2' ht	21.00	12.70	16.70
206	**Aronia melanocarpa**			
	balled and burlapped			
	2' ht	27.00	11.30	18.80
	2 1/2' ht	33.00	17.90	22.80
	3' ht	36.00	18.00	25.80
	bare root			
	2' ht	11.10	5.30	7.60

02950 Shrubs, Temperate

DESCRIPTION	HIGH	LOW	AVG.
208 Azalea exbury, hybrids			
balled and burlapped			
15" ht	27.20	15.80	23.30
18" ht	33.00	19.10	26.70
2' ht	49.50	21.00	29.60
2 1/2' ht	68.00	24.00	38.70
3' ht	48.00	26.30	34.90
container			
2 gal	14.80	12.50	13.20
5 gal	26.30	24.90	25.60
210 Azalea 'Girard', hybrids			
container			
1 gal	7.10	3.60	5.00
2 gal	14.80	9.90	12.50
3 gal	21.00	11.00	17.10
15" ht	18.80	13.70	15.80
18" ht	21.00	18.40	19.50
212 Azalea kaempferi, hybrids			
container			
2 gal	13.00	11.60	12.30
2' ht	22.90	19.40	21.20
214 Berberis julianae			
balled and burlapped			
18" ht	22.50	16.50	19.30
2' ht	33.00	20.30	25.40
2 1/2" ht	43.50	24.00	31.70
3' ht	53.00	30.00	42.80
container			
1 gal	3.90	3.75	3.81
2 gal	25.40	18.80	22.00
216 Berberis x mentorensis			
balled and burlapped			
2' ht	18.00	12.80	14.60
bare root			
18" ht	6.00	4.73	5.40
container			
1 gal	6.80	4.13	5.10
2 gal	16.10	8.90	11.90
5 gal	22.50	11.90	14.80
218 Berberis thunbergii			
balled and burlapped			
18" ht	18.00	11.30	14.20
2' ht	24.00	12.00	17.10
2 1/2' ht	30.00	17.30	22.80
bare root			
15" ht	4.88	4.65	4.76
18" ht	5.60	5.30	5.50
container			
5 gal	12.80	12.20	12.40
220 Berberis thunbergii 'Atropurpurea'			
balled and burlapped			
18" ht	19.70	11.60	15.30
2' ht	24.00	12.80	18.20
2 1/2' ht	30.00	18.00	22.30
bare root			
9" ht	2.85	2.33	2.60
12" ht	3.75	3.23	3.50
15" ht	7.90	4.35	5.30
18" ht	9.00	5.30	6.30

DESCRIPTION	HIGH	LOW	AVG.
container			
1 gal	9.00	3.75	5.10
2 gal	16.10	8.90	11.70
3 gal	16.50	9.80	13.10
5 gal	22.50	12.00	14.80
12" ht	13.80	4.65	9.40
15" ht	13.90	9.90	11.40
18" ht	15.60	11.30	13.20
222 Berberis thunbergii 'Aurea'			
container			
1 gal	8.30	4.13	5.70
2 gal	17.60	8.90	12.60
3 gal	24.00	12.00	16.80
224 Berberis thunbergii 'Crimson Pygmy'			
balled and burlapped			
12" ht	20.30	15.60	17.10
15" ht	24.80	18.40	21.50
container			
1 gal	9.80	4.13	6.10
2 gal	21.60	8.70	12.50
3 gal	28.50	11.60	18.20
12" ht	19.80	13.00	16.80
15" ht	23.40	13.40	17.50
18" ht	28.50	15.80	21.80
226 Berberis thunbergii 'Rosy Glow'			
balled and burlapped			
18" ht	19.10	15.80	17.10
2' ht	22.50	18.80	20.10
container			
1 gal	9.80	4.13	6.00
2 gal	17.60	8.70	12.00
3 gal	24.00	11.30	15.50
12" ht	15.80	8.60	13.10
15" ht	19.80	12.60	15.50
228 Buddlea davidii, varities			
container			
1 gal	5.10	3.60	4.26
2 gal	18.00	7.50	11.50
3 gal	18.40	9.80	13.40
5 gal	18.80	12.80	15.00
230 Buxus microphylla japonica			
container			
1 gal	4.28	3.38	3.93
2 gal	9.90	8.90	9.80
3 gal	11.60	9.00	10.90
5 gal	14.90	12.00	13.50
15 gal	56.00	53.00	54.00
232 Buxus microphylla koreana 'Wintergreen'			
balled and burlapped			
15" ht	43.50	16.50	32.60
18" ht	53.00	20.60	40.40
container			
1 gal	6.80	3.90	4.77
2 gal	20.60	8.60	13.30
5 gal	22.50	11.60	15.90
234 Buxus sempervirens			
balled and burlapped			
12" ht	18.00	15.80	17.00
15" ht	24.00	18.00	21.20

PLANTING

DESCRIPTION	HIGH	LOW	AVG.
18" ht	30.00	20.00	30.00
2' ht	50.00	40.00	40.00
2 1/2' ht	70.00	50.00	60.00
container			
12" ht	20.00	10.00	20.00
236 Calycanthus floridus			
balled and burlapped			
2' ht	40.00	10.00	20.00
238 Camellia sasanqua, varieties			
container			
1 gal	7.10	4.88	5.80
5 gal	21.00	15.00	18.40
15 gal	75.00	64.00	69.00
240 Caragana arborescens 'Pendula'			
balled and burlapped			
1 1/2" cal	132.00	123.00	130.00
2" cal	162.00	125.00	141.00
2 1/2" cal	209.00	150.00	179.00
242 Chaenomeles speciosa 'Texas Scarlet'			
balled and burlapped			
2' ht	24.00	20.00	22.60
3' ht	36.00	27.00	32.90
container			
2 gal	12.20	8.90	10.70
18" ht	15.80	12.20	13.90
244 Chaenomeles speciosa, varieties			
balled and burlapped			
15" ht	16.50	9.00	13.10
18" ht	21.00	11.30	15.60
2' ht	22.50	11.30	17.30
3' ht	36.00	12.80	21.00
bare root			
18" ht	0.00	0.00	0.00
2' ht	0.00	0.00	0.00
container			
1 gal	4.88	3.60	4.28
2 gal	12.20	9.40	10.90
5 gal	15.80	12.00	13.70
246 Clethra alnifolia			
container			
2 gal	19.10	10.10	15.70
18" ht	16.50	12.50	14.30
248 Cornus alba 'Sibirica'			
balled and burlapped			
3' ht	27.40	11.30	17.50
4' ht	39.40	17.00	24.40
5' ht	59.00	21.20	33.40
6' ht	82.00	25.50	48.80
bare root			
2' ht	7.90	4.50	5.60
3' ht	10.10	5.90	7.40
4' ht	11.90	7.00	8.80
250 Cornus mas			
balled and burlapped			
3' ht	74.00	20.70	41.10
4' ht	86.00	25.50	50.00
5' ht	104.00	35.60	64.00

DESCRIPTION	HIGH	LOW	AVG.
6' ht	105.00	83.00	86.00
8' ht	147.00	113.00	131.00
252 Cornus mas 'Elegantissima'			
balled and burlapped			
2' ht	18.00	15.00	16.30
2 1/2' ht	18.80	15.80	17.10
3' ht	22.50	16.50	20.10
4' ht	29.30	19.50	25.70
container			
2 gal	15.00	8.90	12.20
254 Cornus racemosa			
balled and burlapped			
2' ht	13.50	9.80	12.50
2 1/2' ht	19.50	13.20	15.90
3' ht	22.50	11.30	17.40
4' ht	27.00	16.50	21.30
5' ht	33.00	22.50	27.90
6' ht	50.00	30.00	39.10
bare root			
2' ht	7.90	4.73	6.00
3' ht	9.60	6.10	7.30
4' ht	11.90	7.40	9.20
256 Cornus sericea			
balled and burlapped			
2' ht	20.30	9.80	15.20
3' ht	27.40	11.30	20.40
4' ht	39.00	14.30	25.80
5' ht	39.30	20.90	26.60
bare root			
2' ht	5.30	4.43	4.71
3' ht	6.80	5.60	6.10
4' ht	8.30	6.80	7.30
container			
1 gal	5.30	4.50	5.00
5 gal	22.50	12.00	14.70
258 Cornus sericea 'Baileyi'			
balled and burlapped			
2' ht	19.90	12.00	15.20
3' ht	20.30	13.40	15.70
4' ht	30.00	15.40	21.90
5' ht	31.50	17.60	23.00
6' ht	50.00	25.50	32.60
bare root			
2' ht	4.50	3.68	4.32
3' ht	7.50	3.75	5.60
container			
1 gal	5.10	4.65	4.88
5 gal	15.80	12.20	13.90
260 Cornus sericea 'Flaviramea'			
balled and burlapped			
2' ht	20.30	10.50	15.50
3' ht	27.40	13.50	20.40
4' ht	30.00	15.80	20.80
bare root			
2' ht	7.90	4.05	5.70
3' ht	9.60	5.20	6.80
container			
1 gal	5.30	4.65	4.97
5 gal	17.00	12.00	14.30
2' ht	18.00	10.50	13.80
3' ht	25.50	11.30	18.60

02950 Shrubs, Temperate

	DESCRIPTION	HIGH	LOW	AVG.
262	**Corylus avellana 'Contorta'**			
	balled and burlapped			
	2' ht	60.00	37.50	51.00
	2 1/2' ht	83.00	46.80	71.00
	3' ht	135.00	53.00	85.00
	4' ht	225.00	75.00	120.00
	container			
	2 gal	29.90	27.00	28.20
264	**Cotinus coggygria**			
	balled and burlapped			
	4' ht	116.00	21.00	52.00
	5' ht	143.00	24.00	57.00
	6' ht	170.00	27.00	90.00
266	**Cotinus coggygria 'Royal Purple'**			
	balled and burlapped			
	2' ht	33.60	17.30	26.00
	3' ht	42.00	27.00	35.00
268	**Cotoneaster acutifolius**			
	balled and burlapped			
	2 1/2" cal	15.80	13.10	14.90
	3' ht	27.70	14.80	19.50
	4' ht	27.80	16.20	20.70
	5' ht	29.90	22.40	26.00
	bare root			
	18" ht	3.15	2.55	2.90
	2' ht	4.20	3.68	3.99
	3' ht	5.40	4.65	5.10
	container			
	1 gal	5.30	4.28	4.76
	5 gal	15.00	12.20	14.00
	3' ht	46.50	14.10	25.10
270	**Cotoneaster adpressus praecox**			
	container			
	1 gal	4.65	3.75	4.17
	2 gal	12.80	8.40	10.90
	12" ht	11.30	10.10	10.60
	15" ht	13.50	11.20	12.30
	18" ht	18.00	12.80	15.30
272	**Cotoneaster congestus**			
	container			
	3 gal	18.80	11.60	15.20
	5 gal	24.00	15.00	19.50
274	**Cotoneaster dammeri 'Skogsholmen'**			
	container			
	18" ht	23.40	15.30	19.30
276	**Cotoneaster divaricatus**			
	balled and burlapped			
	2' ht	19.50	8.20	17.30
	3' ht	39.40	8.30	23.50
	container	0.00	0.00	0.00
	1 gal	4.65	3.75	4.23
	3 gal	13.50	11.60	12.60
	5 gal	15.00	13.10	14.00
	12" ht	11.30	4.65	8.20
	18" ht	14.20	9.70	12.00
	2' ht	14.30	9.80	12.30
	3' ht	15.60	11.30	14.10

	DESCRIPTION	HIGH	LOW	AVG.
278	**Cotoneaster horizontalis**			
	container			
	1 gal	8.30	3.38	4.80
	2 gal	13.50	10.10	12.10
	3 gal	18.80	11.60	14.60
	5 gal	24.00	12.00	15.70
	15" ht	13.50	11.20	12.40
	18" ht	18.00	12.80	15.50
280	**Deutzia gracilis**			
	balled and burlapped			
	18" ht	15.80	10.10	12.40
	2' ht	19.50	14.60	16.40
	bare root			
	18" ht	10.10	7.40	8.60
	container			
	1 gal	5.70	3.75	4.46
	3 gal	20.30	8.30	14.70
	15" ht	13.40	11.40	12.40
282	**Dievilla sessilifolia**			
	balled and burlapped			
	3' ht	18.80	14.90	16.20
	4' ht	24.80	19.80	22.30
284	**Elaeagnus angustifolia**			
	bare root			
	2' ht	7.90	6.20	6.80
	3' ht	9.60	7.70	8.70
	4' ht	11.30	9.20	10.50
	container			
	5 gal	15.80	15.00	15.40
286	**Elaeagnus ebbingei**			
	container			
	1 gal	4.28	3.75	4.10
	5 gal	15.30	15.00	15.20
288	**Elaeagnus pungens 'Fruitlandii'**			
	container			
	1 gal	4.28	3.75	4.05
	3 gal	13.50	11.30	12.00
	5 gal	15.30	13.70	14.60
290	**Elaeagnus umbellata**			
	container			
	3' ht	29.60	11.30	18.60
	4' ht	38.30	22.50	27.80
	5' ht	46.10	30.00	35.40
	bare root			
	2' ht	7.90	4.50	6.20
	3' ht	9.60	6.00	7.70
292	**Euonymus alata**			
	balled and burlapped			
	18" ht	24.40	14.90	19.70
	2' ht	30.00	15.40	23.60
	2 1/2' ht	42.00	16.90	30.30
	3' ht	63.00	18.00	40.20
	4' ht	65.00	45.00	55.00
	5' ht	84.00	60.00	72.00
	bare root			
	12" ht	8.60	4.88	6.30
	15" ht	10.10	7.10	8.20
	18" ht	11.60	8.10	9.30
	2' ht	11.60	9.60	9.80

PLANTING

	DESCRIPTION	HIGH	LOW	AVG.
	container			
	5 gal	19.50	16.70	18.10
294	**Euonymus alata 'Compacta'**			
	balled and burlapped			
	15" ht	23.60	13.50	16.90
	18" ht	27.00	15.00	21.10
	2' ht	33.80	19.50	25.60
	3' ht	66.00	24.00	42.40
	3 1/2' ht	80.00	30.00	59.00
	4' ht	95.00	72.00	80.00
	bare root			
	12" ht	9.60	5.80	6.90
	15" ht	12.40	8.00	9.60
	18" ht	14.60	8.00	11.10
	container			
	1 gal	6.00	3.38	4.88
	2 gal	23.00	10.10	14.10
	3 gal	23.10	16.10	18.60
	15" ht	21.80	12.40	16.60
	18" ht	27.00	15.50	20.10
	2' ht	25.50	18.60	23.20
296	**Euonymus fortunei 'Emerald Gaiety'**			
	container			
	1 gal	10.50	4.13	6.40
	2 gal	21.00	9.00	14.00
	5 gal	23.90	15.80	20.70
	12" ht	15.80	11.50	13.50
	15" ht	21.00	13.40	16.00
298	**Euonymus fortunei 'Emerald 'n Gold'**			
	container			
	1 gal	10.50	3.75	6.20
	2 gal	21.00	8.30	13.30
	3 gal	27.00	13.90	18.70
	12" ht	15.80	11.50	13.80
	15" ht	19.50	13.40	16.20
	18" ht	20.30	18.80	18.80
300	**Euonymus fortunei 'Gracilis'**			
	container			
	1 gal	4.28	3.75	4.05
302	**Euonymus fortunei 'Sarcoxie'**			
	balled and burlapped			
	18" ht	35.90	11.30	22.50
	2' ht	40.50	15.00	29.00
	container			
	1 gal	5.30	4.65	5.00
	3 gal	14.60	10.50	12.50
	12" ht	13.50	10.40	11.60
	15" ht	15.80	11.90	14.00
	18" ht	16.90	14.50	15.60
304	**Euonymus fortunei 'Silver Queen'**			
	container			
	1 gal	4.65	3.90	4.20
	5 gal	24.00	13.10	17.00
306	**Euonymus japonica**			
	container			
	1 gal	4.13	3.38	3.80
	5 gal	13.90	12.00	13.00

	DESCRIPTION	HIGH	LOW	AVG.
308	**Euonymus japonica 'Albo-marginata'**			
	container			
	1 gal	9.00	3.38	4.70
	2 gal	24.80	8.60	13.60
	5 gal	30.00	12.00	17.70
	15 gal	56.00	56.00	56.00
310	**Euonymus japonica 'Aureo-variegata'**			
	container			
	1 gal	9.00	3.38	4.82
	2 gal	24.80	10.10	14.60
	5 gal	30.00	12.00	17.70
312	**Euonymus japonica 'Microphylla'**			
	container			
	1 gal	4.58	3.38	4.02
	5 gal	13.10	12.00	12.60
314	**Euonymus japonica 'Silver King'**			
	container			
	1 gal	9.00	3.38	4.92
	2 gal	24.80	10.10	13.70
	5 gal	30.00	12.00	16.60
	12" ht	12.60	10.40	11.40
	15" ht	19.80	13.10	16.20
316	**Euonymus kiatschovicus 'Manhattan'**			
	balled and burlapped			
	18" ht	17.40	10.90	14.90
	2' ht	28.10	13.50	20.70
	2 1/2' ht	28.40	19.50	23.10
	container			
	1 gal	6.80	3.68	4.49
	2 gal	16.10	11.00	12.80
	3 gal	18.00	9.80	12.90
	5 gal	24.00	13.90	18.70
318	**Forsythia intermedia 'Arnold Dwarf'**			
	balled and burlapped			
	18" ht	14.60	11.00	12.20
	2' ht	16.50	11.30	13.80
	3' ht	19.90	16.10	18.00
320	**Forsythia intermedia 'Beatrix Farr'**			
	balled and burlapped			
	3' ht	16.10	11.30	13.60
	4' ht	20.60	18.00	19.10
322	**Forsythia intermedia 'Lynwood Gold'**			
	balled and burlapped			
	2' ht	18.00	9.00	12.00
	3' ht	21.00	10.50	14.60
	4' ht	27.00	13.10	19.10
	5' ht	33.00	15.80	24.40
	6' ht	41.40	28.50	35.00
	bare root			
	2' ht	5.30	3.75	4.47
	3' ht	7.60	4.88	6.20
	4' ht	7.80	6.40	6.90
	container			
	1 gal	6.80	3.53	4.97
	2 gal	8.90	8.90	8.90
	3 gal	12.50	11.30	11.90
	5 gal	22.50	12.20	15.90
	12" ht	8.20	4.35	6.30
	2' ht	15.00	10.40	12.00

02950 Shrubs, Temperate

DESCRIPTION	HIGH	LOW	AVG.
324 Forsythia intermedia 'Spectablis'			
balled and burlapped			
2' ht	14.60	9.80	11.90
3' ht	19.10	11.30	14.80
4' ht	24.00	15.00	18.80
5' ht	33.00	18.00	24.60
bare root			
2' ht	6.80	3.75	5.00
3' ht	7.90	4.88	6.30
4' ht	10.10	6.80	8.10
container			
4' ht	22.50	14.30	17.30
326 Forsythia intermedia 'Spring Glory'			
balled and burlapped			
2' ht	18.00	9.80	12.30
3' ht	21.00	11.30	14.70
4' ht	24.00	13.50	18.60
5' ht	33.00	19.50	25.20
bare root			
2' ht	5.30	2.78	4.07
3' ht	6.80	4.50	5.60
4' ht	7.50	6.50	6.90
container			
1 gal	6.80	3.53	4.82
5 gal	22.50	12.80	15.90
328 Forsythia suspensa			
balled and burlapped			
2' ht	15.00	9.80	12.20
3' ht	18.80	11.30	15.80
4' ht	24.00	18.80	20.60
5' ht	45.80	22.50	31.10
bare root			
2' ht	9.60	5.30	6.80
3' ht	12.40	6.80	8.60
330 Forsythia viridissima 'Bronxensis'			
balled and burlapped			
15" ht	15.80	12.80	14.80
18" ht	18.00	14.40	16.10
2' ht	19.50	16.50	17.90
bare root			
12" ht	7.90	4.65	5.70
container			
1 gal	5.30	4.28	4.77
5 gal	12.80	12.00	12.40
12" ht	20.30	10.90	15.40
18" ht	26.40	11.50	17.80
332 Hamamelis virginiana			
balled and burlapped			
2' ht	24.80	13.50	20.80
2 1/2' ht	31.40	15.80	27.70
3' ht	66.00	16.50	37.40
4' ht	90.00	19.50	48.50
5' ht	113.00	22.50	68.00
6' ht	120.00	25.50	77.00
334 Hibiscus syriacus, varieties			
balled and burlapped			
18" ht	21.90	9.00	14.30
2' ht	25.90	9.80	15.60
3' ht	25.50	12.00	17.90
4' ht	28.90	13.50	23.80
5' ht	40.50	30.00	36.00

DESCRIPTION	HIGH	LOW	AVG.
bare root			
18" ht	7.90	3.15	5.10
2' ht	8.90	4.13	6.10
3' ht	9.00	4.43	6.40
container			
1 gal	5.30	3.60	4.35
3 gal	17.00	11.60	13.50
5 gal	25.00	12.40	16.70
3' ht	16.10	13.80	14.90
336 Hydrangea arborescens 'Annabelle'			
balled and burlapped			
18" ht	22.50	18.80	20.20
2' ht	26.40	22.40	23.80
2 1/2' ht	33.00	26.90	29.90
container			
2 gal	13.40	8.90	10.90
5 gal	15.70	12.80	14.20
338 Hydrangea macrophylla, varieties			
container			
1 gal	7.40	3.98	5.20
2 gal	15.00	5.30	11.40
3 gal	20.30	6.80	13.20
5 gal	22.50	11.30	15.70
340 Hydrangea paniculata 'Grandiflora'			
balled and burlapped			
18" ht	24.00	10.50	15.10
2' ht	26.30	12.80	18.90
3' ht	27.00	14.30	22.60
bare root			
18" ht	7.50	4.73	5.70
2' ht	14.20	6.10	8.80
container			
5 gal	39.80	15.70	28.50
18" ht	21.90	9.30	16.70
2' ht	25.10	12.40	18.40
3' ht	39.80	14.20	28.80
342 Hydrangea quercifolia			
balled and burlapped			
18" ht	24.80	10.50	18.80
2' ht	31.50	12.00	22.80
3' ht	62.00	13.50	30.60
container			
1 gal	4.43	4.13	4.26
18" ht	20.60	12.80	17.40
344 Hypericum x moseranum			
container			
1 gal	4.43	3.38	4.01
5 gal	13.70	12.00	12.80
346 Ilex 'Nellie R. Stevens'			
balled and burlapped			
3' ht	60.00	33.00	45.00
4' ht	113.00	53.00	77.00
5' ht	173.00	72.00	110.00
6' ht	239.00	98.00	142.00
7' ht	383.00	113.00	220.00
8' ht	520.00	326.00	404.00
container			
1 gal	5.30	3.68	4.31
5 gal	17.30	12.40	14.80
7 gal	47.30	31.50	38.70

PLANTING

DESCRIPTION	HIGH	LOW	AVG.
10 gal	48.80	48.80	48.80
15 gal	90.00	59.00	70.00
348 Ilex x altaclarensis 'Wilsonii'			
container			
1 gal	4.50	3.38	3.93
5 gal	14.60	12.00	13.30
15 gal	60.00	56.00	58.00
350 Ilex cornuta 'Bufordii'			
container			
1 gal	5.70	3.38	4.25
2 gal	10.40	8.40	9.50
3 gal	11.60	11.40	11.60
5 gal	15.80	12.00	14.30
15 gal	68.00	56.00	61.00
352 Ilex cornuta 'Dwarf Buford'			
container			
1 gal	5.30	3.38	4.19
2 gal	10.50	8.40	9.80
3 gal	16.50	11.40	13.20
5 gal	17.30	12.00	14.30
354 Ilex cornuta 'Rotunda'			
container			
1 gal	4.50	3.38	4.04
2 gal	10.40	8.30	9.20
3 gal	11.60	11.40	11.60
5 gal	15.80	12.00	14.30
15 gal	59.00	56.00	57.00
356 Ilex crenata 'Compacta'			
container			
1 gal	5.30	3.68	4.28
2 gal	17.60	8.50	12.20
3 gal	21.80	11.50	14.00
15" ht	16.40	10.40	13.40
18" ht	18.80	14.60	16.40
358 Ilex crenata 'Convexa'			
balled and burlapped			
15" ht	18.00	12.80	15.40
18" ht	27.40	13.50	19.80
2' ht	37.10	22.50	28.70
2 1/2' ht	51.00	28.50	39.20
3' ht	63.00	37.50	52.00
360 Ilex crenata 'Helleri'			
container			
1 gal	9.00	3.68	5.80
2 gal	18.80	7.90	12.40
3 gal	21.80	9.00	14.10
12" ht	12.40	9.00	10.80
15" ht	16.50	13.40	15.30
18" ht	21.80	15.40	18.50
362 Ilex crenata 'Hetzii'			
balled and burlapped			
15" ht	20.60	12.80	16.70
18" ht	27.40	13.50	21.40
2' ht	37.10	22.50	30.80
2 1/2' ht	51.00	28.50	43.60
3' ht	63.00	37.50	49.20
container			
1 gal	5.30	3.68	4.43

DESCRIPTION	HIGH	LOW	AVG.
2 gal	17.60	8.30	11.90
3 gal	24.00	11.60	16.50
15" ht	22.50	10.40	16.40
18" ht	25.50	15.80	20.00
364 Ilex crenata 'Microphylla'			
balled and burlapped			
2' ht	24.00	22.50	23.30
3' ht	40.50	30.00	35.30
366 Ilex crenata 'Rotundifolia'			
balled and burlapped			
15" ht	18.80	12.80	15.70
18" ht	19.50	13.50	15.90
2' ht	43.10	23.30	30.10
2 1/2' ht	51.00	28.50	37.90
container			
1 gal	4.13	3.83	3.98
3 gal	11.60	11.50	11.60
368 Ilex glabra			
balled and burlapped			
15" ht	19.90	15.00	16.60
18" ht	34.10	18.80	24.20
2' ht	40.90	25.90	31.70
370 Ilex glabra 'Compacta'			
balled and burlapped			
15" ht	31.50	14.30	21.20
18" ht	37.10	17.30	25.80
2' ht	40.50	22.50	31.40
container			
2 gal	18.40	9.80	13.50
15" ht	19.90	14.60	16.50
372 Ilex x meserveae, varieties			
balled and burlapped			
18" ht	53.00	18.00	30.20
2' ht	69.00	24.80	44.50
2 1/2' ht	84.00	33.00	61.00
3' ht	101.00	41.30	74.00
4' ht	149.00	56.00	115.00
5' ht	257.00	79.00	179.00
container			
1 gal	11.30	4.13	7.10
2 gal	24.80	9.80	15.50
3 gal	24.90	11.60	18.80
5 gal	32.90	16.70	23.40
7 gal	60.00	39.00	46.60
12" ht	14.90	12.80	13.60
15" ht	22.50	15.00	18.60
18" ht	40.50	16.40	26.60
2' ht	43.50	24.70	35.20
374 Ilex opaca			
balled and burlapped			
4' ht	98.00	37.50	81.00
7' ht	240.00	188.00	212.00
8' ht	375.00	263.00	312.00
376 Ilex opaca 'Fosteri'			
balled and burlapped			
6' ht	135.00	68.00	103.00
7' ht	180.00	132.00	161.00
8' ht	263.00	179.00	215.00

02950 Shrubs, Temperate

	DESCRIPTION	HIGH	LOW	AVG.
378	**Ilex opaca 'Fosteri II'**			
	balled and burlapped			
	4' ht	56.00	45.00	51.00
	5' ht	161.00	68.00	97.00
	6' ht	192.00	98.00	124.00
	7' ht	195.00	135.00	137.00
	8' ht	243.00	180.00	211.00
380	**Ilex verticillata**			
	balled and burlapped			
	2' ht	39.40	18.80	25.80
	3' ht	52.00	22.50	36.20
382	**Ilex vomitoria 'Nana'**			
	container			
	1 gal	4.50	4.13	4.29
	5 gal	15.80	13.10	14.40
384	**Ilex vomitoria 'Schillings Dwarf'**			
	container			
	1 gal	4.13	3.68	3.87
	2 gal	9.80	8.30	8.80
	3 gal	11.60	9.00	10.90
386	**Ilex vomitoria 'Stokes Dwarf'**			
	container			
	1 gal	4.50	4.28	4.38
	5 gal	15.00	13.90	14.50
388	**Jasminum floridum**			
	container			
	1 gal	4.28	3.75	4.01
390	**Kalmia latifolia**			
	balled and burlapped			
	18" ht	28.50	26.30	27.20
	2' ht	37.50	33.00	34.70
	3' ht	53.00	45.00	48.50
	4' ht	75.00	60.00	70.00
392	**Kolkwitzia amabilis**			
	balled and burlapped			
	2' ht	18.00	11.30	14.70
	3' ht	22.50	15.00	18.80
	container			
	5 gal	20.30	13.70	16.30
394	**Lagerstroemia indica, varieties**			
	balled and burlapped			
	3' ht	30.00	21.80	26.00
	4' ht	54.00	23.90	37.90
	5' ht	60.00	36.00	50.00
	6' ht	83.00	56.00	71.00
	7' ht	105.00	65.00	91.00
	8' ht	150.00	90.00	122.00
	10' ht	242.00	113.00	175.00
	container			
	1 gal	5.90	3.53	4.68
	3 gal	13.50	11.30	12.20
	5 gal	18.80	11.60	15.50
	15 gal	71.00	56.00	63.00
	24" box	246.00	270.00	218.00
396	**Leucothoe axillaris (L. cataesbaei)**			
	balled and burlapped			
	18" ht	39.00	18.80	26.30

	DESCRIPTION	HIGH	LOW	AVG.
	container			
	1 gal	15.00	4.13	8.10
	2 gal	20.30	9.80	14.80
	15" ht	18.80	16.30	17.70
398	**Leucothoe fontanesiana, varieties**			
	container			
	2 gal	18.80	12.70	15.10
	12" ht	18.00	12.70	14.70
	15' ht	19.50	13.40	15.50
400	**Ligustrum amurense**			
	bare root			
	2' ht	3.38	2.93	3.09
	3' ht	4.88	4.05	4.47
402	**Ligustrum x ibolium**			
	bare root			
	2' ht	3.90	2.93	3.18
	3' ht	5.10	3.38	4.25
	4' ht	8.10	4.50	6.20
404	**Ligustrum japonicum**			
	container			
	1 gal	4.28	3.90	4.02
	5 gal	15.00	13.10	14.10
	15 gal	60.00	50.00	56.00
	24" box	240.00	225.00	233.00
406	**Ligustrum japonicum 'Texanum'**			
	container			
	1 gal	4.28	3.38	3.87
	5 gal	15.00	12.00	13.40
	15 gal	66.00	50.00	58.00
408	**Ligustrum obtusifolium regelianum**			
	balled and burlapped			
	2' ht	16.80	8.30	13.00
	2 1/2' ht	18.30	11.30	15.80
	3' ht	20.30	11.40	16.70
	bare root			
	18" ht	4.88	3.00	4.10
	2' ht	6.40	4.50	5.20
410	**Ligustrum ovalifolium**			
	bare root			
	18" ht	3.38	1.13	2.22
	2' ht	3.90	2.93	3.30
	3' ht	7.10	3.38	4.82
	4' ht	8.10	4.50	6.20
412	**Ligustrum x vicaryi**			
	container			
	1 gal	6.80	3.60	4.94
	2 gal	15.70	8.40	10.50
	3 gal	15.80	11.30	13.40
	5 gal	22.50	12.80	15.80
	15" ht	15.00	10.00	13.10
	18" ht	17.40	8.40	13.10
414	**Ligustrum vulgare 'Cheyenne'**			
	balled and burlapped			
	4' ht	16.00	14.30	15.10
	5' ht	19.40	16.10	18.10

PLANTING

	DESCRIPTION	HIGH	LOW	AVG.
416	**Ligustrum vulgare 'Lodense'**			
	container			
	1 gal	6.80	4.28	5.50
	2 gal	16.10	12.80	14.40
	5 gal	22.50	13.10	16.90
418	**Lonicera fragrantissima**			
	balled and burlapped			
	2' ht	16.50	10.50	12.80
	3' ht	21.00	12.00	16.40
	bare root			
	2' ht	9.00	4.05	6.50
	3' ht	10.80	4.95	7.30
420	**Lonicera korolkowii zabelii**			
	balled and burlapped			
	2' ht	11.30	9.80	10.50
	3' ht	18.00	11.30	13.80
	4' ht	19.40	14.60	17.70
	5' ht	41.90	22.50	29.60
	bare root			
	2' ht	6.80	3.75	4.88
	3' ht	8.40	5.30	6.20
	4' ht	10.10	6.60	7.90
422	**Lonicera tatarica 'Arnold's Red'**			
	balled and burlapped			
	3' ht	16.80	12.00	14.00
	4' ht	18.40	16.50	17.50
424	**Lonicera tatarica, varieties**			
	balled and burlapped			
	2' ht	18.00	9.80	12.80
	3' ht	24.00	11.30	15.70
	bare root			
	2' ht	6.80	4.58	5.50
	3' ht	8.40	5.40	6.80
426	**Lonicera x xylosteoides 'Claveys Dwarf'**			
	balled and burlapped			
	18" ht	13.90	11.30	12.50
	2' ht	15.60	12.00	14.30
	2 1/2' ht	18.00	12.80	15.90
	3' ht	22.50	12.80	18.10
	4' ht	25.50	18.80	22.20
	bare root			
	15" ht	3.15	2.55	2.85
	18" ht	5.30	3.38	4.16
	2' ht	6.00	4.13	4.83
428	**Magnolia stellata**			
	balled and burlapped			
	3' ht	105.00	25.50	56.00
	4' ht	135.00	30.00	72.00
	5' ht	165.00	60.00	97.00
	6' ht	210.00	90.00	142.00
	container			
	15 gal	68.00	60.00	64.00
	24" box	240.00	225.00	233.00
430	**Magnolia stellata 'Royal Star'**			
	balled and burlapped			
	2' ht	39.00	33.00	35.70
	3' ht	55.00	35.30	45.80
	4' ht	108.00	48.00	78.00
	5' ht	141.00	67.00	101.00

	DESCRIPTION	HIGH	LOW	AVG.
	container			
	5 gal	30.30	13.50	21.70
	7 gal	60.00	37.50	48.20
432	**Magnolia virginiana**			
	balled and burlapped			
	4' ht	59.00	47.30	53.00
	5' ht	71.00	67.00	68.00
	6' ht	113.00	83.00	98.00
	8' ht	225.00	98.00	145.00
434	**Magnolia virginiana 'Glauca'**			
	balled and burlapped			
	4' ht	46.50	46.50	46.50
	5' ht	63.00	57.00	61.00
	6' ht	95.00	86.00	92.00
436	**Mahonia aquifolium**			
	container			
	1 gal	7.50	5.30	6.10
	5 gal	24.80	13.10	19.60
	15 gal	60.00	56.00	58.00
438	**Mahonia aquifolium 'Compacta'**			
	container			
	1 gal	7.50	6.90	7.20
	5 gal	22.40	14.60	19.10
440	**Mahonia bealei**			
	container			
	1 gal	5.00	4.13	4.61
	5 gal	16.90	13.50	15.40
442	**Myrica pensylvanica**			
	balled and burlapped			
	18" ht	25.50	9.80	18.90
	2' ht	39.00	12.80	24.20
	2 1/2' ht	59.00	18.80	32.80
	container			
	2 gal	17.60	11.20	13.70
	3 gal	21.00	11.30	15.30
	12" ht	14.90	4.80	10.70
	15" ht	15.00	11.20	12.50
	18" ht	19.50	15.70	16.80
444	**Nandina domestica**			
	container			
	1 gal	4.50	3.38	3.99
	3 gal	13.50	11.60	12.10
	5 gal	15.30	12.00	13.70
	15 gal	60.00	53.00	56.00
446	**Nandina domestica 'Compacta'**			
	container			
	1 gal	6.50	4.13	5.10
	3 gal	11.60	11.60	11.60
	5 gal	18.00	13.50	15.50
448	**Osmanthus heterophyllus 'Variegatus'**			
	container			
	1 gal	4.65	4.35	4.50
	5 gal	16.10	12.00	14.30
				0.00

02950 Shrubs, Temperate

	DESCRIPTION	HIGH	LOW	AVG.
450	**Philadelphus coronarius**			
	balled and burlapped			
	4' ht	25.50	18.80	22.10
	5' ht	31.90	22.50	27.20
452	**Philadelphus x virginalis**			
	balled and burlapped			
	2' ht	13.50	9.00	10.90
	3' ht	18.00	10.50	13.40
	bare root			
	2' ht	8.40	5.00	6.40
	3' ht	10.10	6.20	7.60
	container			
	5 gal	15.00	12.00	13.50
454	**Philadelphus x virginalis 'Minnesota Snowflake'**			
	balled and burlapped			
	2' ht	24.80	9.00	15.00
	3' ht	32.60	10.50	17.20
	4' ht	45.40	12.00	23.30
	bare root			
	2' ht	5.30	4.35	4.77
	3' ht	7.90	5.50	6.40
	container			
	5 gal	13.10	12.80	12.90
	18" ht	13.10	6.80	9.90
	2' ht	14.50	10.50	12.00
456	**Photinia Fraseri (Red Tip)**			
	balled and burlapped			
	6' ht	72.00	66.00	69.00
	7' ht	98.00	90.00	94.00
	8' ht	132.00	120.00	126.00
	container			
	1 gal	6.00	3.38	4.16
	3 gal	15.00	7.50	11.80
	5 gal	15.30	12.00	13.80
	7 gal	37.50	30.00	33.80
	15 gal	68.00	53.00	58.00
	24" box	240.00	225.00	233.00
458	**Physocarpus opulifolius 'Dart's Gold'**			
	balled and burlapped			
	3' ht	18.80	16.80	17.80
	4' ht	25.40	19.90	22.60
	container			
	5 gal	12.20	10.50	11.30
460	**Physocarpus opulifolius 'Nanus'**			
	bare root			
	2' ht	3.75	3.45	3.60
462	**Pieris japonica (Andromeda japonica)**			
	balled and burlapped			
	15" ht	26.30	18.80	22.50
	18" ht	33.80	19.50	25.60
	2' ht	56.00	22.50	37.20
	2 1/2' ht	87.00	33.80	55.00
	container			
	1 gal	7.10	4.13	6.10
	3 gal	21.40	11.60	18.50
	12" ht	14.80	9.00	11.90
	15" ht	22.50	11.30	16.40
	18" ht	33.00	15.80	23.30
464	**Potentilla fruticosa 'Abbottswood'**			
	container			
	1 gal	7.50	3.38	5.00
	2 gal	16.10	7.50	10.40
	3 gal	17.00	9.00	13.20
	12" ht	15.80	8.60	12.50
	15" ht	15.90	10.20	13.10
	18" ht	20.30	11.50	14.70
466	**Potentilla fruticosa 'Gold Drop'**			
	balled and burlapped			
	18" ht	14.80	10.40	12.10
	2' ht	16.80	11.60	13.80
	2 1/2' ht	18.80	14.30	17.10
	bare root			
	12" ht	3.90	3.53	3.74
	15" ht	4.73	3.60	4.44
	18" ht	5.80	3.68	4.98
	2' ht	6.80	3.98	5.80
	container			
	1 gal	5.30	3.38	4.44
	5 gal	14.30	10.50	12.30
	18" ht	20.30	11.50	14.50
468	**Potentilla parvifolia 'Jackmannii'**			
	balled and burlapped			
	15" ht	10.50	9.90	10.30
	18" ht	15.00	10.40	12.60
	2' ht	18.00	11.60	15.20
	2 1/2' ht	18.80	14.30	16.10
	bare root			
	12" ht	3.90	3.53	3.74
	15" ht	4.73	3.83	4.44
	18" ht	5.80	3.90	4.98
	2' ht	6.80	5.50	6.30
	container			
	1 gal	7.50	4.43	5.70
	2 gal	16.10	8.30	11.90
	5 gal	22.50	10.50	15.00
	18" ht	15.00	11.50	12.80
470	**Potentilla parvifolia 'Katherine Dykes'**			
	container			
	1 gal	4.73	3.38	4.04
	5 gal	14.30	12.20	13.20
472	**Prunus americana**			
	balled and burlapped			
	6' ht	78.00	66.00	72.00
	8' ht	105.00	103.00	104.00
474	**Prunus cistena**			
	balled and burlapped			
	2' ht	23.60	15.00	17.60
	3' ht	28.50	15.40	21.50
	4' ht	63.00	21.00	32.30
	5' ht	65.00	26.30	39.60
	6' ht	105.00	44.60	60.00
	bare root			
	18" ht	6.60	4.13	5.70
	2' ht	7.70	6.80	7.30
	3' ht	8.90	6.80	8.20
	container			
	1 gal	7.50	4.65	5.90
	2 gal	13.50	8.90	11.60
	5 gal	22.50	12.80	16.80

PLANTING

| 02950 Shrubs, Temperate | | | | | | 1994 |

	DESCRIPTION	HIGH	LOW	AVG.
	2' ht	22.50	13.40	18.20
	3' ht	33.00	18.80	25.00
	4' ht	42.00	34.90	39.10
	5' ht	60.00	40.50	50.00
476	**Prunus glandulosa, varieties**			
	balled and burlapped			
	18" ht	19.40	10.80	15.20
	2' ht	25.90	10.90	16.70
	2 1/2' ht	33.80	18.00	23.50
	container			
	2 gal	13.50	11.30	12.40
	5 gal	22.40	15.80	18.00
	18" ht	15.80	11.80	13.40
478	**Prunus laurocerasus 'Schipkaensis'**			
	balled and burlapped			
	18" ht	20.30	19.90	20.10
	2' ht	26.30	24.00	25.10
	2 1/2' ht	34.10	31.50	32.80
	3' ht	44.30	39.00	41.60
480	**Prunus tomentosa**			
	balled and burlapped			
	3' ht	17.70	14.90	15.80
	4' ht	37.50	17.30	23.50
	5' ht	53.00	21.50	34.00
482	**Prunus triloba**			
	balled and burlapped			
	3' ht	22.90	21.00	21.90
	4' ht	28.10	27.00	27.60
484	**Pyracantha angustifolia 'Gnome'**			
	container			
	1 gal	6.80	4.65	5.70
	5 gal	22.50	15.80	20.20
486	**Pyracantha coccinea 'Kasan'**			
	container			
	1 gal	5.00	4.13	4.44
	5 gal	21.40	11.90	15.60
488	**Pyracantha coccinea 'Lalandei'**			
	container			
	1 gal	6.80	3.38	4.67
	5 gal	24.00	12.00	16.70
	2' ht	24.00	7.50	15.60
490	**Pyracantha coccinea 'Wyatti'**			
	container			
	1 gal	6.80	4.58	5.70
	5 gal	22.50	15.40	19.70
492	**Pyracantha fortuneana 'Graberi'**			
	container			
	1 gal	5.10	3.38	4.32
	5 gal	16.50	12.00	14.50
	15 gal	64.00	56.00	60.00
494	**Pyracantha x mohave**			
	container			
	1 gal	5.00	4.43	4.79
	5 gal	16.50	13.10	15.50
	18" ht	15.00	4.80	11.30
	2' ht	19.90	4.95	14.00

	DESCRIPTION	HIGH	LOW	AVG.
496	**Rhamnus frangula 'Columnaris'**			
	balled and burlapped			
	3' ht	24.80	11.30	15.70
	4' ht	33.00	15.00	19.70
	5' ht	63.00	19.90	29.20
	6' ht	58.00	23.10	35.30
	bare root			
	2' ht	8.30	4.73	6.20
	3' ht	9.30	6.00	7.40
	4' ht	9.40	7.50	8.00
	container			
	5 gal	17.00	7.70	13.60
498	**Rhododendron carolinianum, varieties**			
	balled and burlapped			
	2 1/2" ht	45.00	37.50	41.30
500	**Rhododendron catawbiense, hybrids**			
	balled and burlapped			
	15" ht	36.00	22.50	28.50
	18" ht	45.00	22.70	32.20
	2' ht	63.00	26.30	42.80
	2 1/2' ht	72.00	33.80	55.00
	3' ht	75.00	45.00	61.00
	4' ht	76.00	60.00	63.00
	container			
	1 gal	11.30	3.45	6.50
	2 gal	23.10	11.30	17.70
	3 gal	32.30	17.70	24.50
	7 gal	63.00	31.50	41.40
	12" ht	18.10	16.40	17.50
	15" ht	32.60	16.90	21.80
	18" ht	40.50	22.50	30.70
	2' ht	51.00	27.00	37.70
	2 1/2' ht	63.00	36.00	47.30
502	**Rhododendron PJM**			
	balled and burlapped			
	15" ht	38.60	22.50	30.00
	18" ht	45.00	26.30	35.80
	2' ht	63.00	30.00	45.80
	2 1/2' ht	77.00	33.80	58.00
	3' ht	92.00	37.50	66.00
	container			
	2 gal	23.10	11.30	16.30
	3 gal	31.50	20.30	28.50
	5 gal	32.90	30.30	31.60
	7 gal	42.80	33.00	37.50
	15" ht	32.60	12.40	19.00
	18" ht	40.50	15.80	28.90
	2' ht	51.00	27.00	37.10
504	**Rhus aromatica**			
	balled and burlapped			
	2' ht	22.50	15.50	18.90
	3' ht	28.10	15.50	21.90
	bare root			
	18" ht	5.30	4.20	4.70
	2' ht	6.80	5.20	5.80
506	**Rhus aromatica 'Gro-Low'**			
	balled and burlapped			
	18" ht	16.20	15.80	16.00
	2' ht	32.30	18.80	22.50
	2 1/2' ht	36.00	21.20	26.40

02950 Shrubs, Temperate

DESCRIPTION	HIGH	LOW	AVG.
container			
2 gal	13.50	8.90	11.80
3 gal	17.00	13.90	15.90
508 Rhus glabra			
balled and burlapped			
5' ht	28.90	19.50	25.10
bare root			
2' ht	6.40	3.75	4.85
3' ht	8.60	4.43	6.10
510 Rhus typhina			
balled and burlapped			
5' ht	42.00	19.50	29.20
6' ht	54.00	38.00	48.60
8' ht	132.00	60.00	108.00
10' ht	210.00	75.00	165.00
bare root			
2' ht	6.40	3.75	4.71
3' ht	8.60	4.43	5.90
512 Rhus typhina 'Laciniata'			
container			
5 gal	18.80	12.60	15.50
514 Ribes alpinum			
balled and burlapped			
15" ht	15.00	11.30	13.70
18" ht	18.80	13.40	15.60
2' ht	24.00	16.40	19.60
2 1/2' ht	30.00	19.50	23.20
3' ht	37.50	21.50	26.70
bare root			
18" ht	6.70	5.10	5.60
2' ht	8.20	6.20	7.10
container			
1 gal	5.30	4.73	4.98
3 gal	15.00	12.60	13.80
516 Rosa banksiae 'Lutea'			
container			
1 gal	5.30	4.88	5.10
5 gal	19.90	13.90	16.00
518 Rosa rugosa			
bare root			
18" ht	5.60	4.50	5.10
2' ht	8.10	5.30	6.30
3' ht	9.60	7.10	8.00
container			
1 gal	6.00	4.58	5.10
2 gal	12.20	9.80	11.10
3 gal	18.00	13.50	15.70
12" ht	11.60	4.58	7.60
15" ht	12.80	9.80	11.30
18" ht	18.00	10.40	13.80
2' ht	18.80	11.90	16.20
520 Rosemarinus officinalis, varieties			
container			
1 gal	4.88	3.38	4.08
5 gal	15.00	12.00	13.50
522 Salix caprea			
bare root			
3' ht	6.50	3.90	5.00

DESCRIPTION	HIGH	LOW	AVG.
524 Salix discolor			
balled and burlapped			
2' ht	21.00	9.80	13.70
3' ht	26.30	10.50	16.00
4' ht	33.00	12.80	20.50
5' ht	45.00	15.00	30.00
bare root			
3' ht	6.00	3.90	5.00
526 Spiraea bumalda x 'Anthony Waterer'			
balled and burlapped			
15" ht	14.30	11.90	13.20
18" ht	20.30	10.00	15.20
2' ht	24.00	10.10	17.70
bare root			
12" ht	6.80	4.35	5.30
15" ht	7.90	5.00	5.90
container			
1 gal	9.00	3.60	5.30
2 gal	16.10	7.50	11.20
3 gal	18.00	11.30	14.20
5 gal	22.50	12.00	15.20
12" ht	15.00	10.50	13.20
15" ht	19.80	14.00	16.30
18" ht	23.40	15.00	17.10
528 Spiraea bumalda x 'Froebelii'			
balled and burlapped			
15" ht	14.30	11.90	12.90
18" ht	18.00	12.90	15.30
2' ht	24.00	14.00	18.30
2 1/2' ht	24.80	16.40	20.30
bare root			
18" ht	6.20	4.43	5.10
2' ht	6.50	5.30	5.80
container			
1 gal	9.00	4.43	6.40
2 gal	16.10	7.50	11.40
3 gal	18.00	8.30	13.30
5 gal	22.50	11.30	15.30
530 Spiraea bumalda x 'Gold Flame'			
balled and burlapped			
15" ht	14.30	11.90	12.70
18" ht	18.00	10.10	14.80
2' ht	22.90	14.00	18.30
2 1/2' ht	27.40	16.40	21.70
3' ht	31.50	19.40	24.10
bare root			
12" ht	4.88	4.20	4.50
15" ht	6.20	4.95	5.40
18" ht	6.90	5.80	6.30
2' ht	7.50	6.50	7.10
container			
1 gal	9.00	2.55	5.20
2 gal	16.10	7.50	10.20
3 gal	18.00	8.30	13.70
5 gal	22.50	11.30	14.90
12" ht	15.00	8.90	11.60
15" ht	19.80	11.50	15.10
18" ht	23.40	11.90	15.80
532 Spiraea japonica 'Little Princess'			
balled and burlapped			
18" ht	22.50	14.10	19.00
2' ht	26.30	15.80	22.50

PLANTING

DESCRIPTION	HIGH	LOW	AVG.
container			
1 gal	9.00	2.55	5.40
2 gal	16.10	7.50	10.60
3 gal	22.50	8.30	13.40
5 gal	22.80	11.30	15.40
15" ht	22.20	12.40	17.70
18" ht	29.40	12.50	19.00
534 Spiraea nipponica 'Snowmound'			
balled and burlapped			
15" ht	14.30	11.30	13.30
18" ht	20.30	11.40	16.40
2' ht	24.00	11.80	18.30
2 1/2' ht	27.40	12.30	19.70
3' ht	34.10	13.50	24.70
bare root			
12" ht	4.73	3.90	4.37
15" ht	6.20	4.80	5.40
18" ht	6.90	5.60	6.10
2' ht	7.40	6.80	7.10
container			
1 gal	7.50	4.28	5.40
2 gal	16.30	8.50	11.40
3 gal	16.40	8.60	12.40
5 gal	22.50	11.30	15.20
15" ht	15.00	10.80	12.40
18" ht	19.80	11.90	14.80
2' ht	23.40	13.10	18.00
2 1/2' ht	28.20	22.50	24.80
536 Spiraea prunifolia			
balled and burlapped			
2' ht	19.20	15.00	17.10
538 Spiraea x vanhouttei			
balled and burlapped			
18" ht	20.30	9.00	14.60
2' ht	22.90	10.10	14.80
2 1/2' ht	27.40	14.60	18.00
3' ht	32.60	12.80	18.50
4' ht	33.00	18.80	22.90
bare root			
18" ht	5.30	3.30	4.20
2' ht	6.80	4.20	5.20
3' ht	8.00	5.60	6.50
container			
1 gal	4.43	2.55	3.74
3 gal	16.50	9.00	13.70
5 gal	16.60	12.00	14.00
2' ht	15.00	10.40	12.90
540 Symphoricarpos albus			
bare root			
2' ht	5.30	4.35	4.79
3' ht	6.80	5.00	5.90
542 Symphoricarpos chenaulti 'Hancock'			
bare root			
18" ht	7.50	4.58	6.10
2' ht	8.60	5.30	7.20
544 Symphoricarpos orbiculatus			
container			
1 gal	6.50	4.88	5.70

DESCRIPTION	HIGH	LOW	AVG.
546 Syringa chinensis			
balled and burlapped			
3' ht	27.00	15.00	19.40
4' ht	53.00	18.80	30.00
container			
5 gal	17.30	12.20	14.70
548 Syringa meyeri 'Palibin'			
balled and burlapped			
2' ht	29.60	19.50	24.70
2 1/2' ht	31.50	24.00	29.00
3' ht	74.00	24.80	44.00
bare root			
12" ht	6.80	4.35	5.30
15" ht	11.20	4.88	6.80
18" ht	12.70	5.70	7.60
2' ht	13.90	7.10	9.30
container			
1 gal	6.80	4.95	5.60
2 gal	21.00	8.90	13.30
18" ht	17.20	14.00	15.50
538 Syringa patula 'Miss Kim'			
balled and burlapped			
15" ht	21.00	13.50	17.40
18" ht	26.30	17.30	20.70
2' ht	39.00	20.30	26.90
2 1/2' ht	41.30	24.80	29.60
3' ht	52.00	28.50	36.30
bare root			
18" ht	12.70	6.10	9.00
2' ht	23.60	7.40	15.00
container			
2 gal	21.00	8.90	13.10
5 gal	33.00	12.80	21.00
18" ht	18.80	11.00	14.60
552 Syringa persica			
balled and burlapped			
3' ht	33.00	12.00	22.00
4' ht	42.00	24.80	30.50
554 Syringa vulgaris			
balled and burlapped			
18" ht	21.00	9.00	14.30
2' ht	29.30	11.30	19.60
2 1/2' ht	36.00	17.50	24.30
3' ht	48.00	17.60	27.10
4' ht	69.00	22.10	35.40
5' ht	83.00	37.50	56.00
bare root			
12" ht	5.60	3.15	4.02
18" ht	6.80	4.13	5.10
2' ht	7.90	4.88	6.20
3' ht	9.50	8.20	8.90
container			
1 gal	5.30	5.10	5.20
5 gal	22.50	12.20	16.20
556 Syringa vulgaris, French hybrids			
balled and burlapped			
2' ht	33.00	13.90	22.20
3' ht	54.00	18.00	30.90
4' ht	56.00	24.00	39.40
bare root			
12" ht	6.80	5.40	6.10

02950 Shrubs, Temperate

	DESCRIPTION	HIGH	LOW	AVG.
	18" ht	10.90	6.50	8.40
	2' ht	10.10	8.00	9.10
	container			
	5 gal	17.60	15.70	16.50
	18" ht	17.30	12.90	15.80
558	**Viburnum burkwoodi**			
	balled and burlapped			
	18" ht	30.00	13.50	22.80
	2' ht	35.30	13.70	24.00
	2 1/2' ht	42.00	17.30	31.30
	3' ht	49.50	19.50	34.70
	4' ht	75.00	28.50	48.90
	5' ht	125.00	39.00	73.00
	container			
	1 gal	7.50	4.73	5.80
	2 gal	17.20	11.60	15.00
	5 gal	22.50	15.40	19.20
560	**Viburnum carlcephalum**			
	balled and burlapped			
	18" ht	30.00	11.30	24.30
	2' ht	45.00	14.60	34.70
562	**Viburnum carlesii**			
	balled and burlapped			
	18" ht	30.00	15.00	23.50
	2' ht	74.00	18.00	33.00
	3' ht	81.00	28.50	48.00
	4' ht	129.00	37.50	71.00
	container			
	5 gal	25.00	12.80	18.90
	18" ht	24.00	15.40	19.20
564	**Viburnum dentatum**			
	balled and burlapped			
	2' ht	24.40	11.00	18.50
	3' ht	33.80	13.50	23.70
	4' ht	43.10	19.50	29.30
	5' ht	53.00	30.40	39.00
	6' ht	75.00	48.20	61.00
	bare root			
	18" ht	8.60	4.73	6.10
	2' ht	10.10	6.40	7.50
	3' ht	13.10	8.30	9.30
	container			
	1 gal	7.50	6.00	6.80
	5 gal	22.50	12.00	16.10
566	**Viburnum dilataum**			
	balled and burlapped			
	2' ht	25.90	6.80	18.20
	3' ht	34.50	8.30	25.30
	4' ht	43.50	27.80	34.60
	5' ht	62.00	37.50	49.20
568	**Viburnum lantana**			
	balled and burlapped			
	3' ht	24.80	18.40	21.50
	4' ht	35.40	22.10	29.00
	container			
	5 gal	15.70	12.00	13.80
570	**Viburnum lantana 'Mohican'**			
	balled and burlapped			
	2 1/2' ht	24.80	19.80	23.00

	DESCRIPTION	HIGH	LOW	AVG.
	3' ht	30.80	19.90	25.40
	4' ht	38.30	25.10	32.10
	5' ht	48.00	37.50	41.50
	container			
	2' ht	20.20	13.50	15.90
	3' ht	22.70	16.40	19.00
572	**Viburnum lentago**			
	balled and burlapped			
	2' ht	22.50	12.00	16.20
	3' ht	28.50	16.50	23.30
	4' ht	37.50	20.90	29.00
	5' ht	60.00	29.90	39.60
	6' ht	98.00	36.00	60.00
	8' ht	128.00	54.00	102.00
	bare root			
	2' ht	10.10	6.30	7.50
	3' ht	10.90	8.30	9.10
	4' ht	11.00	10.10	10.50
	contianer			
	5 gal	48.00	13.50	25.10
574	**Viburnum opulus**			
	balled and burlapped			
	2' ht	22.50	13.50	19.80
	3' ht	30.00	13.70	22.80
	4' ht	63.00	18.80	31.40
	5' ht	68.00	30.40	45.20
	bare root			
	18" ht	8.60	4.58	6.10
	2' ht	10.10	6.40	7.60
	3' ht	10.90	8.30	9.80
576	**Viburnum opulus 'Compactum'**			
	balled and burlapped			
	15" ht	25.50	22.50	24.20
	18" ht	33.80	22.70	28.50
	2' ht	39.30	28.50	36.00
578	**Viburnum opulus 'Roseum' sterile**			
	balled and burlapped			
	2' ht	21.00	13.50	17.40
	3' ht	27.00	20.30	22.90
	4' ht	37.50	25.70	30.80
	5' ht	48.00	32.10	39.70
	6' ht	60.00	38.40	47.80
	bare root			
	18" ht	5.30	4.58	4.92
	2' ht	7.10	6.20	6.60
	container			
	1 gal	5.60	3.75	4.64
	2 gal	11.30	6.50	9.50
	3 gal	13.50	12.00	12.80
	5 gal	15.80	12.20	14.30
580	**Viburnum plicatum tomentosum**			
	balled and burlapped			
	2' ht	25.90	13.50	17.70
	3' ht	43.50	16.50	28.80
	4' ht	60.00	20.30	37.00
	5' ht	87.00	29.30	54.00
	bare root			
	3' ht	32.20	8.30	16.50

PLANTING

	DESCRIPTION	HIGH	LOW	AVG.
582	**Viburnum plicatum tomentosum 'Mariesii'**			
	balled and burlapped			
	2' ht	30.80	21.00	23.80
	2 1/2' ht	33.00	22.50	27.60
	3' ht	39.80	23.30	29.30
	4' ht	49.50	27.80	38.80
	5' ht	70.00	42.00	55.00
	container			
	1 gal	7.50	4.73	5.70
	5 gal	22.50	13.50	16.80
	18" ht	18.00	11.90	14.70
	2' ht	22.50	13.50	17.00
584	**Viburnum prunifolium**			
	balled and burlapped			
	2' ht	34.40	19.40	23.50
	2 1/2' ht	44.90	19.50	33.10
	3' ht	65.00	19.90	36.70
	4' ht	87.00	25.10	48.80
	5' ht	111.00	37.50	70.00
	6' ht	138.00	69.00	97.00
	8' ht	195.00	113.00	152.00
	bare root			
	18" ht	9.60	7.10	8.00
586	**Viburnum rhytidophyllum**			
	balled and burlapped			
	2' ht	28.10	21.80	23.80
	3' ht	40.40	26.30	33.00
	4' ht	52.00	44.30	47.00
588	**Viburnum trilobum**			
	balled and burlapped			
	2' ht	19.50	15.00	17.40
	2 1/2' ht	21.00	15.80	18.50
	3' ht	27.00	18.00	22.70
	4' ht	43.10	23.30	30.80
	5' ht	53.00	33.80	40.60
	6' ht	75.00	51.00	64.00
	bare root			
	2' ht	9.70	6.80	7.70
	3' ht	14.20	8.30	10.50
	container			
	5 gal	22.50	12.00	16.70
590	Weigela florida 'Eva Rathke'			
	balled and burlapped			
	2' ht	10.50	9.80	10.10
	3' ht	15.00	13.50	14.30
	4' ht	22.50	16.50	19.50
592	Weigela florida 'Java Red'			
	balled and burlapped			
	2' ht	18.80	11.30	16.30
	container			
	2' ht	28.20	12.20	18.20
594	Weigela florida 'Newport Red'			
	balled and burlapped			
	2' ht	13.50	10.50	12.10
	3' ht	17.30	11.30	14.80
	4' ht	22.50	15.80	20.30
	bare root			
	2' ht	7.40	4.43	5.50
	3' ht	9.00	5.60	6.80

	DESCRIPTION	HIGH	LOW	AVG.
596	**Weigela florida 'Red Prince'**			
	balled and burlapped			
	3' ht	32.30	18.80	23.70
	container			
	1 gal	7.90	4.65	5.80
	5 gal	15.80	13.40	14.60
	18" ht	20.40	15.80	18.70
598	**Weigela florida 'Rosea'**			
	balled and burlapped			
	2' ht	10.50	9.00	9.80
	3' ht	15.00	10.50	12.30
	4' ht	22.50	12.00	18.50
	bare root			
	2' ht	7.40	4.43	5.60
	3' ht	9.00	5.60	7.00
	4' ht	10.90	7.50	9.10
	container			
	2' ht	14.50	11.30	12.80
600	**Weigela florida 'Variegata'**			
	balled and burlapped			
	3' ht	27.00	15.00	20.30
602	**Yucca filamentosa**			
	balled and burlapped			
	2' ht	22.50	11.60	17.40
	2 1/2' ht	24.00	22.50	23.30
	container			
	1 gal	7.50	3.75	5.30
	2 gal	14.80	8.30	11.80
	5 gal	24.00	11.90	17.00
	12" ht	11.60	4.73	9.00
	15" ht	13.50	12.20	12.80
604	**Yucca glauca**			
	container			
	1 gal	5.10	5.00	5.10

SHRUBS, WARM TEMPERATE AND SUBTROPIC

	DESCRIPTION	HIGH	LOW	AVG.
200	**Agapanthus orientalis (africanus)**			
	container			
	1 gal	6.50	3.38	4.26
	5 gal	15.00	12.00	13.30
202	**Agapanthus orientalis 'Albidus' (afr albidus)**			
	container			
	1 gal	4.28	3.38	3.89
	5 gal	15.00	12.00	13.30
204	**Aspidistra elatior (A. lurida)**			
	container			
	1 gal	7.50	4.50	5.70
	5 gal	22.50	12.80	17.60
206	**Aucuba japonica**			
	container			
	1 gal	4.28	3.60	3.87
208	**Aucuba japonica 'Picturata'**			
	container			
	1 gal	5.30	3.75	4.35
	3 gal	11.80	11.60	11.70
	5 gal	16.50	14.30	15.40

	DESCRIPTION	HIGH	LOW	AVG.
210	**Aucuba japonica 'Variegata'**			
	container			
	1 gal	4.80	3.60	4.16
	2 gal	10.10	8.60	9.40
	3 gal	11.80	11.60	11.70
	5 gal	15.80	12.80	14.30
212	**Brunfelsia pauciflora calycina**			
	container			
	1 gal	4.28	4.05	4.14
	5 gal	15.00	12.80	13.80
214	**Calliandra haematocephala (C. inaequilatera)**			
	container			
	1 gal	4.43	3.38	4.02
	5 gal	15.00	12.00	13.60
	15 gal	56.00	53.00	54.00
216	**Callistemon citrinus**			
	container			
	1 gal	4.50	3.38	4.05
	5 gal	15.00	12.00	13.30
	15 gal	60.00	50.00	56.00
218	**Camellia japonica, varieties**			
	container			
	1 gal	7.10	4.88	5.80
	5 gal	21.00	15.00	18.30
	15 gal	75.00	60.00	66.00
220	**Carissa grandiflora 'Tuttlei'**			
	container			
	1 gal	4.28	3.38	3.95
	5 gal	15.00	12.00	13.50
222	**Cassia artemisioides**			
	container			
	1 gal	4.28	3.38	3.89
	5 gal	15.00	12.00	13.50
224	**Cortaderia selloana**			
	container			
	1 gal	6.80	3.38	4.17
	3 gal	11.40	10.90	11.30
	5 gal	15.80	12.00	14.00
226	**Cytisus racemosus, varieties**			
	container			
	1 gal	9.00	4.05	5.70
	5 gal	24.00	13.70	17.20
228	**Dizygotheca elegantissima (Aralia elegantissima)**			
	container			
	1 gal	4.50	3.98	4.23
	5 gal	14.60	12.80	13.70
	15 gal	64.00	60.00	62.00
230	**Dodonaea viscosa 'Purpurea'**			
	container			
	1 gal	4.35	3.38	3.98
	5 gal	15.00	12.00	13.70
	15 gal	66.00	50.00	58.00
232	**Escallonia x exoniensis 'Frades'**			
	container			
	1 gal	4.28	3.38	3.95

	DESCRIPTION	HIGH	LOW	AVG.
	5 gal	15.00	12.00	13.30
	15 gal	60.00	50.00	56.00
234	**Fatshedera lizei**			
	container			
	1 gal	5.10	4.13	4.61
	5 gal	16.10	13.90	15.00
236	**Fatsia japonica**			
	container			
	1 gal	4.28	3.38	3.89
	5 gal	15.00	12.00	13.40
	15 gal	60.00	50.00	56.00
238	**Feijoa sellowiana**			
	container			
	1 gal	5.30	3.38	4.13
	5 gal	15.00	12.00	13.70
	15 gal	66.00	50.00	58.00
	24" box	240.00	225.00	233.00
240	**Gardenia jasminoides, varieties**			
	container			
	1 gal	6.40	3.60	4.67
	2 gal	11.60	9.00	10.90
	5 gal	22.50	12.80	16.10
	7 gal	53.00	45.00	48.80
	15 gal	60.00	59.00	59.00
242	**Grewia caffra (G. occidentalis)**			
	container			
	1 gal	4.28	3.38	3.89
	5 gal	15.00	12.00	13.50
244	**Hibbertia scandens (H. volubilis)**			
	container			
	1 gal	5.10	3.98	4.53
	5 gal	16.10	13.50	14.80
246	**Hibiscus rosa-sinensis, varieties**			
	container			
	1 gal	5.40	3.60	4.55
	5 gal	17.30	12.40	15.20
	15 gal	60.00	59.00	59.00
248	**Jasminum nitidum**			
	container			
	1 gal	4.50	4.13	4.29
	5 gal	15.00	14.30	14.60
250	**Leucophyllum frutescens 'Compactum'**			
	container			
	1 gal	4.88	3.38	4.31
	5 gal	15.80	12.00	14.10
252	**Ligustrum lucidium**			
	container			
	1 gal	4.13	3.38	3.80
	3 gal	11.60	11.30	11.40
	5 gal	13.50	12.00	12.80
	15 gal	56.00	53.00	54.00
254	**Ligustrum lucidium 'Recurvifolium'**			
	container			
	1 gal	4.13	2.25	3.38
	3 gal	11.60	6.00	9.70

PLANTING

DESCRIPTION	HIGH	LOW	AVG.
256 Nerium oleander, varieties			
container			
1 gal	5.60	3.38	4.41
5 gal	17.30	13.10	14.40
15 gal	69.00	53.00	61.00
24" box	240.00	225.00	229.00
36" box	610.00	600.00	600.00
258 Osmanthus fragrans			
container			
1 gal	4.88	3.75	4.26
3 gal	15.00	11.90	12.90
5 gal	16.10	12.00	14.10
15 gal	58.00	53.00	56.00
260 Philodendron selloum			
container			
1 gal	4.28	3.38	3.95
5 gal	15.00	12.00	13.60
15 gal	60.00	56.00	58.00
262 Phyllostachys aurea			
container			
5 gal	71.00	14.30	29.10
15 gal	83.00	56.00	69.00
264 Pittosporum tobira			
container			
1 gal	5.40	3.38	4.13
5 gal	15.00	12.00	13.30
15 gal	60.00	50.00	57.00
266 Pittosporum tobira 'Variegata'			
container			
1 gal	4.28	3.60	3.95
3 gal	14.30	7.10	11.00
5 gal	15.00	12.40	13.50
15 gal	60.00	50.00	57.00
268 Pittosporum tobira 'Wheeler's Dwarf'			
container			
1 gal	4.28	3.60	3.95
2 gal	10.10	8.40	9.20
3 gal	14.30	11.30	12.80
5 gal	15.00	12.40	13.50
15 gal	60.00	50.00	57.00
270 Pittosporum undulatum			
container			
1 gal	5.60	3.60	4.41
5 gal	18.00	13.70	15.50
15 gal	60.00	53.00	57.00
24" box	240.00	225.00	230.00
36" box	610.00	600.00	600.00
272 Plumbago auriculata			
container			
1 gal	4.13	3.38	3.84
5 gal	13.10	12.00	12.60
274 Punica granatum 'Nana'			
container			
1 gal	4.58	3.60	4.19
5 gal	13.70	12.00	12.80

DESCRIPTION	HIGH	LOW	AVG.
276 Pyracantha koidzumii' Santa Cruz'			
container			
1 gal	4.28	3.38	3.85
5 gal	15.00	12.00	13.30
278 Pyracantha koidzumii 'Victory'			
container			
1 gal	4.80	4.28	4.53
5 gal	16.50	15.00	15.80
280 Raphiolepis indica, varieties			
container			
1 gal	5.80	3.98	4.44
2 gal	11.60	9.80	10.60
3 gal	13.90	8.60	11.60
5 gal	26.30	13.50	16.20
15 gal	75.00	53.00	62.00
282 Spiraea cantoniensis (S. reevesiana)			
container			
1 gal	4.28	3.60	3.99
2 gal	10.10	7.50	9.20
5 gal	15.00	13.50	14.30
284 Tecomaria capensis			
container			
1 gal	4.28	3.38	3.90
5 gal	15.00	12.00	13.40
15 gal	56.00	50.00	54.00
286 Ternstroemia gymnanthera (Cleyera japonica)			
container			
1 gal	4.88	3.98	4.31
3 gal	12.40	12.00	12.20
5 gal	16.50	13.50	14.90
7 gal	37.50	33.00	35.30
15 gal	68.00	59.00	63.00
288 Trachelospermum asiaticum			
container			
1 gal	4.35	3.38	3.90
290 Trachelospermum jasminoides			
container			
1 gal	4.50	3.53	4.02
5 gal	15.00	12.00	13.50
15 gal	60.00	56.00	58.00
292 Viburnum davidii			
container			
1 gal	5.30	4.88	5.10
5 gal	17.40	13.90	15.90
294 Viburnum japonicum			
container			
1 gal	4.28	3.38	3.84
5 gal	15.00	12.00	13.40
15 gal	60.00	50.00	56.00
296 Viburnum suspensum			
container			
1 gal	4.28	3.38	3.84
5 gal	15.00	12.00	13.40
15 gal	60.00	50.00	56.00

02950 Shrubs, Warm Temperate and Subtropic 1994

DESCRIPTION	HIGH	LOW	AVG.
298 Viburnum tinus, varieties			
container			
1 gal	4.35	3.38	3.95
5 gal	15.00	12.00	13.70
15 gal	69.00	50.00	59.00
300 Xylosma congestum (X. senticosum)			
container			
1 gal	4.88	3.38	4.25
5 gal	15.80	12.00	13.80
15 gal	69.00	53.00	59.00
24" box	248.00	240.00	244.00
302 Yucca aloifolia			
container			
1 gal	4.43	3.53	4.02
5 gal	15.40	13.90	14.60
304 Yucca gloriosa			
container			
5 gal	16.10	12.00	13.90
15 gal	68.00	56.00	64.00
24" box	248.00	240.00	244.00

GROUND COVERS AND VINES

DESCRIPTION	HIGH	LOW	AVG.
200 Aegopodium podagraria, varieties			
container			
2 1/4" pot	0.93	0.78	0.86
1 quart	2.48	1.49	2.09
1 gal	5.40	3.68	4.32
202 Ajuga reptans, varieties			
container			
50/flat	0.74	0.39	0.56
2 1/4" pot	1.20	0.53	0.81
4" pot	1.65	1.38	1.50
1 quart	2.33	2.25	2.28
1 gal	6.80	3.68	4.56
204 Arctostaphylos uva-ursi			
container			
1 gal	8.60	4.73	7.40
206 Campsis radicans			
container			
1 gal	13.10	3.98	6.50
5 gal	18.90	13.50	16.20
208 Clematis, varieties			
container			
1 gal	10.50	5.30	7.80
2 gal	15.80	10.90	14.10
5 gal	31.50	19.50	25.20
210 Coronilla varia, varieties			
container			
50/flat	0.43	0.41	0.42
212 Cotoneaster apiculata			
container			
1 gal	8.30	3.60	5.30
2 gal	17.30	3.75	10.90
5 gal	24.00	13.80	18.90

DESCRIPTION	HIGH	LOW	AVG.
12" ht	15.00	5.90	10.80
15" ht	21.00	11.20	14.70
18" ht	24.80	12.20	16.50
214 Cotoneaster dammeri 'Skolgsholmen'			
container			
2 gal	13.50	12.30	12.80
15" ht	12.80	11.20	12.10
216 Cotoneaster salicifolius 'Repens'			
container			
1 gal	4.73	3.60	4.22
2 gal	12.80	8.30	10.80
12" ht	11.20	4.80	8.70
218 Euonymus fortunei 'Colorata'			
container			
100/flat	0.29	0.20	0.24
50/flat	0.71	0.39	0.54
2 1/4" pot	1.20	0.71	0.98
4" pot	1.65	1.20	1.40
1 quart	1.95	1.28	1.62
1 gal	6.80	3.38	4.59
220 Euonymus fortunei 'Vegata'			
container			
1 gal	5.30	4.65	4.88
2 gal	11.00	9.00	10.00
3 gal	17.00	12.20	14.60
222 Ficus pumila			
container			
1 gal	5.30	4.13	4.80
5 gal	18.00	12.80	15.40
224 Gelsemium sempervirens			
container			
1 gal	5.60	4.13	4.94
5 gal	18.90	12.80	16.30
15 gal	68.00	60.00	64.00
226 Hedera canariensis			
container			
4" pot	1.49	1.35	1.41
1 gal	5.10	3.75	4.17
5 gal	18.00	12.80	15.40
228 Hedera helix			
container			
100/flat	0.21	0.29	0.24
2 1/4" pot	1.20	0.53	0.81
4" pot	1.38	1.20	1.29
1 gal	6.50	3.75	4.83
5 gal	18.00	12.80	15.90
230 Hedera helix, varieties			
container			
100/flat	0.24	0.29	0.26
2 1/4" pot	1.80	0.59	0.92
4" pot	4.13	1.20	2.15
1 gal	9.30	3.75	5.20
4 gal	18.00	12.80	15.60
232 Hosta fortunei 'Albo-marginata'			
container			
1 quart	5.40	3.90	4.65

PLANTING

DESCRIPTION	HIGH	LOW	AVG.
1 gal	7.10	3.75	5.10
2 gal	9.00	6.00	7.20
234 Hosta lancifolia			
container			
1 gal	6.40	3.90	4.98
236 Hosta sieboldiana 'Elegans'			
container			
1 gal	8.90	4.35	6.70
2 gal	10.10	6.80	8.40
238 Hosta undulata 'Albo-marginata'			
container			
1 quart	3.00	2.42	2.70
1 gal	5.30	3.75	4.50
2 gal	10.10	6.00	7.60
240 Hosta undulata 'Variegated'			
container			
1 quart	3.00	2.42	2.70
1 gal	6.80	3.90	4.94
2 gal	10.10	6.80	8.70
242 Hydrangea anomala petiolaris			
container			
1 gal	15.80	7.10	10.10
2 gal	19.10	11.30	15.50
244 Hypericum calycinum			
container			
1 quart	2.48	2.25	2.33
1 gal	7.50	3.75	4.76
246 Juniperus horizontalis 'Bar Harbor'			
container			
1 gal	8.30	3.45	4.86
2 gal	17.30	8.30	11.30
3 gal	19.50	9.80	14.60
5 gal	24.00	13.90	17.70
12" ht	15.00	4.73	10.10
15" ht	19.80	10.90	14.10
18" ht	23.40	13.20	17.00
248 Juniperus horizontalis 'Prince of Wales'			
container			
1 gal	7.10	3.45	4.64
2 gal	17.30	8.30	10.90
3 gal	19.50	11.30	14.50
5 gal	21.80	12.00	16.10
12" ht	13.50	11.00	12.20
15" ht	16.50	13.90	15.20
18" ht	19.50	15.60	17.30
250 Juniperus horizontalis 'Wiltonii'			
container			
1 gal	7.50	3.45	5.00
2 gal	19.20	3.38	11.40
3 gal	22.50	11.30	16.00
5 gal	24.00	12.00	17.20
12" ht	15.00	7.10	11.90
15" ht	21.00	10.90	15.20
18" ht	24.00	14.60	18.20

DESCRIPTION	HIGH	LOW	AVG.
252 Liriope muscari			
container			
1 gal	4.13	3.38	3.84
254 Liriope muscari 'Big Blue'			
container			
4" pot	3.38	1.20	1.98
1 quart	3.75	2.63	3.21
1 gal	8.90	3.15	5.10
256 Liriope muscari 'Variegata'			
container			
1 quart	4.13	3.00	3.68
1 gal	8.90	3.38	5.10
258 Liriope spicata			
container			
2 1/4" pot	0.81	0.75	0.78
1 quart	3.30	2.63	2.96
1 gal	5.40	3.75	4.61
260 Lonicera heckrottii			
bare root			
2 yr, #1	4.20	2.85	3.51
container			
1 gal	6.00	4.58	5.40
262 Lonicera japonica 'Halliana'			
bare root			
2 yr, #1	4.05	2.85	3.44
container			
50/flat	0.74	0.54	0.63
2 1/4" pot	1.20	0.74	0.96
1 gal	6.80	3.60	4.91
264 Lonicera japonica 'Purpurea'			
container			
1 gal	4.43	3.75	4.14
266 Macfadyena unguis-cati (Doxantha unguis-cati)			
container			
1 gal	5.90	3.98	5.10
5 gal	18.90	13.50	16.80
268 Miscanthus sinensis, varieties			
container			
1 gal	9.40	4.13	5.70
2 gal	13.50	6.40	9.10
3 gal	14.30	9.80	11.80
5 gal	26.30	15.80	20.60
270 Ophiopogon japonicus			
container			
4" pot	1.38	1.20	1.29
1 quart	3.30	3.30	3.29
1 gal	4.20	3.53	3.99
272 Pachysandra terminalis			
container			
100/flat	0.29	0.20	0.21
48/flat	0.51	0.39	0.45
2 1/4" pot	1.80	0.53	0.83
4" pot	1.65	1.35	1.50
1 gal	4.35	3.75	4.04

02950 Ground Covers and Vines — 1994

DESCRIPTION	HIGH	LOW	AVG.
274 Pachysandra terminalis 'Green Carpet'			
container			
48/flat	0.54	0.39	0.47
2 1/4" pot	1.07	0.65	0.84
4" pot	1.65	1.49	1.56
1 gal	4.35	3.98	4.22
276 Parthenocissus quinquefolia			
container			
1 gal	9.30	4.13	6.20
278 Parthenocissus tricuspidata			
container			
1 gal	11.30	3.98	6.50
5 gal	27.00	12.80	18.50
280 Parthenocissus tricuspidata 'Veitchii'			
container			
1 gal	5.60	3.53	4.85
5 gal	18.00	16.10	17.00
282 Passiflora x alatocaerulea			
container			
1 gal	5.60	5.10	5.30
5 gal	18.00	16.10	17.10
284 Polygonum aubertii			
container			
1 gal	8.00	4.95	6.10
258 Liriope muscari, varieties			
container			
lg peat pot	2.40	1.20	1.94
1 quart	3.75	1.34	2.58
1 gal	8.60	3.38	4.70
286 Vinca major, varieties			
container			
2 1/2" pot	0.75	0.75	0.78
1 quart	2.25	1.73	1.98
1 gal	5.60	3.38	4.08
288 Vinca minor, varieties			
container			
48/flat	0.57	0.43	0.50
2 1/4" pot	1.20	0.60	0.83
3" pot	1.50	0.75	0.99
4" pot	1.88	1.13	1.44
290 Wisteria floribunda			
container			
5 gal	49.50	22.50	31.30
292 Wisteria sinensis			
bare root			
2 yr, #1	6.40	3.08	4.73
container			
1 gal	5.60	4.88	5.20
5 gal	32.30	13.90	21.20
15 gal	83.00	60.00	67.00

DESCRIPTION	HIGH	LOW	AVG.
FERNS			
200 Adiantum pedatum			
container			
1 gal	5.60	4.43	5.10
202 Asparagus densiflorus 'Meyers'			
container			
1 gal	5.60	4.50	5.30
5 gal	18.00	14.60	16.20
204 Asparagus densiflorus 'Sprengeri'			
container			
1 gal	4.05	1.50	3.20
5 gal	13.70	12.00	12.80
206 Athyrium filix-femina, varieties			
container			
2 quart	3.45	3.00	3.30
1 gal	7.10	4.35	5.60
208 Dennstaedtia punctilobula, varieties			
container			
1 quart	3.75	2.22	2.99
210 Dryopteris marginalis			
container			
1 gal	9.00	5.30	6.60
212 Osmunda cinnamomea			
container			
1 quart	4.05	2.22	3.15
1 gal	7.10	4.43	5.60
214 Osmunda regalis			
container			
1 quart	3.75	2.22	2.97
216 Polystichum acrostichoides			
container			
1 quart	4.05	2.22	3.15
1 gal	7.40	4.43	6.00
218 Pteris nodulosa (Matteuccia pensylvanica)			
container			
1 quart	3.75	2.63	3.15
2 quart	4.05	3.75	3.75
PERENNIALS			
200 Acanthus hungaricus			
container			
1 gal	7.50	6.50	7.00
202 Acanthus spinosus			
container			
1 gal	7.50	6.50	7.00
204 Achillea filipendulina, varieties			
container			
1 quart	2.48	2.25	2.33
1 gal	4.88	3.38	4.07
2 gal	9.00	6.80	7.90

PLANTING

	DESCRIPTION	HIGH	LOW	AVG.
206	**Alchemilla mollis**			
	container			
	1 quart	2.48	2.25	2.30
	1 gal	5.90	4.13	4.67
208	**Aquilegia, varieties**			
	container			
	1 quart	2.48	2.25	2.33
	1 gal	6.80	3.60	4.46
210	**Aster novi belgii, varieties**			
	container			
	1 gal	4.88	2.42	4.01
212	**Astilbe, varieties**			
	container			
	2 quart	4.80	3.90	4.34
	1 gal	9.00	4.05	5.70
	2 gal	11.60	6.00	8.70
214	**Bergenia cordifolia, varieties**			
	container			
	1 quart	3.75	2.25	2.82
	1 gal	5.40	3.60	4.53
216	**Campanula carpatica, varieties**			
	container			
	1 quart	2.48	2.25	2.33
	1 gal	6.80	3.60	4.59
218	**Chrysanthemum maximum, varieties**			
	container			
	1 quart	2.48	2.25	2.36
	1 gal	5.90	3.60	4.37
220	**Convallaria majalis**			
	container			
	1 quart	2.48	2.25	2.34
222	**Coreopsis lanceolata, varieties**			
	container			
	1 quart	2.48	2.25	2.37
	1 gal	6.80	3.60	4.34
224	**Delphinum, varieties**			
	container			
	1 gal	3.68	3.60	3.63
226	**Dianthus deltoides, varieties**			
	container			
	1 quart	2.48	2.34	2.40
	1 gal	4.88	3.60	3.99
228	**Dicentra eximia, varieties**			
	contianer			
	1 quart	3.90	2.25	2.85
	1 gal	5.40	4.05	4.86
230	**Dicentra spectabilis**			
	container			
	1 gal	6.50	4.13	5.00
	2 gal	9.00	7.50	8.30
232	**Digitalis mertonensis**			
	container			
	1 quart	2.48	2.25	2.33

	DESCRIPTION	HIGH	LOW	AVG.
234	**Echinacea purpurea, varieties**			
	container			
	1 quart	3.90	2.25	2.64
	1 gal	6.80	3.60	4.50
	2 gal	9.00	6.00	7.70
236	**Gaillardi grandiflora, varieties**			
	container			
	1 quart	2.48	2.25	2.36
	1 gal	6.80	3.60	4.40
238	**Galium odoratum**			
	container			
	1 quart	2.48	2.25	2.36
	1 gal	5.40	3.68	4.32
240	**Hemerocallis 'Stella de Oro''**			
	container			
	1 gal	10.90	4.35	6.40
242	**Hemerocallis, varieties**			
	container			
	1 gal	10.90	3.38	5.90
	2 gal	13.10	6.80	9.70
	5 gal	16.10	12.00	14.10
244	**Heuchera Bressingham, hybrids**			
	container			
	1 quart	2.48	2.25	2.33
	1 gal	5.40	3.60	4.31
246	**Iberis sempervirens, varieties**			
	container			
	1 quart	2.48	2.25	2.33
	1 gal	5.40	3.45	4.13
248	**Iris cristata, varieties**			
	container			
	1 quart	3.90	2.42	3.12
250	**Iris ensata, varieties**			
	container			
	1 gal	5.10	4.88	4.98
	2 gal	10.10	7.50	8.80
252	**Iris versicolor, varieties**			
	container			
	1 gal	4.13	2.25	3.18
254	**Lavandula angustifolia, varieties**			
	container			
	1 quart	2.48	2.25	2.34
	1 gal	6.80	3.38	4.44
256	**Liatris spicata**			
	container			
	1 quart	2.48	2.25	2.33
	1 gal	6.80	3.75	4.76
	2 gal	9.00	6.00	7.20
258	**Lobelia cardinalis**			
	container			
	1 quart	2.48	2.25	2.33

02950 Perennials

	DESCRIPTION	HIGH	LOW	AVG.
260	**Oenothera missouriensis**			
	container			
	1 quart	2.48	2.34	2.40
	1 gal	4.13	3.68	3.89
262	**Paeonia lactiflora, varieties**			
	container			
	2 gal	16.10	8.60	12.30
264	**Papaver orientale, varieties**			
	container			
	1 quart	5.30	2.25	3.08
	1 gal	5.30	3.60	4.47
266	**Phlox divaricata**			
	container			
	1 quart	2.48	2.25	2.33
	1 gal	4.95	4.05	4.62
268	**Phlox subulata**			
	container			
	1 gal	7.50	3.45	4.43
	2 gal	10.90	6.00	8.60
270	**Polemonium caeruleum, varieties**			
	container			
	1 quart	2.48	2.25	2.33
272	**Polygonatum multiflorum**			
	container			
	1 quart	3.90	2.25	3.05
274	**Rudbeckia fulgida 'Goldsturm'**			
	container			
	1 quart	2.48	2.25	2.33
	1 gal	6.80	2.34	4.32
	2 gal	9.00	6.80	8.20
276	**Rudbeckia maximum**			
	container			
	1 quart	3.90	2.25	3.06
	1 gal	4.80	4.13	4.46
278	**Sedum, varieties**			
	container			
	4" pot	1.65	1.35	1.50
	1 quart	3.75	2.25	2.57
	1 gal	6.80	3.68	4.55
	2 gal	9.00	6.00	7.40
280	**Sempervivum, varieties**			
	container			
	1 gal	4.50	3.68	4.10
282	**Solidago, varieties**			
	container			
	1 quart	2.48	2.25	2.33
	1 gal	4.88	3.68	4.11

DESCRIPTION	HIGH	LOW	AVG.

PLANTING

	DESCRIPTION	HIGH	LOW	AVG.
	Use this page to note costs for additional plant materials			

	DESCRIPTION	HIGH	LOW	AVG.

02970 Landscape Maintenance — 1994

KEY	DESCRIPTION	UNIT	CREW AND EQUIPMENT	PER DAY	INSTALLATION COST	MATERIALS COST	TOTAL + 25%
10	**LAWNS**						
	Mow lawn						
100	20-22" walking mower	MSF	1J,73	115	1.87		2.52
110	32-36" walking mower	MSF	1J,73	200	1.10		1.48
120	36-42" riding mower	MSF	1J,74	355	0.63		0.85
130	48-60" riding mower	MSF	1J,75	630	0.37		0.50
140	3 gang reel mower	MSF	1G,50	910	0.37		0.50
150	5 gang reel mower	MSF	1G,51	2480	0.15		0.20
	Aerate lawn						
160	walk behind aerator	MSF	1J,76	90	2.44		3.29
170	48" aerator	MSF	1G,50	770	0.43		0.59
180	72" aerator	MSF	1G,51	1155	0.32		0.44
	Edge lawn						
	at pavement						
190	by hand	LF	1J	3200	0.06		0.08
200	power edger	MLF	1J,77	16	13.41		18.10
	at planting bed						
210	by hand	LF	1J	1335	0.14		0.19
220	power edger	MLF	1J,77	4	53.64		72.00
230	Water lawn, per 1" of water	MSF	1J	20	9.48		12.80
240	Rake, by hand	MSF	1J	7	27.08		36.60
	Fertilize lawn, see Section 02920, "Soil Preparation"						
20	**BEDS, FLOWER AND GROUND COVER**						
	Weed						
100	mulched bed	MSF	1J	20	9.48		12.80
110	unmulched bed	MSF	1J	7	27.08		36.60
120	Cultivate bed	MSF	1J	13	14.58		19.70
130	Fertilize bed (see Section 02920, "Soil Preparation" for material prices)	MSF	1J	80	2.37		3.20
140	Clean up litter	MSF	1J	27	7.02		9.50
150	Fall clean up of flower bed	MSF	1J	1	189.55		256.00
30	**SHRUBS**						
100	Hoe or weed shrub bed	MSF	1J	8	23.69		32.00
	Water						
110	shrub	Ea	1J	32	5.92		8.00
120	shrub bed, per 1" water	MSF	1J	20	9.48		12.80
	Prune						
	shrub						
130	under 3' height	Ea	1J	195	0.97		1.31
140	3'-6' height	Ea	1J	95	2.00		2.69
150	over 6' height	Ea	1J	50	3.79		5.10
160	shrub bed	MSF	1J	7	27.08		36.60
170	Fertilize shrub bed (see Section 02920, "Soil Preparation" for material prices)	MSF	1J	80	2.37		3.20
180	Clean up litter	MSF	1J	27	7.02		9.50
40	**TREES**						
	Pruning, see Sections 02115, "Selective Clearing" and 02950, "Trees, Plants, and Ground Covers"						
	Water tree						
100	under 1" caliper	Ea	1J	32	5.92		8.00
110	1" - 3" caliper	Ea	1J	16	11.85		16.00
120	3" - 4" caliper	Ea	1J	10	18.96		25.60
130	over 4" caliper	Ea	1J	8	23.69		32.00

PLANTING

KEY	DESCRIPTION	UNIT	CREW AND EQUIPMENT	PER DAY	INSTALLATION COST	MATERIALS COST	TOTAL + 25%
50	**WALKS AND PAVING**						
100	Sweep walk	MSF	1J	14	13.54		18.30
110	Snow removal, by hand	MSF	1J	5	37.91		51.00

03110 Structural Cast-in-Place Concrete Formwork						1994
KEY	DESCRIPTION	UNIT	CREW AND EQUIPMENT	PER DAY	INSTALLATION COST	MATERIALS COST	TOTAL + 25%

KEY	DESCRIPTION	UNIT	CREW AND EQUIPMENT	PER DAY	INSTALLATION COST	MATERIALS COST	TOTAL + 25%
10	**FOOTING FORMS, 3 USES**						
	Wall type footing forms						
100	depths from grade to 4'	SF	2C1L,81	275	2.60	0.46	3.83
110	depths from 5' to 8'	SF	2C1L,81	260	2.75	0.46	4.01
	Pad type footing forms						
120	depths from grade to 4'	SF	2C1L,81	260	2.75	0.50	4.06
130	depths from 5' to 8'	SF	2C1L,81	250	2.86	0.50	4.20
20	**WALL AND GRADE BEAM FORMS, 3 USES**						
	Forms						
100	grade to 4' depth	SF	3C1L,81	250	3.87	0.48	5.40
110	5' to 8' depth	SF	3C1L,81	240	4.03	0.50	5.70
120	grade to 4' height	SF	3C1L,81	240	4.03	0.48	5.60
130	5' to 8' height	SF	3C1L,81	230	4.21	0.50	5.90
140	Curved walls and grade beams, add	SF	1C	380	0.67	0.12	0.98
150	Retaining and battered walls, add	SF	1C	380	0.67	0.05	0.89
160	Brick and stone ledges, add	LF	1C	245	1.03	0.12	1.44
170	Openings in walls, add	SF	1C	140	1.81	0.58	2.98
30	**CURB AND EDGE FORMS**						
100	Grade to 12" below or above, 3 uses	SF	2C1L,81	270	2.65	0.49	3.92
	Ground slab openings, 3 uses						
110	square	LF	2C1L,81	250	2.86	0.43	4.11
120	circle	LF	2C1L,81	200	3.58	0.43	5.00
130	Screeds, 4" high, 4 uses	LF	2C1L,81	600	1.19	0.22	1.76
40	**STAIRS AND LANDINGS, 2 USES**						
100	On ground, stringers and risers	SF	3C1L,81	175	5.53	0.74	7.80
110	Structural, soffits, stringers and risers	SF	3C1L,81	100	9.68	1.09	13.50
50	**FORM FINISHES AND SPECIAL EFFECTS**						
100	Solid boards, 1 use, add to form cost	SF	1C	280	0.90	0.71	2.02
110	Bevel edge strips, 1 use, add	LF	1C	130	1.95	0.48	3.03
120	Square edge strips, 1 use, add	LF	1C	115	2.20	0.43	3.29
130	Textured form liners, 1 use, add	SF	1C	300	0.84	0.60	1.80
60	**COLUMN FORMS**						
	Wood, square (3 uses)						
100	8" x 8"	LF	2C	50	10.12	2.81	16.20
110	10" x 10"	LF	2C	40	12.64	3.40	20.10
120	12" x 12"	LF	2C	35	14.45	4.19	23.30
	Fiber, round (1 use)						
130	8" diameter	LF	2C	100	5.06	2.37	9.30
140	10" diameter	LF	2C	100	5.06	3.03	10.10
150	12" diameter	LF	2C	100	5.06	3.68	10.90

CONCRETE REINFORCEMENT

03210 Reinforcing Steel   1994

KEY	DESCRIPTION	UNIT	CREW AND EQUIPMENT	PER DAY	INSTALLATION COST	MATERIALS COST	TOTAL + 25%
10	**REINFORCING STEEL**						
	Bars in footings and slabs						
	plain						
100	#3 bar	LF	4I	6700	0.17	0.15	0.40
110	#4 bar	LF	4I	5200	0.22	0.28	0.62
120	#5 bar	LF	4I	4200	0.27	0.42	0.86
130	#6 bar	LF	4I	3300	0.34	0.60	1.18
	galvanized						
140	#3 bar	LF	4I	6700	0.17	0.24	0.51
150	#4 bar	LF	4I	5200	0.22	0.42	0.80
160	#5 bar	LF	4I	4200	0.27	0.61	1.10
170	#6 bar	LF	4I	3300	0.34	0.89	1.54
	epoxy coated						
180	#3 bar	LF	4I	6700	0.17	0.33	0.62
190	#4 bar	LF	4I	5200	0.22	0.58	1.00
200	#5 bar	LF	4I	4200	0.27	0.89	1.45
210	#6 bar	LF	4I	3300	0.34	1.31	2.07
	Bars in walls						
	plain						
220	#3 bar	LF	4I	5200	0.22	0.15	0.46
230	#4 bar	LF	4I	3900	0.29	0.28	0.71
240	#5 bar	LF	4I	3300	0.34	0.42	0.95
250	#6 bar	LF	4I	2600	0.44	0.60	1.29
	galvanized						
260	#3 bar	LF	4I	5200	0.22	0.24	0.57
270	#4 bar	LF	4I	3900	0.29	0.42	0.89
280	#5 bar	LF	4I	3300	0.34	0.61	1.19
290	#6 bar	LF	4I	2600	0.44	0.89	1.66
	epoxy coated						
300	#3 bar	LF	4I	5200	0.22	0.33	0.68
310	#4 bar	LF	4I	3900	0.29	0.58	1.09
320	#5 bar	LF	4I	3300	0.34	0.89	1.54
330	#6 bar	LF	4I	2600	0.44	1.31	2.18
	Bending bars, fieldwork						
340	#3 or #4 bar	Ea	1I	265	1.07		1.33
350	#5 or #6 bar	Ea	1I	200	1.41		1.77
	Hooking bars, fieldwork						
360	#3 or #4 bar	Ea	1I	175	1.62		2.02
370	#5 or #6 bar	Ea	1I	135	2.09		2.62

03220 Welded Wire Fabric

KEY	DESCRIPTION	UNIT	CREW AND EQUIPMENT	PER DAY	INSTALLATION COST	MATERIALS COST	TOTAL + 25%
10	**WELDED WIRE FABRIC**						
	6" x 6" welded wire fabric						
100	10/10	SF	4I	7700	0.15	0.07	0.27
110	8/8	SF	4I	6600	0.17	0.12	0.36
120	6/6	SF	4I	5800	0.20	0.17	0.46
130	4/4	SF	4I	4600	0.25	0.21	0.57
	4" x 4" welded wire fabric						
180	8/8	SF	4I	5200	0.22	0.30	0.65
190	6/6	SF	4I	4700	0.24	0.31	0.69
200	4/4	SF	4I	3600	0.31	0.34	0.82

03250 Concrete Accessories — 1994

KEY	DESCRIPTION	UNIT	CREW AND EQUIPMENT	PER DAY	INSTALLATION COST	MATERIALS COST	TOTAL + 25%
	See also Section 02510, "Walk, Road, and Parking Paving" for joint materials in concrete paving, and Section 04150, "Masonry Accessories for joint materials in masonry.						
10	**FLEXIBLE JOINT FILLER**						
	Gray sponge rubber						
100	1/2" x 4"	LF	1L	400	0.66	1.77	3.03
110	1/2" x 8"	LF	1L	350	0.75	3.50	5.30
120	1" x 4"	LF	1L	400	0.66	3.54	5.20
130	1" x 8"	LF	1L	350	0.75	6.90	9.60
	Polyethylene foam backer rod						
140	1/2" diameter	LF	1L	500	0.52	0.11	0.79
150	1/2" x 2"	LF	1L	490	0.54	0.22	0.94
160	1/2" x 4"	LF	1L	450	0.58	0.34	1.15
170	1/2" x 8"	LF	1L	350	0.75	0.57	1.65
180	1" diameter	LF	1L	490	0.54	0.22	0.94
190	1" x 4"	LF	1L	450	0.58	0.55	1.42
200	1" x 8"	LF	1L	350	0.75	0.99	2.17
20	**KEYWAYS**						
	Asphalt hardboard, premolded tongue and groove and joint metal stakes						
100	1/8" x 3 1/2"	LF	1C	500	0.51	0.44	1.18
110	1/8" x 5 1/2"	LF	1C	500	0.51	0.53	1.29
120	1/4" x 4"	LF	1C	500	0.51	0.70	1.51
130	1/4" x 8"	LF	1C	500	0.51	0.98	1.86
	Keyed Kold 24 gauge metal joint and stakes						
140	3 1/2"	LF	1C	500	0.51	0.46	1.21
150	5 1/2"	LF	1C	500	0.51	0.66	1.46
160	7 1/2"	LF	1C	480	0.53	0.97	1.87
30	**SEALANTS, LIQUID SELF SEALING**						
	Neoprene, cold poured						
100	1/2" x 1"	LF	1L	350	0.75	1.35	2.62
110	1" x 2"	LF	1L	300	0.87	5.00	7.30
	Polyurethane, one part tar modified or two part						
120	1/2" x 1"	LF	1L	350	0.75	1.60	2.94
130	1" x 2"	LF	1L	300	0.87	6.40	9.10
40	**ANCHORS IN CONCRETE**						
	Anchor bolt, nut, washer and template						
	plain steel						
100	1/2" x 12"	Ea	1C	100	2.53	0.60	3.91
110	5/8" x 12"	Ea	1C	80	3.16	1.20	5.50
120	3/4" x 12"	Ea	1C	60	4.21	1.50	7.10
	galvanized steel						
130	1/2" x 12"	Ea	1C	100	2.53	1.10	4.54
140	5/8" x 12"	Ea	1C	80	3.16	1.85	6.30
150	3/4" x 12"	Ea	1C	60	4.21	2.65	8.60
50	**INSERTS, WALL AND BEAM TYPE**						
	Dovetail anchor slot, galvanized						
100	24 gauge	LF	1C	500	0.51	0.23	0.92
110	22 gauge	LF	1C	480	0.53	0.40	1.16
	Wedge type insert, cast iron, including 5/8" bolt, nut and washer						
140		Ea	1C	80	3.16	2.65	7.30
	Threaded insert, cast iron, for threaded bolt or rod						
150	1/2" diameter	Ea	1C	105	2.41	2.07	5.60
160	5/8" diameter	Ea	1C	100	2.53	2.92	6.80
170	3/4" diameter	Ea	1C	95	2.66	2.87	6.90

CONCRETE ACCESSORIES

KEY	DESCRIPTION	UNIT	CREW AND EQUIPMENT	PER DAY	INSTALLATION COST	MATERIALS COST	TOTAL + 25%
60	**WATERSTOPS**						
	Polyvinyl chloride, center bulb						
100	6" x 3/16"	LF	1C	200	1.26	0.97	2.79
110	9" x 3/16"	LF	1C	180	1.40	1.50	3.63
120	6" x 3/8"	LF	1C	195	1.30	1.45	3.43
130	9" x 3/8"	LF	1C	175	1.45	2.18	4.53

03310 Structural Concrete — 1994

KEY	DESCRIPTION	UNIT	CREW AND EQUIPMENT	PER DAY	INSTALLATION COST	MATERIALS COST	TOTAL + 25%
00	**COMPOSITE COSTS**						
	Retaining wall, normal concrete finish, includes excavation and backfill						
	gravity type						
100	4' high, toe to top ***	LF					64.00
110	6' high, toe to top ***	LF					105.00
120	8' high, toe to top ***	LF					202.00
	cantilever type, reinforced						
130	6' high, footing to top ***	LF					122.00
140	8' high, footing to top ***	LF					200.00
	Freestanding wall, reinforced, normal concrete finish, includes excavation and backfill						
150	4' high, footing to top	LF					72.00
160	6' high, footing to top	LF					106.00
10	**CAST-IN-PLACE CONCRETE**						
	The following costs do not include formwork, reinforcing steel, or excavation						
	Footing, wall and column						
100	truck chuted	CY	3L	7	87.44	59.00	183.00
	continuous footing						
105	16" x 8"	LF	3L	210	2.91	2.06	6.20
110	18" x 9"	LF	3L	170	3.60	2.61	7.80
120	20" x 10"	LF	3L	135	4.53	3.22	9.70
130	24" x 12"	LF	3L	95	6.44	4.64	13.90
140	36" x 12"	LF	3L	65	9.42	6.90	20.40
	pier or spread footing						
150	24" x 24" x 12"	Ea	3L	50	12.24	9.30	26.90
160	36" x 36" x 14"	Ea	3L	20	30.60	33.70	80.00
170	48" x 48" x 16"	Ea	3L	10	61.21	49.50	138.00
180	crane and bucket	CY	1A8L,95	170	13.68	60.00	92.00
	Foundation						
190	heavy mat	CY	3L	10	61.21	59.00	150.00
200	medium mat	CY	3L	8	76.51	59.00	169.00
	Wall, below grade to 5' deep						
210	truck chuted	CY	3L	7	87.44	67.00	193.00
220	8" thick	SF	3L	285	2.15	1.74	4.86
230	12" thick	SF	3L	190	3.22	2.64	7.30
240	16" thick	SF	3L	150	4.08	3.50	9.50
250	20" thick	SF	3L	110	5.56	4.37	12.40
260	crane and bucket	CY	1A8L,95	160	14.54	67.00	102.00
	Wall, grade to 8' high, normal finish						
270	ramps and barrows	CY	3L	6	102.02	67.00	211.00
280	8" thick	SF	3L	245	2.50	1.74	5.30
290	12" thick	SF	3L	160	3.83	2.64	8.10
300	16" thick	SF	3L	120	5.10	3.50	10.80
310	20" thick	SF	3L	95	6.44	4.37	13.50
320	crane and bucket	CCY	1A8L,95	160	14.54	67.00	102.00
	Slab on grade						
330	truck chuted	CCY	3L	7	87.44	59.00	183.00
340	crane and bucket	CCY	1A8L,95	160	14.54	59.00	92.00
350	Toppings	CCY	3L	7	87.44	67.00	193.00

CAST-IN-PLACE CONCRETE

03345 Concrete Finishing 1994

KEY	DESCRIPTION	UNIT	CREW AND EQUIPMENT	PER DAY	INSTALLATION COST	MATERIALS COST	TOTAL + 25%
10	**FLOORS**						
100	Aluminum oxide grits	SF	1F	920	0.26	0.13	0.49
110	Carborundum grits	SF	1F	920	0.26	0.18	0.56
	See also Section 02515 "Portland Cement Concrete Paving" for floor finishing						
20	**WALLS**						
100	Patch tie holes and honeycombs	SF	1F	550	0.44	0.08	0.65
	Rub wall						
110	burlap and grout	SF	1F	500	0.49	0.09	0.72
120	carborundum on fins	SF	1F	700	0.35	0.18	0.66

03350 Special Concrete Finishing

KEY	DESCRIPTION	UNIT	CREW AND EQUIPMENT	PER DAY	INSTALLATION COST	MATERIALS COST	TOTAL + 25%
10	**SPECIAL CONCRETE FINISHES**						
	Bush hammered finish						
100	green concrete	SF	1F	200	1.22	0.09	1.63
110	cured concrete	SF	1F	150	1.62	0.11	2.17
	Sandblasted finish						
120	light	SF	2F1L,86	1000	0.76	0.12	1.09
130	heavy	SF	2F1L,86	500	1.51	0.38	2.36

04150 Masonry Accessories						1994
KEY	DESCRIPTION	UNIT	CREW AND EQUIPMENT	PER DAY	INSTALLATION COST	MATERIALS COST	TOTAL + 25%

KEY	DESCRIPTION	UNIT	CREW AND EQUIPMENT	PER DAY	INSTALLATION COST	MATERIALS COST	TOTAL + 25%
10	**JOINT REINFORCEMENT**						
	Horizontal joint reinforcement						
	#9 galvanized steel wire						
100	8" wide ladur	LF	1B	2300	0.11	0.08	0.24
110	12" wide ladur	LF	1B	2100	0.12	0.09	0.27
120	8" wide truss	LF	1B	1900	0.14	0.11	0.31
130	12" wide truss	LF	1B	1700	0.15	0.12	0.34
	Bars for reinforcing brick walls						
	placed horizontal						
140	#3 bars	LF	1B	1700	0.15	0.16	0.39
150	#4 bars	LF	1B	1500	0.17	0.30	0.59
160	#5 bars	LF	1B	1300	0.20	0.47	0.84
	placed vertical						
170	#3 bars	LF	1B	1300	0.20	0.16	0.45
180	#4 bars	LF	1B	1200	0.22	0.30	0.65
190	#5 bars	LF	1B	1100	0.24	0.47	0.88
	Bars for vertical reinforcement of concrete block walls, includes concrete						
200	#4 bars	LF	1B	1000	0.26	1.42	2.10
210	#5 bars	LF	1B	1000	0.26	1.50	2.20
20	**ANCHORS AND TIE SYSTEMS**						
	Anchor bolts, galvanized						
100	1/2" x 10"	Ea	1B	195	1.34	0.61	2.43
110	5/8" x 12"	Ea	1B	170	1.53	1.23	3.45
120	3/4" x 16"	Ea	1B	140	1.86	1.82	4.60
	Dovetail anchors						
130	16 ga. galv. x 3 1/2"	Ea	1B	1300	0.20	0.11	0.39
140	12 ga. galv. x 3 1/2"	Ea	1B	1300	0.20	0.14	0.43
	Stone anchors						
	galvanized						
160	1/8" x 1" x 6"	Ea	1B	1300	0.20	0.61	1.01
170	3/16" x 1 1/4" x 8"	Ea	1B	1300	0.20	1.16	1.70
	Wall ties						
	corrugated galvanized						
200	24 gauge, 7/8" x 7"	Ea	1B	1300	0.20	0.07	0.34
210	16 gauge, 7/8" x 7"	Ea	1B	1300	0.20	0.03	0.29
30	**CONTROL JOINTS**						
	Molded rubber or PVC						
100	regular	LF	1B	425	0.61	1.67	2.85
110	wide flange	LF	1B	350	0.74	2.33	3.84

UNIT MASONRY

KEY	DESCRIPTION	UNIT	CREW AND EQUIPMENT	PER DAY	INSTALLATION COST	MATERIALS COST	TOTAL + 25%
00	**COMPOSITE COSTS**						
	Retaining wall, gravity type, face brick veneer, includes excavation and backfill						
	common brick backup						
100	4' high, toe to top ***	LF					146.00
110	6' high, toe to top ***	LF					270.00
120	8' high, toe to top ***	LF					444.00
	concrete block backup						7.00
130	4' high, toe to top ***	LF					87.00
140	6' high, toe to top ***	LF					196.00
	plain concrete backup						
150	4' high, toe to top ***	LF					126.00
160	6' high, toe to top ***	LF					204.00
170	8' high, toe to top ***	LF					340.00
	Retaining wall, cantilver type, face brick veneer, reinforced concrete backup and base, includes excavation and backfill						
180	6' high, toe to top	LF					203.00
190	8' high, toe to top	LF					302.00
	Freestanding wall, face brick, includes excavation, and backfill						
200	4' high, 8" thick ***	LF					101.00
210	6' high, 12" thick ***	LF					172.00
10	**BACKUP WALLS**						
	See Sections 03310, "Structural Concrete", 04220, "Concrete Unit Masonry", and this section						
20	**BRICK WALL VENEERS**						
	Face brick, extruded hard red, 4" veneer						
	standard 3 3/4 x 8" x 2 1/4"						
100	running bond	SF	4B3L	315	5.49	2.05	9.40
110	common bond	SF	4B3L	245	7.06	2.51	12.00
120	English bond	SF	4B3L	170	10.17	3.22	16.70
130	Flemish bond, alternate full headers and stretchers every course	SF	4B3L	200	8.64	3.08	14.70
140	Flemish headers every 6th course	SF	4B3L	240	7.20	2.15	11.70
150	Flemish cross bond, headers every 2nd course	SF	4B3L	230	7.52	2.65	12.70
160	double-stretcher, garden wall bond	SF	4B3L	210	8.23	2.71	13.70
170	triple-stretcher, garden wall bond	SF	4B3L	220	7.86	2.60	13.10
	modular 3 5/8" x 7 5/8" x 2 1/4"						
180	running bond	SF	4B3L	290	5.96	2.00	10.00
190	common bond	SF	4B3L	220	7.86	2.45	12.90
200	English bond	SF	4B3L	155	11.15	3.16	17.90
210	Flemish bond, alternate full headers and stretchers every course	SF	4B3L	185	9.34	3.04	15.50
220	Flemish headers every 6th course	SF	4B3L	220	7.86	2.11	12.50
230	Flemish cross bond, headers every 2nd course	SF	4B3L	210	8.23	2.35	13.20
240	double-stretcher, garden wall bond	SF	4B3L	190	9.10	2.40	14.40
250	triple-stretcher, garden wall bond	SF	4B3L	200	8.64	2.28	13.70

04210 Brick Masonry — 1994

KEY	DESCRIPTION	UNIT	CREW AND EQUIPMENT	PER DAY	INSTALLATION COST	MATERIALS COST	TOTAL + 25%
	special modular sizes, running bond						
260	economy 8, 3 5/8" x 3 5/8" x 7 5/8"	SF	4B3L	295	5.86	2.26	10.10
270	double, 3 5/8" x 5" x 7 5/8"	SF	4B3L	145	11.92	2.55	18.10
280	norman, 3 5/8" x 2 1/4" x 11 5/8"	SF	4B3L	370	4.67	2.24	8.60
290	economy 12, 3 5/8" x 3 5/8" x 11 5/8"	SF	4B3L	415	4.17	2.47	8.30
30	**SOLID BRICK WALLS**						
	Common brick wall						
	standard 3 3/4" x 8" x 2 1/4"						
100	4" thick	SF	4B3L	315	5.49	1.57	8.80
110	8" thick	SF	4B3L	160	10.80	3.23	17.50
120	12" thick	SF	4B3L	110	15.71	4.88	25.70
130	16" thick	SF	4B3L	90	19.21	6.60	32.30
140	20" thick	SF	4B3L	70	24.69	8.10	41.00
150	24" thick	SF	4B3L	60	28.81	10.00	48.50
	modular 3 5/8" x 7 5/8" x 2 1/4"						
160	4" thick	SF	4B3L	290	5.96	1.54	9.40
170	8" thick	SF	4B3L	150	11.52	3.16	18.40
180	12" thick	SF	4B3L	105	16.46	4.80	26.60
190	16" thick	SF	4B3L	80	21.61	6.40	35.00
200	20" thick	SF	4B3L	65	26.59	8.00	43.20
210	24" thick	SF	4B3L	55	31.43	9.80	52.00
	Face brick, extruded hard red						
220	4" thick serpentine	SF	4B3L	245	7.06	1.78	11.00
230	8" thick English or Flemish	SF	4B3L	130	13.30	3.66	21.20
40	**BRICK STEPS**						
	Brick pavers, treads and risers set on concrete, extruded hard red						
100	3 3/4" x 8" x 2 1/4"	M	2B1L	0.68	1102.59	540.00	2050.00
110	3 3/4" x 8" x 1 5/8"	M	2B1L	0.7	1071.09	500.00	1960.00
120	3 5/8" x 7 5/8" x 2 1/4"	M	2B1L	0.76	986.53	510.00	1870.00
130	3 5/8" x 7 5/8" x 1 5/8"	M	2B1L	0.79	949.06	474.00	1780.00

Brick laid flat requires 4 bricks per SF for 3 3/4" x 8",
4.5 bricks per SF for 3 5/8" x 7 5/8"

Brick laid on edge requires 6.3 bricks per SF for
3 3/4" x 8" x 2 1/4", 6.9 bricks per SF for
3 5/8" x 7 5/8" x 2 1/4"

04220 Concrete Unit Masonry

KEY	DESCRIPTION	UNIT	CREW AND EQUIPMENT	PER DAY	INSTALLATION COST	MATERIALS COST	TOTAL + 25%
10	**CONCRETE BLOCK WALL**						
	Concrete block, sand and gravel, not reinforced, exposed joints tooled						
	backup, 8" x 16" block						
100	8" thick	SF	4B2L	430	3.37	1.39	6.00
110	10" thick	SF	4B2L	420	3.45	1.71	6.50
120	12" thick	SF	4B2L	400	3.62	1.93	6.90
	freestanding, 8" x 16" block						
130	8" thick	SF	4B2L	415	3.49	1.26	5.90
140	10" thick	SF	4B2L	400	3.62	1.47	6.40
150	12" thick	SF	4B2L	390	3.72	1.71	6.80

UNIT MASONRY

KEY	DESCRIPTION	UNIT	CREW AND EQUIPMENT	PER DAY	INSTALLATION COST	MATERIALS COST	TOTAL + 25%
	foundations, 8" x 16" block						
160	8" thick	SF	4B2L	450	3.22	1.26	5.60
170	10" thick	SF	4B2L	435	3.33	1.26	5.70
180	12" thick	SF	4B2L	420	3.45	1.71	6.50
190	16" thick	SF	4B2L	300	4.83	2.38	9.00
	solid, 8" x 16" block						
200	8" thick	SF	4B2L	400	3.62	1.62	6.60
210	12" thick	SF	4B2L	360	4.03	2.35	8.00
	Decorative block, 1 face, add to above						
	exposed aggregate	SF					30%
	fluted	SF					15%
	shadow	SF					5%
	split face	SF					10%
	split rib	SF					20%

04410 Rough Stone — 1994

KEY	DESCRIPTION	UNIT	CREW AND EQUIPMENT	PER DAY	INSTALLATION COST	MATERIALS COST	TOTAL + 25%
00	**COMPOSITE COSTS**						
	Rubble stone retaining wall, includes excavation and backfill						
	in mortar						
100	4' high, toe to top ***	LF					141.00
110	6' high, toe to top ***	LF					295.00
120	dry set, 4' high, toe to top ***	LF					144.00
	Freestanding rubble stone wall, includes excavation and backfill						
	in mortar						
130	4' high, toe to top ***	LF					88.00
140	6' high, toe to top ***	LF					176.00
	dry set						
150	4' high, toe to top ***	LF					105.00
160	6' high, toe to top ***	LF					198.00
10	**RUBBLE STONE WALL**						
	Rubble stone wall						
	in mortar						
100	12" thick	CF	2L2M	120	7.78	9.30	21.30
110	18" thick	CF	2L2M	130	7.18	8.80	20.00
120	24" thick	CF	2L2M	140	6.66	11.50	22.70
	dry set						
130	12" thick	CF	2L2M	160	5.83	7.90	17.20
140	18" thick	CF	2L2M	165	5.65	7.60	16.60
150	24" thick	CF	2L2M	170	5.49	6.80	15.40

04420 Cut Stone

KEY	DESCRIPTION	UNIT	CREW AND EQUIPMENT	PER DAY	INSTALLATION COST	MATERIALS COST	TOTAL + 25%
00	**COMPOSITE COSTS**						
	Retaining wall, 4" stone veneer, includes excavation and backfill						
	gravity type						
	concrete block backup						
100	4' high, toe to top	LF					127.00
110	6' high, toe to top	LF					222.00
	plain concrete backup						
120	4' high, toe to top	LF					172.00
130	6' high, toe to top	LF					301.00
140	8' high, toe to top	LF					486.00
	cantilever type, reinforced backup and base						
150	6' high, footing to top	LF					311.00
160	8' high, footing to top	LF					492.00
	Freestanding wall, includes excavation and backfill						
	mortar set						
170	4' high, toe to top, 12" thick	LF					184.00
180	8' high, toe to top, 18" thick	LF					378.00
	dry set						
190	4' high, toe to top, 12" thick	LF					115.00
200	6' high, toe to top, 18" thick	LF					248.00

STONE

KEY	DESCRIPTION	UNIT	CREW AND EQUIPMENT	PER DAY	INSTALLATION COST	MATERIALS COST	TOTAL + 25%
10	**STONE WALL VENEER**						
	Ashlar veneer, 4" thick						
	coursed						
100	limestone	SF	2L2M	120	8.30	8.70	21.20
110	marble	SF	2L2M	100	9.96	22.60	40.70
120	granite	SF	2L2M	80	12.45	9.90	27.90
	random						
130	limestone	SF	2L2M	90	11.07	6.50	22.00
140	marble	SF	2L2M	90	11.07	13.70	31.00
150	sandstone	SF	2L2M	95	10.48	7.10	22.00
160	granite	SF	2L2M	70	14.23	5.60	24.80
20	**STONE DRY SET**						
	Random ashlar, random range limestone						
100	12" thick	CF	2L2M	160	6.22	16.40	28.30
110	18" thick	CF	2L2M	165	6.04	15.90	27.40
120	24" thick	CF	2L2M	170	5.86	15.30	26.40
30	**STONE COPINGS AND STEPS**						
	Stone copings, steps, etc.						
100	limestone	CF	2L2M	25	39.83	40.20	100.00
110	marble	CF	2L2M	22	45.27	115.00	200.00
120	granite	CF	2L2M	20	49.79	37.40	109.00
130	slate, 1 1/2"	SF	2L2M	90	11.07	16.50	34.50

05520 Handrails and Railings — 1994

KEY	DESCRIPTION	UNIT	CREW AND EQUIPMENT	PER DAY	INSTALLATION COST	MATERIALS COST	TOTAL + 25%
10	**PAVEMENT MOUNTED HANDRAILS**						
	Handrail, 1 1/2" pipe						
	steel, welded joints, painted						
100	single rail, 1'-6" high ***	LF	2I	110	5.14	13.90	23.80
110	double rail, 2'-8" high ***	LF	2I	95	5.95	20.90	33.60
120	triple rail, 3'-6" high ***	LF	2I	85	6.65	26.60	41.60
	aluminum, flush joints						
130	single rail, 1'-6" high ***	LF	2I	95	5.95	26.50	40.60
140	double rail, 2'-8" high ***	LF	2I	85	6.65	42.10	61.00
150	triple rail, 3'-6" high ***	LF	2I	75	7.54	56.00	79.00
	Center stair rail, 1 1/2" pipe						
160	steel, welded joints, painted	LF	2I	80	7.07	21.30	35.50
170	aluminum, flush joints	LF	2I	70	8.08	49.20	72.00
20	**WALL BRACKETED HANDRAILS**						
	Handrail, 1 1/2" pipe						
100	steel, painted ***	LF	2I	120	4.71	9.80	18.10
110	aluminum ***	LF	2I	100	5.66	20.50	32.70

ORNAMENTAL METAL

KEY	DESCRIPTION	UNIT	CREW AND EQUIPMENT	PER DAY	INSTALLATION COST	MATERIALS COST	TOTAL + 25%
10	**PAVEMENT MOUNTED HANDRAILS**						
	Pavement mounted handrail						
	mild steel bars, channels and molded caps, painte						
	minimum design						
100	2'-8" high ***	LF	2I	40	14.14	22.30	45.50
110	3'-6" high ***	LF	2I	35	16.16	27.60	55.00
	special design						
120	2'-8" high ***	LF	3I	35	24.24	35.40	75.00
130	3'-6" high ***	LF	3I	30	28.28	42.10	88.00
	alumnium bars, channels and tubing, anodized finish						
	minimum design						
140	1'-6" high ***	LF	2I	35	16.16	35.20	64.00
150	2'-8" high ***	LF	2I	30	18.85	44.90	80.00
160	3'-6" high ***	LF	2I	25	22.62	63.00	107.00
	monumental design						
170	1'-6" high ***	LF	2I	30	18.85	56.00	94.00
180	2'-8" high ***	LF	2I	25	22.62	77.00	125.00
190	3'-6" high ***	LF	2I	20	28.28	100.00	160.00
	bronze bars, channels, tubing and casting						
	minimum design						
200	1'-6" high ***	LF	2I	30	18.85	65.00	105.00
210	2'-8" high ***	LF	2I	25	22.62	112.00	168.00
220	3'-6" high ***	LF	2I	20	28.28	144.00	215.00
	monumental design						
230	1'-6" high ***	LF	2I	25	22.62	131.00	192.00
240	2'-8" high ***	LF	2I	20	28.28	196.00	280.00
250	3'-6" high ***	LF	2I	15	37.70	262.00	375.00
	Center stair rail						
	mild steel posts, molded caps, painted						
260	single rails ***	LF	2I	35	16.16	35.50	65.00
270	double rails, brackets	LF	2I	25	22.62	49.90	91.00
	aluminum tube posts, rails, anodized finish						
280	single rails	LF	2I	35	16.16	63.00	99.00
290	double rails, brackets	LF	2I	25	22.62	110.00	166.00
	composite metal and wood						
300	high	LF	2I	30	18.85	160.00	224.00
310	low	LF	2I	20	28.28	320.00	435.00
20	**WALL BRACKETED HANDRAILS**						
	Wall bracketed handrails						
	mild steel channels, molded caps and wrought brackets, painted						
100	minimum design	LF	2I	100	5.66	13.10	23.40
110	special design	LF	2I	80	7.07	26.30	41.70
	aluminum channels, tubing and brackets, anodized finish						
120	minimum design	LF	2I	80	7.07	22.50	37.00
130	monumental design ***	LF	2I	70	8.08	43.70	65.00
	bronze channels, tubing and castings						
140	minimum design	LF	2I	70	8.08	58.00	83.00
150	monumental design ***	LF	2I	40	14.14	112.00	158.00

06110 Wood Framing — 1994

KEY	DESCRIPTION	UNIT	CREW AND EQUIPMENT	PER DAY	INSTALLATION COST	MATERIALS COST	TOTAL + 25%
00	**COMPOSITE COSTS**						
	Deck, 20' x 16', 30" above grade, 2" x 6" decking,						
	4" x 8" beams and rim joists, 2" x 8" joists -						
	2' O.C., 4" x 4" posts, concrete footings						
100	fir, pine or spruce, treated ***	SF					14.80
110	western cedar ***	SF					15.20
120	redwood ***	SF					9.40
	Deck railing, 3' high, two 2" x 4" railings,						
	2" x 4" posts						
130	fir, pine or spruce, treated ***	LF					21.50
140	western cedar ***	LF					20.30
150	redwood ***	LF					13.10
	Exterior stairs, 3' wide, 2" x 12" stringers and						
	treads (two 2 x 6's), railings not included						
160	fir, pine or spruce, treated ***	LF					53.00
170	western cedar ***	LF					48.90
180	redwood ***	LF					30.80
	Stain, 2 coats, add to above						
190	deck	SF					2.87
200	deck railing	LF					1.38
210	exterior stairs, 3' wide	LF					5.50
	Wood construction, lineal feet of members in place,						
	fir, pine, or spruce, pressure treated						
	posts and columns						
220	4" x 4"	LF					7.00
230	4" x 6"	LF					8.80
240	6" x 6"	LF					12.60
	beams						
250	4" x 6"	LF					6.70
260	4" x 8"	LF					8.80
270	4" x 10"	LF					10.60
	joists and headers						
280	2" x 6"	LF					3.89
290	2" x 8"	LF					5.10
	ledgers and nailers						
300	2" x 4"	LF					2.54
310	2" x 6"	LF					4.04
	plates						
320	2" x 4"	LF					3.53
330	2" x 6"	LF					5.20
	decking						
340	2" x 4"	LF					2.03
350	2" x 6"	LF					3.35
	fascia and trim						
360	1" x 4"	LF					2.45
370	1" x 6"	LF					3.07
380	1" x 8"	LF					3.34
	stair stringers						
390	2" x 10"	LF					12.30
400	2" x 12"	LF					14.10
	stair treads						
410	2" x 6"	LF					5.50
420	2" x 12"	LF					10.30
	railings, benches, etc.						
430	2" x 4"	LF					3.53
440	2" x 6"	LF					5.60
450	2" x 8"	LF					7.40
460	2" x 10"	LF					9.10

ROUGH CARPENTRY

KEY	DESCRIPTION	UNIT	CREW AND EQUIPMENT	PER DAY	INSTALLATION COST	MATERIALS COST	TOTAL + 25%
10	**FRAMING**						
	To compute board feet, see Appendix P, "Board Measure"						
	Framing installation (add material)						
	beams						
100	4" x 6"	BF	2C,81	600	1.26		1.57
110	4" x 8"	BF	2C,81	650	1.16		1.45
120	4" x 10"	BF	2C,81	700	1.08		1.35
	bridging, solid						
130	2" x 6"	BF	2C,81	285	2.65		3.31
140	2" x 8"	BF	2C,81	300	2.52		3.15
150	2" x 10"	BF	2C,81	320	2.36		2.95
	decking						
160	2" x 4"	BF	2C,81	770	0.98		1.23
170	2" x 6"	BF	2C,81	840	0.90		1.12
	fascia and exterior trim						
180	1" x 4"	BF	2C,81	160	4.72		5.90
190	1" x 6"	BF	2C,81	200	3.78		4.72
200	1" x 8"	BF	2C,81	260	2.91		3.63
	joists and headers						
210	2" x 6"	BF	2C,81	550	1.37		1.72
220	2" x 8"	BF	2C,81	600	1.26		1.57
230	2" x 10"	BF	2C,81	650	1.16		1.45
	ledgers and nailers						
240	2" x 4"	BF	2C,81	450	1.68		2.10
250	2" x 6"	BF	2C,81	500	1.51		1.89
	plates						
260	2" x 4"	BF	2C,81	250	3.02		3.78
270	2" x 6"	BF	2C,81	300	2.52		3.15
	posts and columns						
280	4" x 4"	BF	2C,81	325	2.33		2.91
290	4" x 6"	BF	2C,81	350	2.16		2.70
300	6" x 6"	BF	2C,81	375	2.02		2.52
	railings, benches, etc.						
310	2" x 4"	BF	2C,81	250	3.02		3.78
320	2" x 6"	BF	2C,81	260	2.91		3.63
330	2" x 8"	BF	2C,81	270	2.80		3.50
340	2" x 10"	BF	2C,81	280	2.70		3.37
	stair stringers						
350	2" x 10"	BF	2C,81	145	5.21		6.50
360	2" x 12"	BF	2C,81	155	4.88		6.10
	stair treads						
370	2" x 12"	BF	2C,81	270	2.80		3.50
380	two 2" x 6" 's	BF	2C,81	240	3.15		3.94
	trellis or arbor						
390	1" x 3"	BF	2C,81	600	1.26		1.57
400	2" x 4"	BF	2C,81	700	1.08		1.35
410	2" x 6"	BF	2C,81	480	1.57		1.97
	wood grounds						
420	1" x 2"	BF	2C,81	300	2.52		3.15
	studs						
430	2" x 4"	BF	2C,81	350	2.16		2.70
440	2" x 6"	BF	2C,81	200	3.78		4.72
20	**PRESSURE TREATED LUMBER**						
	Fir, pine, or spruce dimension lumber, pressure treated						
	select structural						
	2" x 4"						
100	high	BF				2.87	3.59
110	low	BF				3.40	4.25

KEY	DESCRIPTION	UNIT	CREW AND EQUIPMENT	PER DAY	INSTALLATION COST	MATERIALS COST	TOTAL + 25%
	2" x 6", 2" x 8"						
120	high	BF				3.40	4.25
130	low	BF				1.05	1.31
	2" x 10", 2" x 12"						
160	high	BF				4.29	5.40
170	low	BF				1.27	1.59
	4" x 4", 4" x 6", 6" x 6"						
200	high	BF				3.25	4.06
210	low	BF				1.75	2.19
	common #2 and better, green						
	2" x 4"						
260	high	BF				1.23	1.54
270	low	BF				0.75	0.94
	2" x 6", 2" x 8"						
280	high	BF				1.60	2.00
290	low	BF				0.79	0.99
	2" x 10", 2" x 12"						
320	high	BF				2.57	3.21
330	low	BF				0.90	1.13
	4" x 4", 4" x 6", 6" x 6"						
360	high	BF				2.39	2.99
370	low	BF				1.39	1.74
30	**PRESSURE TREATED BOARDS**						
	Fir, pine, or spruce boards, pressure treated						
	B and better						
	1" x 4"						
100	high	BF				2.54	3.18
110	low	BF				1.09	1.36
	1" x 6", 1" x 8"						
120	high	BF				2.54	3.18
130	low	BF				1.09	1.36
	C and better						
	1" x 4"						
160	high	BF				1.83	2.29
170	low	BF				0.79	0.99
	1" x 6", 1" x 8"						
180	high	BF				1.80	2.25
190	low	BF				0.79	0.99
40	**CEDAR LUMBER**						
	Western red cedar dimension lumber						
	no. 1 appearance						
	2" x 4"						
100	high	BF				1.97	2.46
110	low	BF				0.97	1.21
	2" x 6", 2" x 8"						
120	high	BF				2.60	3.25
130	low	BF				1.36	1.70
	2" x 10", 2" x 12"						
160	high	BF				3.19	3.99
170	low	BF				1.44	1.80
	4" x 4", 4" x 6", 6" x 6"						
200	high	BF				3.46	4.33
210	low	BF				1.56	1.95
	standard and better, rough						
	2" x 4"						
220	high	BF				0.72	0.90
230	low	BF				0.59	0.74
	2" x 6", 2" x 8"						
240	high	BF				1.00	1.25
250	low	BF				0.76	0.95

ROUGH CARPENTRY

KEY	DESCRIPTION	UNIT	CREW AND EQUIPMENT	PER DAY	INSTALLATION COST	MATERIALS COST	TOTAL + 25%
	2" x 10", 2" x 12"						
280	high	BF				1.10	1.38
290	low	BF				0.81	1.01
	4" x 4", 4" x 6", 6" x 6"						
320	high	BF				0.81	1.01
330	low	BF				0.77	0.96
	standard and better, S4S						
	2" x 4"						
380	high	BF				0.90	1.13
390	low	BF				0.60	0.75
	2" x 6", 2" x 8"						
400	high	BF				0.75	0.94
410	low	BF				0.75	0.94
	2" x 10", 2" x 12"						
440	high	BF				1.01	1.26
450	low	BF				0.55	0.69
	4" x 4", 4" x 6", 6" x 6"						
480	high	BF				1.73	2.16
490	low	BF				0.76	0.95
50	**CEDAR BOARDS**						
	Western red cedar boards						
	clear S4S; C and better						
	1" x 4"						
100	high	BF				2.32	2.90
110	low	BF				1.04	1.30
	1" x 6", 1" x 8"						
120	high	BF				1.46	1.83
130	low	BF				0.80	1.00
	#3 and better, S1S2E						
	1" x 4"						
160	high	BF				1.55	1.94
170	low	BF				0.63	0.79
	1" x 6", 1" x 8"						
180	high	BF				3.17	3.96
190	low	BF				0.90	1.13
60	**REDWOOD LUMBER**						
	Redwood dimension lumber						
	select heart						
	2" x 4"						
100	high	BF				2.49	3.11
110	low	BF				1.09	1.36
	2" x 6", 2" x 8"						
120	high	BF				3.01	3.76
130	low	BF				1.18	1.48
	2" x 10", 2" x 12"						
160	high	BF				3.44	4.30
170	low	BF				1.48	1.85
	4" x 4", 4" x 6", 6" x 6"						
200	high	BF				1.72	2.15
210	low	BF				1.47	1.84
	construction heart						
	2" x 4"						
240	high	BF				1.94	2.43
250	low	BF				1.02	1.28
	2" x 6", 2" x 8"						
260	high	BF				2.20	2.75
270	low	BF				1.02	1.28

06110 Wood Framing — 1994

KEY	DESCRIPTION	UNIT	CREW AND EQUIPMENT	PER DAY	INSTALLATION COST	MATERIALS COST	TOTAL + 25%
	2" x 10", 2" x 12"						
300	high	BF				2.17	2.71
310	low	BF				2.06	2.58
	4" x 4", 4" x 6", 6" x 6"						
340	high	BF				1.99	2.49
350	low	BF				1.27	1.59
70	**REDWOOD BOARDS**						
	Redwood boards						
	clear all heart						
	1" x 4"						
100	high	BF				2.53	3.16
110	low	BF				1.14	1.43
	1" x 6", 1" x 8"						
120	high	BF				2.09	2.61
130	low	BF				1.26	1.58
	clear and better						
	1" x 4"						
160	high	BF				1.60	2.00
170	low	BF				0.78	0.98
	1" x 6", 1" x 8"						
180	high	BF				1.59	1.99
190	low	BF				0.77	0.96

06115 Sheathing

KEY	DESCRIPTION	UNIT	CREW AND EQUIPMENT	PER DAY	INSTALLATION COST	MATERIALS COST	TOTAL + 25%
10	**ROOF SHEATHING**						
	Plywood sheathing						
100	1/2"	SF	2C,81	1150	0.44	0.75	1.49
110	3/8"	SF	2C,81	1090	0.47	0.82	1.61
120	3/4"	SF	2C,81	1030	0.50	0.94	1.80

TIMBER CONSTRUCTION

KEY	DESCRIPTION	UNIT	CREW AND EQUIPMENT	PER DAY	INSTALLATION COST	MATERIALS COST	TOTAL + 25%
00	**COMPOSITE COSTS**						
	Railroad tie retaining wall, includes excavation and backfill						
	gravity type						
100	new ties	SF					11.80
110	used ties	SF					9.80
	with deadmen						
120	new ties	SF					16.40
130	used ties	SF					13.80
	Pressure treated timber retaining wall, includes excavation and backfill						
	gravity type						
140	6" x 6" timber	SF					9.50
150	6" x 8" timber	SF					11.10
	with deadmen						
160	6" x 6" timber	SF					13.40
170	6" x 8" timber	SF					15.50
10	**RAILROAD TIES**						
	Trench excavation and backfill, see Section 02220, "Excavating, Backfilling, & Compacting"						
	Relay railroad tie (approximately 8'-6" long), spiked in place, includes incidental trimming						
100	new tie	Ea	2C,81	36	14.19	16.90	38.90
110	used tie	Ea	2C,81	32	15.97	8.60	30.70
20	**TIMBERS**						
	Trench excavation and backfill, see Section 02220, "Excavating, Backfilling, & Compacting"						
	8' long timber, spiked in place, includes incidental trimming						
	penta soaked						
100	4" x 6"	Ea	2C,81	48	10.65	6.40	21.30
110	5" x 6"	Ea	2C,81	46	11.11	7.90	23.80
120	6" x 6"	Ea	2C,81	44	11.61	9.40	26.30
130	6" x 8"	Ea	2C,81	40	12.77	11.40	30.20
	pressure treated, penta						
150	5" x 6"	Ea	2C,81	46	11.11	9.50	25.80
160	6" x 6"	Ea	2C,81	44	11.61	11.30	28.60
170	6" x 8"	Ea	2C,81	40	12.77	13.70	33.10
	pressure treated, CCA						
180	4" x 6"	Ea	2C,81	48	10.65	7.40	22.60
190	5" x 6"	Ea	2C,81	46	11.11	8.00	23.90
200	6" x 6"	Ea	2C,81	44	11.61	12.00	29.50
210	6" x 8"	Ea	2C,81	40	12.77	16.00	36.00
	pressure treated, CCA, brown						
220	4" x 6"	Ea	2C,81	48	10.65	8.30	23.70
230	5" x 6"	Ea	2C,81	46	11.11	9.00	25.10
240	6" x 6"	Ea	2C,81	44	11.61	12.90	30.60
250	6" x 8"	Ea	2C,81	40	12.77	17.20	37.50

07310 Shingles							**1994**
KEY	DESCRIPTION	UNIT	CREW AND EQUIPMENT	PER DAY	INSTALLATION COST	MATERIALS COST	TOTAL + 25%
10	**ASPHALT COATED FELT**						
100	15 Lb felt underlayment	SF	1C	4500	0.06	0.10	0.20
110	30 Lb shake felt	SF	1C	3500	0.07	0.15	0.28
20	**ASPHALT SHINGLES**						
	Square butt shingles						
100	240#	SF	1C	550	0.46	0.40	1.07
110	310#	SF	1C	335	0.75	0.65	1.76
30	**WOOD SHINGLES AND SHAKES**						
	Red cedar shingles, sawed						
	16" x 5" exposed						
100	#1 grade	SF	1C	300	0.84	1.32	2.70
110	#2 grade	SF	1C	320	0.79	1.07	2.33
120	#3 grade	SF	1C	335	0.75	0.78	1.92
	18" x 5 1/2" exposed						
130	#1 grade	SF	1C	280	0.90	1.34	2.80
140	#2 grade	SF	1C	300	0.84	1.16	2.50
150	#3 grade	SF	1C	315	0.80	1.02	2.28
160	add for fire retardant	SF				1.14	1.43
	Wood shakes, hand split red cedar, 24" x 10" weather						
170	1/2" to 3/4" thickness	SF	1C	270	0.94	1.05	2.48
180	3/4" to 1 1/4" thickness	SF	1C	245	1.03	1.21	2.80
190	add for fire retardant	SF				0.66	0.83

LATH AND PLASTER

KEY	DESCRIPTION	UNIT	CREW AND EQUIPMENT	PER DAY	INSTALLATION COST	MATERIALS COST	TOTAL + 25%
00	**COMPOSITE COSTS**						
	Portland cement stucco, 3 coat application on masonry						
	float finish						
100	ordinary quality workmanship	SY					18.80
110	first quality workmanship	SY					23.00
120	rough cast finish	SY					24.20
	Portland cement stucco, 2 coat application on masonry						
	float finish						
130	ordinary quality workmanship	SY					15.10
140	first quality workmanship	SY					19.10
150	rough cast finish	SY					18.80
	Portland cement stucco, 3 coat application on metal lath over masonry						
	float finish						
160	ordinary quality workmanship	SY					29.30
170	first quality workmanship	SY					33.60
180	rough cast finish	SY					34.70
10	**3 COAT APPLICATION ON MASONRY**						
100	First coat (scratch coat), 3/8" thick	SY	1F1L	130	3.44	0.53	4.96
	Second coat (brown coat), 3/8" thick						
110	ordinary quality workmanship	SY	2F1L	160	4.32	0.88	6.50
120	first quality workmanship	SY	2F1L	135	5.12	0.88	7.50
	Finish coat, float finish, 1/8" thick						
130	ordinary quality workmanship	SY	2F1L	135	5.12	0.73	7.30
140	first quality workmanship	SY	2F1L	90	7.67	0.73	10.50
	white cement stucco						
150	ordinary quality workmanship	SY	2F1L	135	5.12	0.81	7.40
160	first quality workmanship	SY	2F1L	90	7.67	0.81	10.60
20	**2 COAT APPLICATION ON MASONRY**						
	Base coat, 3/8" thick						
100	ordinary quality workmanship	SY	2F1L	160	4.32	0.53	6.10
110	first quality workmanship	SY	2F1L	135	5.12	0.53	7.10
	Finish coat, float finish, 1/4" thick						
120	ordinary quality workmanship	SY	2F1L	120	5.76	1.46	9.00
130	first quality workmanship	SY	2F1L	85	8.13	1.46	12.00
	white cement stucco						
140	ordinary quality workmanship	SY	2F1L	120	5.76	1.62	9.20
150	first quality workmanship	SY	2F1L	85	8.13	1.62	12.20
30	**3 COAT APPLICATION ON METAL LATH**						
	Metal lath, expanded diamond mesh						
100	painted	SY	1L	100	2.04	4.00	7.60
110	galvanized	SY	1L	100	2.04	4.80	8.60
120	First coat (scratch coat), 1/2" thick	SY	1F1L	130	3.44	0.71	5.20
	Second coat (brown coat), 3/8" thick						
130	ordinary quality workmanship	SY	2F1L	135	5.12	1.41	8.20
140	first quality workmanship	SY	2F1L	115	6.01	1.41	9.30
	First coat, float finish, 1/8" thick						
150	ordinary quality workmanship	SY	2F1L	135	5.12	0.73	7.30
160	first quality workmanship	SY	2F1L	90	7.67	0.73	10.50
	white cement stucco						
170	ordinary quality workmanship	SY	2F1L	135	5.12	0.81	7.40
180	first quality workmanship	SY	2F1L	90	7.67	0.81	10.60

09220 Portland Cement Plaster

KEY	DESCRIPTION	UNIT	CREW AND EQUIPMENT	PER DAY	INSTALLATION COST	MATERIALS COST	TOTAL + 25%
40	**FINISH**						
100	Troweled finish, add	SY	1F	200	1.22		1.52
110	Textured finish, add	SY	1F	400	0.61		0.76
	Rough cast finish, deduct finish coat, and add						
120	wet rough cast	SY	2F1L	70	9.87	0.61	13.10
130	dry rough cast (pebble dash)	SY	2F1L	75	9.21	0.62	12.30

PAINTING

KEY	DESCRIPTION	UNIT	CREW AND EQUIPMENT	PER DAY	INSTALLATION COST	MATERIALS COST	TOTAL + 25%
10	**EXTERIOR PAINTING**						
	Paint masonry						
100	primer and 1 coat	SF	1P	500	0.46	0.16	0.77
110	primer and 2 coats	SF	1P	400	0.57	0.23	1.00
	Paint metal railing						
120	primer and 1 coat	LF	1P	500	0.46	0.16	0.77
130	primer and 2 coats	LF	1P	400	0.57	0.23	1.00
	Paint wood surface						
140	primer and 1 coat	SF	1P	650	0.35	0.16	0.64
150	primer and 2 coats	SF	1P	470	0.49	0.23	0.90
	Wood fences, see Section 02830, "Fences and Gates"						

09930 Transparent Finishes

KEY	DESCRIPTION	UNIT	CREW AND EQUIPMENT	PER DAY	INSTALLATION COST	MATERIALS COST	TOTAL + 25%
10	**EXTERIOR STAINING**						
	Stain wood surface						
100	1 coat and sealer	SF	1P	550	0.42	0.14	0.70
110	2 coats and sealer	SF	1P	350	0.65	0.16	1.02
	Wood fences, see Section 02830, "Fences and Gates"						
	Decks, see Section 06110, "Wood Framing"						

10352 Ground Set Flagpoles — 1994

KEY	DESCRIPTION	UNIT	CREW AND EQUIPMENT	PER DAY	INSTALLATION COST	MATERIALS COST	TOTAL + 25%
10	**FOUNDATIONS**						
	Foundation for flagpole, includes excavation						
100	20' height	Ea	2L	4.2	97.16	18.20	144.00
110	25' height	Ea	2L	3.8	107.38	32.10	174.00
120	30' height	Ea	2L	3.4	120.02	36.00	195.00
130	35' height	Ea	2L	3.1	131.63	51.00	228.00
140	40' height	Ea	2L	2.8	145.74	93.00	298.00
150	45' height	Ea	2L	2.6	156.95	90.00	309.00
160	50' height	Ea	2L	2.4	170.03	138.00	385.00
170	60' height	Ea	2L	2.1	194.31	160.00	443.00
180	70' height	Ea	2L	1.9	214.77	241.00	570.00
190	80' height	Ea	2L	1.7	240.04	384.00	780.00
20	**FLAGPOLES**						
	Aluminum flagpole, cone or entasis tapered, with hardware, halyard, and ground sleeve						
	standard weight						
	standard finish						
100	20' height	Ea	2L	6.3	64.77	414.00	600.00
105	25' height	Ea	2L	5.6	72.87	464.00	670.00
110	30' height	Ea	2L	5.1	80.01	750.00	1040.00
115	35' height	Ea	2L	4.6	88.71	1060.00	1440.00
120	40' height	Ea	1D1L,07	4.2	200.23	1470.00	2090.00
125	45' height	Ea	1D1L,07	3.9	215.64	1870.00	2610.00
130	50' height	Ea	1D1L,07	3.6	233.61	2440.00	3340.00
135	60' height	Ea	1D1L,07	3.2	262.81	4230.00	5600.00
140	70' height	Ea	1A1L,95	2.8	320.67	5600.00	7400.00
145	80' height	Ea	1A1L,95	2.6	345.33	7300.00	9600.00
	clear anodized						
150	20' height	Ea	2L	6.3	64.77	580.00	810.00
155	25' height	Ea	2L	5.6	72.87	670.00	930.00
160	30' height	Ea	2L	5.1	80.01	1000.00	1350.00
165	35' height	Ea	2L	4.6	88.71	1550.00	2050.00
170	40' height	Ea	1D1L,07	4.2	200.23	1680.00	2350.00
175	45' height	Ea	1D1L,07	3.9	215.64	2060.00	2840.00
180	50' height	Ea	1D1L,07	3.6	233.61	2770.00	3750.00
185	60' height	Ea	1D1L,07	3.2	262.81	4650.00	6100.00
190	70' height	Ea	1A1L,95	2.8	320.67	6080.00	8000.00
195	80' height	Ea	1A1L,95	2.6	345.33	7830.00	10200.00
	bronze anodized						
200	20' height	Ea	2L	6.3	64.77	600.00	830.00
205	25' height	Ea	2L	5.6	72.87	690.00	950.00
210	30' height	Ea	2L	5.1	80.01	1110.00	1490.00
215	35' height	Ea	2L	4.6	88.71	1710.00	2250.00
220	40' height	Ea	1D1L,07	4.2	200.23	1800.00	2500.00
225	45' height	Ea	1D1L,07	3.9	215.64	2220.00	3040.00
230	50' height	Ea	1D1L,07	3.6	233.61	2880.00	3890.00
235	60' height	Ea	1D1L,07	3.2	262.81	4870.00	6400.00
240	70' height	Ea	1A1L,95	2.8	320.67	6500.00	8500.00
245	80' height	Ea	1A1L,95	2.6	345.33	8200.00	10700.00
	black anodized						
250	20' height	Ea	2L	6.3	64.77	610.00	840.00
255	25' height	Ea	2L	5.6	72.87	700.00	970.00
260	30' height	Ea	2L	5.1	80.01	1230.00	1640.00
265	35' height	Ea	2L	4.6	88.71	1440.00	1910.00
270	40' height	Ea	1D1L,07	4.2	200.23	1820.00	2530.00

FLAGPOLES

10352 Ground Set Flagpoles

KEY	DESCRIPTION	UNIT	CREW AND EQUIPMENT	PER DAY	INSTALLATION COST	MATERIALS COST	TOTAL + 25%
275	45' height	Ea	1D1L,07	3.9	215.64	2240.00	3070.00
280	50' height	Ea	1D1L,07	3.6	233.61	2960.00	3990.00
285	60' height	Ea	1D1L,07	3.2	262.81	5900.00	7700.00
290	70' height	Ea	1A1L,95	2.8	320.67	6600.00	8700.00
295	80' height	Ea	1A1L,95	2.6	345.33	8300.00	10800.00
	extra heavy weight						
	standard finish						
300	30' height	Ea	2L	5.1	80.01	960.00	1300.00
305	35' height	Ea	2L	4.6	88.71	1630.00	2150.00
310	40' height	Ea	1D1L,07	4.2	200.23	2330.00	3160.00
315	45' height	Ea	1D1L,07	3.9	215.64	2830.00	3810.00
320	50' height	Ea	1D1L,07	3.6	233.61	3310.00	4430.00
325	60' height	Ea	1D1L,07	3.2	262.81	4630.00	6100.00
330	70' height	Ea	1A1L,95	2.8	320.67	6400.00	8400.00
335	80' height	Ea	1A1L,95	2.6	345.33	8700.00	11300.00
	clear anodized						
340	30' height	Ea	2L	5.1	80.01	1210.00	1610.00
345	35' height	Ea	2L	4.6	88.71	1590.00	2100.00
350	40' height	Ea	1D1L,07	4.2	200.23	2320.00	3150.00
355	45' height	Ea	1D1L,07	3.9	215.64	2550.00	3460.00
360	50' height	Ea	1D1L,07	3.6	233.61	3110.00	4180.00
365	60' height	Ea	1D1L,07	3.2	262.81	5100.00	6700.00
370	70' height	Ea	1A1L,07	2.8	324.24	6900.00	9000.00
375	80' height	Ea	1A1L,95	2.6	345.33	9300.00	12100.00
	bronze anodized						
380	30' height	Ea	2L	5.1	80.01	1250.00	1660.00
385	35' height	Ea	2L	4.6	88.71	1670.00	2200.00
390	40' height	Ea	1D1L,07	4.2	200.23	2430.00	3290.00
395	45' height	Ea	1D1L,07	3.9	215.64	2690.00	3630.00
400	50' height	Ea	1D1L,07	3.6	233.61	3260.00	4370.00
405	60' height	Ea	1D1L,07	3.2	262.81	5500.00	7200.00
410	70' height	Ea	1A1L,95	2.8	320.67	7100.00	9300.00
415	80' height	Ea	1A1L,95	2.6	345.33	9600.00	12400.00
	black anodized						
420	30' height	Ea	2L	5.1	80.01	1310.00	1740.00
425	35' height	Ea	2L	4.6	88.71	1710.00	2250.00
430	40' height	Ea	1D1L,07	4.2	200.23	2500.00	3380.00
435	45' height	Ea	1D1L,07	3.9	215.64	2770.00	3730.00
440	50' height	Ea	1D1L,07	3.6	233.61	3380.00	4520.00
445	60' height	Ea	1D1L,07	3.2	262.81	5570.00	7300.00
450	70' height	Ea	1A1L,95	2.8	320.67	7400.00	9700.00
455	80' height	Ea	1A1L,95	2.6	345.33	10000.00	12900.00
	Fiberglass flagpole with hardware, internal halyard, and ground sleeve						
465	25' height	Ea	2L	5.6	72.87	1130.00	1500.00
470	30' height	Ea	2L	5.1	80.01	1430.00	1890.00
475	35' height	Ea	2L	4.6	88.71	1840.00	2410.00
480	40' height	Ea	1D1L,07	4.2	200.23	2080.00	2850.00
490	50' height	Ea	1D1L,07	3.6	233.61	4660.00	6100.00
495	60' height	Ea	1D1L,07	3.2	262.81	1240.00	1880.00
	Galvanized steel, cone tampered, with hardware, halyard and ground sleeve						
505	25' height	Ea	2L	6.3	64.77	228.00	366.00
510	30' height	Ea	2L	5.6	72.87	245.00	397.00
515	35' height	Ea	2L	5.1	80.01	304.00	480.00
520	40' height	Ea	2L	4.2	97.16	391.00	610.00

10352 Ground Set Flagpoles — 1994

KEY	DESCRIPTION	UNIT	CREW AND EQUIPMENT	PER DAY	INSTALLATION COST	MATERIALS COST	TOTAL + 25%
	Tilting aluminum flagpole with hardware and halyard						
530	25' height	Ea	2L	5.6	72.87	2210.00	2850.00
535	30' height	Ea	2L	5.1	80.01	2510.00	3240.00
540	35' height	Ea	2L	4.6	88.71	3130.00	4020.00
545	40' height	Ea	1D1L,07	4.2	200.23	3500.00	4630.00
550	45' height	Ea	1D1L,07	3.9	215.64	4000.00	5300.00
555	50' height	Ea	1D1L,07	3.6	233.61	5500.00	7200.00
560	60' height	Ea	1D1L,07	3.2	262.81	8000.00	10300.00
565	70' height	Ea	1A1L,95	2.8	320.67	8700.00	11300.00
	Nautical aluminum flagpole with hardware, halyard, and ground sleeve						
570	30' height	Ea	2L	5.1	80.01	2190.00	2840.00
575	35' height	Ea	2L	4.6	88.71	3000.00	3860.00
580	40' height	Ea	1D1L,07	4.2	200.23	3430.00	4540.00
590	50' height	Ea	1D1L,07	3.6	233.61	4570.00	6000.00
595	60' height	Ea	1D1L,07	3.2	262.81	6300.00	8200.00
	Internal halyard system for flagpole, add						
600	25' height	Ea				600.00	750.00
605	30' height	Ea				630.00	790.00
610	35' height	Ea				650.00	810.00
615	40' height	Ea				680.00	850.00
620	45' height	Ea				700.00	880.00
625	50' height	Ea				730.00	910.00
630	60' height	Ea				750.00	940.00
635	70' height	Ea				790.00	990.00
640	80' height	Ea				820.00	1030.00
30	**FINIALS**						
	Ball finial, standard with all poles						
	Eagle on ball finial						
	gold leafed copper						
100	12" wingspread	Ea				359.00	449.00
110	18" wingspread	Ea				481.00	600.00
120	24" wingspread	Ea				640.00	800.00
130	36" wingspread	Ea				1400.00	1750.00
	gold bronze finish aluminum						
160	12" wingspread	Ea				70.00	88.00
170	18" wingspread	Ea				121.00	151.00
	Weathervane finial, gold leafed copper						
	arrow						
180	12" long	Ea				269.00	336.00
190	18" long	Ea				232.00	290.00
200	24" long	Ea				384.00	480.00
210	36" long	Ea				690.00	860.00
	eagle on arrow						
220	12" wingspread	Ea				700.00	880.00
230	18" wingspread	Ea				790.00	990.00
240	24" wingspread	Ea				990.00	1240.00
250	36" wingspread	Ea				1790.00	2240.00
40	**FLAGS**						
	U.S. flag, heavyweight, exterior						
100	5' x 8' (30-35' pole)	Ea				85.00	106.00
110	6' x 10' (40-45' pole)	Ea				125.00	156.00
120	8' x 12' (50' pole)	Ea				210.00	263.00
130	10' x 15' (60' pole)	Ea				315.00	394.00
140	12' x 18' (70' pole)	Ea				411.00	510.00
150	15' x 25' (80' pole)	Ea				690.00	860.00

FLAGPOLES

KEY	DESCRIPTION	UNIT	CREW AND EQUIPMENT	PER DAY	INSTALLATION COST	MATERIALS COST	TOTAL + 25%
	10352 Ground Set Flagpoles						**1994**
	Custom flags and banners						
	simple						
160	5' x 8'	Ea				198.00	248.00
170	6' x 10'	Ea				257.00	321.00
180	8' x 12'	Ea				378.00	473.00
190	10' x 15'	Ea				481.00	600.00
200	12' x 18'	Ea				660.00	830.00
	fancy						
210	5' x 8'	Ea				380.00	475.00
220	6' x 10'	Ea				493.00	620.00
230	8' x 12'	Ea				730.00	910.00
240	10' x 15'	Ea				930.00	1160.00
250	12' x 18'	Ea				1270.00	1590.00

11484 Backstops | 1994

KEY	DESCRIPTION	UNIT	CREW AND EQUIPMENT	PER DAY	INSTALLATION COST	MATERIALS COST	TOTAL + 25%
10	**BACKSTOPS**						
	Hooded backstop, 4' overhang, galvanized chain link						
	10' high						
100	10' wide back, 10' wings	Ea	2l,80	1.6	357.59	1470.00	2280.00
110	20' wide back, 10' wings	Ea	2l,80	1.1	520.13	1830.00	2940.00
120	30' wide back, 10' wings	Ea	2l,80	0.8	715.18	2170.00	3610.00
	12' high						
130	10' wide back, 10' wings	Ea	2l,80	1.4	408.67	1670.00	2600.00
140	20' wide back, 10' wings	Ea	2l,80	1	572.14	2090.00	3330.00
150	30' wide back, 10' wings	Ea	2l,80	0.7	817.35	2190.00	3760.00
	Unhooded, galvanized chain link						
	10' high						
160	10' wide back, no wings	Ea	2l,80	3	190.71	550.00	930.00
170	20' wide back, no wings	Ea	2l,80	1.9	301.13	760.00	1330.00
180	30' wide back, no wings	Ea	2l,80	1.4	408.67	1060.00	1840.00
190	10' wide back, 5' wings	Ea	2l,80	2	286.07	900.00	1480.00
200	10' wide back, 10' wings	Ea	2l,80	1.5	381.43	1150.00	1910.00
	12' high						
210	10' wide back, no wings	Ea	2l,80	2.7	211.90	570.00	980.00
220	20' wide back, no wings	Ea	2l,80	1.7	336.55	820.00	1450.00
230	30' wide back, no wings	Ea	2l,80	1.2	476.79	1200.00	2100.00
240	10' wide back, 5' wings	Ea	2l,80	1.8	317.86	1060.00	1720.00
250	10' wide back, 10' wings	Ea	2l,80	1.4	408.67	1330.00	2170.00

PRE-ENGINEERED STRUCTURES

13121 Pre-engineered Buildings	1994

KEY	DESCRIPTION	UNIT	CREW AND EQUIPMENT	PER DAY	INSTALLATION COST	MATERIALS COST	TOTAL + 25%
10	**BUS STOP SHELTERS**						
	Architectural bronze anodized aluminum 8' high, skylight, bench, 1/4" tinted safety glass walls, surface mounted						
100	4' x 6'	Ea	2I,81	2	285.37	2850.00	3920.00
110	6' x 8'	Ea	2I,81	1.5	380.49	4790.00	6500.00
120	6' x 12'	Ea	2I,81	1	570.74	6600.00	9000.00
20	**GAZEBOS**						
	Octagonal gazebo, 16' diameter, rustic, style, pitched asphalt shingled roof						
100	no floor	Ea	2C,80	1.8	284.66	4630.00	6100.00
110	wood floor	Ea	2C,80	1.5	341.60	11900.00	15300.00
30	**PRE-TENSIONED MEMBRANE STRUCTURES**						
	Vinyl-polyester fiber membrane, open sides (does not include footings, floors)						
	beam, point, or pole supported						
100	5,000 SF ground area	MSF	4L	5	163.22	10600.00	13500.00
110	10,000 SF ground area	MSF	4L	5	163.22	8900.00	11300.00
120	25,000 SF ground area	MSF	1A4L,95	12.5	120.80	6400.00	8200.00
130	50,000 SF ground area	MSF	1A4L,95	16.7	90.42	5600.00	7100.00
	frame supported						
140	5,000 SF ground area	MSF	4L	5	163.22	14000.00	17700.00
150	10,000 SF ground area	MSF	4L	5	163.22	11900.00	15100.00
	hybrid supported						
160	5,000 SF ground area	MSF	4L	5	163.22	10800.00	13700.00
170	10,000 SF ground area	MSF	4L	5	163.22	13700.00	17300.00
180	25,000 SF ground area	MSF	1G4L,95	3.3	451.77	11700.00	15200.00
190	Enclosed sides, add per MSF wall area	MSF	1L	8	25.50	1770.00	2240.00
40	**POST-TENSIONED MEMBRANE STRUCTURES**						
	Air pressure supported vinyl-polyester membrane structure (includes mechanical) (does not include footings, floors, electrical supply)						
	single wall type						
100	5,000 SF ground area	MSF	4L	5	163.22	15300.00	19300.00
110	10,000 SF ground area	MSF	4L	5	163.22	11300.00	14300.00
120	25,000 SF ground area	MSF	6L	7.5	163.22	7600.00	9700.00
130	50,000 SF ground area	MSF	6L	12.5	97.93	6500.00	8200.00
	double wall type						
140	5,000 SF ground area	MSF	4L	5	163.22	25400.00	32000.00
150	10,000 SF ground area	MSF	4L	5	163.22	18800.00	23700.00
160	25,000 SF ground area	MSF	6L	7.5	163.22	12900.00	16300.00
170	50,000 SF ground area	MSF	6L	12.5	97.93	11200.00	14100.00
50	**RESTROOMS, WATER SYSTEMS**						
	Waterwaste system, factory built, delivered, installed, fire safety treated, yellow southern pine frame, pitched roof, fiberglass, shingles, skylights, plumbed, fixtures, storeroom, exterior entrance, privacy screens, slab and site utilities not included						
100	Off-loading at site	Ea	1D1L,95	2	415.49		520.00
	Diagonal wood siding exterior						
110	1 toilet, 1 sink, uni-sex, 8' x 12'	Ea	1C1L	0.3	1523.09	33000.00	43200.00
130	2 toilets, 2 sinks, 8' x 20'	Ea	1C1L	0.3	1523.09	50800.00	65400.00
150	3 toilets, 1 urinal, 2 sinks, 12' x 36'	Ea	1C1L	0.3	1523.09	80900.00	103000.00
170	4 toilets, 2 urinals, 4 sinks, 12' x 32'	Ea	1C1L	0.3	1523.09	95800.00	121700.00

13121 Pre-engineered Structures — 1994

KEY	DESCRIPTION	UNIT	CREW AND EQUIPMENT	PER DAY	INSTALLATION COST	MATERIALS COST	TOTAL + 25%
	Vertical wood siding, economy model						
190	1 toilet, 1 sink, uni-sex, 8' x 12'	Ea	1C1L	0.3	1523.09	25300.00	33500.00
210	2 toilets, 2 sinks, 8' x 20'	Ea	1C1L	0.3	1523.09	39100.00	50800.00
230	3 toilets, 1 urinal, 2 sinks, 12' x 36'	Ea	1C1L	0.3	1523.09	62100.00	79500.00
250	4 toilets, 2 urinals, 4 sinks, 12' x 32'	Ea	1C1L	0.3	1523.09	74200.00	94700.00
	Brick or slump block exterior						
270	1 toilet, 1 sink, uni-sex, 8' x 12'	Ea	1C1L	0.3	1523.09	38400.00	49900.00
280	2 toilets, 2 sinks, 8' x 20'	Ea	1C1L	0.3	1523.09	58600.00	75200.00
290	3 toilets, 1 urinal, 2 sinks, 12' x 36'	Ea	1C1L	0.3	1523.09	91500.00	116300.00
300	4 toilets, 2 urinals, 4 sinks, 12' x 32'	Ea	1C1L	0.3	1523.09	108300.00	137300.00
	Electrical wiring, romex, add						
310	1 toilet	Ea	1E	8	34.87	2330.00	2960.00
320	2 toilets	Ea	1E	8	34.87	2490.00	3160.00
330	3 toilets	Ea	1E	8	34.87	2710.00	3430.00
340	4 toilets	Ea	1E	8	34.87	2710.00	3430.00
60	**RESTROOMS, VAULT SYSTEMS**						
	Vault waste system, factory-built, delivered, installed, fire safety treated, yellow southern pine frame, pitched roof, fiberglass shingles, skylights, fixtures, storeroom, exterior entrance privacy screens, (slab and vault not included)						
100	Off-loading at site	Ea	1D1L,95	4	207.74		260.00
	Diagonal wood siding						
110	1 toilet, no sink, 7' x 7'	Ea	1C1L	0.3	1523.09	27800.00	36700.00
120	3 toilets, 1 urinal, no sink, 12' x 20'	Ea	1C1L	0.3	1523.09	66600.00	85200.00
	Vertical wood siding, economy model						
130	1 toilet, no sink, 7' x 7'	Ea	1C1L	0.3	1523.09	21300.00	28500.00
140	3 toilets, 1 urinal, no sink, 12' x 20'	Ea	1C1L	0.3	1523.09	51200.00	65900.00
	Brick or slump block exterior						
150	1 toilet, no sink, uni-sex, 7' x 7'	Ea	1C1L	0.3	1523.09	32500.00	42500.00
160	3 toilets, no sink, 12' x 20'	Ea	1C1L	0.3	1523.09	75300.00	96000.00
170	Pit-type, polyethylene, uni-sex, 1 toilet, 48" x 45" x 86"	Ea	2L	20	20.40	1040.00	1330.00
70	**CHEMICAL-TYPE, PORTABLE**						
100	Polyethylene, uni-sex, 1 toilet, 48" x 45" x 86"	Ea	2L	20	20.40	980.00	1250.00

13125 Grandstands and Bleachers

KEY	DESCRIPTION	UNIT	CREW AND EQUIPMENT	PER DAY	INSTALLATION COST	MATERIALS COST	TOTAL + 25%
10	**BLEACHERS**						
	Bleachers with galvanized steel frame, 15' long, no footings						
	wood seats						
100	3 row, 30 seater	Ea	2L	16	25.50	630.00	820.00
110	5 row, 50 seater	Ea	2L	11	37.10	920.00	1200.00
120	10 row, 100 seater	Ea	2L	4.6	88.71	2810.00	3620.00
	aluminum seats						
130	3 row, 30 seater	Ea	2L	16	25.50	880.00	1130.00
140	5 row, 50 seater	Ea	2L	11	37.10	1530.00	1960.00
150	10 row, 100 seater	Ea	2L	4.6	88.71	4650.00	5900.00
	fiberglass seats						
160	3 row, 30 seater	Ea	2L	16	25.50	580.00	760.00
170	5 row, 50 seater	Ea	2L	11	37.10	1060.00	1370.00
180	10 row, 100 seater	Ea	2L	4.6	88.71	3820.00	4890.00

PRE-ENGINEERED STRUCTURES

KEY	DESCRIPTION	UNIT	CREW AND EQUIPMENT	PER DAY	INSTALLATION COST	MATERIALS COST	TOTAL + 25%
	galvanized steel seats						
190	3 row, 30 seater	Ea	2L	16	25.50	442.00	580.00
200	5 row, 50 seater	Ea	2L	11	37.10	820.00	1070.00
210	10 row, 100 seater	Ea	2L	4.6	88.71	2460.00	3190.00
	Bleachers with aluminum frame and seats, 15' long, no footings						
220	3 row, 30 seater	Ea	2L	16	25.50	1040.00	1330.00
230	5 row, 50 seater	Ea	2L	11	37.10	1910.00	2430.00
240	10 row, 100 seater	Ea	2L	4.6	88.71	5700.00	7200.00

KEY	DESCRIPTION	UNIT	CREW AND EQUIPMENT	PER DAY	INSTALLATION COST	MATERIALS COST	TOTAL + 25%
10	**EXPOSED CONDUITS**						
	Galvanized conduits, includes fittings						
100	1/2" diameter	LF	1E	95	2.94	1.14	5.10
110	3/4" diameter	LF	1E	85	3.28	1.45	5.90
120	1" diameter	LF	1E	75	3.72	1.70	6.80
130	1 1/2" diameter	LF	1E	60	4.65	2.96	9.50
140	2" diameter	LF	1E	50	5.58	3.55	11.40
150	3" diameter	LF	1E	30	9.30	7.50	21.00
160	4" diameter	LF	1E	20	13.95	11.70	32.10
20	**CONDUITS IN CONCRETE**						
	Conduit, includes fittings						
	galvanized						
100	1/2" diameter	LF	1E	190	1.47	1.06	3.16
110	3/4" diameter	LF	1E	165	1.69	1.30	3.74
120	1" diameter	LF	1E	140	1.99	1.78	4.72
130	1 1/2" diameter	LF	1E	110	2.54	2.79	6.70
140	2" diameter	LF	1E	95	2.94	3.66	8.20
150	3" diameter	LF	1E	50	5.58	7.20	16.00
160	4" diameter	LF	1E	30	9.30	10.80	25.10
	polyvinylchloride						
170	1/2" diameter	LF	1E	225	1.24	0.34	1.97
180	3/4" diameter	LF	1E	195	1.43	0.34	2.21
190	1" diameter	LF	1E	170	1.64	0.48	2.65
200	1 1/2" diameter	LF	1E	125	2.23	0.82	3.81
210	2" diameter	LF	1E	100	2.79	1.49	5.30
220	3" diameter	LF	1E	70	3.99	2.46	8.10
230	4" diameter	LF	1E	40	6.97	3.66	13.30
30	**CONDUITS IN TRENCH**						
	Does not include excavation and backfilling of trench. See Section 02220, "Excavating, Backfilling, & Compacting"						
	Underground utility installations						
	light or medium soil						
100	small vibratory plow	LF	1G1L,25	3000	0.17		0.22
110	large vibratory plow	LF	1G1L,25	4000	0.13		0.16
120	heavy soil, large vibratory plow	LF	1G1L,25	3500	0.15		0.19
	Conduit in trench, includes fittings						
	galvanized						
130	2" diameter	LF	1E	110	2.54	3.66	7.70
140	3" diameter	LF	1E	60	4.65	8.00	15.80
150	4" diameter	LF	1E	40	6.97	12.40	24.20
	polyvinylchloride						
160	2" diameter	LF	1E	150	1.86	1.49	4.19
170	3" diameter	LF	1E	95	2.94	2.39	6.70
180	4" diameter	LF	1E	75	3.72	3.57	9.10

ELECTRICAL MATERIALS

16120 Wires and Cables 1994

KEY	DESCRIPTION	UNIT	CREW AND EQUIPMENT	PER DAY	INSTALLATION COST	MATERIALS COST	TOTAL + 25%
10	**WIRES, INSTALLED IN CONDUITS**						
	Copper wire, 600 V, THW insulation						
	3 wire						
100	#14	LF	1E	440	0.63	0.15	0.98
110	#12	LF	1E	395	0.71	0.20	1.13
120	#10	LF	1E	315	0.89	0.31	1.49
130	#8	LF	1E	255	1.09	0.51	2.00
140	#4	LF	1E	180	1.55	0.93	3.10
150	#2	LF	1E	165	1.69	1.37	3.83
160	1/0	LF	1E	120	2.32	2.13	5.60
170	2/0	LF	1E	100	2.79	2.59	6.70
180	3/0	LF	1E	90	3.10	3.18	7.80
190	4/0	LF	1E	80	3.49	3.93	9.30
200	250 MCM	LF	1E	70	3.99	5.00	11.20
210	300 MCM	LF	1E	70	3.99	5.60	12.00
220	400 MCM	LF	1E	60	4.65	7.00	14.60
230	500 MCM	LF	1E	55	5.07	9.40	18.10
20	**CABLES**						
	Insulated moisture-resistive cables installed in ground or exposed location, Copper wire, 600 V, THW insulation						
	2 wire						
100	#14	LF	1E	280	1.00	0.19	1.48
110	#12	LF	1E	250	1.12	0.21	1.66
120	#10	LF	1E	220	1.27	0.35	2.02
	3 wire						
130	#14	LF	1E	245	1.14	0.24	1.72
140	#12	LF	1E	215	1.30	0.35	2.06
150	#10	LF	1E	185	1.51	0.51	2.52
160	#8	LF	1E	165	1.69	0.75	3.05
170	#6	LF	1E	135	2.07	1.18	4.06
180	#4	LF	1E	100	2.79	1.37	5.20

16130 Boxes

KEY	DESCRIPTION	UNIT	CREW AND EQUIPMENT	PER DAY	INSTALLATION COST	MATERIALS COST	TOTAL + 25%
10	**RECEPTACLES**						
	Double receptacle						
100	15 Ampere	Ea	1E	35	7.97	3.92	14.90
110	20 Ampere	Ea	1E	20	13.95	6.50	25.60
	Single receptacle						
120	30 Ampere	Ea	1E	20	13.95	6.50	25.60
130	50 Ampere	Ea	1E	10	27.90	6.60	43.10
20	**OUTLET BOXES**						
100	4" square or octagonal outlet box	Ea	1E	20	13.95	1.80	19.70
30	**JUNCTION BOXES**						
100	4" junction box	Ea	1E	20	13.95	1.85	19.70

16425 Switchboards

KEY	DESCRIPTION	UNIT	CREW AND EQUIPMENT	PER DAY	INSTALLATION COST	MATERIALS COST	TOTAL + 25%
10	**DISTRIBUTION SWITCHBOARDS**						
	Distribution switchboard						
100	200 Ampere	Ea	1E	1.2	232.46	2040.00	2840.00
110	400 Ampere	Ea	1E	0.9	309.95	2310.00	3270.00
120	800 Ampere	Ea	1E	0.5	557.92	3300.00	4820.00

16440 Disconnect Switches

KEY	DESCRIPTION	UNIT	CREW AND EQUIPMENT	PER DAY	INSTALLATION COST	MATERIALS COST	TOTAL + 25%
10	**SERVICE DISCONNECT**						
	Service disconnect						
100	100 Amperes	Ea	1E	3	92.99	140.00	291.00
110	300 Amperes	Ea	1E	2	139.48	185.00	406.00
120	400 Amperes	Ea	1E	1	278.96	436.00	890.00
130	600 Amperes	Ea	1E	0.5	557.92	700.00	1570.00

16450 Secondary Grounding

KEY	DESCRIPTION	UNIT	CREW AND EQUIPMENT	PER DAY	INSTALLATION COST	MATERIALS COST	TOTAL + 25%
10	**GROUNDING**						
	Grounding, includes rods and accessories, copper						
110	1/2"	Ea	1E	5	55.79	78.00	167.00
120	3/4"	Ea	1E	4	69.74	120.00	237.00

16470 Panelboards

KEY	DESCRIPTION	UNIT	CREW AND EQUIPMENT	PER DAY	INSTALLATION COST	MATERIALS COST	TOTAL + 25%
10	**LIGHT AND POWER PANELS**						
	4 wire 120/208 V 100 Amperes						
110	10 circuit	Ea	1E	3	92.99	410.00	630.00
120	12 circuit	Ea	1E	1.5	185.97	428.00	770.00
130	16 circuit	Ea	1E	1.5	185.97	492.00	850.00
	3 wire 120/220 V 100 Amperes						
140	10 circuit	Ea	1E	2.5	111.58	375.00	610.00
150	12 circuit	Ea	1E	2	139.48	388.00	660.00
160	16 circuit	Ea	1E	2	139.48	449.00	740.00

16475 Overcurrent Protective Devices

KEY	DESCRIPTION	UNIT	CREW AND EQUIPMENT	PER DAY	INSTALLATION COST	MATERIALS COST	TOTAL + 25%
10	**CIRCUIT BREAKERS**						
	Primary or secondary circuit breaker						
110	100 Ampere	Ea	1E	3	92.99	226.00	399.00
120	200 Ampere	Ea	1E	2	139.48	580.00	900.00
130	400 Ampere	Ea	1E	1	278.96	930.00	1510.00

SERVICE AND DISTRIBUTION

KEY	DESCRIPTION	UNIT	CREW AND EQUIPMENT	PER DAY	INSTALLATION COST	MATERIALS COST	TOTAL + 25%
10	**SWITCHES**						
	Standard toggle, 15 Amperes						
110	1 pole	Ea	1E	35	7.97	4.98	16.20
120	3 way	Ea	1E	25	11.16	7.40	23.20
130	4 way	Ea	1E	20	13.95	18.10	40.10
	Mercury, 15 Amperes						
140	1 pole	Ea	1E	35	7.97	19.80	34.70
150	3 way	Ea	1E	25	11.16	30.30	52.00
160	4 way	Ea	1E	20	13.95	69.00	104.00

16501 Lamps · 1994

KEY	DESCRIPTION	UNIT	CREW AND EQUIPMENT	PER DAY	INSTALLATION COST	MATERIALS COST	TOTAL + 25%
10	**LAMPS, EXTERIOR**						
	Incandescent lamp						
100	100W	Ea	1E	80	3.49	2.20	7.10
110	200W	Ea	1E	80	3.49	2.45	7.40
	Mercury vapor lamp						
120	40W	Ea	1E	60	4.65	18.30	28.70
130	175W	Ea	1E	60	4.65	22.00	33.30
140	250W	Ea	1E	60	4.65	35.70	50.00
150	400W	Ea	1E	60	4.65	46.50	64.00
160	1000W	Ea	1E	50	5.58	62.00	84.00
	Sodium lamp						
	low pressure						
180	55W	Ea	1E	30	9.30	42.00	64.00
190	135W	Ea	1E	30	9.30	69.00	98.00
200	180W	Ea	1E	30	9.30	77.00	108.00
	high pressure						
210	400W	Ea	1E	15	18.60	65.00	104.00
220	1000W	Ea	1E	10	27.90	173.00	251.00
	Metal halide lamp						
230	175W	Ea	1E	30	9.30	43.80	66.00
240	400W	Ea	1E	25	11.16	59.00	88.00
250	1000W	Ea	1E	20	13.95	114.00	160.00

16503 Poles and Standards

KEY	DESCRIPTION	UNIT	CREW AND EQUIPMENT	PER DAY	INSTALLATION COST	MATERIALS COST	TOTAL + 25%
10	**LIGHT POLES AND BRACKETS**						
	Wood pole						
100	30' high	Ea	1A2E,95	3	417.25	141.00	700.00
110	40' high	Ea	1A2E,95	2	625.88	248.00	1090.00
120	45' high	Ea	1A2E,95	1.5	834.50	354.00	1490.00
130	single bracket, add	Ea	1A2E,95	10	125.18	34.80	200.00
	Steel pole						
140	15' high	Ea	2E	6	92.99	491.00	730.00
150	20' high	Ea	1A2E,95	4	312.94	830.00	1430.00
160	30' high	Ea	1A2E,95	3	417.25	1140.00	1950.00
170	40' high	Ea	1A2E,95	2	625.88	1390.00	2520.00
180	45' high	Ea	1A2E,95	1.5	834.50	1450.00	2860.00
190	single bracket, add	Ea	1A2E,95	8	156.47	57.00	267.00
200	double brackets, add	Ea	1A2E,95	6	208.63	128.00	421.00
	Aluminum pole						
210	20' high	Ea	1A2E,95	3	417.25	560.00	1220.00
220	30' high	Ea	1A2E,95	2	625.88	1010.00	2040.00
230	40' high	Ea	1A2E,95	1.5	834.50	1720.00	3190.00
240	single bracket, add	Ea	1A2E,95	8	156.47	43.40	250.00
250	double brackets, add	Ea	1A2E,95	6	208.63	88.00	371.00
	Ornamental pole						
260	10' high	Ea	2E	2	278.96	1080.00	1700.00
270	15' high	Ea	2E	1.5	371.94	1220.00	1990.00
280	20' high	Ea	1A2E,95	2.5	500.70	1280.00	2230.00
190	30' high	Ea	1A2E,95	2	625.88	1920.00	3180.00
	Concrete pole						
300	15' high	Ea	2E	6	92.99	203.00	370.00
310	20' high	Ea	1A2E,95	4	312.94	266.00	720.00
320	30' high	Ea	1A2E,95	3	417.25	429.00	1060.00
330	40' high	Ea	1A2E,95	2	625.88	600.00	1530.00
340	45' high	Ea	1A2E,95	1	1251.75	672.00	2400.00

LIGHTING

16503 Poles and Standards

KEY	DESCRIPTION	UNIT	CREW AND EQUIPMENT	PER DAY	INSTALLATION COST	MATERIALS COST	TOTAL + 25%
	Fiberglass pole						
350	20' high	Ea	1A2E,95	4	312.94	580.00	1120.00
360	30' high	Ea	1A2E,95	3.5	357.64	1230.00	1980.00
370	40' high	Ea	1A2E,95	3	417.25	1670.00	2610.00
20	**REINFORCED CONCRETE BASES**						
	See section 03311, "Cast-in-Place Concrete"						

16530 Site Lighting

KEY	DESCRIPTION	UNIT	CREW AND EQUIPMENT	PER DAY	INSTALLATION COST	MATERIALS COST	TOTAL + 25%
00	**COMPOSITE COSTS**						
	Composite Costs include service, distribution system, poles, bases, standards, lighting fixtures, control switches, and lamps						
	Site and walkway lighting						
100	plain steel poles, 15' high	Ea					3370.00
	ornamental poles						
110	10' high	Ea					4740.00
120	15' high	Ea					5700.00
	Parking lot lighting						
130	wood poles, 30' high	Ea					7100.00
	steel poles						
140	20' high	Ea					6400.00
150	30' high	Ea					8400.00
	Private roadway lighting						
160	wood poles, 30' high	Ea					4690.00
	steel poles						
170	20' high	Ea					5200.00
180	30' high	Ea					6300.00
	Play field lighting						
190	wood poles, 45' high	Ea					11300.00
200	steel poles, 45' high	Ea					13000.00
	Tennis court lighting						
210	single court	Ea					7100.00
220	2 court battery	Ea					11600.00
230	4 court battery	Ea					18200.00
10	**GARDEN AND LEISURE AREA LUMINAIRES**						
	Cast aluminum with lamps						
	wall fixtures						
100	incandescent 100W	Ea	1E	8	34.87	33.10	85.00
110	mercury vapor 40W	Ea	1E	8	34.87	195.00	287.00
	pole top fixtures						
120	incandescent 100W	Ea	1E	6	46.49	66.00	141.00
130	mercury vapor 40W	Ea	1E	6	46.49	211.00	322.00
20	**PUBLIC AND MONUMENTAL LUMINAIRES**						
	Cast aluminum and prismatic glass or shatter-proof plastic, with lamps						
	wall fixtures						
100	incandescent 200W	Ea	1E	5	55.79	397.00	570.00
110	mercury vapor 175W	Ea	1E	5	55.79	530.00	730.00
120	sodium, low pressure 55W	Ea	1E	5	55.79	590.00	810.00
	pole top fixtures						
130	incandescent 200W	Ea	1E	4	69.74	374.00	550.00
140	mercury vapor 175W	Ea	1E	4	69.74	463.00	670.00
150	sodium, low pressure 55W	Ea	1E	4	69.74	530.00	750.00

LIGHTING

16530 Site Lighting — 1994

KEY	DESCRIPTION	UNIT	CREW AND EQUIPMENT	PER DAY	INSTALLATION COST	MATERIALS COST	TOTAL + 25%
30	**SPORTS AND PARKING AREA LUMINAIRES**						
	Floodlights with lamps						
	mercury vapor						
100	400W	Ea	1E	3	92.99	400.00	620.00
110	1000W	Ea	1E	2.5	111.58	560.00	840.00
	sodium, high pressure						
120	400W	Ea	1E	3	92.99	462.00	690.00
130	1000W	Ea	1E	2.5	111.58	820.00	1160.00
40	**LOW VOLTAGE LANDSCAPE LIGHTING**						
	Transformers						
100	100W	Ea	1E	15	18.60	128.00	183.00
110	150W	Ea	1E	10	27.90	152.00	225.00
120	250W	Ea	1E	10	27.90	200.00	285.00
130	Cables, 12/2 LV	LF	1E	280	1.00	0.87	2.33
	Luminaires, redwood, acrylic diffusers						
	walkway						
140	17" high, 12W	Ea	1E	15	18.60	62.00	101.00
150	22" high, 12W	Ea	1E	15	18.60	73.00	114.00
	bollard walkway						
160	34" high, 24W	Ea	1E	8	34.87	85.00	150.00
170	5" x 5" x 18" post, 18W, prismatic diffuser	Ea	1E	8	34.87	157.00	240.00
	wall						
180	5" x 6" x 16", 24W	Ea	1E	8	34.87	77.00	140.00
190	7" x 7" x 13", 24W	Ea	1E	8	34.87	91.00	157.00
200	post, 5' high, 12V, 50W, prewired	Ea	1E	6	46.49	410.00	570.00
	hanging, 3' chain						
210	5" x 5" x 6", 12W	Ea	1E	5	55.79	57.00	141.00
220	7" x 7" x 10", 24W	Ea	1E	5	55.79	88.00	180.00
230	floodlight, 12V, 18W, sealed beam, lexan lens	Ea	1E	15	18.60	73.00	114.00
240	Luminaires, plastic, glare shield, 12V, 18W, sealed beam	Ea	1E	15	18.60	34.70	67.00
	Lamps						
250	6W	Ea	1E	80	3.49	1.03	5.60
260	12W	Ea	1E	80	3.49	1.03	5.60
270	18W	Ea	1E	80	3.49	1.03	5.60
280	24W	Ea	1E	80	3.49	1.34	6.00
290	18W, sealed beam	Ea	1E	60	4.65	9.60	17.80

16550 Roadway Lighting

KEY	DESCRIPTION	UNIT	CREW AND EQUIPMENT	PER DAY	INSTALLATION COST	MATERIALS COST	TOTAL + 25%
10	**ROADWAY LIGHTING LUMINAIRES**						
	Cast aluminum, prismatic glass, ballast and lamps, not including poles and brackets						
	mercury vapor						
100	400W	Ea	1E	2	139.48	620.00	950.00
110	1000W	Ea	1E	2	139.48	690.00	1040.00
	sodium, low pressure						
120	135W	Ea	1E	2	139.48	146.00	357.00
130	180W	Ea	1E	2	139.48	590.00	910.00

Ac	acre		Hp	horsepower
BCF	bank cubic foot		Ht	height
BCY	bank cubic yard		IPS	inside pipe size
BF	board foot		Lb	pound
Bu	bushel		LCF	loose cubic foot
Cal	caliper		LCY	loose cubic yard
CCF	compacted cubic foot		Ld	load
CCY	compacted cubic yard		LF	lineal foot
CF	cubic foof		M	thousand
Conc	concrete		MSF	thousand square feet
CY	cubic yard		NPS	nominal pipe size
Diam	diameter		OC	on center
DPST	double pole single throw		PLS	pure live seed
Ea	each		PSI	pounds per square inch
FH	feet head		PVC	polyvinyl chloride
4PST	four pole single throw		Qt	quart
Ga	gauage		Reinf	reinforced
Gal	gallon		SF	square foot
Galv	galvanized		SPST	single pole single throw
GPH	gallons per hour		SY	square yard
GPM	gallons per minute		T/M	ton/mile

B. Labor

The labor rates used to develop the costs herein are listed in the first column of the table below, with the code which identifies the trade in the Crew and Equipment column. The number preceding this code in the Crew and Equipment column identifies the number of workers of that trade in the crew. These labor rates are the averages of rates in 28 major U.S. cities, and include fringe benefits, insurance, and taxes. The table also lists rates for each of the 28 cities and provides an adjustment factor (% of 28 city average) which may be used to locally adjust installation costs.

1994 DAILY LABOR RATE BY TRADE
28 METROPOLITAN AREAS

Includes: *Base wages
*Benefits
*Insurance & taxes

Crew Code	Trade	28 City Average	Atlanta	Baltimore	Birmingham	Boston	Chicago
A	Equipment Operator - Medium	273.84	186.81	198.42	170.97	317.54	318.38
B	Brickmason	260.35	137.28	239.71	173.82	348.48	292.09
C	Carpenter	252.90	166.53	221.76	116.16	320.60	288.60
D	Truck Driver	206.95	89.87	215.00	87.33	245.10	199.85
E	Electrician	278.96	231.93	257.66	105.18	231.94	330.74
F	Cement Mason	243.34	176.88	220.18	173.82	332.32	297.05
G	Equipment Operator - Light	254.71	152.59	210.36	127.04	294.62	300.96
I	Ironworker	282.77	223.03	273.93	191.66	319.86	356.61
J	Landscape Laborer	189.55	114.79	156.50	128.20	241.30	246.26
L	Laborer	204.03	114.79	161.46	128.20	241.30	246.26
M	Stonemason	262.48	137.28	239.71	173.82	348.48	292.09
P	Painter	229.07	117.43	203.70	123.34	329.68	269.60
U	Plumber	293.91	236.44	264.11	113.52	353.44	312.47
	Average All Trades	**248.68**	**160.43**	**220.19**	**139.47**	**301.90**	**288.54**
	Percent of 28 City Average (Local adjustment factor)		64.51%	88.54%	56.08%	121.40%	116.03%

Crew Code	Trade	Cincinnati	Cleveland	Dallas	Denver	Detroit	Indianapolis
A	Equipment Operator - Medium	264.95	289.66	190.61	193.99	308.08	221.36
B	Brickmason	234.75	279.00	175.93	167.16	305.40	226.62
C	Carpenter	243.14	283.64	160.51	198.42	266.77	239.29
D	Truck Driver	210.14	227.57	85.01	186.38	238.15	161.52
E	Electrician	256.29	283.70	198.80	236.10	315.85	233.70
F	Cement Mason	182.90	253.12	121.55	176.25	279.73	207.72
G	Equipment Operator - Light	264.00	284.38	133.48	191.77	305.23	220.62
I	Ironworker	266.11	310.89	176.77	205.18	331.35	261.89
J	Landscape Laborer	207.50	204.34	74.03	115.00	111.83	180.58
L	Laborer	184.80	257.14	100.32	115.00	229.47	182.79
M	Stonemason	234.12	279.00	177.62	167.16	305.40	227.78
P	Painter	212.26	277.09	139.08	168.96	267.27	211.73
U	Plumber	275.30	316.59	154.28	238.66	271.50	257.77
	Average All Trades	**233.56**	**272.78**	**145.23**	**181.54**	**272.00**	**217.95**
	Percent of 28 City Average (Local adjustment factor)	93.92%	109.69%	58.40%	73.00%	109.38%	87.64%

APPENDIX

B. Labor

Crew code	Trade	Kansas City	Las Vegas	Los Angeles	Miami	Minneapolis	Newark
A	Equipment Operator - Medium	231.79	331.16	338.98	211.20	240.56	336.65
B	Brickmason	229.15	214.90	342.36	200.64	248.58	345.10
C	Carpenter	232.85	266.11	302.02	170.33	240.13	270.35
D	Truck Driver	211.62	186.81	311.84	90.29	139.50	292.30
E	Electrician	262.84	282.78	358.46	171.37	280.51	275.99
F	Cement Mason	218.38	225.46	311.10	134.32	227.15	345.10
G	Equipment Operator - Light	191.35	327.99	327.04	135.80	237.07	316.48
I	Ironworker	251.64	330.00	343.20	140.34	268.65	261.36
J	Landscape Laborer	195.36	205.29	305.50	76.98	113.52	283.01
L	Laborer	195.36	203.49	305.50	76.98	202.22	283.01
M	Stonemason	229.15	214.58	342.36	200.64	248.48	345.10
P	Painter	215.32	213.95	283.01	109.51	241.08	260.30
U	Plumber	285.75	251.86	366.96	192.40	278.26	377.31
	Average All Trades	**226.97**	**250.34**	**326.03**	**146.98**	**228.13**	**307.08**
	Percent of 28 City Average (Local adjustment factor)	91.27%	100.67%	131.10%	59.11%	91.74%	123.48%

Crew Code	Trade	New Orleans	New York	Philadelphia	Phoenix	Pittsburg	Portland
A	Equipment Operator - Medium	167.48	447.96	336.30	341.62	267.27	264.00
B	Brickmason	179.52	415.96	293.88	321.97	260.62	260.20
C	Carpenter	169.91	428.42	323.03	313.32	258.09	249.74
D	Truck Driver	105.07	365.48	234.14	249.53	207.43	237.71
E	Electrician	251.73	483.01	344.66	360.38	275.11	282.83
F	Cement Mason	159.46	346.58	293.88	304.13	317.80	245.20
G	Equipment Operator - Light	124.08	416.59	288.42	336.12	228.73	259.35
I	Ironworker	182.58	466.22	331.58	356.93	291.77	282.27
J	Landscape Laborer	89.13	331.48	253.33	288.82	172.91	159.98
L	Laborer	89.13	331.48	253.97	300.75	171.79	196.10
M	Stonemason	179.52	445.74	283.43	321.97	260.62	260.20
P	Painter	129.99	346.68	285.44	309.41	248.90	190.92
U	Plumber	196.63	526.52	348.37	356.40	297.26	226.93
	Average All Trades	**155.71**	**411.70**	**297.73**	**320.10**	**250.64**	**239.65**
	Percent of 28 City Average (Local adjustment factor)	62.61%	165.55%	119.72%	128.72%	100.79%	96.37%

Crew Code	Trade	St. Louis	San Diego	San Francisco	Seattle	Washington D.C.
A	Equipment Operator - Medium	239.71	333.80	417.86	282.69	217.64
B	Brickmason	234.64	275.93	398.64	261.89	225.46
C	Carpenter	245.63	285.33	334.80	274.98	210.67
D	Truck Driver	209.14	272.55	305.92	272.66	156.66
E	Electrician	238.84	255.51	431.12	302.65	271.14
F	Cement Mason	240.45	275.09	303.17	284.70	160.09
G	Equipment Operator - Light	227.25	332.75	404.34	282.59	210.88
I	Ironworker	270.12	338.66	343.20	300.12	241.67
J	Landscape Laborer	220.18	251.43	270.34	160.93	149.00
L	Laborer	223.77	251.43	280.37	236.97	149.00
M	Stonemason	234.64	275.93	398.64	261.89	264.00
P	Painter	225.14	284.28	324.83	210.78	214.26
U	Plumber	262.42	360.31	504.82	337.71	265.37
	Average All Trades	**236.30**	**291.77**	**362.93**	**266.97**	**210.45**
	Percent of 28 City Average (Local adjustment factor)	95.02%	117.33%	145.94%	107.35%	84.63%

The equipment rates used to develop the costs herein are listed below, with the code which identifies the equipment in the Crew and Equipment column. The daily equipment rates include fuel, lubrication, maintenance, repairs, tread wear, and depreciation. Equipment operator costs are not included in the equipment rate. The mobilization cost includes mobilization and demobilization, to be added in only once for the job. These mobilization costs allow for travel up to 25 miles.

1994 EQUIPMENT DAILY RATES

CODE	EQUIPMENT	DAILY RATE	MOBILIZATION
00	1/2 ton pickup truck	$70	
01	1 ton pickup truck	90	
02	4 CY dump truck	110	
03	6 CY dump truck	115	
04	8 CY dump truck	140	
05	10 CY dump truck	230	
06	spreader, tailgate or towed	140	
07	boom truck	430	
08	aerial lift truck	210	
09	tank truck, 2500 gallon	155	
10	1/2 CY wheel loader	230	$130
11	1 CY wheel loader	295	170
12	1 1/2 CY wheel loader	340	200
13	small backhoe/loader	105	130
14	1/2 CY hydraulic backhoe	170	320
15	1 CY hydraulic backhoe	280	410
16	3/4 CY track loader	180	170
17	1 CY track loader	260	200
18	1 3/4 CY track loader	370	230
19	3 CY track loader	490	320
20	50 HP crawler tractor with attachment	190	130
21	150 HP crawler tractor with attachment	400	170
22	300 HP crawler tractor with attachment	770	320
23	crawler drill and compressor	850	320
24	12 HP trencher, manually guided	35	
25	25 HP vibratory plow, manually guided	65	
26	30 HP trencher/vibratory plow	70	130
30	10 CY towed scraper	500	380
31	15 CY towed scraper	510	520
32	20 CY towed scraper	910	520
33	15 CY motor scraper	820	520
34	10 CY elevating scraper	490	320
35	20 CY elevating scraper	1020	520
36	65 HP motor grader	230	170
37	125 HP motor grader	310	320
40	pneumatic tire roller, towed, with tractor	240	370
41	sheepsfoot roller, towed, with tractor	220	250
42	vibratory roller, towed, with tractor	330	380
43	10 ton steel roller, self propelled	200	200
44	pneumatic tire roller, self propelled	230	200
45	rammer compactor, manually guided	30	
46	vibratory compactor, manually guided	20	
50	20 HP garden trctor with attachment	40	110
51	40 HP utility trctor with attachment	90	130

CODE	EQUIPMENT	DAILY RATE	MOBILIZATION
60	800 gallon hydraulic planter/mulcher	$175	
61	1500 gallon hydraulic planter/mulcher	250	
62	small power mulcher	170	
63	large power mulcher	245	
64	soil shredder	170	
70	18" sod cutter, walk-behind	30	
71	26" power tiller	30	
72	20-22" walk-behind mower	25	
73	32-36" walk-behind mower	30	
74	36-42" rider mower	35	
75	48-60" rider mower	45	
76	walk behind aerator	30	
77	power lawn edger	25	
80	2 man earth auger	7	
81	power tools	5	
82	chain saw	14	
83	brush saw	12	
84	brush chipper	130	
85	stump chipper	140	
86	air tools and compressor	65	
87	demolition hammer, self-propelled	250	$320
90	asphalt paver	700	520
91	concrete paver	830	520
92	12 CF power buggy and S-6 mixer	125	110
93	curb extruding machine, asphalt or concrete	70	130
94	transverse soil mixer	870	520
95	crane, truck mounted, 15 ton capacity	420	
96	asphalt distributor truck	355	
97	pavement stripper, manually guided	16	

D. U.S. Weights and Measures

Read down for U.S. and metric equivalents.

LINEAR MEASURE

mile	1					
furlong	8	1				
rod	320	40	1			
yard	1,760	220	5.5	1		
foot	5,280	660	16.5	3	1	
inch	63,360	7,920	198	36	12	1
kilometer	1.609					
meter			5.029	0.914		
centimeter					30.48	2.54

D. U.S. Weights and Measures

Read down for U.S. and metric equivalents.

AREA MEASURE

square mile	1					
acre	640	1				
square rod	102,400	160	1			
square yard		4840	30.25	1		
square foot		43560	272.25	9	1	
square inch				1,296	144	1
square kilometer	2.59					
hectare		0.405	0.405			
centare		4,047	25.293	0.836	0.093	
square centimeter						6.451

CUBIC MEASURE

freight ton	1			
cubic yard		1		
cubic foot	40	27	1	
cubic inch		46,656	1,728	1
cubic meter		0.765	0.028	
cubic centimeter				16.387

WEIGHT (AVOIRDUPOIS)

long ton	1			
short ton		1		
pound	2,240	2,000	1	
ounce			16	1
metric ton	1.016	0.907	0.907	
kilogram			0.453	
gram				28.349

LIQUID MEASURE

barrel	1							
gallon	32.5	1						
quart		4	1					
pint		8	2	1				
cup		16	4	2	1			
fluid ounce		128	32	16	8	1		
tablespoon				32	16	2	1	
teaspoon					48	6	3	1
drop								60
liter		3.785	0.946	0.437				
milliliter						29.573	14.787	4.929

DRY MEASURE

barrel	1						
bushel		1					
peck		4	1				
quart	105	32	8	1			
pint		64	16	2	1		
cup		128	32	4	2	1	
tablespoon				64	32	16	1
teaspoon						48	3
liter		35.238	8.809	1.101	0.55	0.275	

Read down for metric and U.S. equivalents

LINEAR MEASURE

kilometer	1			
meter	1,000	1		
centimeter		100	1	
millimeter			10	1
mile	0.62			
yard		1.094		
foot		3.281		
inch		39.37	0.39	0.04

AREA MEASURE

square kilometer	1			
hectare	100	1		
centare (sq. meter)		10,000	1	
square centimeter			10,000	1
square mile	0.386			
acre		2.47		
square foot			10.76	
square inch				0.155

CUBIC MEASURE

stere (cubic meter)	1		
decistere	10	1	
cubic centimeter		100,000	1
cubic yard	1.31		
cubic foot		3.53	
cubic inch			0.061

LIQUID AND DRY MEASURE

kiloliter	1	
liter	1,000	1
milliliter		1,000
liquid quart		1.057
dry quart		0.908

WEIGHT

metric ton	1		
kilogram	1,000	1	
gram		1,000	1
milligram			1,000
short ton	1.1		
pound		2.205	
ounce			0.035

SQUARE

Diagonal = $d = s\sqrt{2}$

Area = $s^2 = 0.5\ d^2$

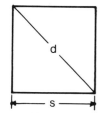

PARALLELOGRAM

Area = ab

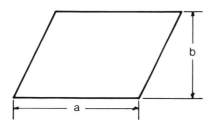

RECTANGLE

Area = $ab = b\sqrt{d^2-b^2}$

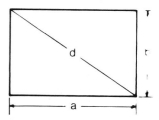

TRAPEZIUM

Area = $1/2\ [a(h+h^1) + bh^1 + ch]$

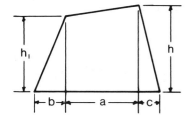

TRIANGLE

Area = $1/2\ bh$

Area = $\sqrt{S(S-a)(S-b)(S-c)}$ when $S = \dfrac{a+b+c}{2}$

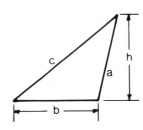 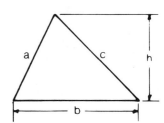

TRAPEZOID

Area = $1/2\ h\ (a+b)$

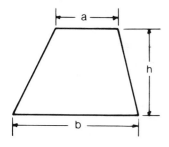

REGULAR POLYGON

n = number of sides

r = short radius

S = length of side

R = long radius

5 sides: Area = $1.7205\ S^2 = 3.633\ r^2$

6 sides: Area = $2.5981\ S^2 = 3.464\ r^2$

7 sides: Area = $3.6339\ S^2 = 3.371\ r^2$

8 sides: Area = $4.8284\ S^2 = 3.314\ r^2$

9 sides: Area = $6.1819\ S^2 = 3.276\ r^2$

10 sides: Area = $7.6942\ S^2 = 3.249\ r^2$

11 sides: Area = $9.3657\ S^2 = 3.230\ r^2$

12 sides: Area = $11.1963\ S^2 = 3.215\ r^2$

SLOPES

Multiply the horizontal area or length of the slope by the following factor to get actual slope area or length.

Slope	Factor
3/4:1	1.667
1:1	1.414
1 1/2:1	1.202
2:1	1.118
2 1/2:1	1.077
3:1	1.054
4:1	1.031
5:1	1.020

CIRCLE

π = 3.1416

A = area

d = diameter

c = circumference

r = radius

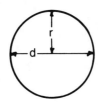

$c = \pi d = 3.1416\,d$

$c = 2\pi r = 6.2832\,r$

$d = \dfrac{c}{\pi} = \dfrac{c}{3.1416}$

$r = \dfrac{c}{2\pi} = \dfrac{c}{6.2832}$

$A = \dfrac{\pi d^2}{4} = 0.7854\,d^2$

$A = \pi r^2 = 3.1416\,r^2$

$c = 2\sqrt{\pi A} = 3.54\sqrt{A}$

$c = \dfrac{2A}{r} = \dfrac{4A}{d}$

$d = 2\sqrt{\dfrac{A}{\pi}} = 1.128\sqrt{A}$

$r = \sqrt{\dfrac{A}{\pi}} = 0.564\sqrt{A}$

$A = \dfrac{c^2}{4\pi} = \dfrac{c^2}{12.57}$

$A = \dfrac{cr}{2} = \dfrac{cd}{4}$

CIRCULAR RING

Area $= \pi(R^2-r^2) = 3.1416\,(R^2-r^2)$

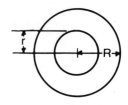

QUADRANT

Area $= \dfrac{\pi r^2}{4} = 0.7854\,r^2 = 0.3927\,c^2$

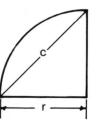

SEGMENT

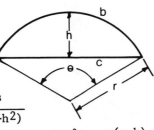

b = length of arc

θ = angle in degrees

Chord $= c = \sqrt{4(2hr-h^2)}$

Area $= 1/2\,[br-c(r-h)] = \pi r^2 \dfrac{\theta}{360} - \dfrac{c(r-h)}{2}$

SECTOR

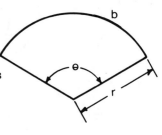

b = length of arc

θ = angle in degrees

Area $= \dfrac{br}{2} = \pi r^2 \dfrac{\theta}{360}$

ELLIPSE

Area $= \pi ab = 3.1416\,ab$

Circumference $= 2\pi\sqrt{\dfrac{a^2+b^2}{2}}$

PARABOLA

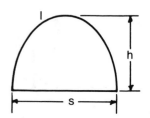

Area $= 2/3\,sh$

G. Material Weights

Material	Lb/LCY	Lb/BCY	Lb/CCY
Clay			
natural	2800	3400	
dry	2500	3100	
wet	2800	3500	
Clay and Gravel			
dry	2400	2800	
wet	2600	3100	
Decomposed Rock			
75% rock, 25% earth	3300	4700	
50% rock, 50% earth	2900	3850	
25% rock, 75% earth	2650	3300	
Earth			
dry	2550	3200	
wet	2700	3400	
loam	2100	2600	
Granite, broken	2800	4600	

Material	Lb/LCY	Lb/BCY	Lb/CCY
Gravel			
pitrun	3250	3650	
dry	2550	2850	
dry, 1/4"-2"	2850	3200	
wet, 1/4"-2"	3400	3800	
Limestone, broken	2600	4400	
Sand			
dry, loose	2400	2700	
damp	2850	3200	
wet	3100	3500	
Sand and Clay	2700	3400	4050
Sand and Gravel			
dry	2900	3250	
wet	3400	3750	
Stone, crushed	2700	4500	
Topsoil	1600	2300	
Traprock, broken	2950	4400	

Soil volume is defined according to its state in the earth moving processes. The three measures of soil volume are:

BCY: Bank Cubic Yard, on cubic yard of material as it lies undisturbed in the natural state.

LCY: Loose Cubic Yard, one cubic yard of material which has been swelled as a result of loading.

CCY: Compacted Cubic Yard, one cubic yard of material which has been compacted and has shrunk as a result of compaction.

BANK MATERIAL

EXPANSION AND COMPACTION FACTORS

MATERIAL	BCY =	LCY =	CCY
Sand	1	1.12	0.98
Sand and Gravel	1	1.11	0.99
Sand and Clay	1	1.27	0.87
Sandy Loam	1	1.20	0.97
Loam	1	1.23	0.95
Clay Loam	1	1.24	0.91
Clay	1	1.25	0.85
Clay and Gravel	1	1.18	0.95
Gravel	1	1.12	0.98
Topsoil	1	1.43	0.80

LOOSE MATERIAL

BANK AND COMPACTION FACTORS

MATERIAL	LCY =	BCY =	CCY
Sand	1	0.89	0.88
Sand and Gravel	1	0.90	0.89
Sand and Clay	1	0.79	0.69
Sandy Loam	1	0.83	0.81
Loam	1	0.81	0.77
Clay Loam	1	0.81	0.73
Clay	1	0.80	0.68
Clay and Gravel	1	0.85	0.81
Gravel	1	0.89	0.88
Topsoil	1	0.70	0.56
Crushed Stone	1		0.60

COMPACTED MATERIAL

BANK AND LOOSE FACTORS

MATERIAL	CCY =	BCY =	LCY
Sand	1	1.02	1.14
Sand and Gravel	1	1.01	1.12
Sand and Clay	1	1.15	1.46
Sandy Loam	1	1.03	1.24
Loam	1	1.05	1.29
Clay Loam	1	1.10	1.36
Clay	1	1.18	1.47
Clay and Gravel	1	1.05	1.24
Gravel	1	1.02	1.14
Topsoil	1	1.25	1.79
Crushed Stone			
Peat Moss	1		1.67
	1		1.80

KEY	DESCRIPTION	UNIT	CREW AND EQUIPMENT	PER DAY	INSTALLATION COST	MATERIALS COST	TOTAL + 25%
	Load loose material on truck						
	light or medium soil						
100	by hand, light soil	LCY	1L	11	18.55		23.20
105	by hand, medium soil	LCY	1L	6.1	33.45		41.80
110	1/2 CY wheel loader	LCY	1G,10	274	1.77		2.21
115	1 CY wheel loader	LCY	1G,11	549	1.00		1.25
120	1 1/2 CY wheel loader	LCY	1G,12	830	0.72		0.90
125	3/4 CY track loader	LCY	1G,16	634	0.69		0.86
130	1 CY track loader	LCY	1G,17	848	0.61		0.76
135	1 3/4 CY track loader	LCY	1G,18	1482	0.42		0.53
140	3 CY track loader	LCY	1G,19	2544	0.29		0.37
	heavy soil						
145	by hand	LCY	1L	5.5	37.10		46.40
150	1/2 CY wheel loader	LCY	1G,10	220	2.20		2.75
155	1 CY wheel loader	LCY	1G,11	433	1.27		1.59
160	1 1/2 CY wheel loader	LCY	1G,12	635	0.94		1.17
165	3/4 CY track loader	LCY	1G,16	506	0.86		1.07
170	1 CY track loader	LCY	1G,17	677	0.76		0.95
175	1 3/4 CY track loader	LCY	1G,18	1189	0.53		0.66
180	3 CY track loader	LCY	1G,19	2031	0.37		0.46
	Excavate and load soil						
	light or medium						
185	by hand, light soil	BCY	2L	8	51.01		64.00
190	by hand, medium soil	BCY	2L	4.9	83.28		104.00
195	1/2 CY wheel loader	BCY	1G,10	205	2.36		2.96
200	1 CY wheel loader	BCY	1G,1L,11	415	1.82		2.27
205	1 1/2 CY wheel loader	BCY	1G,1L,12	620	1.29		1.61
210	3/4 CY track loader	BCY	1G,1L,16	370	1.73		2.16
215	1 CY track loader	BCY	1G,1L,17	495	1.45		1.82
220	1 3/4 CY track loader	BCY	1G,1L,18	865	0.96		1.20
225	3 CY track loader	BCY	1G,1L,19	1485	0.64		0.80
	heavy soil						
230	by hand	BCY	2L	3.7	110.29		138.00
235	1/2 CY wheel loader	BCY	1G,10	165	2.94		3.67
240	1 CY wheel loader	BCY	1G,1L,11	325	2.32		2.90
245	1 1/2 CY wheel loader	BCY	1G,1L,12	490	1.63		2.04
250	3/4 CY track loader	BCY	1G,1L,16	300	2.13		2.66
255	1 CY track loader	BCY	1G,1L,17	395	1.82		2.27
260	1 3/4 CY track loader	BCY	1G,1L,18	690	1.20		1.50
265	3 CY track loader	BCY	1G,1L,19	1185	0.80		1.00
	Haul and dump, light traffic						
	1 mile round trip						
270	1/2 ton pickup truck	LCY	1D,00	19	14.58		18.20
275	1 ton pickup truck	LCY	1D,01	50	5.94		7.40
280	4 CY dump truck	LCY	1D,02	111	2.86		3.57
285	6 CY dump truck	LCY	1D,03	144	2.24		2.79
290	8 CY dump truck	LCY	1D,04	169	2.05		2.57
295	10 CY dump truck	LCY	1D,05	189	2.31		2.89
	2 mile round trip						
300	1/2 ton pickup truck	LCY	1D,00	15	18.46		23.10
305	1 ton pickup truck	LCY	1D,01	39	7.61		9.50
310	4 CY dump truck	LCY	1D,02	96	3.30		4.13
315	6 CY dump truck	LCY	1D,03	127	2.54		3.17
320	8 CY dump truck	LCY	1D,04	152	2.28		2.85
325	10 CY dump truck	LCY	1D,05	171	2.56		3.19
	4 mile round trip						
330	1/2 ton pickup truck	LCY	1D,00	10	27.69		34.60
335	1 ton pickup truck	LCY	1D,01	27	11.00		13.70
340	4 CY dump truck	LCY	1D,02	76	4.17		5.20
345	6 CY dump truck	LCY	1D,03	103	3.13		3.91
350	8 CY dump truck	LCY	1D,04	125	2.78		3.47
355	10 CY dump truck	LCY	1D,05	144	3.03		3.79

APPENDIX

KEY	DESCRIPTION	UNIT	CREW AND EQUIPMENT	PER DAY	INSTALLATION COST	MATERIALS COST	TOTAL + 25%
	6 mile round trip						
360	1/2 ton pickup truck	LCY	1D,00	7.8	35.51		44.40
365	1 ton pickup truck	LCY	1D,01	21	14.14		17.70
370	4 CY dump truck	LCY	1D,02	63	5.03		6.30
375	6 CY dump truck	LCY	1D,03	86	3.74		4.68
380	8 CY dump truck	LCY	1D,04	107	3.24		4.05
385	10 CY dump truck	LCY	1D,05	124	3.52		4.40
	8 mile round trip						
390	1/2 ton pickup truck	LCY	1D,00	6.3	43.96		55.00
395	1 ton pickup truck	LCY	1D,01	17	17.47		21.80
400	4 CY dump truck	LCY	1D,02	53	5.98		7.50
405	6 CY dump truck	LCY	1D,03	74	4.35		5.40
410	8 CY dump truck	LCY	1D,04	93	3.73		4.66
415	10 CY dump truck	LCY	1D,05	109	4.01		5.00
	10 mile round trip						
420	1/2 ton pickup truck	LCY	1D,00	5.3	52.25		65.00
425	1 ton pickup truck	LCY	1D,01	14	21.21		26.50
430	4 CY dump truck	LCY	1D,02	46	6.89		8.60
435	6 CY dump truck	LCY	1D,03	65	4.95		6.20
440	8 CY dump truck	LCY	1D,04	82	4.23		5.30
445	10 CY dump truck	LCY	1D,05	97	4.50		5.60
	20 mile round trip						
450	4 CY dump truck	LCY	1D,02	28	11.32		14.10
455	6 CY dump truck	LCY	1D,03	41	7.85		9.80
460	8 CY dump truck	LCY	1D,04	52	6.67		8.30
465	10 CY dump truck	LCY	1D,05	63	6.94		8.70
	Haul and dump, medium traffic						
	1 mile round trip						
470	1/2 ton pickup truck	LCY	1D,00	16	17.31		21.60
475	1 ton pickup truck	LCY	1D,01	44	6.75		8.40
480	4 CY dump truck	LCY	1D,02	99	3.20		4.00
485	6 CY dump truck	LCY	1D,03	131	2.46		3.07
490	8 CY dump truck	LCY	1D,04	156	2.22		2.78
495	10 CY dump truck	LCY	1D,05	176	2.48		3.10
	2 mile round trip						0.00
500	1/2 ton pickup truck	LCY	1D,00	12	23.08		28.80
505	1 ton pickup truck	LCY	1D,01	32	9.28		11.60
510	4 CY dump truck	LCY	1D,02	80	3.96		4.95
515	6 CY dump truck	LCY	1D,03	108	2.98		3.73
520	8 CY dump truck	LCY	1D,04	131	2.65		3.31
525	10 CY dump truck	LCY	1D,05	150	2.91		3.64
	4 mile round trip						
530	1/2 ton pickup truck	LCY	1D,00	7.8	35.51		44.40
535	1 ton pickup truck	LCY	1D,01	21	14.14		17.70
540	4 CY dump truck	LCY	1D,02	58	5.46		6.80
545	6 CY dump truck	LCY	1D,03	80	4.02		5.00
550	8 CY dump truck	LCY	1D,04	99	3.50		4.38
555	10 CY dump truck	LCY	1D,05	116	3.77		4.71
	6 mile round trip						
560	1/2 ton pickup truck	LCY	1D,00	5.8	47.75		60.00
565	1 ton pickup truck	LCY	1D,01	15	19.80		24.70
570	4 CY dump truck	LCY	1D,02	45	7.04		8.80
575	6 CY dump truck	LCY	1D,03	64	5.03		6.30
580	8 CY dump truck	LCY	1D,04	80	4.34		5.40
585	10 CY dump truck	LCY	1D,05	95	4.60		5.70
	8 mile round trip						
590	1/2 ton pickup truck	LCY	1D,00	4.5	61.54		77.00
595	1 ton pickup truck	LCY	1D,01	12	24.75		30.90
600	4 CY dump truck	LCY	1D,02	37	8.57		10.70
605	6 CY dump truck	LCY	1D,03	53	6.07		7.60
610	8 CY dump truck	LCY	1D,04	67	5.18		6.50
615	10 CY dump truck	LCY	1D,05	80	5.46		6.80

KEY	DESCRIPTION	UNIT	CREW AND EQUIPMENT	PER DAY	INSTALLATION COST	MATERIALS COST	TOTAL + 25%
	I. Hauling						**1994**
	10 mile round trip						
620	1/2 ton pickup truck	LCY	1D,00	3.8	72.88		91.00
625	1 ton pickup truck	LCY	1D,01	10	29.69		37.10
630	4 CY dump truck	LCY	1D,02	31	10.22		12.80
635	6 CY dump truck	LCY	1D,03	45	7.15		8.90
640	8 CY dump truck	LCY	1D,04	58	5.98		7.50
645	10 CY dump truck	LCY	1D,05	69	6.33		7.90
	20 mile round trip						
650	4 CY dump truck	LCY	1D,02	18	17.61		22.00
655	6 CY dump truck	LCY	1D,03	26	12.38		15.50
660	8 CY dump truck	LCY	1D,04	34	10.20		12.80
665	10 CY dump truck	LCY	1D,05	41	10.66		13.30
	Haul and dump, heavy traffic						
	1 mile round trip						
670	1/2 ton pickup truck	LCY	1D,00	15	18.46		23.10
675	1 ton pickup truck	LCY	1D,01	31	9.58		12.00
680	4 CY dump truck	LCY	1D,02	85	3.73		4.66
685	6 CY dump truck	LCY	1D,03	114	2.82		3.53
690	8 CY dump truck	LCY	1D,04	137	2.53		3.17
695	10 CY dump truck	LCY	1D,05	157	2.78		3.48
	2 mile round trip						
700	1/2 ton pickup truck	LCY	1D,00	8.1	34.19		42.70
705	1 ton pickup truck	LCY	1D,01	22	13.50		16.90
710	4 CY dump truck	LCY	1D,02	63	5.03		6.30
715	6 CY dump truck	LCY	1D,03	86	3.74		4.68
720	8 CY dump truck	LCY	1D,04	107	3.24		4.05
725	10 CY dump truck	LCY	1D,05	124	3.52		4.40
	4 mile round trip						
730	1/2 ton pickup truck	LCY	1D,00	5	55.39		69.00
735	1 ton pickup truck	LCY	1D,01	13	22.84		28.60
740	4 CY dump truck	LCY	1D,02	41	7.73		9.70
745	6 CY dump truck	LCY	1D,03	58	5.55		6.90
750	8 CY dump truck	LCY	1D,04	74	4.69		5.90
755	10 CY dump truck	LCY	1D,05	88	4.97		6.20
	6 mile round trip						
760	1/2 ton pickup truck	LCY	1D,00	3.6	76.93		96.00
765	1 ton pickup truck	LCY	1D,01	9.7	30.61		38.30
770	4 CY dump truck	LCY	1D,02	31	10.22		12.80
775	6 CY dump truck	LCY	1D,03	44	7.32		9.10
780	8 CY dump truck	LCY	1D,04	56	6.20		7.70
785	10 CY dump truck	LCY	1D,05	68	6.43		8.00
	8 mile round trip						
790	1/2 ton pickup truck	LCY	1D,00	2.8	98.91		124.00
795	1 ton pickup truck	LCY	1D,01	7.6	39.07		48.80
800	4 CY dump truck	LCY	1D,02	24	13.21		16.50
805	6 CY dump truck	LCY	1D,03	35	9.20		11.50
810	8 CY dump truck	LCY	1D,04	46	7.54		9.40
815	10 CY dump truck	LCY	1D,05	55	7.94		9.90
	10 mile round trip						
820	1/2 ton pickup truck	LCY	1D,00	2.3	120.41		151.00
825	1 ton pickup truck	LCY	1D,01	6.3	47.13		59.00
830	4 CY dump truck	LCY	1D,02	20	15.85		19.80
835	6 CY dump truck	LCY	1D,03	30	10.73		13.40
840	8 CY dump truck	LCY	1D,04	38	9.13		11.40
845	10 CY dump truck	LCY	1D,05	47	9.30		11.60
	20 mile round trip						
850	4 CY dump truck	LCY	1D,02	11	28.81		36.00
855	6 CY dump truck	LCY	1D,03	16	20.12		25.20
860	8 CY dump truck	LCY	1D,04	21	16.52		20.70
865	10 CY dump truck	LCY	1D,05	26	16.81		21.00
870	**Dump charges, rubbish**	LCY					**6.00**

APPENDIX

The following height/caliper relationships are the standards recommended by the American Association of Nurseryman's "American Standard for Nursery Stock."

Small Upright Trees

Height (feet)	Minimum Caliper (inches)
2	5/16
3	7/16
4	9/16
5	11/16
6	7/8

Shade Trees

Caliper (inches)	Average Height (feet)	Maximum Height (feet)
1/2	5-6	8
3/4	6-8	10
1	8-10	11
1 1/4	8-10	12
1 1/2	10-12	14
1 3/4	10-12	14
2	12-14	16
2 1/2	12-14	16
3	14-16	18
3 1/2	14-16	18
4	16-18	22
5	18 &	26

Slower growing shade trees shall have heights not less than 2/3 of the height in the above table

K. Plant Ball Sizes

The following ball sizes are the minimum recommended for nursery grown plants by the American Association of Nurserymen's "American Standard for Nursery Stock." These sizes will apply in most parts of the country. In some parts of the country however, varying growing conditions may result in plants requiring a shallower and wider ball, or a deeper and narrower ball than the recommended size. Plants collected from wild or native stands must have minimum ball sizes equal to those recommended for the next larger size nursery grown stock.

Shade Trees

Caliper Inches	Ball Diameter Inches	Ball Depth Inches
1/2	12	9
3/4	14	10.5
1	16	12
1 1/4	18	13.5
1 1/4	20	13.3
1 3/4	22	14.7
2	24	16
2 1/2	28	18.7
3	32	19.2
3 1/2	38	22.8
4	42	25.2
4 1/2	48	28.8
5	54	32.4

Small Trees

Height Feet	Ball Diameter Inches	Ball Depth Inches
2	10	7.5
3	12	9
4	14	10.5
5	16	12
6	18	13.5
7	20	13.3
8	22	14.7
9	24	16
10	26	17.2

Deciduous Shrubs

Height	Ball Diameter Inches	Ball Depth Inches
12"	8	6
18"	9	6.8
2'	10	7.5
3'	12	9
4'	14	10.5
5'	16	12
6	18	13.3
7'	20	13.5
8'	22	14.7
9'	24	16
10'	26	17.3

K. Plant Ball Sizes

Spreading, Semi-spreading, Globe, and Dwarf Conifers

Spread	Ball Diameter Inches	Ball Depth Inches
18"	10	7.5
2'	12	9
2 1/2'	14	10.5
3'	16	12
3 1/2'	18	13.5
4'	21	14
5'	24	16
6'	28	18.7
7'	32	19.2
8'	36	21.6
16'	46	27.6

Cone and Broad Upright Conifers

Height	Ball Diameter Inches	Ball Depth Inches
18"	10	7.5
2'	12	9
3'	14	10.5
4'	16	12
5'	20	13.3
6'	22	14.7
7'	24	16
8'	27	18
9'	30	20
10'	34	20.4
12'	38	22.8
14'	42	25.2
18'	50	30

Columnar Conifers

Height	Ball Diameter Inches	Ball Depth Inches
18"	10	7.5
2'	12	9
3'	13	9.8
4'	14	10.5
5'	16	12
6'	18	13.5
7'	20	13.3
8'	22	14.7
9'	24	16
10'	27	18
12'	30	20
14'	33	19.8
16'	36	21.6
18'	40	24

Rapid Growing Columnar Conifers

Height	Ball Diameter Inches	Ball Depth Inches
18"	8	6
2'	9	6.8
3'	11	8.3
4'	12	9
5'	14	10.5

Spreading, Semi-spreading, Globe, and Dwarf Broadleaf Evergreens

Spread	Ball Diameter Inches	Ball Depth Inches
18"	10	7.5
2'	12	9
2 1/2'	14	10.5
3'	16	12
3 1/2'	18	13.5
4'	21	14

Cone and Broad Upright Broadleaf Evergreens

Height	Ball Diameter Inches	Ball Depth Inches
18"	10	7.5
2'	12	9
3'	14	10.5
4'	16	12
5'	20	13.3
6'	22	14.7
7'	24	16
8'	27	18
9'	30	20
10'	34	20.4
12'	38	22.8
14'	42	25.2
16'	46	27.6
18'	50	30

APPENDIX

The following root spreads are the minimums recommended for nursery grown plants by the American Association of Nurserymen's "American Standard for Nursery Stock." Plants collected from wild or native stands must have root spreads 1/3 greater than those recommended for nursery grown stock of the same size.

Shade Trees

Caliper Inches	Average Height Feet	Minimum Spread Inches
1/2	5-6	12
3/4	6-8	16
1	8-10	18
1 1/4	8-10	20
1 1/2	10-12	24
1 3/4	10-12	28
2	12-14	32
3	14-16	38

Deciduous Shrubs

Height	Minimum Spread Inches
18"	10
2'	11
3'	14
4'	16
5'	18
6'	20

M. Ball Volumes and Weights

These ball volumes and weights are for soil balls conforming to the diameter/depth ratios recommended by the American Association of Nurserymen's "American Standard for Nursery Stock." See Appendix K for corresponding plant sizes.

The following volumes and weights are for plants grown in standard size containers.

Container Volumes and Weights

Container Size Gallons	Volume Cubic ft	Weight Pounds
.25	0.03	3
1	0.13	12
2	0.27	24
3	0.4	36
4	0.53	48
5	0.67	60
7	0.94	84
15	2.01	180

Ball Volumes and Weights

Ball Diameter Inches	Ball Depth Inches	Ball Volume Cubic ft	Ball Weights Pounds
8	6	0.15	16.5
9	6.8	0.21	23.5
10	7.5	0.29	31.8
11	8.3	0.39	42.8
12	9	0.5	55
14	10.5	0.8	88
16	12	1.2	130
18	13.5	1.7	186
20	13.3	2.1	227
21	14	2.4	263
22	14.7	2.7	302
24	16	3.5	390
26	17.3	4.5	497
27	18	5.1	557
28	18.7	5.6	621
30	20	7	765
32	19.2	7.6	836
33	19.8	8.3	915
34	20.4	9.1	998
36	21.6	10.8	1188
38	22.8	12.7	1400
40	24	14.8	1627
42	25.2	17.1	1887
46	27.6	22.5	2474
50	30	29	3188

For ball sizes not included in the table:

Volume of soil ball, cubic feet = (ball diameter, feet)2 x (ball depth, feet x 2/3)

Weight of soil ball, pounds = volume, cubic feet x 110 pounds

N. Planting Pit Volumes

Planting Pit Excavation

Pit Diameter Inches	Pit Depth Inches	Pit Volume Cubic feet	Pit Diameter Inches	Pit Depth Inches	Pit Volume Cubic feet	Pit Diameter Inches	Pit Depth Inches	Pit Volume Cubic feet
18	9	1.33	48	24	25.1	84	42	135
18	12	1.77	48	30	31.4	84	48	154
18	15	2.21	48	36	37.7	84	54	173
						84	60	192
21	9	1.8	54	24	31.8	84	66	212
21	12	2.4	54	30	39.8			
21	15	3.01	54	36	47.7	90	42	155
21	18	3.61	54	42	55.7	90	48	177
						90	54	199
24	12	3.14	60	30	49.1	90	60	221
24	15	3.93	60	36	58.9	90	66	243
24	18	4.71	60	42	68.7	90	72	265
			60	48	78.5			
30	15	6.14				96	48	201
30	18	7.36	66	30	59.4	96	54	226
30	21	8.59	66	36	71.3	96	60	276
30	24	9.82	66	42	83.1	96	72	302
			66	48	95			
36	18	10.6	66	54	107			
36	21	12.4						
36	24	14.1	72	36	85			
36	30	17.7	72	42	99			
			72	48	113			
42	18	12.8	72	54	127			
42	21	15						
42	24	17.1	78	36	100			
42	30	21.4	78	42	116			
42	36	25.7	78	48	133			
			78	54	149			
			78	60	166			

For pit sizes not included in the table:

Pit volume, cubic feet = x (pit diameter, feet)2 - 4 x (pit depth, feet)

O. Backfill Volumes

To compute backfill volume for balled and burlapped or container plants, subtract ball or container volume (from Appendix M) from pit volume (from Appendix N).

Rough lumber is sold by the "Foot Board-Measure", which is the equivalent of a board 1 foot wide, 1 foot long, and 1 inch thick. To compute the board-measure in any board, lumber, or timber, divide the nominal sectional area in inches by 12, and multiply by the length in feet. The following table can be used to esti-mate the number of board feet in lumber of standard sizes. The top row lists the product of the nominal dimensions of lumber in square inches. The left column lists the length of lumber in even feet. The matrix lists the number of feet in board-measure for various dimensions of lumber.

Table of Board Measure

Board Length Feet	Nominal Sectional Area in Square Inches									
	2	4	6	8	10	12	14	16	18	20
2	0.3	0.7	1.0	1.3	1.7	2.0	2.3	2.7	3.0	3.3
4	0.7	1.3	2.0	2.7	3.3	4.0	4.7	5.3	6.0	6.7
6	1.0	2.0	3.0	4.0	5.0	6.0	7.0	8.0	9.0	10.0
8	1.3	2.7	4.0	5.3	6.7	8.0	9.3	10.7	12.0	13.3
10	1.7	3.3	5.0	6.7	8.3	10.0	11.7	13.3	15.0	16.7
12	2.0	4.0	6.0	8.0	10.0	12.0	14.0	16.0	18.0	20.0
14	2.3	4.7	7.0	9.3	11.7	14.0	16.3	18.7	21.0	23.3
16	2.7	5.3	8.0	10.7	13.3	16.0	18.7	21.3	24.0	26.7
18	3.0	6.0	9.0	12.0	15.0	18.0	21.0	24.0	27.0	30.0
20	3.3	6.7	10.0	13.3	16.7	20.0	23.3	26.7	30.0	33.3
22	3.7	7.3	11.0	14.7	18.3	22.0	25.7	29.3	33.0	36.7
24	4.0	8.0	12.0	16.0	20.0	24.0	28.0	32.0	36.0	40.0
26	4.3	8.7	13.0	17.3	21.7	26.0	30.3	34.7	39.0	43.3
28	4.7	9.3	14.0	18.7	23.3	28.0	32.7	37.3	42.0	46.7
30	5.0	10.0	15.0	20.0	25.0	30.0	35.0	40.0	45.0	50.0
32	5.3	10.7	16.0	21.3	26.7	32.0	37.3	42.7	48.0	53.3
34	5.7	11.3	17.0	22.7	28.3	34.0	39.7	45.3	51.0	56.7
36	6.0	12.0	18.0	24.0	30.0	36.0	42.0	48.0	54.0	60.0
38	6.3	12.7	19.0	25.3	31.7	38.0	44.3	50.7	57.0	63.3
40	6.7	13.3	20.0	26.7	33.3	40.0	46.7	53.3	60.0	66.7

Board Length Feet	Nominal Sectional Area in Square Inches									
	24	28	30	32	36	40	42	48	56	60
2	4.0	4.7	5.0	5.3	6.0	6.7	7.0	8.0	9.3	10.0
4	8.0	9.3	10.0	10.7	12.0	13.3	14.0	16.0	18.7	20.0
6	12.0	14.0	15.0	16.0	18.0	20.0	21.0	24.0	28.0	30.0
8	16.0	18.7	20.0	21.3	24.0	26.7	28.0	32.0	37.3	40.0
10	20.0	23.3	25.0	26.7	30.0	33.3	35.0	40.0	46.7	50.0
12	24.0	28.0	30.0	32.0	36.0	40.0	42.0	48.0	56.0	60.0
14	28.0	32.7	35.0	37.3	42.0	46.7	49.0	56.0	65.3	70.0
16	32.0	37.3	40.0	42.7	48.0	53.3	56.0	64.0	74.7	80.0
18	36.0	42.0	45.0	48.0	54.0	60.0	63.0	72.0	84.0	90.0
20	40.0	46.7	50.0	53.3	60.0	66.7	70.0	80.0	93.3	100.0
22	44.0	51.3	55.0	58.7	66.0	73.3	77.0	88.0	102.7	110.0
24	48.0	56.0	60.0	64.0	72.0	80.0	84.0	96.0	112.0	120.0
26	52.0	60.7	65.0	69.3	78.0	86.7	91.0	104.0	121.3	130.0
28	56.0	65.3	70.0	74.7	84.0	93.3	98.0	112.0	130.7	140.0
30	60.0	70.0	75.0	80.0	90.0	100.0	105.0	120.0	140.0	150.0
32	64.0	74.7	80.0	85.3	96.0	106.7	112.0	128.0	149.3	160.0
34	68.0	79.3	85.0	90.7	102.0	113.3	119.0	136.0	158.7	170.0
36	72.0	84.0	90.0	96.0	108.0	120.0	126.0	144.0	168.0	180.0
38	76.0	88.7	95.0	101.3	114.0	126.7	133.0	152.0	177.3	190.0
40	80.0	93.3	100.0	106.7	120.0	133.3	140.0	160.0	186.7	200.0

Q. Reinforcing Steel

Concrete Reinforcing Bars
Standard Sizes and Weights

Bar Number	Inches Diameter	Pounds Per Foot
2	1/4	0.167
3	3/8	0.376
4	1/2	0.668
5	5/8	1.043
6	3/4	1.502
7	7/8	2.044
8	1	2.670

Welded Steel Fabric Reinforcing
570 Square Feet Per Roll

Style	Pounds Per 100 SF
6" x 6" - 10/10	21
6" x 6" - 8/8	30
6" x 6" - 6/6	42
6" x 6" - 4/4	58
4" x 4" - 10/10	31
4" x 4" - 8/8	44
4" x 4" - 6/6	62
4" x 4" - 4/4	85

R. Plant Name Index

LATIN NAMES	COMMON NAMES
Abelia	Abelia
x grandiflora	Glossy Abelia
Abies	Fir
balsamea 'Nana'	Balsam Fir
concolor	White Fir
fraseri	Fraser Fir
Acacia	Mimosa
baileyana	Golden Mimosa
latifolia	Broadleaf Latifolia
Acer	Maple
campestre	Hedge Maple
ginnala	Amur Maple
negundo	Boxelder
palmatum	Japanese Maple
'Atropurpureum'	Red Japanese Maple
platanoides	Norway Maple
'Schwedleri'	Schwedler Maple
rubrum	Red Maple
saccharinum	Silver Maple
saccharum	Sugar Maple
Aegopodium podagraria	Bishop's Weed
Aesculus glabra	Ohio Buckeye
Aesculus hippocastanum	Common Horsechestnut
Ajuga reptans	Carpet Bugle
Albizia julibrissin	Mimosa
Amelanchier canadensis	Shadblow Serviceberry
Araucaria heterophylla	Norfolk Island Pine
Archontophoenix cunninghamiana	Piccabeen Palm
Arctostaphylos uva-ursi	Bearberry
Arecastrum romanzoffianum	Pygmy Date Palm
Aronia	Chokecherry
melanocarpa	Black Chokecherry
Asparagus densiflorus	Asparagus
'Meyers'	Meyers Asparagus
'Sprengeri'	Aparagus Fern
Aspidistra elatior	Bar-room Plant
Athyrium filix-femina	Ladyfern
Aucuba japonica	Japanese Laurel
'Variegata'	Gold Dust Plant
Azalea	Asalea

LATIN NAMES	COMMON NAMES
Bauhinia purpurea	Purple Bauhinia
Berberis	Barberry
julianae	Wintergreen Barberry
x mentorensis	Mentor Barberry
thunbergii	Japanese Barberry
'Atropurpurea'	Redleaf Japanese Barberry
'Crimson Pygmy'	Crimson Pygmy
Betula	Birch
maximowicziana	Monarch Birch
nigra	River Birch
papyrifera	Paper Birch
pendula	European White Birch
'Youngii'	Young's Weeping Birch
Brachychiton populneus	Bottle Tree
Buxus	Boxwood
microphylla japonica	Japanese Littleleaf Boxwood
microphylla koreana	Korean Barberry
sempervirens	Common Box
Calliandra haematocephala	Red Powderpuff
Callistemon citrinus	Lemon Bottlebrush
Calycanthus floridus	Common Sweetshrub
Camellia	Camellia
japonica	Japanese Camellia
sasanqua	Sasanqua Camellia
Caragana arborescens	Siberian Peashrub
Carissa grandiflora	Natal Plum
Carpinus	Hornbeam
betulus	European Hornbeam
caroliniana	American Hornbeam
Cassia artemisioides	Wormwood Senna
Catalpa speciosa	Northern Catalpa
Cedrus	Cedar
atlantica	Atlas Cedar
deodara	Deodara Cedar
Celastrus scandens	American Bittersweet
Celtis occidentalis	Common Hackberry
Ceratonia silique	Carob
Cercidiphyllum japonicum	Katsuratree
Cercis canadensis	Eastern Redbud
Chaenomeles speciosa	Common Floweringquince
Chamaecyparis	Cypress
obtusa	Hinoki Cypress
pisifera	Japanese Falsecypress
Chamaerops humilis	Dwarf Fan Palm
Chrysanthemum maximum	Shasta Daisy
Cinnamomum camphora	Camphor Tree
Cladrastis lutea	American Yellowwood
Clematis	Clematis
Convallaria majalis	Lily-of-the-Valley
Cordyline indivisa	Blue Dracena
Cornus	Dogwood
alba 'Sibirica'	Siberian Dogwood
alternifolia	Pagoda Dogwood
florida	Flowering Dogwood
'Rubra'	Pink Dogwood
kousa	Kousa Dogwood
kousa chinensis	Chinese Dogwood

LATIN NAMES

COMMON NAMES

Cornus, continued

Latin	Common
mas	Corneliancherry Dogwood
racemosa	Gray Dogwood
sericea	Redosier Dogwood
Baileyi	Bailey Dogwood
'Flaviramea'	Golden Twig Dogwood
Coronilla varia	Crown Vetch
Cortaderia selloana	Pampas Grass
Corylus avellana 'Contorta'	Harry Lauder's Walkingstick
Cotinus coggrgria	Common Smoketree
'Royal Purple'	Smoke Bush
Cotoneaster	Cotoneaster
acutifolius	Peking Cotoneaster
adpressus	Creeping Cotoneaster
apiculata	Cranberry Cotoneaster
congestus	Pyrenees Cotoneaster
dammeri	Bearberry Cotoneaster
divaricatus	Spreading Cotoneaster
horizontalis	Rock Cotoneaster
salicifolius	Willowleaf Cotoneaster
Crataegus	Hawthorn
crus-galli	Cockspur Hawthorn
crus-galli inermis	Thornless Cockspur
laevigata	English Hawthorn
x lavallei	Lavalle Hawthorn
phaenopyrum	Washington Howthorn
toba	Toba Hawthorn
viridis 'Winter King'	Green Hawthorn
Cryptomeria japonica	Japanese Cedar
Cupressocyparis leylandii	Leyland Cypress
Cupressus sempervirens	Italian Cypress
Cycas revolta	Sago Palm
Cytisus	Broom

Deutzia

Latin	Common
	Deutzia
gracilis	Slender Deutzia
scabra 'Pride of Rochester'	Pride of Rochester Deutzia
Diervilla sessilifolia	Southern Bush-honeysuckle
Dizygotheca elegantissima	False Arelia

Echinacea purpurea

Latin	Common
	Purple Coneflower
Elaeagnus	Olive
angustifolia	Russian-olive
pungens	Thorny Elaeagnus
umbellata	Autumn-olive
Eriobotrya	Eriobotrya
japonica	Loquat
Eucalyptus	Gum
camaldulensis	Red Gum
cinerea	Silver Dollar Tree
citriodora	Lemon Scented Gum
ficifolia	Red Flowering Gum
nicholii	Black Peppermint
polyanthemos	Silver Dollar Gum
rudis	Desert Gum
viminalis	White Gum
Euonymus	Euonymous
alata	Winged Euonymous
'Compacta'	Dwarfed Winged Euonymus
fortunei	Wintercreeper Euonymus
'Vegeta'	Bigleaf Wintercreeper
japonica	Japonese Euonymus
kiautschovica 'Manhattan'	Evergreen Euonymous

LATIN NAMES

COMMON NAMES

LATIN NAMES	COMMON NAMES
Fagus	Beech
grandifolia	American Beech
sylvatica	European Beech
'Riversii'	River's Purple Beech
Fatshedera lizei	Aralia Ivy
Fatsia japonica	Japanese Fatsia
Feijoa sellowiana	Guava
Ficus	Fig
benjamina	Java Fig
pumila	Climbing Fig
retusa	Indian Laurel
rubiginosa	Port Jackson Fig
Forsythia	Forsythia
intermedia	Border Forsythia
x 'Spectablis'	Showy Border Forsythia
x 'Spring Glory'	Primrose Yellow
suspensa	Weeping Forsythia
viridissima	Greenstem Forsythia
Fraxinus	Ash
americana	White Ash
pennsylvanica lanceolata	Green Ash
velutina	Velvet Ash
velutina glabra 'Modesto'	Modesto Ash
Gardenia jasminoides	Cape Jasmine
Gelsemium sempervirens	Carolina Yellow Jessamine
Ginko biloba	Ginko
Gleditsia triacanthos inermis	Thornless Common Honeylocust
Grevillea robusta	Silk-oak Grevillea
Gymnocladus dioica	Kentucky Coffeetree
Hamamelis virginiana	Vernal Witchhazel
Hedera	Ivy
canariensis	Algerian Ivy
helix	English Ivy
Hemerocallis	Daylilly
Hibbertia scandens	Snake Vine
Hibiscus	Mallow
rosa-sinensis	Chinese Hibiscus
syriacus	Rose-of-Sharon
Hosta	Plantain Lilly
Hydrangea	Hydrangea
arborescens	Hills-of-Snow
macrophylla	Bigleaf Hydrangea
paniculata 'Grandiflora'	PeeGee Hydrangea
quercifolia	Oakleaf Hydrangea
Hypericum x moseranum	Moser's St. Johnswort
Ilex	Holly
x altaclarensis	Altaclara Holly
cornuta	Chinese Holly
'Bufordii'	Buford Holly
crenata	Japanese Holly
'Rotundifolia'	Bigleaf Japanese Holly
glabra	Inkberry
x meserveae	Meserve Holly
x Nellie R. Stevens	Nellie R. Stevens Holly
opaca	American Holly
verticillata	Common Winterberry
vomitoria	Yaupon
Jacaranda mimosifolia	Sharpleaf Jacaranda
Jasminum	Jasmine
nitidum	Star Jasmine
floridum	Showy Jasmine

LATIN NAMES	COMMON NAMES
Juniperus	Juniper
chinensis	Chinese Juniper
communis 'Hibernica'	Irish Juniper
conferta	Shore Juniper
horizontalis	Creeping Juniper
'Plumosa'	Andorra Juniper
'Wiltonii'	Blue Rug Juniper
sabina	Savin Juniper
scopulorum	Rocky Mountain Juniper
virginiana	Eastern Redcedar
Kalmia latifolia	Mountain-laurel
Koelreuteria paniculata	Panicled Goldenraintree
Laburnum x watereri 'Vossii'	Goldenchain Tree
Lagerstroemia indica	Common Crapemyrtle
Larix decidua	European Larch
Laurus nobilis	Bay Laurel
Leptospermum laevigatum	Australian Tea Tree
Leucophyllum frutescens	Barometer Bush
Leucothoe	Leucothoe
axillaris	Coast Leucothoe
fontanesiana	Drooping Leucothoe
Ligustrum	Privet
amurense	Amur Privet
x ibolium	Ibolium Privet
japonicum	Japanese Privet
lucidium	Waxleaf Privet
obtusifolium regelianum	Regel Privet
ovalifolium	California Privet
x vicaryi	Golden Privet
vulgare	European Privet
'Cheyenne'	Cheyenne Privet
Liquidambar styraciflua	American Sweetgum
Liriodendron tulipifera	Tuliptree
Liriope muscari	Big Blue Lilyturf
Lonicera	Honesuckle
fragrantissima	Winter Honeysuckle
heckrottii	Goldflame Honeysuckle
japonica	Japanese Honeysuckle
'Halliana'	Hall's Japanese Honeysuckle
korolkowii zabelii	Blueleaf Honeysuckle
tatarica	Tatarian Honeysuckle
x xylosteoides 'Clavey's Dwarf	Clavey's Dwarf Honeysuckle
Macfadyena unguis-cati	Cat's-Claw
Magnolia	Magnolia
grandiflora	Southern Magnolia
x loebneri	Loebner Magnolia
x soulangiana	Saucer Magnolia
stellata	Star Magnolia
virginiana	Sweet Bay Magnolia
Mahonia	Mahonia
aquifolium	Oregon Grapeholly
bealei	Leatherleaf Mahonia
Malus	Crabapple
x atrosanguinea	Carmine Crabapple
baccata	Siberian Crabapple
floribunda	Japanese Flowering Crabapple
hupehensis	Tea Crabapple
ioensis	Prairie Crabapple
sargentii	Sargent Crabapple
Metasequoia glyptostroboides	Dawn Redwood
Morus alba	White Mulberry

LATIN NAMES	COMMON NAMES
Myrica pensylvanica	Northern Bayberry
Nandina domestica	Heavenly Bamboo
Nerium oleander	Oleander
Nyssa sylvatica	Black Tupelo
Olea europaea	Common Olive
Ophiopogon japonicus	Dwarf Lilyturf
Osmanthus	Osmanthus
fragrans	Fragrant Tea Olive
heterophyllus	Holly Olive
Osmunda cinnamonea	Cinnamon Fern
Ostrya virginiana	American Hophornbeam
Oxydendrum arboreum	Sourwood
Pachysandra terminalis	Japanese Pachysandra
Parthenocissus	Creeper
quinquefolia	Virginia Creeper
'Engelmannii'	Engleman Ivy
tricuspidata	Japanese Creeper
Passiflora x alatocaerulea	Passion Flower
Phellodendron amurense	Amur Corktree
Philadelphus	Mockorange
coronarius	Sweet Mockorange
x virginalis	Virginia Mockorange
Photinia x fraseri	Fraser Photinia
Phyllostachys aurea	Fishpole Bamboo
Physocarpus opulifolius	Common Ninebark
Picea	Spruce
abies	Norway Spruce
'Nidiformis'	Bird's Nest Spruce
glauca	White Spruce
'Conica'	Dwarf White Spruce
'Densata'	Black Hills Spruce
omorika	Serbian Spruce
pungens	Colorado Spruce
'Glauca'	Colorado Blue Spruce
Pieris japonica	Japanese Pieris
Pinus	Pine
canariensis	Canary Island Pine
halepensis	Aleppo Pine
mugo	Swiss Mountain Pine
mugo	Mugo Pine
nigra	Austrian Pine
pinea	Italian Stone Pine
ponderosa	Ponderosa Pine
resinosa	Red Pine
strobus	Eastern White Pine
sylvestris	Scotch Pine
taeda	Loblolly Pine
thunbergiana	Japanese Black Pine
Pistacia chinensis	Chinese Pistache
Pittosporum	Pittosporum
tobira	Japanese Pittosporum
undulatum	Victorian Box
Platanus	Planetree
x acerifolia	London Planetree
occidentalis	American Planetree
Platycladus orientalis	Oriental Arborvitae
Plumbago auriculata	Cape Leadwort
Podocarpus	Podocarpus
macrophyllus	Yew Podocarpus
macrophyllus maki	Maki Podocarpus
Polygonum aubertii	Silvervine Fleeceflower

LATIN NAMES	COMMON NAMES
Populus	Poplar
alba 'Pyramidalis'	Lombardy Poplar
nigra 'Italica'	Lombardy Black Poplar
tremuloides	Quaking Aspen
Potentilla	Cinquefoil
fruticosa	Shrubby Cinquefoil
Prunus	Prunus
x blireiana	Blireiana Plum
caroliniana	Carolina Cherrylaurel
cerasifera	Cherry Plum
x cistena	Purpleleaf Sand Cherry
glandulosa	Dwarf Flowering Almond
laurocerasus	Cherry Laurel
sargentii	Sargent Cherry
serrulata	Japanese Flowering Cherry
subhirtella	Higan Cherry
tomentosa	Manchu Cherry
triloba	Flowering Almond
virginiana	Chokecherry
yedoensis	Yoshino Cherry
Pseudotsugo menziesii	Douglas Fir
Punica granatum 'Nana'	Dwarf Pomegranate
Pyracantha	Firethorn
coccinea	Scarlet Firethorn
koldzumii	Formosa Firethorn
Pyrus	Pear
calleryana	Callery Pear
'Bradford'	Bradford Pear
kawakamii	Evergreen Pear
Quercus	Oak
acutissima	Sawtooth Oak
alba	White Oak
bicolor	Swamp White Oak
coccinea	Scarlet Oak
macrocarpa	Bur Oak
nigra	Water Oak
palustris	Pin Oak
phellos	Willow Oak
robur	English Oak
rubra	Red Oak
shumardii	Shumard Oak
virginiana	Live Oak
Raphiolepis indica	Indian Hawthorn
Rhamnus frangula	Alder Buckthorn
Rhododendron	Rhododendron
catawbiense	Catawba Rhododendron
Rhus	Sumac
aromatica	Fragrant Sumac
glabra	Smooth Sumac
typhina	Staghorn Sumac
Ribes alpinum	Alpine Currant
Robinia pseudoacacia	Black Locust
Rosa	Rose
banksiae	Banksia Rose
hugonis	Father Hugo Rose
rugosa	Rugosa Rose
Rosemarinus officinalis	Rosemary
Rudbeckia hirta	Black-Eyed Susan

LATIN NAMES	COMMON NAMES
Salix	Willow
alba 'Tristis'	Golden Weeping Willow
babylonica	Babylon Weeping Willow
caprea	Goat Willow
discolor	Pussy Willow
matsudana 'Tortuosa'	Corkscrew Hankow Willow
Sambucus canadensis	American Elder
Schinus	Schinus
molle	Pepper Tree
terebinthifolius	Brazilian Pepper Tree
Sedum acre	Gold Moss
Sequoia sempervirens	Redwood
Sophora japonica	Japanese Pagodatree
Sorbus aucuparia	European Mountainash
Spiraea	Spirea
bumalda	Bumald Spirea
cantoniensis	Reeves Spirea
nipponica 'Snowmound'	Snowmound Nippon Spirea
prunifolia	Bridalwreath Spirea
thunbergii	Thunberg Spirea
x vanhoutei	Vanhoutte Spirea
Strelitzia	Strelitzia
nicolia	Bird-of-Paradise Tree
reginae	Queen's Bird-of-Paradise
Symphoricarpos	Coralberry
albus	Common Snowberry
orbiculatus	Indiancurrant Coralberry
Syringa	Lilac
x chinensis	Chinese Lilac
meyeri	Meyer Lilac
patula	Manchurian Lilac
x persica	Persian Lilac
reticulata	Japanese Tree Lilac
vulgaris	Common Lilac
Syzygium paniculatum	Brush Cherry
Taxodium distichum	Common Baldcypress
Taxus	Yew
baccata 'Repandens'	Dwarf English Yew
cuspidata	Japanese Yew
x media	Anglojap Yew
Tecomaria capensis	Cape Honeysuckle
'Aurea'	Yellow Cape Honeysuckle
Thuja occidentalis	Eastern Arborvitae
Tilia	Linden
americana	American Linden
cordata	Littleleaf Linden
x euchlora	Crimean Linden
Trachelospermum	Jasmine
asiaticum	Japanese Star Jasmine
jasminoides	Confederate Jasmine
Tristania conferta	Brisbane Box
Tsuga canadensis	Eastern Hemlock
Ulmus	Elm
parvifolia	Chinese Elm
pumila	Siberian Elm
Viburnum	Viburnum
x burkwoodii	Burkwood Viburnum
x carlcephalum	Fragrant Viburnum
carlesii	Koreanspice Viburnum
davidii	David Viburnum

LATIN NAMES

COMMON NAMES

Viburnum, continued
dentatum
japonicum
lantana
lentago
opulus
  'Roseum'
plicatum tomentosum
prunifolium
rhytidophyllum
suspensum
tinus
trilobum
Vinca minor

Arrowwood Viburnum
Japonese Viburnum
Wayfaringtree Viburnum
Nannyberry Viburnum
European Cranberrybush Viburnum
European Snowball
Doublefile Viburnum
Blackhaw Viburnum
Lantanaphyllum Viburnum
Sandankwa Viburnum
Laurustinus
American Cranberrybush Viburnum
Common Periwinkle

Washingtonia robusta
Weigela florida
Wisteria
  floribunda
  sinensis

Thread Palm
Old Fashioned Weigela
Wisteria
Japanese Wisteria
Chinese Wisteria

Xylosma congestum

Shiny Xylosma

Yucca
aloifolia
filamentosa
gloriosa

Yucca
Spanish-Bayonet
Adam's-needle Yucca
Spanish-dagger

Zelkova serrata

Japanese Zelkova

PAVEMENT · 6" x 12" CONCRETE · GRAVEL

SCALE 3/4" = 1'-0"
02525.00.100

18" · CONCRETE · PAVEMENT · 6" · GRAVEL

SCALE 3/4" = 1'-0"
02525.00.120

ASPHALT CONCRETE CURB · 8" · 6"

SCALE 3/4" = 1'-0"
02525.10.100

PAVEMENT · 6" x 24" CONCRETE · GRAVEL

02525.20.140

20" GRATE AND FRAME · PRECAST CONCRETE · 6" PRECAST CONCRETE BASE · INLET/OUTLET

SCALE 3/8" = 1'-0"
02720.00.100

20" GRATE AND FRAME · BRICK CORBEL · RADIAL CONCRETE BLOCK · INLET/OUTLET · CONCRETE BASE

SCALE 3/8" = 1'-0"
02720.00.130

22" GRATE AND FRAME · 24" CONCRETE PIPE · OUTLET CONCRETE · CONC.

SCALE 3/8" = 1'-0"
2720.20.160

CONCRETE · NATURAL GRADE · GRAVEL · MEASURED HEIGHT OF WALL

SCALE 3/8" = 1'-0"
03310.00.110

REINFORCED CONCRETE · #4 REINF. BARS · NATURAL GRADE · GRAVEL · #6 REINF. BARS · MEASURED HEIGHT OF WALL · #4 BARS · #6 BARS

SCALE 3/8" = 1'-0"
03310.00.130

S. Illustrated Composites

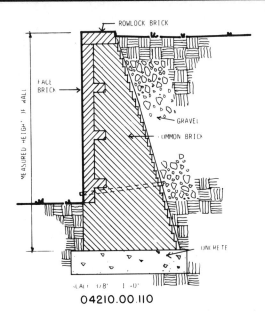

04210.00.110

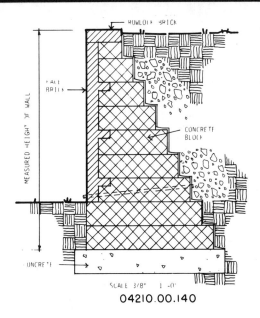

04210.00.140

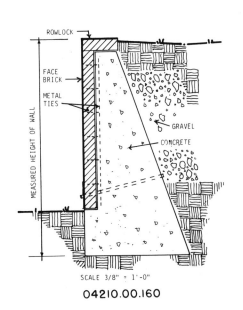

04210.00.160

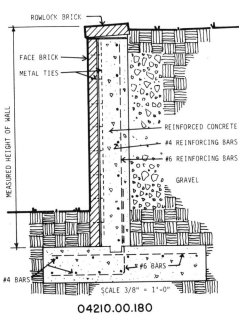

04210.00.180

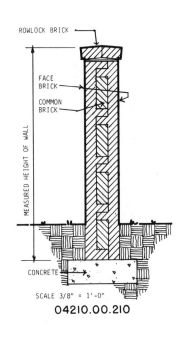

04210.00.210

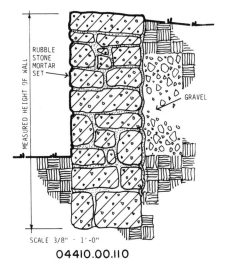

04410.00.110

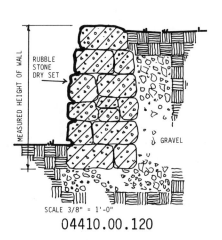

04410.00.120

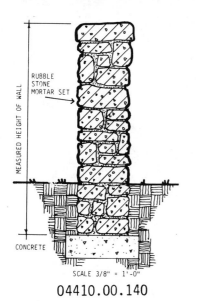

RUBBLE STONE MORTAR SET

MEASURED HEIGHT OF WALL

CONCRETE

SCALE 3/8" = 1'-0"

04410.00.140

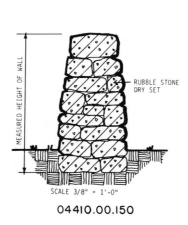

MEASURED HEIGHT OF WALL

RUBBLE STONE DRY SET

SCALE 3/8" = 1'-0"

04410.00.150

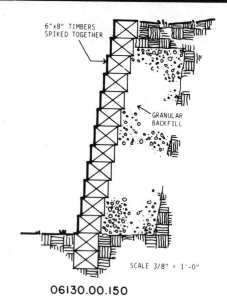

6"x8" TIMBERS SPIKED TOGETHER

GRANULAR BACKFILL

SCALE 3/8" = 1'-0"

06130.00.150

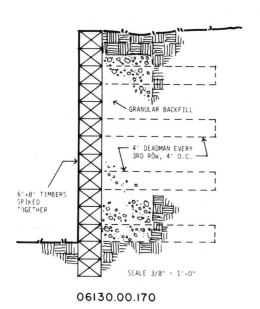

GRANULAR BACKFILL

4' DEADMAN EVERY 3RD ROW, 4' O.C.

6"x8" TIMBERS SPIKED TOGETHER

SCALE 3/8" = 1'-0"

06130.00.170

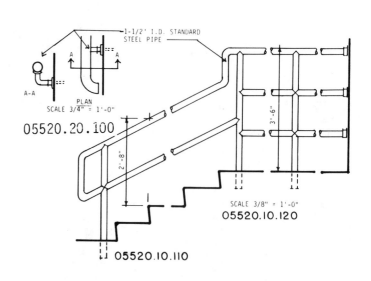

1-1/2" I.D. STANDARD STEEL PIPE

A-A
PLAN
SCALE 3/4" = 1'-0"

05520.20.100

3'-6"

2'-8"

SCALE 3/8" = 1'-0"

05520.10.120

05520.10.110

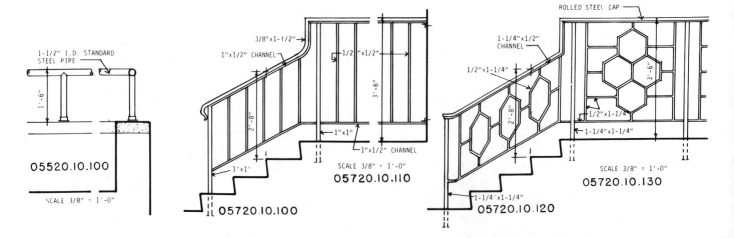

1-1/2" I.D. STANDARD STEEL PIPE

1'-6"

05520.10.100

SCALE 3/8" = 1'-0"

3/8"x1-1/2"
1"x1/2" CHANNEL
1/2"x1/2"
3'-6"
2'-8"
1"x1"
1"x1/2" CHANNEL
1'x1'
SCALE 3/8" = 1'-0"
05720.10.110
05720.10.100

ROLLED STEEL CAP
1-1/4"x1/2" CHANNEL
1/2"x1-1/4"
3'-6"
2'-8"
1/2"x1-1/4
1-1/4"x1-1/4"
SCALE 3/8" = 1'-0"
05720.10.130
1-1/4"x1-1/4"
05720.10.120

S. Illustrated Composites

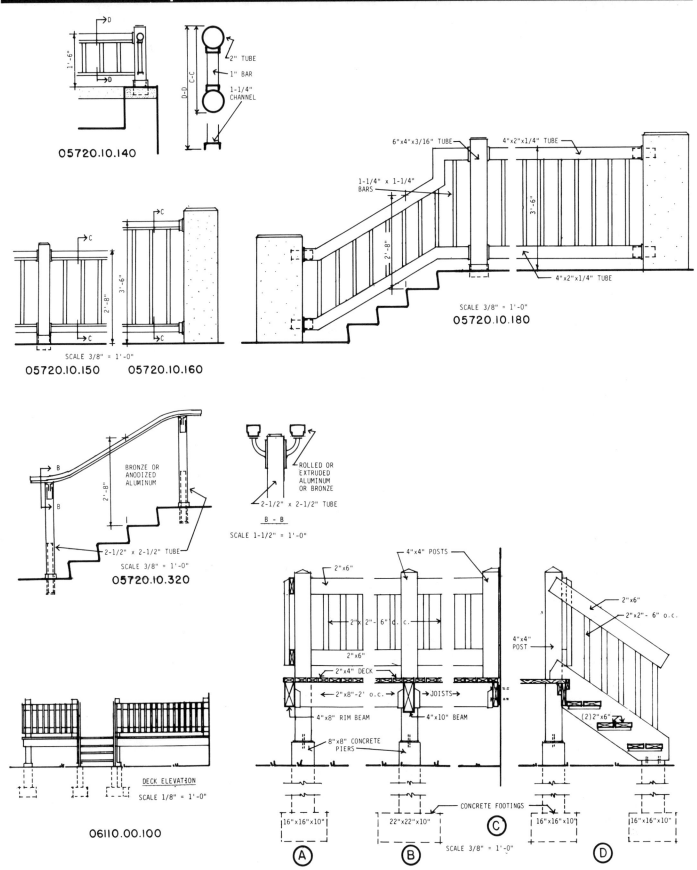

05720.10.140

2" TUBE
1" BAR
1-1/4" CHANNEL

05720.10.150   05720.10.160

SCALE 3/8" = 1'-0"

6"x4"x3/16" TUBE   4"x2"x1/4" TUBE

1-1/4" x 1-1/4" BARS

4"x2"x1/4" TUBE

SCALE 3/8" = 1'-0"
05720.10.180

BRONZE OR ANODIZED ALUMINUM

ROLLED OR EXTRUDED ALUMINUM OR BRONZE

2-1/2" x 2-1/2" TUBE

2-1/2" x 2-1/2" TUBE

B - B
SCALE 1-1/2" = 1'-0"

SCALE 3/8" = 1'-0"
05720.10.320

DECK ELEVATION
SCALE 1/8" = 1'-0"

06110.00.100

4"x4" POSTS
2"x6"
2"x2"- 6" o.c.
2"x6"
2"x4" DECK
2"x8"-2' o.c.   JOISTS
4"x8" RIM BEAM   4"x10" BEAM
8"x8" CONCRETE PIERS
2"x6"
2"x2"- 6" o.c.
4"x4" POST
(2)2"x6"
CONCRETE FOOTINGS
16"x16"x10"   22"x22"x10"   16"x16"x10"   16"x16"x10"
SCALE 3/8" = 1'-0"

Ⓐ   Ⓑ   Ⓒ   Ⓓ

INDEX